PEARSON EDEXCEL INTERNA
GCSE (9–1)

FURTHER PURE MATHEMATICS

Student Book

Ali Datoo
Greg Attwood, Keith Pledger, David Wilkins, Alistair Macpherson,
Bronwen Moran, Joseph Petran and Geoff Staley

Published by Pearson Education Limited, 80 Strand, London, WC2R 0RL.

www.pearsonglobalschools.com

Copies of official specifications for all Pearson qualifications may be found on the website: https://qualifications.pearson.com

Text © Pearson Education Limited 2017
Edited by Linnet Bruce, Keith Gallick and Susan Lyons
Designed by Cobalt id
Typeset by Tech-Set Ltd, Gateshead, UK
Cover design by Pearson Education Limited
Picture research by Debbie Gallagher
Cover photo © Getty Images: Naahushi Kavuri / EyeEm

Inside front cover: **Shutterstock.com**: Dmitry Lobanov

The rights of Ali Datoo, Greg Attwood, Keith Pledger, David Wilkins, Alistair Macpherson, Bronwen Moran, Joseph Petran and Geoff Staley to be identified as authors of this work have been asserted by them in accordance with the Copyright, Designs and Patents Act 1988.

First published 2017

25 24 23 22 21 20

IMP 10 9 8 7 6 5

British Library Cataloguing in Publication Data
A catalogue record for this book is available from the British Library

ISBN 978 0 435 18854 2

Printed in Slovakia by Neografia

Acknowledgements
(Key: b-bottom; c-centre; l-left; r-right; t-top)

Images:
123RF.com: ealisa 143; **Alamy Stock Photo**: Ammit 3; **Getty Images**: Christoph Hetzmannseder 2, David Crunelle / EyeEm 160, Ditto 24, EyeEm 136, hohl 74, Julia Antonio / EyeEm 60, Krzysztof Dydynski 106, Martin Barraud 124, Ozgur Donmaz 36, sebastian-julian 96, View Pictures / UIG 182; **Shutterstock.com**: Africa Studio 75, Akhenaton Images 90, Aleksandr Markin 128, andrea crisante 107t, Anette Holmberg 37, Brian Kinney 161, cigdem 148, IM_photo 123, Jacques Durocher 49t, jordache 180, Maridav 83, MCorfield 92, Miami2you 130, migrean 107b, Mikael Damkier 160, Nando 11, Nattawadee Supchapo 137, Neil Lockhart 61, Nicku 80, oksmit 125, Ondrej Prosicky 183, Patricia Hofmeester 131, Pavel L Photo and Video 154, photofriday 77t, Rawpixel.com 9, Sergey Edentod 47, Steve Noakes 25, Svetlana Privezentseva 49b, Syda Productions 77b, wavebreakmedia 121, worradirek 10, Zhukov Oleg 5

All other images © Pearson Education

ABOUT THIS BOOK

This book is written for students following the Pearson Edexcel International GCSE (9–1) Further Pure Maths specification and covers both years of the course. The specification and sample assessment materials for Further Pure Maths can be found on the Pearson Qualifications website.

In each chapter, there are concise explanations and worked examples, plus numerous exercises that will help you build up confidence.

There are also exam practice questions and a chapter summary to help with exam preparation. Answers to all exercises are included at the back of the book as well as a glossary of Maths-specific terminology.

Points of Interest put the maths you are about to learn in a real-world context.

Learning Objectives show what you will learn in each chapter.

Hint boxes give you tips and reminders.

THE QUADRATIC FUNCTION   CHAPTER 2   25

2 THE QUADRATIC FUNCTION

The path followed by a bottlenose dolphin jumping out of the water is called a parabola. A parabola is a **visual realisation** of the quadratic function $y = -x^2 + k$. Using this formula, scientists can calculate the height of a dolphin's jump (on the y-axis) and the distance travelled (on the x-axis).

There is no scientific agreement about why dolphins jump. Some scientists believe it is because they are trying to conserve energy, some believe it is to help them find food, and others believe they do it just for fun.

The parabola is a beautiful and elegant shape, commonly seen in nature. It is also seen in many man-made structures such as bridges and buildings.

LEARNING OBJECTIVES

- **Factorise** quadratic expressions where the **coefficient** of x^2 is greater than 1
- Complete the square and use this to solve quadratic equations
- Solve quadratic equations using the quadratic formula

- Understand and use the discriminant to identify whether the roots are (i) equal and real, (ii) unequal and real or (iii) not real
- Understand the roots a and β and know how to use them

STARTER ACTIVITIES

1 ▶ Factorise

   a $6x^2 + 9x$ b $2b^2 + 8b$ c $9qm^2 - 27m$

   d $9xy^2 + 36x^2y$ e $24x - 64x^2$

2 ▶ Factorise

   a $x^2 + 9x + 18$ b $x^2 - 7x + 12$ c $x^2 - 2x - 3$

   d $x^2 + 15x + 36$ e $x^2 + 12x + 27$

3 ▶ Factorise

   a $x^2 - 9$ b $x^2 - 25$

   c $9x^2 - 16$ d $25x^2 - 16$

HINT

All the parts in question 3 are examples of the difference of two squares.

Examples provide a clear, instructional framework. The blue highlighted text gives further explanation of the method.

Language is graded for speakers of English as an additional language (EAL), with advanced Maths-specific terminology highlighted and defined in the glossary at the back of the book.

Key Points boxes summarise the essentials.

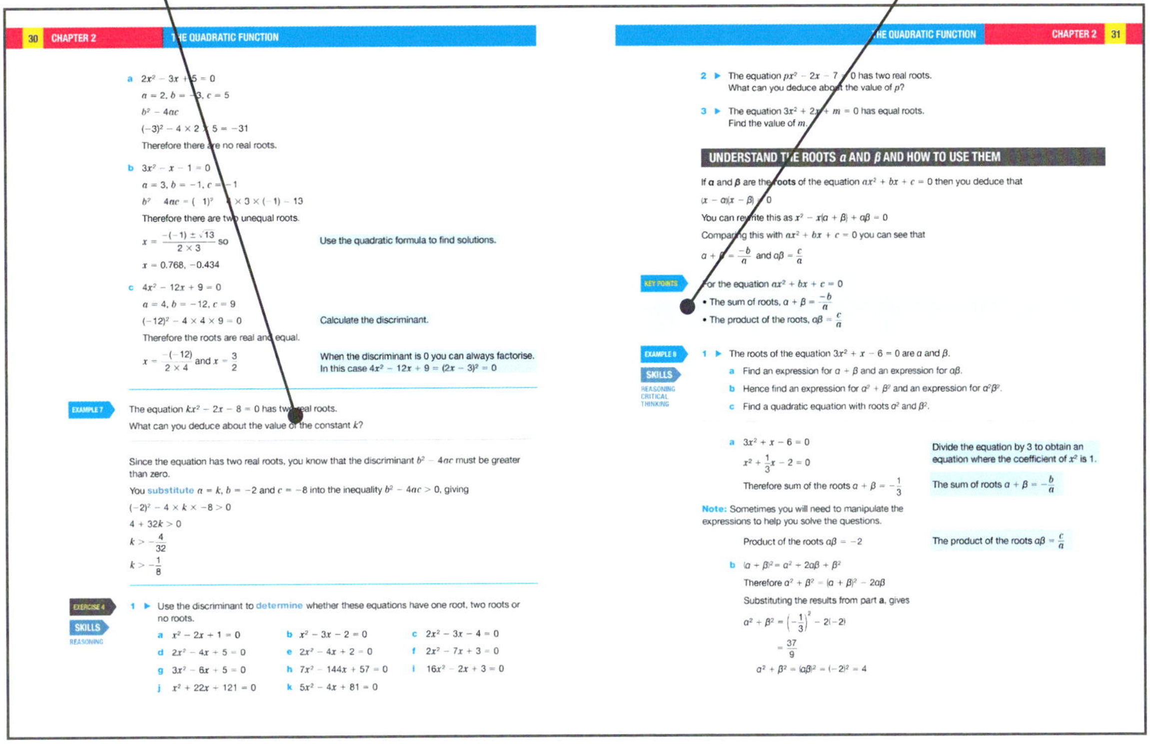

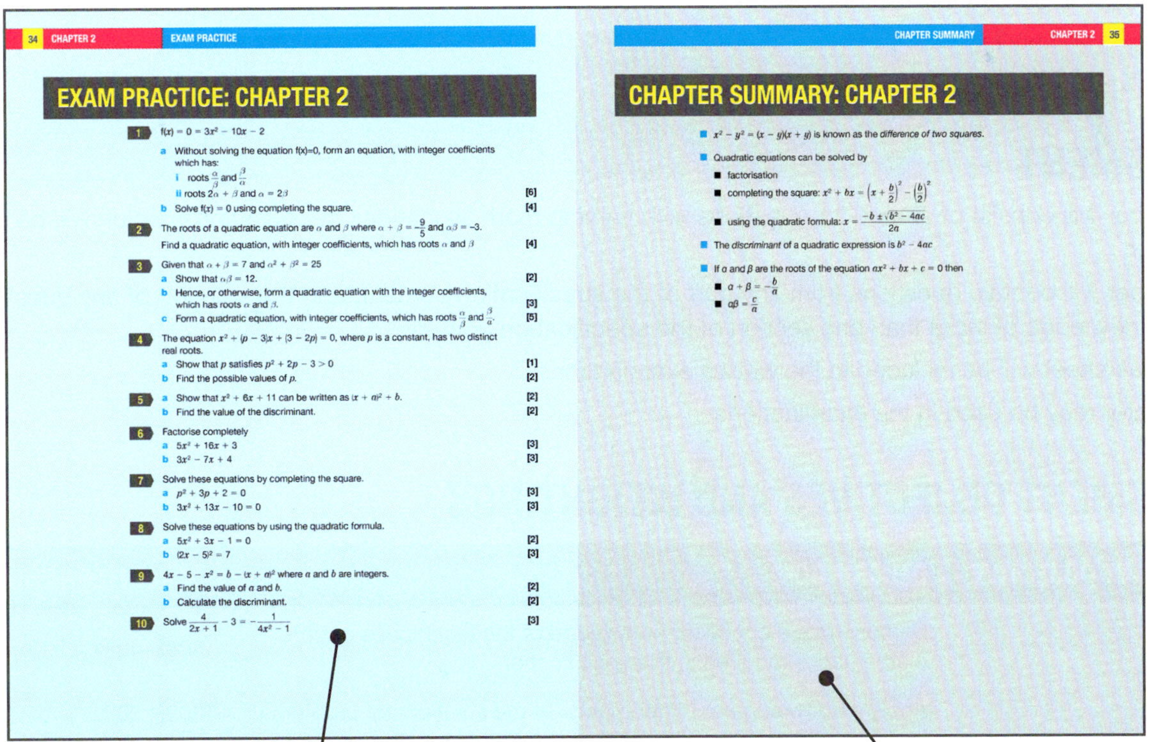

Left textbook page (30 CHAPTER 2 — THE QUADRATIC FUNCTION)

a $2x^2 - 3x + 5 = 0$

$a = 2, b = -3, c = 5$

$b^2 - 4ac$

$(-3)^2 - 4 \times 2 \times 5 = -31$

Therefore there are no real roots.

b $3x^2 - x - 1 = 0$

$a = 3, b = -1, c = -1$

$b^2 - 4ac = (-1)^2 - 4 \times 3 \times (-1) = 13$

Therefore there are two unequal roots.

$x = \dfrac{-(-1) \pm \sqrt{13}}{2 \times 3}$ so

$x = 0.768, -0.434$

Use the quadratic formula to find solutions.

c $4x^2 - 12x + 9 = 0$

$a = 4, b = -12, c = 9$

$(-12)^2 - 4 \times 4 \times 9 = 0$

Therefore the roots are real and equal.

$x = \dfrac{-(-12)}{2 \times 4}$ and $x = \dfrac{3}{2}$

Calculate the discriminant.

When the discriminant is 0 you can always factorise. In this case $4x^2 - 12x + 9 = (2x - 3)^2 = 0$

EXAMPLE 7 The equation $kx^2 - 2x - 8 = 0$ has two real roots. What can you deduce about the value of the constant k?

Since the equation has two real roots, you know that the discriminant $b^2 - 4ac$ must be greater than zero.

You substitute $a = k, b = -2$ and $c = -8$ into the inequality $b^2 - 4ac > 0$, giving

$(-2)^2 - 4 \times k \times -8 > 0$

$4 + 32k > 0$

$k > -\dfrac{4}{32}$

$k > -\dfrac{1}{8}$

EXERCISE 4

SKILLS REASONING

1 ▶ Use the discriminant to determine whether these equations have one root, two roots or no roots.

a $x^2 - 2x + 1 = 0$ **b** $x^2 - 3x - 2 = 0$ **c** $2x^2 - 3x - 4 = 0$

d $2x^2 - 4x + 5 = 0$ **e** $2x^2 - 4x + 2 = 0$ **f** $2x^2 - 7x + 3 = 0$

g $3x^2 - 6x + 5 = 0$ **h** $7x^2 - 144x + 57 = 0$ **i** $16x^2 - 2x + 3 = 0$

j $x^2 + 22x + 121 = 0$ **k** $5x^2 - 4x + 81 = 0$

Right textbook page (THE QUADRATIC FUNCTION — CHAPTER 2 31)

2 ▶ The equation $px^2 - 2x - 7 = 0$ has two real roots. What can you deduce about the value of p?

3 ▶ The equation $3x^2 + 2x + m = 0$ has equal roots. Find the value of m.

UNDERSTAND THE ROOTS α AND β AND HOW TO USE THEM

If α and β are the roots of the equation $ax^2 + bx + c = 0$ then you deduce that

$(x - \alpha)(x - \beta) = 0$

You can rewrite this as $x^2 - x(\alpha + \beta) + \alpha\beta = 0$

Comparing this with $ax^2 + bx + c = 0$ you can see that

$\alpha + \beta = -\dfrac{b}{a}$ and $\alpha\beta = \dfrac{c}{a}$

KEY POINTS For the equation $ax^2 + bx + c = 0$
- The sum of roots, $\alpha + \beta = -\dfrac{b}{a}$
- The product of the roots, $\alpha\beta = \dfrac{c}{a}$

EXAMPLE 8

SKILLS REASONING / CRITICAL THINKING

1 ▶ The roots of the equation $3x^2 + x - 6 = 0$ are α and β.

a Find an expression for $\alpha + \beta$ and an expression for $\alpha\beta$.

b Hence find an expression for $\alpha^2 + \beta^2$ and an expression for $\alpha^2\beta^2$.

c Find a quadratic equation with roots α^2 and β^2.

a $3x^2 + x - 6 = 0$

$x^2 + \dfrac{1}{3}x - 2 = 0$

Divide the equation by 3 to obtain an equation where the coefficient of x^2 is 1.

Therefore sum of the roots $\alpha + \beta = -\dfrac{1}{3}$

The sum of roots $\alpha + \beta = -\dfrac{b}{a}$

Note: Sometimes you will need to manipulate the expressions to help you solve the questions.

Product of the roots $\alpha\beta = -2$

The product of the roots $\alpha\beta = \dfrac{c}{a}$

b $\alpha^2 + \beta^2 = \alpha^2 - 2\alpha\beta + \beta^2$

Therefore $\alpha^2 + \beta^2 = (\alpha + \beta)^2 - 2\alpha\beta$

Substituting the results from part **a**, gives

$\alpha^2 + \beta^2 = \left(-\dfrac{1}{3}\right)^2 - 2(-2)$

$= \dfrac{37}{9}$

$\alpha^2 + \beta^2 = \alpha^2\beta^2 = (-2)^2 = 4$

Bottom left textbook page (34 CHAPTER 2 — EXAM PRACTICE)

EXAM PRACTICE: CHAPTER 2

1 $f(x) = 0 = 3x^2 - 10x - 2$

a Without solving the equation f(x)=0, form an equation, with integer coefficients which has:

  i roots $\dfrac{\alpha}{\beta}$ and $\dfrac{\beta}{\alpha}$

  ii roots 2α and β and $\alpha = 2\beta$ [6]

b Solve f(x) = 0 using completing the square. [4]

2 The roots of a quadratic equation are α and β where $\alpha + \beta = -\dfrac{9}{5}$ and $\alpha\beta = -3$. Find a quadratic equation, with integer coefficients, which has roots α and β [4]

3 Given that $\alpha + \beta = 7$ and $\alpha^2 + \beta^2 = 25$

a Show that $\alpha\beta = 12$. [2]

b Hence, or otherwise, form a quadratic equation with the integer coefficients, which has roots α and β. [3]

c Form a quadratic equation, with integer coefficients, which has roots $\dfrac{\alpha}{\beta}$ and $\dfrac{\beta}{\alpha}$. [5]

4 The equation $x^2 + (p - 3)x + (3 - 2p) = 0$, where p is a constant, has two distinct real roots.

a Show that p satisfies $p^2 + 2p - 3 > 0$ [1]

b Find the possible values of p. [2]

5 a Show that $x^2 + 6x + 11$ can be written as $(x + a)^2 + b$. [2]

b Find the value of the discriminant. [2]

6 Factorise completely

a $5x^2 + 16x + 3$ [3]

b $3x^2 - 7x + 4$ [3]

7 Solve these equations by completing the square.

a $p^2 + 3p + 2 = 0$ [3]

b $3x^2 + 13x - 10 = 0$ [3]

8 Solve these equations by using the quadratic formula.

a $5x^2 + 3x - 1 = 0$ [2]

b $(2x - 5)^2 = 7$ [3]

9 $4x - 5 - x^2 = b - (x + a)^2$ where a and b are integers.

a Find the value of a and b. [2]

b Calculate the discriminant. [2]

10 Solve $\dfrac{4}{2x + 1} - 3 = -\dfrac{1}{4x^2 - 1}$ [3]

Bottom right textbook page (CHAPTER SUMMARY — CHAPTER 2 35)

CHAPTER SUMMARY: CHAPTER 2

- $x^2 - y^2 = (x - y)(x + y)$ is known as the *difference of two squares*.
- Quadratic equations can be solved by
  - factorisation
  - completing the square: $x^2 + bx = \left(x + \dfrac{b}{2}\right)^2 - \left(\dfrac{b}{2}\right)^2$
  - using the quadratic formula: $x = \dfrac{-b \pm \sqrt{b^2 - 4ac}}{2a}$
- The *discriminant* of a quadratic expression is $b^2 - 4ac$
- If α and β are the roots of the equation $ax^2 + bx + c = 0$ then
  - $\alpha + \beta = -\dfrac{b}{a}$
  - $\alpha\beta = \dfrac{c}{a}$

Exam Practice tests cover the whole chapter and provide quick, effective feedback on your progress.

Chapter Summaries state the most important points of each chapter.

ASSESSMENT OVERVIEW

The following tables give an overview of the assessment for the Edexcel International GCSE in Further Pure Mathematics.

We recommend that you study this information closely to help ensure that you are fully prepared for this course and know exactly what to expect in the assessment.

PAPER 1	PERCENTAGE	MARK	TIME	AVAILABILITY
Written examination paper Paper code 4PM1/01C Externally set and assessed by Edexcel	50%	100	2 hours	January and June examination series First assessment June 2019

PAPER 2	PERCENTAGE	MARK	TIME	AVAILABILITY
Written examination paper Paper code 4PM1/02 Externally set and assessed by Edexcel	50%	100	2 hours	January and June examination series First assessment June 2019

CONTENT SUMMARY

- Number
- Algebra and calculus
- Geometry and calculus

ASSESSMENT

- Each paper will consist of around 11 questions with varying mark allocations per questions, which will be stated on the paper
- Each paper will contain questions from any part of the specification content, and the solution of any questions may require knowledge of more than one section of the specification content
- A formulae sheet will be included in the written examinations
- A calculator may be used in the examinations

ASSESSMENT OBJECTIVES AND WEIGHTINGS

ASSESSMENT OBJECTIVE	DESCRIPTION	% IN INTERNATIONAL GCSE
AO1	Demonstrate a confident knowledge of the techniques of pure mathematics required in the specification	30%–40%
AO2	Apply a knowledge of mathematics to the solutions of problems for which an immediate method of solution is not available and which may involve knowledge of more than one topic in the specification	20%–30%
AO3	Write clear and accurate mathematical solutions	35%–50%

RELATIONSHIP OF ASSESSMENT OBJECTIVES TO UNITS

UNIT NUMBER	ASSESSMENT OBJECTIVE		
	AO1	AO2	AO3
Paper 1	15%–20%	10%–15%	17.5%–25%
Paper 2	15%–20%	10%–15%	17.5%–25%
Total for International GCSE	30%–40%	20%–30%	35%–50%

ASSESSMENT SUMMARY

The Edexcel International GCSE in Further Pure Mathematics requires students to demonstrate application and understanding of the following topics.

Number
• Use numerical skills in a purely mathematical way and in real-life situations.

Algebra and calculus
• Use algebra and calculus to set up and solve problems.
• Develop competence and confidence when manipulating mathematical expressions.
• Construct and use graphs in a range of situations.

Geometry and trigonometry
• Understand the properties of shapes, angles and transformations.
• Use vectors and rates of change to model situations.
• Use coordinate geometry.
• Use trigonometry.

Students will be expected to have a thorough knowledge of the content common to the Pearson Edexcel International GCSE in Mathematics (Specification A) (Higher Tier) or Pearson Edexcel International GCSE in Mathematics (Specification B).

Questions may be set which assumes knowledge of some topics covered in these specifications, however knowledge of statistics and matrices will not be required.
Students will be expected to carry out arithmetic and algebraic manipulation, such as being able to change the subject of a formula and evaluate numerically the value of any variable in a formula, given the values of the other variables.
The use and notation of set theory will be adopted where appropriate.

CALCULATORS

Students will be expected to have access to a suitable electronic calculator for all examination papers. The electronic calculator should have these functions as a minimum:
$+, -, \times, \div, \pi, x^2, \sqrt{x}, \frac{1}{x}, x^y, \ln x, e^x$, sine, cosine and tangent and their inverses in degrees and decimals of a degree or radians.

Prohibitions
Calculators with any of the following facilities are prohibited in all examinations:
    databanks
    retrieval of text or formulae
    QWERTY keyboards
    built-in symbolic algebra manipulations
    symbolic differentiation or integration.

FORMULAE SHEET

These formulae will be provided for you during the examination.

MENSURATION

Surface area of sphere $= 4\pi r^2$

Curved surface area of cone $= \pi r \times$ slant height

Volume of sphere $= \dfrac{4}{3}\pi r^3$

SERIES

Arithmetic series

Sum to n terms $S_n = \dfrac{n}{2}[2a + (n-1)d]$

Geometric series

Sum to n terms, $S_n = \dfrac{a(1 - r^n)}{(1 - r)}$

Sum to infinity, $S_\infty = \dfrac{a}{1 - r}$ $\qquad\qquad |r| < 1$

Binomial series

$(1 + x)^n = 1 + nx + \dfrac{n(n - 1)}{2!}x^2 + \ldots + \dfrac{n(n - 1)\ldots(n - r + 1)}{r!}x^r + \ldots$ for $|x| < 1, n \in \mathbb{Q}$

CALCULUS

Quotient rule (differentiation)

$\dfrac{\mathrm{d}}{\mathrm{d}x}\left(\dfrac{f(x)}{g(x)}\right) = \dfrac{f'(x)g(x) - f(x)g'(x)}{[g(x)]^2}$

TRIGONOMETRY

Cosine rule

In triangle ABC: $a^2 = b^2 + c^2 - 2bc \cos A$

$\tan\theta = \dfrac{\sin\theta}{\cos\theta}$

$\sin(A + B) = \sin A \cos B + \cos A \sin B$ $\qquad$ $\sin(A - B) = \sin A \cos B - \cos A \sin B$

$\cos(A + B) = \cos A \cos B - \sin A \sin B$ $\qquad$ $\cos(A - B) = \cos A \cos B + \sin A \sin B$

$\tan(A + B) = \dfrac{\tan A + \tan B}{1 - \tan A \tan B}$ $\qquad$ $\tan(A - B) = \dfrac{\tan A - \tan B}{1 + \tan A \tan B}$

LOGARITHMS

$\log_a x = \dfrac{\log_b x}{\log_b a}$

FORMULAE TO KNOW

The following are formulae that you are expected to know and remember during the examination. These formulae **will not** be provided for you. Note that this list is not exhaustive.

LOGARITHMIC FUNCTIONS AND INDICES

$\log_a xy = \log_a x + \log_a y$

$\log_a \dfrac{x}{y} = \log_a x - \log_a y$

$\log_a x^k = k \log_a x$

$\log_a \dfrac{1}{x} = -\log_a x$

$\log_a a = 1$

$\log_a 1 = 0$

$\log_a b = \dfrac{1}{\log_b a}$

QUADRATIC EQUATIONS

$a x^2 + bx + c = 0$ has roots given by $x = \dfrac{-b \pm \sqrt{b^2 - 4ac}}{2a}$

When the roots of $ax^2 + bx + c = 0$ are α and β then $\alpha + \beta = -\dfrac{b}{a}$ and $\alpha\beta = \dfrac{c}{a}$ and the equation can be written $x^2 - (\alpha + \beta)x + \alpha\beta = 0$

SERIES

Arithmetic series: nth term $= l = a + (n - 1)d$

Geometric series: nth term $= a r^{n-1}$

COORDINATE GEOMETRY

The gradient of the line joining two points (x_1, y_1) and (x_2, y_2) is $\dfrac{y_2 - y_1}{x_2 - x_1}$

The distance d between two points (x_1, y_1) and (x_2, y_2) is given by
$d^2 = (x_1 - x_2)^2 + (y_1 - y_2)^2$

The coordinates of the point dividing the line joining (x_1, y_1) and (x_2, y_2) in the ratio $m : n$ are
$\left(\dfrac{n x_1 - m x_2}{m + n}, \dfrac{n y_1 - m y_2}{m + n} \right)$

CALCULUS

Differentiation:

function	derivative
x^n	nx^{n-1}
$\sin ax$	$a\cos ax$
$\cos ax$	$-a\sin ax$
e^{ax}	ae^{ax}
$f(x)g(x)$	$f'(x)g(x) + f(x)g'(x)$
$f(g(x))$	$f'(g(x))g'x$

Integration:

function	derivative
x^n	$\dfrac{1}{n+1}x^{n+1} + c \quad n \neq -1$
$\sin ax$	$-\dfrac{1}{a}\cos ax + c$
$\cos ax$	$\dfrac{1}{a}\sin ax + c$
e^{ax}	$\dfrac{1}{a}e^{ax} + c$

AREA AND VOLUME

Area between a curve and the x-axis $= \int_a^b y\,dx$, $y \geqslant 0$

$\left| \int_a^b y\,dx \right|$, $y < 0$

Area between a curve and the y-axis $= \int_c^d x\,dy$, $x \geqslant 0$

$\left| \int_c^d x\,dy \right|$, $x < 0$

Area between $g(x)$ and $f(x) = \int_a^b |g(x) - f(x)|\,dx$

Volume of revolution $= \int_a^b \pi y^2\,dx$ or $\int_c^d \pi x^2\,dy$

TRIGONOMETRY

Radian measure:

length of arc $= r\theta$

area of sector $= \dfrac{1}{2}r^2\theta$

In a triangle ABC:

$\dfrac{a}{\sin A} = \dfrac{b}{\sin B} = \dfrac{c}{\sin C}$

$\cos^2\theta + \sin^2\theta = 1$

area of a triangle $= \dfrac{1}{2}ab\,\sin C$

CHAPTER 1

1 SURDS AND LOGARITHMIC FUNCTIONS

The Richter scale, which describes the energy released by an earthquake, uses the base 10 logarithm as its unit. An earthquake of **magnitude** 9 is 10 times as powerful as one of magnitude 8, and 100 000 times as powerful as one of magnitude 4.

The **devastating** 2004 earthquake in the Indian Ocean had a magnitude of 9. Thankfully, such events are rare. The most common earthquakes, which occur over 100 000 times a year, are magnitude 2 to 3, so humans can hardly feel them.

LEARNING OBJECTIVES

- Write a number exactly using surds
- Rationalise the denominator of a surd
- Be familiar with the **functions** a^x and $\log_b x$ and recognise the shapes of their graphs
- Be familiar with functions including e^x and similar terms, and use them in graphs
- Use graphs of functions to solve equations
- Rewrite expressions including powers using logarithms instead
- Understand and use the laws of logarithms
- Change the base of a logarithm
- Solve equations of the form $a^x = b$

STARTER ACTIVITIES

1 ▶ Simplify

   a $y^6 \times y^5$
   b $2q^3 \times 4q^4$
   c $3k^2 \times 3k^7 \times 3k^{-3}$

   d $(x^2)^4$
   e $(a^4)^2 \div a^3$
   f $64x^4y^6 \div 4xy^2$

2 ▶ Simplify

   a $(m^3)^{\frac{1}{2}}$
   b $3p^{\frac{1}{2}} \times p^3$
   c $28c^{\frac{2}{3}} \div 7c^{\frac{1}{3}}$

   d $6b^{\frac{1}{2}} \times 3b^{-\frac{1}{2}}$
   e $27p^{\frac{2}{3}} \div 9p^{\frac{1}{6}}$
   f $5y^6 \times 3y^{-7}$

3 ▶ Evaluate

   a $16^{\frac{1}{2}}$
   b $125^{\frac{1}{3}}$
   c 8^{-2}
   d $(-2)^{-3}$

   e $\left(\frac{6}{7}\right)^0$
   f $81^{-\frac{1}{4}}$
   g $\left(\frac{9}{16}\right)^{-\frac{3}{2}}$

WRITE A NUMBER EXACTLY USING A SURD

A surd is a number that cannot be simplified to remove a square root (or a cube root, fourth root etc). Surds are irrational numbers.

HINT

An irrational number is a number that cannot be expressed as a fraction, for example π.

NUMBER	DECIMAL	IS IT A SURD?
$\sqrt{1}$	1	No
$\sqrt{2}$	1.414213...	Yes
$\sqrt{4}$	2	No
$\sqrt{\dfrac{1}{4}}$	0.5	No
$\sqrt{\dfrac{2}{3}}$	0.816496...	Yes

You can **manipulate** surds using these rules:

$$\sqrt{ab} = \sqrt{a} \times \sqrt{b}$$

$$\sqrt{\frac{a}{b}} = \frac{\sqrt{a}}{\sqrt{b}}$$

EXAMPLE 1

SKILLS

CRITICAL THINKING

Simplify

a $\sqrt{12}$

b $\dfrac{\sqrt{20}}{2}$

c $5\sqrt{6} - 2\sqrt{24} + \sqrt{294}$

---

a $\sqrt{12}$

$= \sqrt{4 \times 3}$

$= \sqrt{4} \times \sqrt{3}$ Use the rule $\sqrt{ab} = \sqrt{a} \times \sqrt{b}$

$= 2\sqrt{3}$ $\sqrt{4} = 2$

b $\dfrac{\sqrt{20}}{2}$ $\sqrt{20} = \sqrt{4} \times \sqrt{5}$

$= \dfrac{\sqrt{4 \times 5}}{2}$ $\sqrt{4} = 2$

$= \dfrac{2 \times \sqrt{5}}{2}$

$= \sqrt{5}$

c $5\sqrt{6} - 2\sqrt{24} + \sqrt{294}$

$= 5\sqrt{6} - 2\sqrt{6}\sqrt{4} + \sqrt{6}\sqrt{49}$ $\sqrt{6}$ is a common factor

$= \sqrt{6}(5 - 2\sqrt{4} + \sqrt{49})$ Work out the square roots $\sqrt{4}$ and $\sqrt{49}$

$= \sqrt{6}(5 - 2 \times 2 + 7)$ $5 - 4 + 7 = 8$

$= 8\sqrt{6}$

EXERCISE 1

SKILLS

CRITICAL
THINKING

1 ▶ Simplify without using a calculator

    a $\sqrt{18}$ **b** $\sqrt{50}$ **c** $\sqrt{125}$

    d $\sqrt{128}$ **e** $\sqrt{132}$ **f** $\sqrt{8625}$

2 ▶ Simplify without using a calculator

    a $\dfrac{\sqrt{60}}{2}$ **b** $\dfrac{\sqrt{135}}{2}$ **c** $\dfrac{\sqrt{128}}{8}$

    d $\dfrac{\sqrt{68}}{4}$ **e** $\dfrac{\sqrt{96}}{6}$

3 ▶ Simplify without using a calculator

    a $6\sqrt{3} - 2\sqrt{3}$ **b** $7\sqrt{3} - \sqrt{12} + \sqrt{48}$ **c** $\sqrt{112} + 2\sqrt{172} - \sqrt{63}$

    d $6\sqrt{48} - 3\sqrt{12} + 2\sqrt{27}$ **e** $3\sqrt{578} - \sqrt{162} + 4\sqrt{32}$ **f** $2\sqrt{5} \times 3\sqrt{5}$

    g $6\sqrt{7} \times 4\sqrt{7}$ **h** $4\sqrt{8} \times 6\sqrt{8}$

4 ▶ Simplify without using a calculator

    a $6(4 - \sqrt{12})$ **b** $9(6 - 3\sqrt{29})$ **c** $4(1 + \sqrt{3}) + 3(3 + 2\sqrt{3})$

    d $3(\sqrt{2} - \sqrt{7}) - 5(\sqrt{2} + \sqrt{7})$ **e** $(4 + \sqrt{3})(4 - \sqrt{3})$

    f $(2\sqrt{7} - \sqrt{6})(\sqrt{7} - 2\sqrt{6})$ **g** $(\sqrt{8} + \sqrt{5})(\sqrt{8} - \sqrt{5})$

5 ▶ A garden is $\sqrt{30}$ m long and $\sqrt{8}$ m wide. The garden is covered in grass except for a small rectangular pond which is $\sqrt{2}$ m long and $\sqrt{6}$ m wide.

Express the area of the pond as a percentage of the area of the garden.

6 ▶ Find the value of $2p^2 - 3pq$ when $p = \sqrt{2} + 3$ and $q = \sqrt{2} - 2$

RATIONALISE THE DENOMINATOR OF A SURD

HINT

In the denominator, the multiplication gives the difference of two squares, with the result $a^2 - b^2$, which means the surd disappears.

Rationalising the denominator of a surd means removing a root from the denominator of a fraction. You will usually need to rationalise the denominator when you are asked to *simplify* it.

The rules for rationalising the denominator of a surd are:

- For fractions in the form $\sqrt{\dfrac{1}{a}}$, multiply the numerator and denominator by $\sqrt{a}$

- For fractions in the form $\dfrac{1}{a + \sqrt{b}}$, multiply the numerator and denominator by $a - \sqrt{b}$

- For fractions in the form $\dfrac{1}{a - \sqrt{b}}$, multiply the numerator and denominator by $a + \sqrt{b}$

EXAMPLE 2

Rationalise the denominator of

a $\dfrac{1}{\sqrt{3}}$ **b** $\dfrac{1}{3 + \sqrt{2}}$ **c** $\dfrac{\sqrt{5} + \sqrt{2}}{\sqrt{5} - \sqrt{2}}$

a $\dfrac{1}{\sqrt{3}}$

$\quad = \dfrac{1 \times \sqrt{3}}{\sqrt{3} \times \sqrt{3}}$ Multiply the top and bottom by $\sqrt{3}$

$\quad = \dfrac{\sqrt{3}}{3}$ $\sqrt{3} \times \sqrt{3} = (\sqrt{3})^2 = 3$

b $\dfrac{1}{3 + \sqrt{2}}$

$\quad = \dfrac{1 \times (3 - \sqrt{2})}{(3 + \sqrt{2})(3 - \sqrt{2})}$ Multiply the top and bottom by $3 - \sqrt{2}$

$\quad = \dfrac{3 - \sqrt{2}}{9 - 3\sqrt{2} + 3\sqrt{2} - 2}$ $\sqrt{2} \times \sqrt{2} = 2$

$\quad = \dfrac{3 - \sqrt{2}}{7}$ $9 - 2 = 7,\ -3\sqrt{2} + 3\sqrt{2} = 0$

c $\dfrac{\sqrt{5} + \sqrt{2}}{\sqrt{5} - \sqrt{2}}$

$\quad = \dfrac{(\sqrt{5} + \sqrt{2})(\sqrt{5} + \sqrt{2})}{(\sqrt{5} - \sqrt{2})(\sqrt{5} + \sqrt{2})}$ Multiply the top and bottom by $\sqrt{5} + \sqrt{2}$

$\quad = \dfrac{5 + \sqrt{5}\sqrt{2} + \sqrt{2}\sqrt{5} + 2}{5 - 2}$ $\sqrt{5}\sqrt{2} - \sqrt{2}\sqrt{5} = 0$ in the denominator

$\quad = \dfrac{7 + 2\sqrt{10}}{3}$ $\sqrt{5}\sqrt{2} = \sqrt{10}$

EXERCISE 2

SKILLS

EXECUTIVE
FUNCTION

1 ▶ Rationalise

a $\dfrac{1}{\sqrt{13}}$ **b** $\dfrac{1}{\sqrt{7}}$ **c** $\dfrac{2}{\sqrt{3}}$ **d** $\dfrac{\sqrt{6}}{\sqrt{3}}$

e $\dfrac{12}{\sqrt{3}}$ **f** $\dfrac{3\sqrt{5}}{\sqrt{3}}$ **g** $\dfrac{9\sqrt{12}}{2\sqrt{18}}$ **h** $\dfrac{1}{2 - \sqrt{3}}$

2 ▶ Rationalise

a $\dfrac{\sqrt{6}}{\sqrt{3} + \sqrt{6}}$ **b** $\dfrac{2 + \sqrt{3}}{2 - \sqrt{3}}$ **c** $\dfrac{\sqrt{2} - \sqrt{3}}{\sqrt{2} + \sqrt{3}}$

d $\dfrac{4\sqrt{2} - 2\sqrt{3}}{\sqrt{2} + \sqrt{3}}$ **e** $\dfrac{\sqrt{2} + 2\sqrt{5}}{\sqrt{5} - \sqrt{2}}$ **f** $\dfrac{\sqrt{7} + \sqrt{3}}{\sqrt{7} - \sqrt{3}}$

g $\dfrac{\sqrt{11} + 2\sqrt{5}}{\sqrt{11} + 3\sqrt{5}}$ **h** $\dfrac{2\sqrt{5} - 3\sqrt{7}}{5\sqrt{6} + 4\sqrt{2}}$ **i** $\dfrac{2 + \sqrt{10}}{\sqrt{2} + \sqrt{5}}$

j $\dfrac{ab}{a\sqrt{b} - b\sqrt{a}}$ **k** $\dfrac{a - b}{a\sqrt{b} - b\sqrt{a}}$

BE FAMILIAR WITH THE FUNCTIONS a^x AND $\log_a x$ AND RECOGNISE THE SHAPES OF THEIR GRAPHS

You need to be familiar with functions in the form $y = a^x$ where $a > 0$.

Look at a table of values for $y = 2^x$

x	-3	-2	-1	0	1	2	3
y	$\frac{1}{8}$	$\frac{1}{4}$	$\frac{1}{2}$	1	2	4	8

Note: $2^0 = 1$ In fact a^0 is always equal to 1 if a is positive.

$$2^{-3} = \frac{1}{2^3} = \frac{1}{8}$$ A negative index turns the number into its **reciprocal**.

The graph of $y = 2^x$ looks like this:

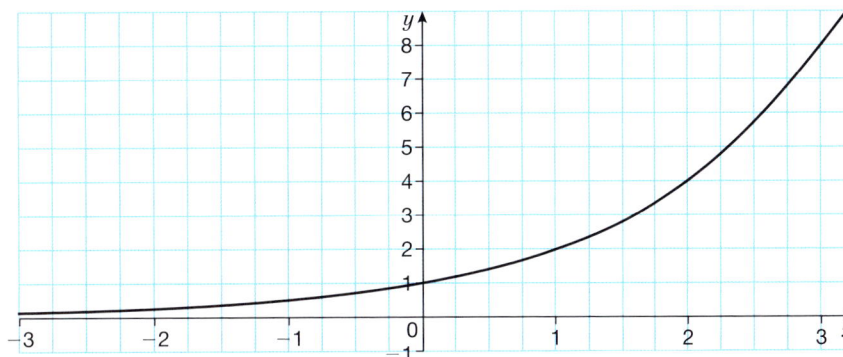

Note: the x-axis is an **asymptote** to the curve.

Other graphs of the type $y = a^x$ have similar shapes, always passing through $(0, 1)$.

EXAMPLE 3

SKILLS

ANALYSIS

a On the same axes, **sketch** the graphs of $y = 3^x$, $y = 2^x$ and $y = 1.5^x$

b On another set of axes, sketch the graphs of $y = \left(\frac{1}{2}\right)^x$ and $y = 2^x$

a For all three graphs, $y = 1$ when $x = 0$ $a^0 = 1$

When $x > 0$, $3^x > 2^x > 1.5^x$

When $x < 0$, $3^x < 2^x < 1.5^x$ Work out the relative positions of the graphs

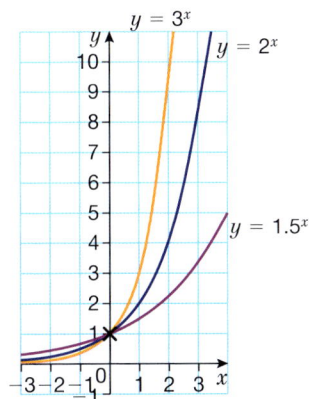

b $\dfrac{1}{2} = 2^{-1}$

so, $y = \left(\dfrac{1}{2}\right)^{x}$ is the same as $y = (2^{-1})^{x} = 2^{-x}$ $(a^{m})^{n} = a^{mn}$

Therefore the graph of $y = \left(\dfrac{1}{2}\right)^{x}$ is a reflection in the y-axis of the graph of $y = 2^{x}$

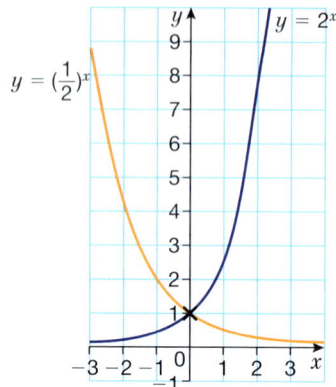

EXAMPLE 4   If you compare the graphs of $y = 2^{x}$ and $y = \log_{2} x$ you see the following relationship:

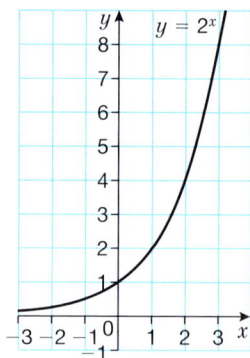

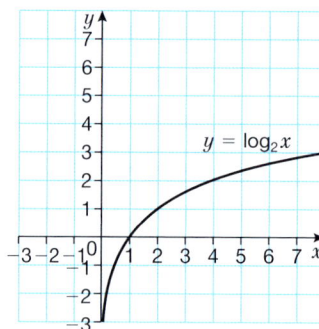

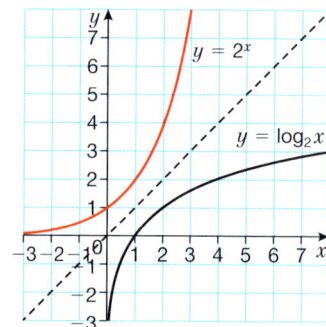

EXAMPLE 5   On the same set of axes sketch the graphs $y = \log_{2} x$ and $y = \log_{5} x$

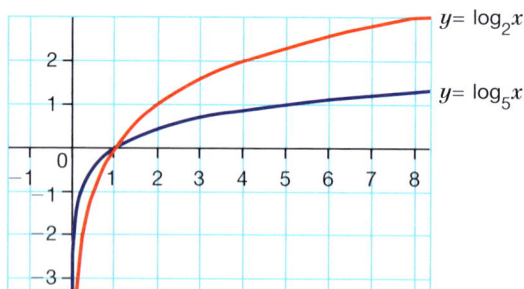

Note:

For both graphs $y = 0$ when $x = 1$, since $\log_{a} 1$ where is a > 1.

$\log_{2} 2 = 1$ so $y = \log_{2} x$ passes through $(2, 1)$

and $\log_{5} 5 = 1$ so $y = \log_{5} x$ passes through $(5, 1)$.

EXERCISE 3

SKILLS

ANALYSIS
REASONING

1 ▶ On the same set of axes sketch the graphs of

    a $y = 5^{x}$ **b** $y = 7^{x}$ **c** $y = \left(\dfrac{1}{3}\right)^{x}$

2 ▶ On the same set of axes sketch the graphs of

    a $y = \log_5 x$ **b** $y = \log_7 x$

    c   Write down the coordinates of the point of intersection of these two graphs.

3 ▶ On the same set of axes sketch the graphs of

    a $y = 3^x$ **b** $y = \log_3 x$

4 ▶ On the same set of axes sketch the graphs of

    a $y = \log_3 x$ **b** $y = \log_5 x$ **c** $y = \log_{0.5} x$ **d** $y = \log_{0.25} x$

BE FAMILIAR WITH EXPRESSIONS OF THE TYPE e^x AND USE THEM IN GRAPHS

Consider this example: Zainab opens an account with $1.00. The account pays 100% interest per year. If the interest is credited once, at the end of the year, her account will contain $2.00. How much will it contain after a year if the interest is calculated and credited more frequently? Let us investigate this more thoroughly.

HOW OFTEN INTEREST IS CREDITED INTO THE ACCOUNT	VALUE OF ACCOUNT AFTER 1 YEAR ($)
Yearly	$\left(1 + \dfrac{1}{1}\right)^1 = 2$
Semi-annually	$\left(1 + \dfrac{1}{2}\right)^2 = 2.25$
Quarterly	$\left(1 + \dfrac{1}{4}\right)^4 = 2.441406...$
Monthly	$\left(1 + \dfrac{1}{12}\right)^{12} = 2.61303529...$
Weekly	$\left(1 + \dfrac{1}{52}\right)^{52} = 2.69259695...$
Daily	$\left(1 + \dfrac{1}{365}\right)^{365} = 2.71456748...$
Hourly	$\left(1 + \dfrac{1}{8760}\right)^{8760} = 2.71812669...$
Every minute	$\left(1 + \dfrac{1}{525\,600}\right)^{525\,600} = 2.7182154...$
Every second	$\left(1 + \dfrac{1}{31\,536\,000}\right)^{31\,536\,000} = 2.71828247...$

The amount in her account gets bigger and bigger the more often the interest is compounded, but the rate of growth slows. As the number of compounds increases, the calculated value appears to be approaching a fixed value. This value gets closer and closer to a fixed value of 2.71828247254.......This number is called 'e'.

The number e is called Euler's number or Euler's constant. It is a naturally occurring number that is the base of the natural logarithm. It arises naturally in mathematics and has numerous real life applications.

EXAMPLE 6

SKILLS

ANALYSIS
INTERPRETATION

Draw the graphs of e^x and e^{-x}

x	−2	−1	0	1	2	3	4
e^x	0.14	0.37	1	2.7	7.4	20	55

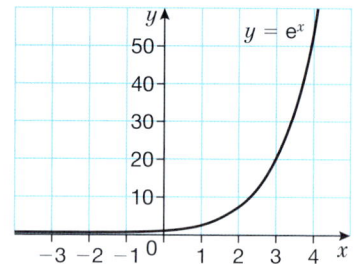

x	−4	−3	−2	−1	0	1	2
e^{-x}	55	20	7.4	2.7	1	0.37	0.14

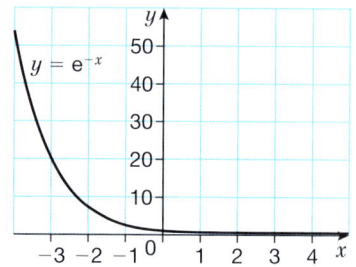

EXAMPLE 7

Draw the graphs of these **exponential functions.**

a $y = e^{2x}$

b $y = 10e^{-x}$

c $y = 3 + 4e^{\frac{1}{2}x}$

a

x	−2	−1	0	1	2
e^{2x}	0.02	0.1	1	7.4	55

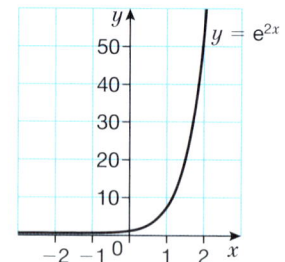

b

x	−2	−1	0	1	2
$10e^{-x}$	73	27	10	3.7	1.4

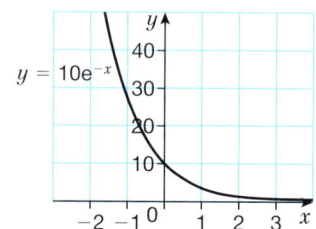

c

x	-2	-1	0	1	2
$3 + 4e^{\frac{1}{2}x}$	4.5	5.4	7	9.6	13.9

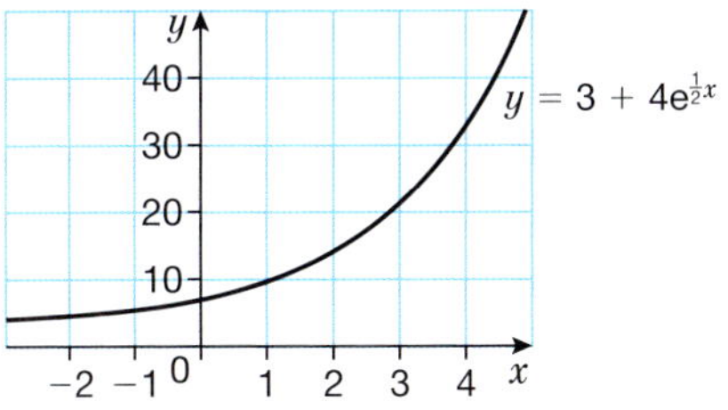

On pages 7–9 you saw the connection between $y = \log_a x$ and and $y = a^x$. The **function** $y = \log_e x$ is particularly important in mathematics and so it has a special notation:

$$\log_e x \equiv \ln x$$

Your calculator should have a special button for evaluating $\ln x$.

EXAMPLE 8   Solve these equations.

a $e^x = 3$

b $\ln x = 4$

a When $e^x = 3$

$\quad\quad x = \ln 3$

b When $\ln x = 4$

$\quad\quad x = e^4$

As you can see, the inverse of e^x is $\ln x$ (and vice versa).

EXAMPLE 9   Sketch these graphs on the same set of axes.

a $y = \ln x$

b $y = \ln (3 - x)$

c $y = 3 + \ln (2x)$

a–c

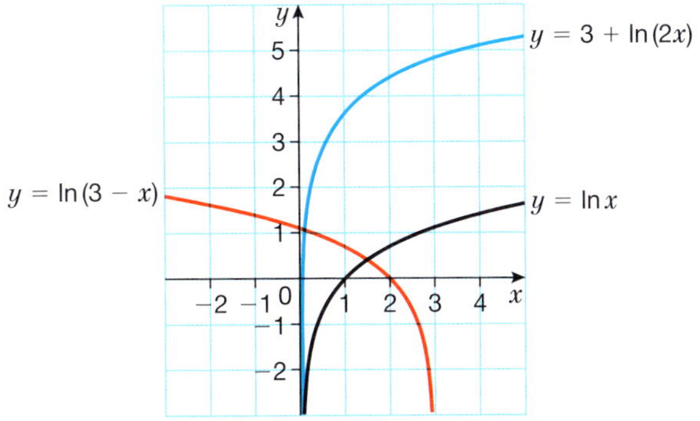

EXERCISE 4

SKILLS

ANALYSIS REASONING

1 ▶ Sketch these graphs.

a $y = e^x + 1$

b $y = 4e^{-2x}$

c $y = 2e^x - 3$

d $y = 6 + 10^{\frac{1}{2}x}$

e $y = 100e^{-x} + 10$

2 ▶ Sketch these graphs, stating any vertical asymptotes.

a $y = \ln (x + 1)$

b $y = \ln x$

c $y = \ln 2x$

d $y = \ln (4 - x)$

e $y = \ln (2 + x) + 4$

BE ABLE TO USE GRAPHS OF FUNCTIONS TO SOLVE EQUATIONS

EXAMPLE 10

a Complete the table of values for: $y = e^{\frac{1}{2}x} - 2$
Giving your answers to two decimal places where appropriate.

b Draw the graph of $y = e^{\frac{1}{2}x} - 2$ for $0 \leqslant x \leqslant 5$.

c Use your graph to estimate, to 2 significant figures, the solution of the equation $e^{\frac{1}{2}x} = 8$
Show your method clearly.

d By drawing a suitable line on your graph, estimate to 2 significant figures the solution to the equation $x = 2 \ln(7 - 2x)$.

a

x	-1	0	1	2	3	4	5
y	-1.39	-1	-0.35	0.72	2.48	5.39	10.18

b

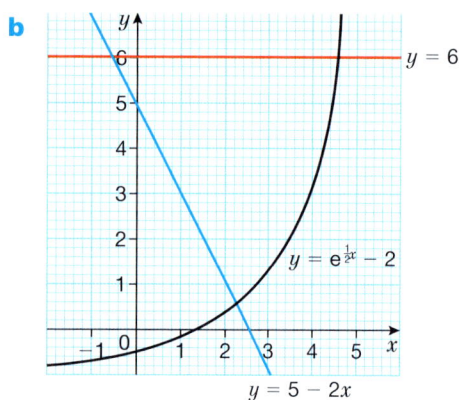

HINT

Make the
LHS $= e^{\frac{1}{2}x} - 2$
i.e. the equation
of the graph.
To do this, you
need to subtract
2 from 8 and
draw the line
$y = 6$ (as shown
in the diagram).

c $e^{\frac{1}{2}x} = 8$

$e^{\frac{1}{2}x} - 2 = 8 - 2$

$e^{\frac{1}{2}x} = 6$

So the solution is the intersection of the curve $y = e^{\frac{1}{2}x}$ and $y = 6$

$x \approx 4.15$ (In the exam you will be allowed a range of values.)

HINT

Make the **LHS**
equal to the
given equation
i.e $e^{\frac{1}{2}x} - 2$.
Draw the line
$y = 5 - 2x$ (as
shown in the
diagram) on
your graph and
find points of
intersection.

d $x = 2 \ln(7 - 2x)$

$\dfrac{x}{2} = \ln(7 - 2x)$

$e^{\frac{1}{2}x} = 7 - 2x$

$e^{\frac{1}{2}x} - 2 = 7 - 2x - 2$

$e^{\frac{1}{2}x} = 5 - 2x$

So, the solution is the intersection of the curve and $y = e^{\frac{1}{2}x}$ and the line $y = 5 - 2x$, $x \approx 2.1$

EXAMPLE 11

a Complete the table below of values of $y = 2 + \ln x$, giving your values of y to decimal places.

x	0.1	0.5	1	1.5	2	3	4
y	-0.3	1.31		2.41	2.69	3.10	

b Draw the graph of $y = 2 + \ln x$ for $0.1 \leqslant x \leqslant 4$

c Use your graph to estimate, to 2 significant figures, the solution of the equation $\ln x = 0.5$

d By drawing a suitable line on your graph estimate, to 1 significant figure, the solution of the equation $x = e^{x-2}$

a

x	0.1	0.5	1	1.5	2	3	4
y	-0.3	1.31	2	2.41	2.69	3.10	3.39

b

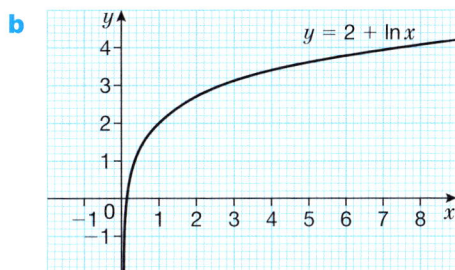

c $\ln x = 0.5$ Make the LHS $= 2 + \ln x$, i.e the equation of the graph.
Therefore you need to add 2

$2 + \ln x = 2.5$ and so draw the line $y = 2.5$

$y = 2.5$

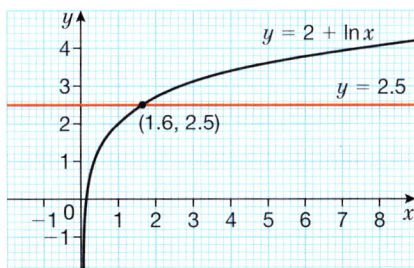

The solution is the intersection of the curve and the line $y = 2.5$. From the graph this is approximately 1.6. In the exam you will be given a small range of answers.

d $x = e^{x-2}$

$\ln x = x - 2$ Using the properties of logs

$\ln x + 2 = x - 2 + 2$ Make the LHS equal to the given equation i.e. $\ln x + 2$.

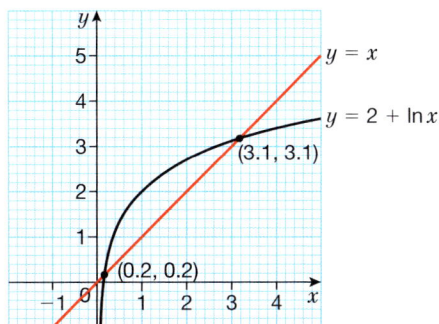

1 ▶ a Draw the graph $y = 3 + 2e^{-\frac{1}{2}x}$ for $0 \le x \le 6$

b Use your graph to estimate, to 1 decimal place, the solution to the equation $e^{-\frac{1}{2}x} = 0.5$, showing your method clearly.

c By drawing a suitable line, estimate, to 1 decimal place, the solution of the equation $x = -2 \ln\left(\dfrac{x-2}{2}\right)$

2 ▶ a Draw the graph $y = 2 + \dfrac{1}{3}e^x$ for $-1 \le x \le 3$

b Use your graph to estimate, to 1 decimal place, the solution to the equation $e^x = 12$ showing your method clearly.

c By drawing a suitable line, estimate, to 1 decimal place, the solution to the equation $x = \ln(6 - 6x)$

3 ▶ a Complete the table below of values of $y = 5 \sin 2x - 2 \cos x$, giving your values of y to 2 decimal places.

x	0°	15°	30°	45°	60°	75°	90°
y	−2	0.57		3.59	3.33		0

b Draw the graph of $y = 5 \sin 2x - 2 \cos x$ for $0 \le x \le 90°$

c Use your graph to estimate, to 1 decimal place, the solutions of the equation $2(1 + \cos x) = 5 \sin 2x$ showing your method clearly.

WRITING AN EXPRESSION AS A LOGARITHM

In the exam $\log_{10}$ will be written as lg. This textbook uses lg for $\log_{10}$.

$\log_a n = x$ **means that** $a^x = n$, **where** a **is called the base of the logarithm**.

- $\log_a 1 = 0 \ (a > 0)$, **because** $a^0 = 1$
- $\log_a a = 1 \ (a > 0)$, **because** $a^1 = a$

EXAMPLE 12

Write as a logarithm $2^5 = 32$

SKILLS

ADAPTABILITY

$2^5 = 32$

So $\log_2 32 = 5$ ⟶ Here $a = 2$, $x = 5$, $n = 32$

Here 2 is the base, 5 is the logarithm. In words, you would say '2 to the power of 5 equals 32'. You would also say 'the logarithm of 32, to base 2, is 5'.

EXAMPLE 13

Rewrite using a logarithm

a $10^3 = 1000$ **b** $5^4 = 625$ **c** $2^{10} = 1024$

a $\lg 1000 = 3$ **b** $\log_5 625 = 4$ **c** $\log_2 1024 = 10$

EXAMPLE 14

Find the value of

a $\log_3 81$ **b** $\log_4 0.25$ **c** $\log_{0.5} 4$ **d** $\log_a(a^5)$

a $\log_3 81 = 4$ $3^4 = 81$

b $\log_4 0.25 = -1$ $4^{-1} = \dfrac{1}{4} = 0.25$

c $\log_{0.5} 4 = -2$ $0.5^{-2} = \left(\dfrac{1}{2}\right)^{-2} = 2^2 = 4$

d $\log_a (a^5) = 5$ $a^5 = a^5$

EXERCISE 6

SKILLS

CRITICAL THINKING

1 ▶ Rewrite these exponentials as logarithms.

   a $4^3 = 64$ **b** $5^{-2} = \dfrac{1}{25}$ **c** $8^6 = 262\,144$

   d $3^x = 9$ **e** $8^x = 1$ **f** $2^x = \dfrac{1}{4}$

2 ▶ Write these logarithms in exponential form.

   a $\log_3 81 = 4$ **b** $\log_3 729 = 6$ **c** $\log_5 625 = 4$

   d $\log_{16} 4 = \dfrac{1}{2}$ **e** $\log_3\left(\dfrac{1}{27}\right) = -3$ **f** $\log_{10} 0.01 = -2$

3 ▶ Without a calculator find the value of

   a $\log_2 4$ **b** $\log_3 27$ **c** $\log_3 81$ **d** $\log_5 625$

   e $\log_5\left(\dfrac{1}{125}\right)$ **f** $\lg\sqrt{10}$ **g** $\log_3\sqrt{27}$ **h** $\log_3\sqrt[5]{3}$

4 ▶ Find the value of x for which

   a $\log_3 x = 4$ **b** $\log_6 x = 3$ **c** $\log_x 64 = 3$

   d $\log_x 16 = \dfrac{4}{3}$ **e** $\log_x 64 = \dfrac{2}{3}$

5 ▶ Find using your calculator

   a $\lg 20$ **b** $\lg 14$ **c** $\lg 0.25$ **d** $\lg 0.3$ **e** $\lg 54.6$

UNDERSTAND AND USE THE LAWS OF LOGARITHMS

$2^5 = 32$ and $\log_2 32 = 5$

The rules of logarithms follow the **rules of indices**.

EXPONENT (POWERS)	LOGARITHMS	LAW
$c^x \times c^x = c^{x+y}$	$\log_c xy = \log_c x + \log_c y$	Multiplication Law
$c^x \div c^y = c^{x-y}$	$\log_c \dfrac{x}{y} = \log_c x - \log_c y$	Division Law
$(c)^q$	$\log_c(x^q) = q\log_c x$	Power Law
$\dfrac{1}{c} = c^{-1}$	$\log_c\left(\dfrac{1}{x}\right) = -\log_c x$	
$c^1 = c$	$\log_c(c) = 1$	
$c^0 = 1$	$\log_c(1) = 0$	

EXAMPLE 15

SKILLS

DECISION MAKING

Write as a single logarithm

a $\log_3 6 + \log_3 7$ **b** $\log_2 15 - \log_2 3$ **c** $2\log_5 3 + 3\log_5 2$ **d** $\lg 3 - 4\lg\left(\dfrac{1}{2}\right)$

---

a $\log_3(6 \times 7)$

$= \log_3(42)$

Use the multiplication law

b $\log_2(15 \div 3)$

$= \log_2 5$

Use the division law

c $2\log_5 3 + 3\log_5 2$

$= \log_5(3^2) + \log_5(2^3)$

Apply the power law to both expressions

$= \log_5 9 + \log_5 8$

Use the multiplication law

$= \log_5 72$

d $\lg 3 - 4\lg\left(\dfrac{1}{2}\right)$

Use the power law

$= \lg 3 - \lg\left(\dfrac{1}{2}\right)^4$

$= \lg\left(3 \div \dfrac{1}{16}\right)$

$= \lg 48$

Use the division law

EXAMPLE 16

Find the value, in terms of $\log_a x$, $\log_a y$ and $\log_a z$

a $\log_a(x^2yz^3)$ **b** $\log_a\left(\dfrac{x}{y^3}\right)$ **c** $\log_a\left(\dfrac{x\sqrt{y}}{z}\right)$ **d** $\log_a\left(\dfrac{x}{a^4}\right)$

---

a $\log_a(x^2yz^3)$

$= \log_a(x^2) + \log_a(y) + \log_a(z^3)$

$= 2\log_a(x) + \log_a(y) + 3\log_a(z)$

b $\log_a\left(\dfrac{x}{y^3}\right)$

$= \log_a(x) - \log_a(y^3)$

$= \log_a(x) - 3\log_a(y)$

c $\log_a\left(\dfrac{x\sqrt{y}}{z}\right)$

$= \log_a(x\sqrt{y}) - \log_a(z)$

$= \log_a(x) + \log_a(\sqrt{y}) - \log_a(z)$

$= \log_a(x) + \dfrac{1}{2}\log_a(y) - \log_a(z)$

Use the power law $\sqrt{y} = y^{\frac{1}{2}}$

d $\log_a\left(\dfrac{x}{a^4}\right)$

$= \log_a(x) - \log_a(a^4)$

$$= \log_a(x) - 4\log_a(a)$$

$$= \log_a(x) - 4 \qquad\qquad \boxed{\log_a a = 1}$$

EXERCISE 7

SKILLS

CRITICAL THINKING

1 ▶ Write as a single logarithm

a $\log_4 8 + \log_4 8$

b $\log_9 3 + \log_9 2$

c $\log_5 27 + \log_5 3$

d $\log_4 24 + \log_4 15 - \log_5 3$

e $2\log_6 9 - 10\log_6 81$

f $\dfrac{1}{2}\log_2 25 + 2\log_2 3$

g $\log_8 25 + \log_8 10 - 3\log_8 5$

h $2\log_{12} 3 + 4\log_{12} 2$

i $2\lg 20 - (\lg 5 + \lg 8)$

2 ▶ Write in terms of $\log_a x$, $\log_a y$, $\log_a z$

a $\log_a x^4 y^3 z$

b $\log_a \dfrac{x^6}{y^3}$

c $\log_a ((xz)^2)$

d $\log_a \dfrac{1}{xyz}$

e $\log_a \sqrt{xy}$

f $\log_a \sqrt{x^4 y^2 z^3}$

g $\log_a \dfrac{\sqrt{x^3 y^7}}{z^3}$

CHANGE THE BASE OF A LOGARITHM

Working in base a, suppose that $\qquad\qquad \log_a x = m$

Writing this as a power $\qquad\qquad a^m = x$

Taking logs to a different base b $\qquad\qquad \log_b(a^m) = \log_b(x)$

Using the power law $\qquad\qquad m\log_b a = \log_b x$

Writing m as $\log_a x$ $\qquad\qquad \log_a x \times \log_b a = \log_b x$

This can be written as $\qquad\qquad \log_a x = \dfrac{\log_b x}{\log_b a}$

Using this rule, notice in particular that $\log_a b = \dfrac{\log_b b}{\log_b a}$,

$$\text{but } \log_b b = 1$$

$$\text{so, } \log_a b = \dfrac{1}{\log_b a}$$

EXAMPLE 17

SKILLS

EXECUTIVE FUNCTION

Find, to 3 significant figures, the value of $\log_8(11)$

One method is to use the change of base rule

$$\log_8 11 = \dfrac{\lg 11}{\lg 8}$$

$$= 1.15$$

Another method is to solve $8^x = 11$

$$\text{Let } x = \log_8(11)$$

$$8^x = 11$$

$$\lg (8^x) = \lg 11$$ Take logs to base 10 of each side

$$x \lg 8 = \lg 11$$ Use the power law

$$x = \frac{\lg 11}{\lg 8}$$ Divide by $\lg 8$

$$x = 1.15 \text{ (3 s.f.)}$$

EXAMPLE 18   Solve the equation $\log_5 x + 6\log_x 5 = 5$

$$\log_5 x + \frac{6}{\log_5 x} = 5$$ Use change of base rule, special case

$$\text{Let } \log_5(x) = y$$

$$y + \frac{6}{y} = 5$$

$$y^2 + 6 = 5y$$ Multiply by y

$$y^2 - 5y + 6 = 0$$

$$(y - 3)(y - 2) = 0$$

$$\text{So } y = 3 \text{ or } y = 2$$

$$\log_5 x = 3 \text{ or } \log_5 x = 2$$

$$x = 5^3 \text{ or } x = 5^2$$ Write as powers

$$x = 125 \text{ or } x = 25$$

EXERCISE 8

SKILLS

EXECUTIVE FUNCTION

1 ▶ Find, to 3 significant figures

a $\log_8 785$ b $\log_5 15$ c $\log_6 32$

d $\log_{12} 4$ e $\log_{15} \frac{1}{7}$

2 ▶ Solve, giving your answer to 3 significant figures

a $6^x = 15$ b $9^x = 751$

c $15^x = 3$ d $3^x = 17.3$

e $3^{2x} = 25$ f $4^{3x} = 64$

g $7^{3x} = 152$

HINT

If no base is given in a question, you should assume base 10.

3 ▶ Solve, giving your answers in an exact form

a $\log_2 x = 8 + 9\log_x 2$ b $\log_6 x + 3\log_x 6 = 4$

c $\lg x + 5\log_x 10 = -6$ d $\log_2 x + \log_4 x = 2$

SOLVE EQUATIONS OF THE FORM $a^x = b$

You need to be able to solve equations of the form $a^x = b$.

EXAMPLE 19   Solve the equation $3^x = 20$, giving your answer to 3 significant figures.

SKILLS

PROBLEM SOLVING ANALYSIS

$$3^x = 20$$

$$\lg (3^x) = \lg 20$$ Take logs to base 10 on each side

$x \lg 3 = \lg 20$ Use the power law

$x = \dfrac{\lg 20}{\lg 3}$ Divide by $\lg 3$

$x = \dfrac{1.3010...}{0.4771...}$ Use your calculator for logs to base 10

$= 2.73$ (3 s.f.)

Or, a simpler version

$3^x = 20$

$x = \log_3 20$

$x = 2.73$

EXAMPLE 20 Solve the equation $7^{x+1} = 3^{x+2}$

$(x + 1) \lg 7 = (x + 2) \lg 3$ Use the power law

$x \lg 7 + \lg 7 = x \lg 3 + 2 \lg 3$ Multiply out

$x \lg 7 - x \lg 3 = 2 \lg 3 - \lg 7$ Collect x terms on left and numerical terms on right

$x(\lg 7 - \lg 3) = 2 \lg 3 - \lg 7$ Factorise

$x = \dfrac{2 \lg 3 - \lg 7}{\lg 7 - \lg 3}$ Divide by $\lg 7 - \lg 3$

$x = 0.297$ (3 s.f.)

EXAMPLE 21 Solve the equation $5^{2x} + 7(5^x) - 30 = 0$, giving your answer to 2 decimal places.

Let $y = 5^x$

$y^2 + 7y - 30 = 0$ Use $5^{2x} = (5^x)^2 = y^2$

So $(y + 10)(y - 3) = 0$

So $y = -10$ or $y = 3$

If $y = -10$, $5^x = -10$, has no solution 5^x cannot be negative

If $y = 3$, $5^x = 3$

$\lg (5^x) = \lg 3$ Solve as in previous examples

$x \lg (5) = \lg 3$

$x = \dfrac{\lg 3}{\lg 5}$

$x = 0.683$ (3 s.f.)

EXERCISE 9

1 ▶ Solve, giving your answer to 3 significant figures

    a $4^x = 12$ **b** $5^x = 20$

    c $15^x = 175$ **d** $7^x = \dfrac{1}{4}$

    e $4^{x+1} = 30$ **f** $7^{2x+1} = 36$

    g $4^{x+1} = 9^{x+2}$ **h** $2^{3y-2} = 3^{2y+5}$

    i $7^{2x+6} = 11^{3x-2}$ **j** $3^{4-3x} = 4^{x+5}$

2 ▶ Solve, giving your answer to 3 significant figures

    a $4^{2x} + 4^x - 12 = 0$ **b** $6^{2x} - 10(6^x) + 8 = 0$

    c $5^{2x} - 6(5^x) - 7 = 0$ **d** $4^{2x+1} + 7(4^x) - 15 = 0$

    e $3^{2x} - 5(3^x) = -4$ **f** $3^{2x+1} = 26(3^x) + 9$

EXAM PRACTICE: CHAPTER 1

1   Simplify $\sqrt{32} + \sqrt{18}$, giving your answer in the form $p\sqrt{2}$, where p is an integer.   **[2]**

2   Simplify $\dfrac{\sqrt{32} + \sqrt{18}}{3 + \sqrt{2}}$ giving your answer in the form $a\sqrt{2} + b$,

where a and b are integers.   **[3]**

3   **a**   Expand and simplify $(7 + \sqrt{5})(3 - \sqrt{5})$ **[2]**

    b   Express $\dfrac{7 + \sqrt{5}}{3 + \sqrt{5}}$ in the form $a + b\sqrt{5}$, where a and b are integers.   **[2]**

4   Write $\sqrt{75} - \sqrt{27}$ in the form $k\sqrt{x}$, where k and x are integers.   **[2]**

5   A rectangle A has a length of $(1 + \sqrt{5})$ cm and an area of $\sqrt{80}$ cm².

Calculate the width of A in cm, giving your answer in the form $a + b\sqrt{5}$, where a and b are integers to be found.   **[3]**

6   Sketch the graph of $y = 8^x$, showing the coordinates of any points at which the graph crosses the axes.   **[3]**

7   Solve the equation $8^{2x} - 4(8^x) = 3$, giving your answer to 3 significant figures.   **[3]**

8   **a**   Given that $y = 6x^2$, Show that $\log_6 y = 1 + 2\log_6 x$ **[2]**

    b   Hence, or otherwise, solve the equation $1 + 2\log_3 x = \log_3 (28x - 9)$ **[3]**

9   Find the values of x such that: $2\log_3 x - \log_3 (x - 2) - 2 = 0$ **[2]**

10   Find the values of y such that: $\dfrac{\log_2 32 + \log_2 16}{\log_2 y} - \log_2 y = 0$ **[3]**

11   Given that $\log_b y + 3\log_b 2 = 5$, express y in terms of b in its simplest form.   **[2]**

12   Solve $5^{2x} = 12(5^x) - 35$ **[4]**

13   Find, giving your answer to 3 significant figures where appropriate, the value of x for which $5^x = 10$ **[3]**

14   Given that $\log_3 (3b + 1) - \log_3 (a - 2) = -1$, $a > 2$, express b in terms of a.   **[2]**

15   Solve $3^{3x-2} = \sqrt[3]{9}$ **[4]**

16   Solve $25^t + 5^{t+1} = 24$, giving your answer to 3 significant figures.   **[3]**

17 Given that $\log_2 x = p$, find, in terms of p, the simplest form of

   a $\log_2(16x)$, [1]

   b $\log_2\left(\dfrac{x^4}{2}\right)$. [1]

   c Hence, or otherwise, solve

   $$\log_2(16x) - \log_2\left(\dfrac{x^4}{2}\right) = \dfrac{1}{2}$$

   Give your answer in its simplest surd form. [3]

18 Solve $\log_3 t + \log_3 5 = \log_3(2t + 3)$ [3]

19 **a** Draw the graph $y = 2 + \ln x$ for $0.1 \leqslant x \leqslant 4$ [2]

   b Use your graph to estimate, to 2 significant figures, the solution to $\ln x = 0.5$, showing clearly your method. [2]

   c By drawing a suitable line, estimate to 2 significant figures, the solution of the equation $x = e^{x-2}$ [2]

CHAPTER SUMMARY: CHAPTER 1

■ You can simplify expressions by using the power (indices) laws

$c^x \times c^x = c^{x+y}$
$c^x \div c^y = c^{x-y}$
$(c^p)^q = c^{p \times q}$
$\dfrac{1}{c} = c^{-1}$
$c^1 = c$
$c^0 = 1$

■ You can manipulate surds using these rules:

  ■ $\sqrt{ab} = \sqrt{a} \times \sqrt{b}$

  ■ $\sqrt{\dfrac{a}{b}} = \dfrac{\sqrt{a}}{\sqrt{b}}$

    ■ The rules for rationalising surds are:

      ■ If you have a fraction in the form $\dfrac{1}{\sqrt{a}}$ then multiply top and bottom by $\sqrt{a}$

      ■ If you have a fraction in the form $\dfrac{1}{1 + \sqrt{a}}$ then multiply top and bottom by $(1 - \sqrt{a})$

      ■ If you have a fraction in the form $\dfrac{1}{1 - \sqrt{a}}$ then multiply top and bottom by $(1 + \sqrt{a})$

■ $\log_a n = x$ can be rewritten as $a^x = n$ where a is the base of the logarithm

■ The laws of logarithms are:

$\log_a xy = \log_a x + \log_a y$
$\log_a \dfrac{x}{y} = \log_a x - \log_a y$
$\log_a (x^q) = q\log_a x$
$\log_a \left(\dfrac{1}{x}\right) = -\log_a x$
$\log_a (c) = 1$
$\log_a (1) = 0$

■ The change of base rule for logarithms can be written as $\log_a x = \dfrac{\log_b x}{\log_b a}$

■ From the change of base you can derive $\log_a b = \dfrac{1}{\log_b a}$

■ The natural logarithm is defined as: $\log_e x \equiv \ln x$

■ The graph of $y = e^x$ is shown below   ■ The graph of $y = \ln x$ is shown below

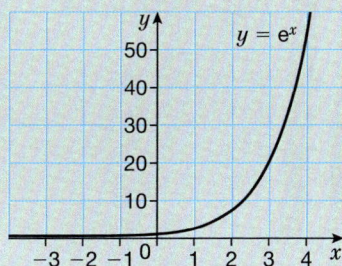

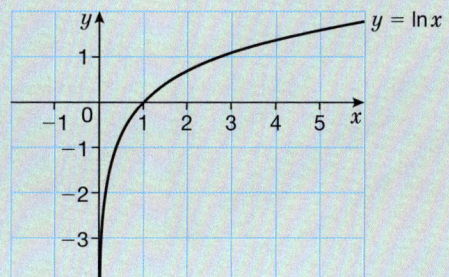

CHAPTER 2

2 THE QUADRATIC FUNCTION

The path followed by a bottlenose dolphin jumping out of the water is called a parabola. A parabola is a **visual realisation** of the quadratic function $y = -x^2 + k$. Using this formula, scientists can calculate the height of a dolphin's jump (on the y-axis) and the distance travelled (on the x-axis).

There is no scientific agreement about why dolphins jump. Some scientists believe it is because they are trying to conserve energy, some believe it is to help them find food, and others believe they do it just for fun.

The parabola is a beautiful and elegant shape, commonly seen in nature. It is also seen in many man-made structures such as bridges and buildings.

LEARNING OBJECTIVES

- **Factorise** quadratic expressions where the **coefficient** of x^2 is greater than 1

- Complete the square and use this to solve quadratic equations

- Solve quadratic equations using the quadratic formula

- Understand and use the discriminant to identify whether the roots are (i) equal and real, (ii) unequal and real or (iii) not real

- Understand the roots a and β and know how to use them

STARTER ACTIVITIES

1 ▶ Factorise

   a $6x^2 + 9x$ b $2b^2 + 8b$ c $9qm^2 - 27m$

   d $9xy^2 + 36x^2y$ e $24x - 64x^2$

2 ▶ Factorise

   a $x^2 + 9x + 18$ b $x^2 - 7x + 12$ c $x^2 - 2x - 3$

   d $x^2 + 15x + 36$ e $x^2 + 12x + 27$

3 ▶ Factorise

   a $x^2 - 9$ b $x^2 - 25$

   c $9x^2 - 16$ d $25x^2 - 16$

HINT

All the parts in question 3 are examples of the difference of two squares.

FACTORISE QUADRATIC EXPRESSIONS WHERE THE COEFFICIENT OF x^2 IS GREATER THAN 1

EXAMPLE 1

SKILLS

DECISION MAKING CRITICAL THINKING

Factorise $3x^2 + 5x - 2$

You need to find two numbers:

They must **add** together to make $+5$ (the coefficient of x), and they must **multiply** together to give -6 (the coefficient of $x^2 \times$ the **constant** term, in this case 3×-2)

$$6 \times -1 = -6 \qquad \text{and} \qquad 6 + (-1) = 5$$

These numbers are then used to split the $5x$ into two terms, $6x$ and $-1x$

$3x^2 + 5x - 2 = 3x^2 + 6x - x - 2$ The $5x$ term has been split into $6x$ and $-x$

$\qquad\qquad\quad = 3x(x + 2) - (x + 2)$

$\qquad\qquad\quad = (x + 2)(3x - 1)$ $3x^2 + 6x$ and $-x - 2$ have both been factorised

EXAMPLE 2

SKILLS

CRITICAL THINKING DECISION MAKING

Factorise $6x^2 - 5x - 4$

Find two numbers that add together to make -5 and multiply together to give -24

(the coefficient of x^2 multiplied by the constant term, in this case 6×-4)

$$3 \times -8 = -24 \qquad \text{and} \qquad 3 + -8 = -5$$

$6x^2 - 5x - 4 = 6x^2 + 3x - 8x - 4$ The $-5x$ term has been split into $3x$ and $-8x$

$\qquad\qquad\quad = 3x(2x + 1) - 4(2x + 1)$

$\qquad\qquad\quad = (2x + 1)(3x - 4)$ $6x^2 + 3x$ and $-8x - 4$ have both been factorised

EXERCISE 1

SKILLS

CRITICAL THINKING DECISION MAKING

1 ▶ Factorise

     a $3x^2 - 7x - 6$ **b** $2x^2 + 11x + 5$

     c $2x^2 - 7x - 4$ **d** $5x^2 - 16x + 3$

     e $6x^2 + x - 12$ **f** $9x^2 - 6x + 1$

     g $9x^2 - 18x - 7$

2 ▶ Solve

     a $2x^2 + 5x + 2 = 0$ **b** $4x^2 + 17x + 4 = 0$

     c $3x^2 - 13x = -4$ **d** $6x^2 - 10x + 4 = 0$

     e $3(x^2 - 2) = -17x$ **f** $15x^2 + 42x - 9 = 0$

     g $3x(3x - 4) = -4$

COMPLETE THE SQUARE AND USE THIS TO SOLVE QUADRATIC EQUATIONS

A perfect square quadratic is in the form:

$$x^2 + 2bx + b^2 = (x + b)^2 \quad \text{or} \quad x^2 - 2bx + b^2 = (x - b)^2$$

In order to complete the square you will need to manipulate the expression.

To complete the square of the function $x^2 + 2bx$ you need a further term b^2.

So the completed square form is:

$$x^2 + 2bx = (x + b)^2 - b^2$$

Similarly

$$x^2 - 2bx = (x - b)^2 - b^2$$

Completing the square: $x^2 + bx = \left(x + \dfrac{b}{2}\right)^2 - \left(\dfrac{b}{2}\right)^2$

EXAMPLE 3

SKILLS

REASONING
EXECUTIVE
FUNCTION

Complete the square for

a $x^2 + 12x$
b $2x^2 - 10x$

a $x^2 + 12x$ 　　　　　　　　　　$2b = 12$ so $b = 6$

$= (x + 6)^2 - 6^2$

$= (x + 6)^2 - 36$

b $2x^2 - 10x$ 　　　　　　Here the coefficient of x^2 is 2

$= 2(x^2 - 5x)$ 　　　　　　So take out the coefficient of x^2

$= 2\left[\left(x - \dfrac{5}{2}\right)^2 - \left(\dfrac{5}{2}\right)^2\right]$ 　　Complete the square on $(x^2 - 5x)$

$= 2\left(x - \dfrac{5}{2}\right)^2 - \dfrac{25}{2}$

Any quadratic equation can be solved by completing the square.

EXAMPLE 4

Complete the square to solve

a $x^2 + 8x + 10 = 0$
b $2x^2 - 8x + 7 = 0$

a $x^2 + 8x + 10 = 0$ 　　　　Check coefficient of $x^2 = 1$

$x^2 + 8x = -10$ 　　　　Subtract 10 to get the LHS in the form $ax^2 + bx$

$(x + 4)^2 - 4^2 = -10$ 　　Complete the square for $(x^2 + 8x)$

$(x + 4)^2 = -10 + 16$ 　　Add 4^2 to both sides

$(x + 4)^2 = 6$

$(x + 4) = \pm\sqrt{6}$ 　　　　Square root both sides

$x = -4 \pm \sqrt{6}$ 　　　　Subtract 4 from both sides

Then the solutions of $x^2 + 8x + 10 = 0$ are either

$x = -4 + \sqrt{6}$ or $x = -4 - \sqrt{6}$ 　　Leave your answer in surd form

b $2x^2 - 8x + 7 = 0$ The coefficient of x^2 is 2

$x^2 - 4x + \dfrac{7}{2} = 0$ So divide by 2

$x^2 - 4x = -\dfrac{7}{2}$ Subtract $\dfrac{7}{2}$ from both sides

$(x - 2)^2 - 2^2 = -\dfrac{7}{2}$ Complete the square for $x^2 - 4x$

$(x - 2)^2 = -\dfrac{7}{2} + 4$ Add 2^2 to both sides

$(x - 2)^2 = \dfrac{1}{2}$ Combine the RHS

$(x - 2) = \pm\sqrt{\dfrac{1}{2}}$ Square root both sides

$x = 2 \pm \dfrac{1}{\sqrt{2}}$ Add 2 to both sides

So the roots are either

$x = 2 + \dfrac{1}{\sqrt{2}}$ or $x = 2 - \dfrac{1}{\sqrt{2}}$

EXERCISE 2

SKILLS

PROBLEM SOLVING

1 ▶ Complete the square for these expressions.

     a $x^2 + 4x$ **b** $x^2 - 16x$ **c** $3x^2 - 24x$

     d $x^2 - x - 12$ **e** $x^2 + x - 1$ **f** $3x^2 - 6x + 1$

     g $2x^2 + 3x - 1$ **h** $4x^2 + 6x - 1$

2 ▶ Solve these quadratic equations by completing the square.

Leave your answer in surd form where appropriate.

     a $6x^2 - 11x - 10 = 0$ **b** $x^2 + 2x - 2 = 0$ **c** $2x^2 - 6x + 1 = 0$

     d $2x^2 + 3x - 6 = 0$ **e** $4x^2 - 59x - 15 = 0$ **f** $4x^2 + 8x - 9 = 0$

     g $15 - 6x - 2x^2 = 0$ **h** $4x^2 - x - 8 = 0$

3 ▶ Show by completing the square that the solutions to $ax^2 + bx + c = 0$ are $x = \dfrac{-b \pm \sqrt{b^2 - 4ac}}{2a}$

SOLVE QUADRATIC EQUATIONS USING THE QUADRATIC FORMULA

The quadratic formula $x = \dfrac{-b \pm \sqrt{b^2 - 4ac}}{2a}$

can be used to solve any quadratic equation of the form $ax^2 + bx + c = 0$ if a is not zero.

EXAMPLE 5

Use the quadratic formula to solve $4x^2 - 3x - 2 = 0$

SKILLS

PROBLEM SOLVING

$x = \dfrac{-(-3) \pm \sqrt{(-3)^2 - 4(4)(-2)}}{2 \times 4}$ Use $x = \dfrac{-b \pm \sqrt{b^2 - 4ac}}{2a}$, where $a = 4, b = -3, c = -2$

$x = \dfrac{3 \pm \sqrt{(9 + 32)}}{8}$ $-4 \times 4 \times -2 = 32$

$x = \dfrac{3 \pm \sqrt{41}}{8}$

Then $x = \dfrac{3 + \sqrt{41}}{8}$ or $x = \dfrac{3 - \sqrt{41}}{8}$ Leave your answer in surd form

EXERCISE 3

SKILLS

EXECUTIVE
FUNCTION

1 ▶ Solve these equations using the quadratic formula.
Leave your answer in surd form where appropriate.

a $x^2 = 6x$
b $2x^2 + 50x = 0$
c $x^2 - x - 6 = 0$

d $p^2 - 4p + 2 = 0$
e $m^2 + 2m - 2 = 0$
f $x^2 + 7x + 10 = 0$

g $t^2 - 5t - 6 = 0$
h $x^2 + 2x - 35 = 0$
i $n^2 - 4n + 4 = 0$

j $x^2 + 6x + 6 = 0$

2 ▶ Solve these equations, leaving your answer in surd form if appropriate.

a $9x^2 - 6x - 25 = 0$
b $3x^2 - 6x + 2 = 0$
c $6x^2 - 5x - 6 = 0$

d $2x^2 + 3x - 1 = 0$
e $2x^2 + 7x + 3 = 0$
f $3x^2 + 7x + 1 = 0$

g $4x^2 - 16x + 15 = 0$
h $7x^2 + 5x - 3 = 0$
i $10x^2 - 15x - 8 = 0$

j $x^2 + 3x - 6 = 0$
k $(x - 7)^2 = 63$
l $4x^2 + 15x + 13 = 0$

3 ▶ The diagram shows the floor plan of a bedroom.
The total area is $35.5\,\text{m}^2$ Find the value of x.

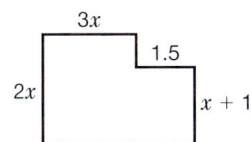

UNDERSTAND AND USE THE DISCRIMINANT TO IDENTIFY WHETHER THE ROOTS ARE (i) EQUAL AND REAL, (ii) UNEQUAL AND REAL OR (iii) NOT REAL

The equation $ax^2 + bx + c = 0$ has two solutions where a is not zero

$$x = \frac{-b + \sqrt{b^2 - 4ac}}{2a} \text{ and } x = \frac{-b - \sqrt{b^2 - 4ac}}{2a}$$

These two solutions may be the same or different, real numbers or not real numbers.

The nature of the roots (solutions) of the equation will clearly depend on the expression $b^2 - 4ac$. This expression $b^2 - 4ac$ is called the *discriminant*, as it allows us to identify (*discriminate*) whether the roots of a particular equation are equal and real, unequal and real or not real at all.

$b^2 - 4ac > 0$ the roots of the equation are **unequal and real** (**two roots**)	$b^2 - 4ac = 0$ the roots of the equation are **equal and real** (**one repeated root**)	$b^2 - 4ac < 0$ there are **no real roots** of the equation (**no real roots**)

EXAMPLE 6

SKILLS

REASONING

What can you **deduce** from the values of the discriminants of these equations? Find the roots where possible.

a $2x^2 - 3x + 5 = 0$
b $3x^2 - x - 1 = 0$
c $4x^2 - 12x + 9 = 0$

a $2x^2 - 3x + 5 = 0$

$a = 2, b = -3, c = 5$

$b^2 - 4ac$

$(-3)^2 - 4 \times 2 \times 5 = -31$

Therefore there are no real roots.

b $3x^2 - x - 1 = 0$

$a = 3, b = -1, c = -1$

$b^2 - 4ac = (-1)^2 - 4 \times 3 \times (-1) = 13$

Therefore there are two unequal roots.

$x = \dfrac{-(-1) \pm \sqrt{13}}{2 \times 3}$ so

$x = \dfrac{1 \pm \sqrt{13}}{6}$

Use the quadratic formula to find solutions

c $4x^2 - 12x + 9 = 0$

$a = 4, b = -12, c = 9$

$(-12)^2 - 4 \times 4 \times 9 = 0$

Calculate the discriminant

Therefore the roots are real and equal.

$x = \dfrac{-(-12)}{2 \times 4}$ and $x = \dfrac{3}{2}$

When the discriminant is 0 you can always factorise. In this case $4x^2 - 12x + 9 = (2x - 3)^2 = 0$

EXAMPLE 7

The equation $kx^2 - 2x - 8 = 0$ has two real roots.

What can you deduce about the value of the constant k?

Since the equation has two real roots, you know that the discriminant $b^2 - 4ac$ must be greater than zero.

You **substitute** $a = k, b = -2$ and $c = -8$ into the inequality $b^2 - 4ac > 0$, giving

$(-2)^2 - 4 \times k \times (-8) > 0$

$4 + 32k > 0$

$k > -\dfrac{4}{32}$

$k > -\dfrac{1}{8}$ (where k is not zero)

EXERCISE 4

SKILLS

REASONING

1 ▶ Use the discriminant to **determine** whether these equations have one repeated root, two distinct roots or no roots.

    a $x^2 - 2x + 1 = 0$ **b** $x^2 - 3x - 2 = 0$ **c** $2x^2 - 3x - 4 = 0$

    d $2x^2 - 4x + 5 = 0$ **e** $2x^2 - 4x + 2 = 0$ **f** $2x^2 - 7x + 3 = 0$

    g $3x^2 - 6x + 5 = 0$ **h** $7x^2 - 144x + 57 = 0$ **i** $16x^2 - 2x + 3 = 0$

    j $x^2 + 22x + 121 = 0$ **k** $5x^2 - 4x + 81 = 0$

2 ▶ The equation $px^2 - 2x - 7 = 0$ has two real roots.
What can you deduce about the value of p?

3 ▶ The equation $3x^2 + 2x + m = 0$ has equal roots.
Find the value of m.

UNDERSTAND THE ROOTS α AND β AND HOW TO USE THEM

If α and β are the **roots** of the equation $ax^2 + bx + c = 0$ then you deduce that

$(x - \alpha)(x - \beta) = 0$

You can rewrite this as $x^2 - x(\alpha + \beta) + \alpha\beta = 0$

Comparing this with $ax^2 + bx + c = 0$ you can see that

$\alpha + \beta = \dfrac{-b}{a}$ and $\alpha\beta = \dfrac{c}{a}$

KEY POINTS

For the equation $ax^2 + bx + c = 0$

• The sum of roots, $\alpha + \beta = \dfrac{-b}{a}$

• The product of the roots, $\alpha\beta = \dfrac{c}{a}$

EXAMPLE 8

SKILLS

REASONING
CRITICAL
THINKING

1 ▶ The roots of the equation $3x^2 + x - 6 = 0$ are α and β.

   a Find an expression for $\alpha + \beta$ and an expression for $\alpha\beta$.

   b Hence find an expression for $\alpha^2 + \beta^2$ and an expression for $\alpha^2\beta^2$.

   c Find a quadratic equation with roots α^2 and β^2.

   a $3x^2 + x - 6 = 0$

      $x^2 + \dfrac{1}{3}x - 2 = 0$

Divide the equation by 3 to obtain an equation where the coefficient of x^2 is 1

      Therefore sum of the roots $\alpha + \beta = -\dfrac{1}{3}$

The sum of roots $\alpha + \beta = -\dfrac{b}{a}$

Note: Sometimes you will need to manipulate the expressions to help you solve the questions.

      Product of the roots $\alpha\beta = -2$

The product of the roots $\alpha\beta = \dfrac{c}{a}$

   b $(\alpha + \beta)^2 = \alpha^2 + 2\alpha\beta + \beta^2$

      Therefore $\alpha^2 + \beta^2 = (\alpha + \beta)^2 - 2\alpha\beta$

      Substituting the results from part **a**, gives

      $\alpha^2 + \beta^2 = \left(-\dfrac{1}{3}\right)^2 - 2(-2)$

            $= \dfrac{37}{9}$

      $\alpha^2\beta^2 = (\alpha\beta)^2 = (-2)^2 = 4$

c Let the equation be $x^2 + px + q = 0$

$p = (a^2 + \beta^2) = -\dfrac{37}{9}$ Use $p = -$sum of the roots

$q = a^2\beta^2 = 4$ $q = $ product of the roots

So the equation is: $x^2 - \dfrac{37}{9}x + 4 = 0$ Simplify the equations in order for the all the coefficients to be integers

OR $9x^2 - 37x + 36 = 0$

Note: This question can be answered without finding a and β.

EXAMPLE 9

The roots of the equation $x^2 - 3x - 2 = 0$ are a and β.

Without finding the value of a and β, find the equations with the roots

a $3a, 3\beta$ **b** $\dfrac{1}{a}, \dfrac{1}{\beta}$ **c** a^2, β^2

If a and β are the roots of $x^2 - 3x - 2 = 0$ then $a + \beta = 3$ and $a\beta = -2$

a If the roots are $3a$ and 3β then

Sum of the roots $= 3(a + \beta) = 3 \times 3 = 9$ Using $a + \beta = 3$ and $a\beta = -2$

Product of the roots $= 3a \times 3\beta = 9a\beta = -18$

Equation is $x^2 - 9x - 18 = 0$

b If the roots are $\dfrac{1}{a}, \dfrac{1}{\beta}$

Sum of roots $\dfrac{1}{a} + \dfrac{1}{\beta} = \dfrac{\beta + a}{a\beta}$

$\qquad\qquad = -\dfrac{3}{2}$

Product of roots: $\dfrac{1}{a} \times \dfrac{1}{\beta} = \dfrac{1}{a\beta}$ Using $a + \beta = 3$ and $a\beta = -2$

$\qquad\qquad = -\dfrac{1}{2}$

Equation is: $x^2 + \dfrac{3}{2}x - \dfrac{1}{2} = 0$

so $2x^2 + 3x - 1 = 0$

c If the roots are a^2, β^2 then

Sum of roots $= a^2 + \beta^2 = (a + \beta)^2 - 2a\beta$

$\qquad\qquad = 3^2 - 2(-2) = 13$

Product of roots $= a^2\beta^2 = (a\beta)^2 = (-2)^2 = 4$

Therefore equation is $x^2 - 13x + 4 = 0$

EXERCISE 5

SKILLS

REASONING
CRITICAL
THINKING

1 ▶ The roots of the equation $x^2 + 5x + 2 = 0$ are α and β.
Find an equation whose roots are

   a $2\alpha + 1$ and $2\beta + 1$

   b $\alpha\beta$ and $\alpha^2\beta^2$

2 ▶ The roots of the equation $x^2 + 6x + 1 = 0$ are α and β.
Find an equation whose roots are

   a $\alpha + 3$ and $\beta + 3$

   b $\dfrac{\alpha}{\beta}$ and $\dfrac{\beta}{\alpha}$

3 ▶ The roots of the equation $x^2 - x - 1 = 0$ are α and β.
Find an equation whose roots are

   a $\dfrac{1}{\alpha}$ and $\dfrac{1}{\beta}$

   b $\dfrac{\alpha}{\alpha + \beta}$ and $\dfrac{\beta}{\alpha + \beta}$

EXAM PRACTICE: CHAPTER 2

1 $f(x) = 0 = 3x^2 - 10x - 2$

   a   Without solving the equation $f(x)=0$, form an equation, with integer coefficients which has:

     i   roots $\dfrac{\alpha}{\beta}$ and $\dfrac{\beta}{\alpha}$

     ii   roots $2\alpha + \beta$ and $\alpha + 2\beta$ **[6]**

   b   Solve $f(x) = 0$ by completing the square.   **[4]**

2   The roots of a quadratic equation are α and β where $\alpha + \beta = -\dfrac{9}{5}$ and $\alpha\beta = -3$.

   Find a quadratic equation, with integer coefficients, which has roots α and β **[4]**

3   Given that $\alpha + \beta = 7$ and $\alpha^2 + \beta^2 = 25$

   a   Show that $\alpha\beta = 12$.   **[2]**

   b   Hence, or otherwise, form a quadratic equation with integer coefficients, which has roots α and β.   **[3]**

   c   Form a quadratic equation, with integer coefficients, which has roots $\dfrac{\alpha}{\beta}$ and $\dfrac{\beta}{\alpha}$.   **[5]**

4   The equation $x^2 + (p - 3)x + (3 - 2p) = 0$, where p is a constant, has two distinct real roots.

   a   Show that p satisfies $p^2 + 2p - 3 > 0$ **[1]**

   b   Find the possible values of p.   **[2]**

5   **a**   Show that $x^2 + 6x + 11$ can be written as $(x + a)^2 + b$.   **[2]**

   b   Find the value of the discriminant.   **[2]**

6   Factorise completely

   a $5x^2 + 16x + 3$ **[3]**

   b $3x^2 - 7x + 4$ **[3]**

7   Solve these equations by completing the square.

   a $p^2 + 3p + 2 = 0$ **[3]**

   b $3x^2 + 13x - 10 = 0$ **[3]**

8   Solve these equations by using the quadratic formula.

   a $5x^2 + 3x - 1 = 0$ **[2]**

   b $(2x - 5)^2 = 7$ **[3]**

9 $4x - 5 - x^2 = b - (x + a)^2$ where a and b are integers.

   a   Find the value of a and b.   **[2]**

   b   Calculate the discriminant.   **[2]**

10   Solve $\dfrac{4}{2x + 1} - 3 = -\dfrac{1}{4x^2 - 1}$ **[3]**

CHAPTER SUMMARY: CHAPTER 2

- $x^2 - y^2 = (x - y)(x + y)$ is known as the *difference of two squares*

- Quadratic equations can be solved by

  - factorisation
  - completing the square: $x^2 + bx = \left(x + \dfrac{b}{2}\right)^2 - \left(\dfrac{b}{2}\right)^2$
  - using the quadratic formula: $x = \dfrac{-b \pm \sqrt{b^2 - 4ac}}{2a}$

- The *discriminant* of a quadratic expression is $b^2 - 4ac$

- If α and β are the roots of the equation $ax^2 + bx + c = 0$ then

  - $\alpha + \beta = -\dfrac{b}{a}$
  - $\alpha\beta = \dfrac{c}{a}$

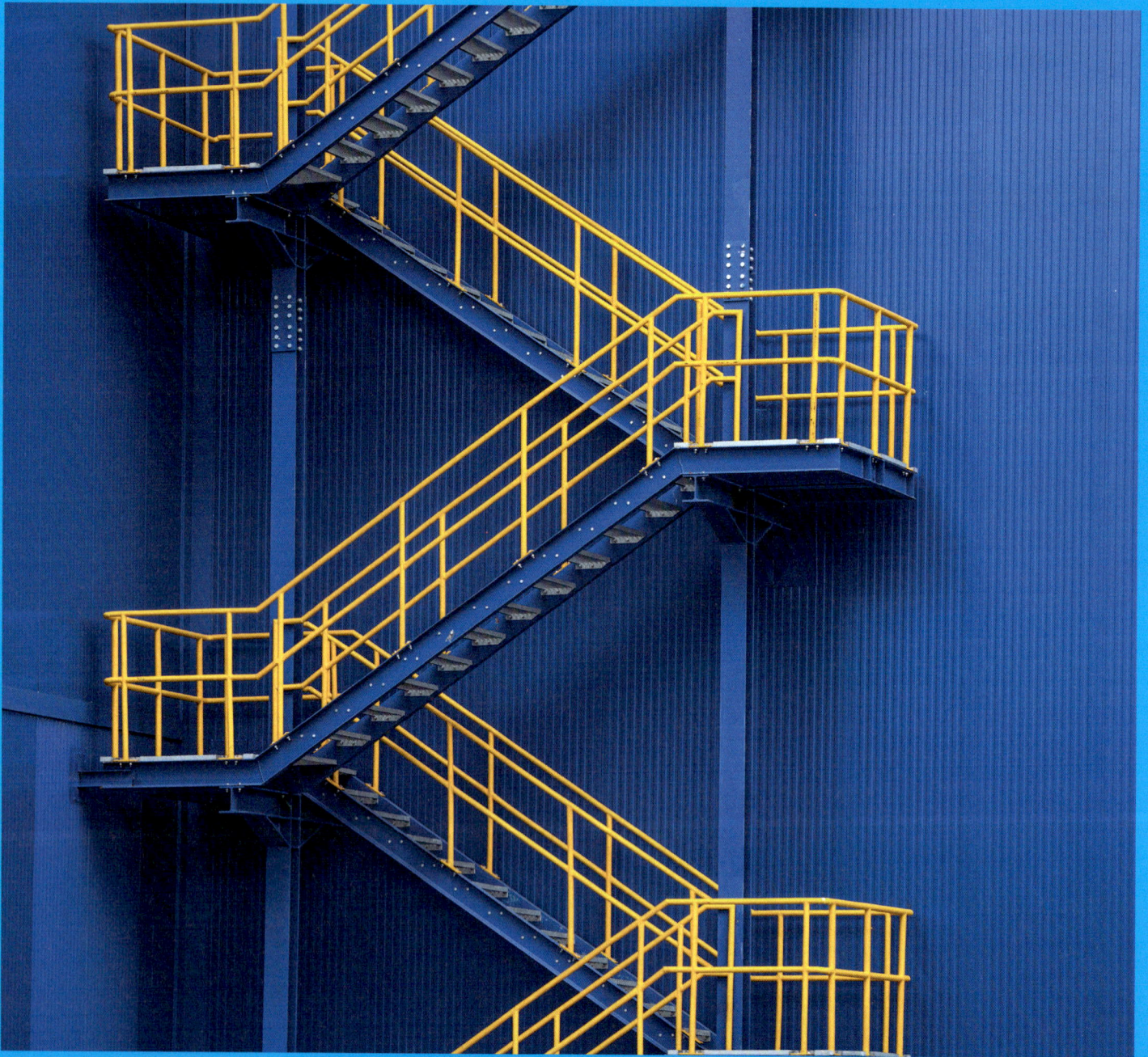

CHAPTER 3

3 INEQUALITIES AND IDENTITIES

The only value at which Fahrenheit and Celsius are the same temperature is -40.

If you substitute $F = C$ into the **linear** equation $F = 1.8C + 32$ you get: $C = F = -40$.

In this chapter you will learn about **simultaneous equations**, inequalities and linear programming (a form of **mathematical modelling**).

All of these mathematical tools are vital for research into **global warming**. Mathematical modelling enables us to predict the effects of global warming, from how it will affect human health to the effect it has on global food production. Scientists, businesses, economists and politicians all use mathematical models to plan ways of limiting the consequences of global warming.

LEARNING OBJECTIVES

- Solve two simultaneous equations, one linear and one quadratic
- Solve linear inequalities
- Solve quadratic inequalities
- **Graph** linear inequalities in two **variables**

- Use inequalities to solve linear programming problems
- Divide a **polynomial** by $(x \pm p)$
- Factorise a polynomial by using the **factor theorem**
- Use the **remainder theorem** to find the **remainder** when a polynomial is divided by $(ax - b)$

STARTER ACTIVITIES

1 ▶ Using substitution, solve these simultaneous equations, writing your answers as **Cartesian** coordinates.

    a $x + y = 15$ $x - y = 3$ **b** $2x - 3y = 2$ $x + 2y = 8$

    c $x + y = 7$ $2x - 3y = 9$ **d** $11y + 15x = -23$ $7y - 2x = 20$

2 ▶ Sketch these equations on one graph.

    a $y = x^2$ **b** $y = 2x^2$ **c** $y = -x^2$

    d $y = 5x^2 + 2$ **e** $y = -3x^2 - 4$

3 ▶ Use **long division** to solve these equations, giving answers to 3 significant figures.

    a $435 \div 25$ **b** $460 \div 25$ **c** $511 \div 30$ **d** $739 \div 19$

SOLVE SIMULTANEOUS EQUATIONS, ONE LINEAR AND ONE QUADRATIC

EXAMPLE 1

Solve

a $x + 2y = 3$

$x^2 + 3xy = 10$

b $3x - 2y = 1$

$x^2 + y^2 = 25$

---

a $x = 3 - 2y$ Rearrange the linear equation to get $x = \ldots$ or $y = \ldots$

$(3 - 2y)^2 + 3y(3 - 2y) = 10$ Substitute this into the quadratic equation, in place of x

$9 - 12y + 4y^2 + 9y - 6y^2 = 10$ $(3 - 2y)^2 = (3 - 2y) \times (3 - 2y)$

$-2y^2 - 3y - 1 = 0$

$2y^2 + 3y + 1 = 0$

$(2y + 1)(y + 1) = 0$ Solve for y using factorisation

$y = -\dfrac{1}{2}$ or $y = -1$

So $x = 4$ or $x = 5$

Solutions are $x = 4$, $y = -\dfrac{1}{2}$ and $x = 5$, $y = -1$.

There are two solution pairs. The graph of the linear equation (straight line) intersects the graph of the quadratic (curve) at two points.

b $3x - 2y = 1$

$x^2 + y^2 = 25$

$2y = 3x - 1$

$y = \dfrac{3x - 1}{2}$ Find $y = \ldots$ from linear equation

$x^2 + \left(\dfrac{3x - 1}{2}\right)^2 = 25$ Substitute $y = \dfrac{3x - 1}{2}$ into the quadratic equation to form an equation in x

$x^2 + \left(\dfrac{9x^2 - 6x + 1}{4}\right) = 25$ Now multiply by 4

$4x^2 + 9x^2 - 6x + 1 = 100$

$13x^2 - 6x - 99 = 0$

$(13x + 33)(x - 3) = 0$

So $x = -\dfrac{33}{13}$ or $x = 3$

$y = -\dfrac{56}{13}$ or $y = 4$ Substitute x-values into $y = \dfrac{3x - 1}{2}$

The solutions are $x = 3$, $y = 4$ and $x = -\dfrac{33}{13}$, $y = -\dfrac{56}{13}$

EXERCISE 1

SKILLS

PROBLEM
SOLVING

1 ▶ Solve these simultaneous equations.

   a $3 - x^2 = y, x + 1 = y$ **b** $2x + 1 = y, x^2 - x + 3 - y = 0$

   c $x^2 + y^2 = 5, x + y = 3$ **d** $y = x^2 + 2x - 3, y = 2x + 1$

   e $y = x^2 - 3x + 1, y = 2x - 5$ **f** $x = 3 + 2y, x^2 + 2y^2 = 27$

   g $2x^2 + xy + y^2 = 22, x + y = 1$ **h** $2y + 4x = 6, 2x^2 - 3xy = 14$

   i $2x + 4y = 6, x^2 - 2y + 4y^2 = 18$

   j $xy = 14, 4x + 3y = 29$

   k $x^2 + 4y^2 + 3x + 2y - 56 = 0, 5x - 2y + 7 = 0$

   l $2x + 4y = 9, 4x^2 + 16y^2 - 20x - 4y + 19 = 0$

   m Find the coordinates of the point where the line $2x + 2y = 18$ meets the circle
       $(x - 2)^2 + (y - 3)^2 = 16$

2 Find the coordinates of the intersection of the given curves.

   a $y = 4x^2 + 11x$
       $y = x^3 + 3x^2 - x$

   b $y = x^3 + 3x$
       $y = x^2 + 5x$

   c $y + 8x^2 = 2x^3$
       $y + x^2 + 3x = 0$

   d $y = 2x^2 - x$
       $y = 2x^3 + 3x^2 - 7x$

SOLVE LINEAR INEQUALITIES

You can use the skills learnt in solving linear *equations* to solve linear *inequalities*.

EXAMPLE 2

Find the set of values of x for which

a $2x - 5 < 7$

b $5x + 9 > x + 20$

c $12 - 3x < 27$

d $3(x - 5) > 5 - 2(x - 8)$

a $2x - 5 < 7$

        $2x < 12$ Add 5 to both sides

         $x < 6$ Divide both sides by 2

b $5x + 9 > x + 20$

$\quad 4x + 9 > 20$ Subtract x from both sides

$\quad\quad\; 4x > 11$ Subtract 9 from both sides

$\quad\quad\;\; x > \dfrac{11}{4}$ Divide both sides by 4

c $12 - 3x < 27$

$\quad\quad\; -3x < 15$ Subtract 12 from both sides

$\quad\quad\quad x > -5$ Divide both sides by -3. You therefore need to reverse the inequality sign

Alternative approach

$12 - 3x < 27$

$\quad\quad\; 12 < 27 + 3x$ Add $3x$ to both sides

$\quad\quad\; -15 < 3x$ Subtract 27 from both sides

$\quad\quad\quad -5 < x$ Divide both sides by 3

$\quad\quad\quad\; x > -5$ Rewrite with x on the **LHS**

d $3(x - 5) > 5 - 2(x - 8)$

$\quad 3x - 15 > 5 - 2x + 16$ Expand

$\quad\quad\quad 5x > 5 + 16 + 15$ Add $2x + 15$ to both sides

$\quad\quad\quad 5x > 36$

$\quad\quad\quad\; x > \dfrac{36}{5}$ Divide both sides by 5

EXAMPLE 3   Find the set of values of x for which

$3x - 5 < x + 8$ and $5x > x - 8$

$3x - 5 < x + 8$ gives

$2x - 5 < 8$

$\quad 2x < 13$

$\quad\;\; x < \dfrac{13}{2}$

$5x > x - 8$ gives

$4x > -8$

$\quad x > -2$

Draw a number line to illustrate the two inequalities.

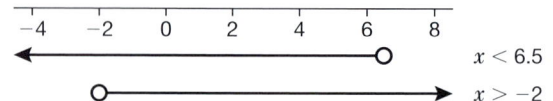

$x < 6.5$

$x > -2$

So the required set of values is $-2 < x < \dfrac{13}{2}$

Note: Draw a number line.

EXAMPLE 4

Find the set of values of x for which $4x + 7 > 3$ and $17 < 11 + 2x$

$4x + 7 > 3$ gives

$\quad 4x > -4$

$\quad x > -1$

$17 < 11 + 2x$ gives

$\quad 6 < 2x$

$\quad 3 < x$

$\quad x > 3$

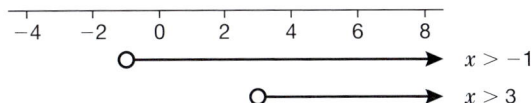

Note: Draw a number line.

So the required set of values is $x > 3$

EXERCISE 2

SKILLS

REASONING

1 ▶ Find the set of values of x for which

    a $5x - 8 < 6 - 2x$ **b** $7x - 17 > 7 - 7x$

    c $15x + 3 \leqslant 27x - 3$ **d** $16x - 3 \geqslant 3 - 2x$

    e $85x + 15 > 7 + 3x$ **f** $16x + 25 < 27 + 3x$

    g $9x + 71 \leqslant 16 + 8x$ **h** $2x + 69 \geqslant -3x + 52$

2 ▶ Find the set of values of x for which

    a $2(3x + 5) \geqslant 4x + 3$ **b** $3(5x + 15) < 6x$

    c $4(x + 7) > 3(x + 2)$ **d** $5(3x - 6) \geqslant 7(5x + 2)$

    e $4(4x - 3) \leqslant 6(7x - 3)$ **f** $22(3x + 8) > 3(5 - x)$

    g $16(4 - 2x) \leqslant 7(3 - x)$ **h** $-7(3x + 3) > -6(4 - x)$

3 ▶ Find the set of values of x for which

    a $3(x - 2) > x - 4$ and $4x + 12 > 2x + 17$

    b $4(x + 3) > 2$ and $5x + 5 > 6$

    c $5(3 - x) \geqslant 2(3x - 3)$ and $2(5x + 3) \geqslant 4(2 - x)$

    d $3(3 + 2x) < 2(4x + 1)$ and $6(2x + 3) < 3(x - 4)$

    e $9(2x - 3) \geqslant 4$ and $15(6x + 3) \geqslant 5$

    f $4(2 - x) > 3(3x + 3)$ and $6(x - 2) < 4(2x + 2)$

SOLVE QUADRATIC INEQUALITIES

To solve quadratic inequalities you need to

i Solve the quadratic equation

ii Sketch the corresponding quadratic function

iii Use your sketch to find the required set of values.

HINT

To solve the quadratic **inequality**, you may have to rearrange it so that all the terms are on one side.

EXAMPLE 5

Find the set of values of x for which $x^2 - 4x - 5 < 0$ and draw a sketch to show this.

SKILLS

INTERPRETATION
CRITICAL
THINKING

$x^2 - 4x - 5 = 0$ Quadratic equation

$(x + 1)(x - 5) = 0$ Factorise

$x = -1$ or $x = 5$ -1 and 5 are called critical values

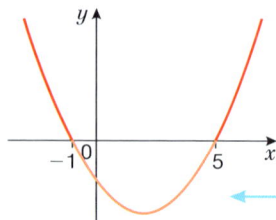

Your sketch does not need to be accurate. All you really need to know is that the graph is 'U-shaped' and crosses the x-axis at -1 and 5

$x^2 - 4x - 5 < 0$ $(y < 0)$ for the part of the graph below the x-axis.

So the required set of values is $-1 < x < 5$

KEY POINTS

Be careful how you write your answers

$-1 < x < 5$ is fine, showing that x is between -1 and 5.

But it is wrong to write something like $5 < x < -1$ or $-1 > x > 5$ because x cannot be less than -1 and greater than 5 at the same time.

This type of solution needs to be written in two separate parts, $x < -1$, $x > 5$.

EXAMPLE 6

Find the set of values of x for which $3 - 5x - 2x^2 < 0$ and sketch the graph of $y = 3 - 5x - 2x^2$

$3 - 5x - 2x^2 = 0$ Quadratic equation

$2x^2 + 5x - 3 = 0$ Multiply by -1, so it's easier to factorise

$(2x - 1)(x + 3) = 0$

$x = \dfrac{1}{2}$ or $x = -3$ $\dfrac{1}{2}$ and -3 are the critical values

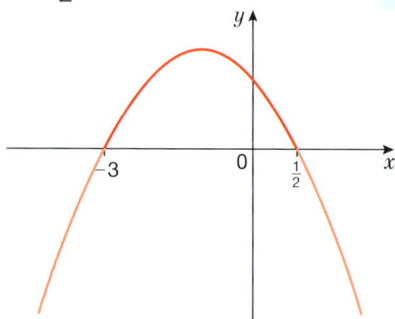

Since the coefficient of x^2 is negative, the graph is 'upside-down U-shaped', and crosses the x-axis at -3 and $\dfrac{1}{2}$

$3 - 5x - 2x^2 < 0$ $(y < 0)$ for the outer parts of the graph, below the x-axis

So the required set of vales is $x < -3$ or $x > \dfrac{1}{2}$

EXAMPLE 7

Find the set of values of x for which $12 + 4x > x^2$

Method 1: sketch graph

$12 + 4x > x^2$

$12 + 4x - x^2 > 0$

$x^2 - 4x - 12 = 0$

$(x + 2)(x - 6) = 0$

$x = -2$ or $x = 6$

Sketch of $y = 12 + 4x - x^2$

$12 + 4x - x^2 > 0$

Therefore $-2 < x < 6$

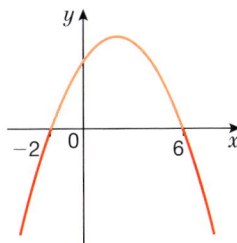

Method 2: table

$12 + 4x > x^2$

$12 + 4x - x^2 < 0$

$x^2 - 4x - 12 < 0$

$x^2 - 4x - 12 = 0$

$(x + 2)(x - 6) = 0$

$x = -2$ or $x = 6$

	$x < -2$	$-2 < x < 6$	$x > 6$
$x + 2$	$-$	$+$	$+$
$x - 6$	$-$	$-$	$+$
$(x + 2)(x - 6)$	$+$	$-$	$+$

Use the critical values to split the real number line into sets

For each set, check whether the set of values makes the value of the bracket positive or negative

For example, if $x < -2$, $x + 2$ is negative, $x - 6$ is negative, and $(x + 2)(x - 6)$ is positive

$x^2 - 4x - 12 < 0$

$(x + 2)(x - 6) < 0$

$(x + 2)(x - 6)$ is negative for $-2 < x < 6$

Therefore $-2 < x < 6$

EXERCISE 3

SKILLS

INTERPRETATION
CRITICAL
THINKING

1 ▶ By sketching graphs, solve these inequalities.

    a $(x - 2)(x + 3) < 0$ **b** $(x + 3)(x - 4) \leqslant 0$ **c** $(2x + 3)(x + 4) < 0$

    d $(7x + 8)(4 - 6x) > 0$ **e** $(6x + 3)(4x - 3) \geqslant 0$ **f** $(4x - 3)(5x - 7) \leqslant 0$

2 ▶ Find the set of values of x which **satisfy** these inequalities.

    a $x^2 - 7x - 18 < 0$ **b** $x^2 + 6x + 9 \leqslant 0$ **c** $x^2 + 13x + 12 \geqslant 0$

    d $x^2 - 14x + 40 < 0$ **e** $x^2 + 7x + 12 > 0$ **f** $7x^2 - 31x - 20 \leqslant 0$

    g $2x^2 + 17x + 21 > 0$ **h** $5x^2 - x - 18 < 0$ **i** $6x^2 + 14x - 12 > 0$

    j $x^2 - 25 \leqslant 0$ **k** $x^2 - 16 \geqslant 0$

GRAPH LINEAR INEQUALITIES IN TWO VARIABLES

Consider the two diagrams below.

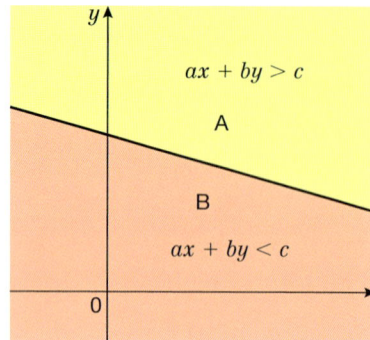

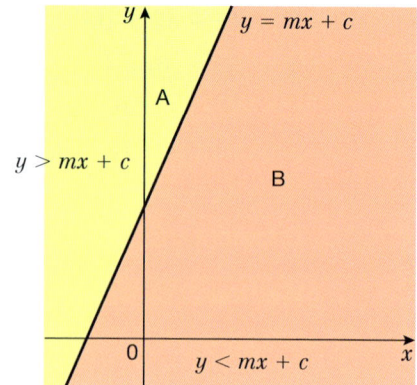

HINT

If the line is to be included in the region you use $\geqslant$ or $\leqslant$ in place of $>$ or $<$.

So points in region A, *including the line*, would be represented by:
$ax + by \geqslant c$ or $y \geqslant mx + c$.

HINT

If the line is to be included in the region you use $\geqslant$ or $\leqslant$ in place of $>$ or $<$.

So points in region A, *including the line*, would be represented by:
$ax + by \geqslant c$ or $y \geqslant mx + c$.

HINT

To decide which side of the line does not satisfy the inequality, choose a convenient point in each region and substitute its coordinates into the inequality to see whether (or not) it satisfies the inequality. Shade the region containing the point that does *not* satisfy the inequality.

- All the points that lie on the line are represented by
  $ax + by = c$ or $y = mx + c$
- All the points that lie above the line, in region A, are represented by
  $ax + by > c$ or $y > mx + c$
- All the points that lie below the line, in region B, are represented by
  $ax + by < c$ or $y < mx + c$

When illustrating an inequality, first draw a straight line and then use shading.

- Inequalities using $>$ or $<$ are represented by a **dashed (or dotted) line**. This indicates the the **line itself** is *not* **included in the region**.
- Inequalities using $\geqslant$ or $\leqslant$ are represented by a **solid line** to show that the **line is included in the region**.

The convention is that the region that does *not* satisfy the inequality is shaded.

The feasible region satisfying several inequalities will therefore be the one left unshaded.

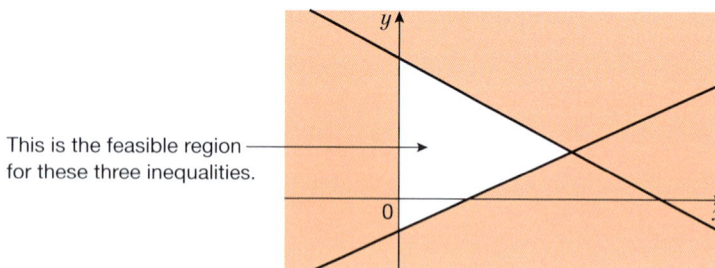

This is the feasible region for these three inequalities.

EXAMPLE 8

SKILLS

ANALYSIS

Write down the inequalities shown by regions A, B, C, D, E, F, G, H, I and J in the diagrams below.

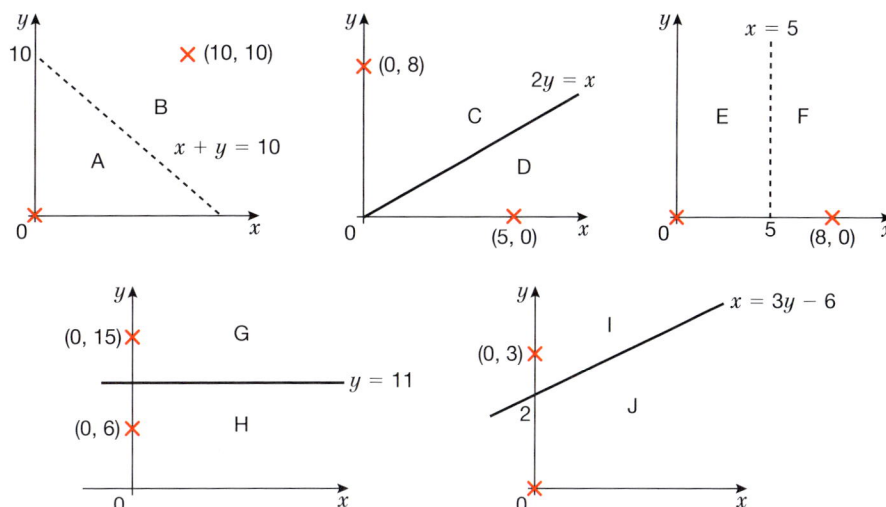

Note: $x = 3y - 6$ could be written in many different forms, such as $3y = x + 6$ or $3y - x = 6$

You must use a coordinate to check the direction of the inequality since the region, I, is given by $x \leq 3y - 6$ or equivalent.

Broken line, so $<$ rather than $\leq$

a Region A $x + y < 10$ Testing point (0, 0): $0 + 0 < 10$

   Region B $x + y > 10$ Testing point (10, 10): $10 + 10 > 10$

Solid line, so $\geq$ rather than $>$

b Region C $2y \geq x$ Testing point (0, 8): $2 \times 8 \geq 0$

   Region D $2y \leq x$ Testing point (5, 0): $2 \times 0 \leq 5$

Broken line, so a strict inequality

c Region E $x < 5$ Testing point (0, 0): $0 < 5$

   Region F $x > 5$ Testing point (8, 0): $8 > 5$

Solid line

d Region G $y \geq 11$ Testing point (0, 15): $15 \geq 11$

   Region H $y \leq 11$ Testing point (0, 6): $6 \leq 11$

Solid line

e Region I $x \leq 3y - 6$ Testing point (0, 3): $0 \leq 3 \times 3 - 6$

   Region J $x \geq 3y - 6$ Testing point (0, 0): $0 \geq 3 \times 0 - 6$

EXAMPLE 9

Illustrate on a diagram the region R, for which:

$x \geq 1$ $4x + 3y < 12$ $2y \leq x$ $x, y \geq 0$

Label the region R.

There are five inequalities here and three lines to add to the axes.

$x \geqslant 1$

Draw $x = 1$

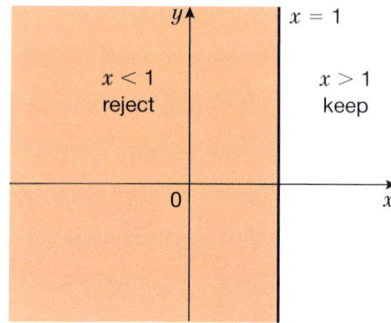

$4x + 3y < 12$

Draw $4x + 3y = 12$ as a broken line.

To draw it, note that when $x = 0$, $y = 4$

When $y = 0$, $x = 3$

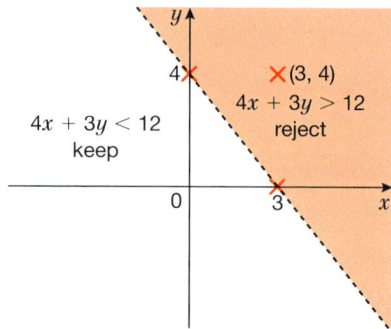

$2y \leqslant x$

To draw the line $2y = x$, note that it passes through (0, 0) and (2, 1)

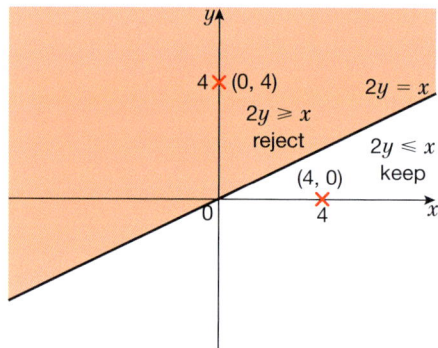

Also draw $x, y > 0$

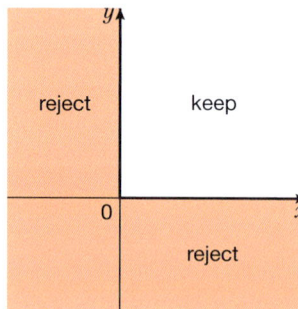

Combine all these on one diagram:

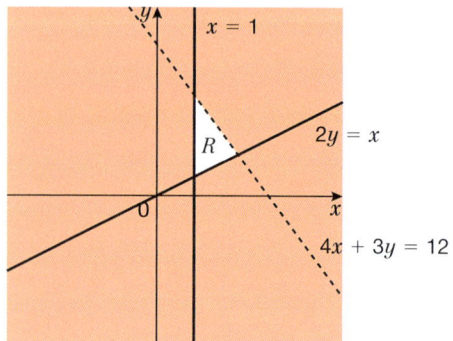

Note: Colour has been used here for clarity. Do not use colour in the examination!

EXAMPLE 10

SKILLS

CRITICAL
THINKING
REASONING
ANALYSIS

Note: This is an example of **Linear Programming**.

A food cart manager sells cheeseburgers and chicken burgers. The cart is open only during the lunch break of 12–2 pm. The manager can cook a maximum of 40 cheeseburgers and a maximum of 70 chicken burgers. He cannot cook more than 90 burgers in total. The profit on a cheeseburger is 33 pence and the profit on a chicken burger is 21 pence. How many of each kind of burger should the manager sell to maximise profit?

Step 1

Formulate the problems into linear equations.

Let x = number of cheeseburgers

Let y = number of chicken burgers

$x \geqslant 0$ and $y \geqslant 0$ You cannot have a negative number of burgers

Number of each burger

$x \leqslant 40$ and $y \leqslant 70$ These equations are created from information in the question

Total number of burgers

$x + y \leqslant 90$

Step 2

Obtain a profit inequality

$0.33(x) + 0.21(y)$ = profit   Convert pence to pounds

Step 3

Now draw these equations on a graph.

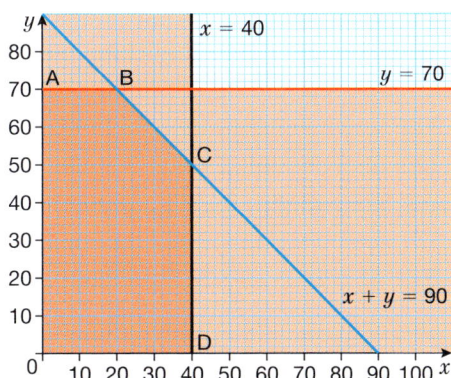

The region shaded in red is the only region that satisfies all the inequalities. Any value in this region will work but the maximum profit value will be close to one of the vertices of the regions marked A, B, C, D.

Step 4

Find the coordinates of the vertices:

The coordinates of A are (0, 70).

The coordinates of B are (20, 70).

The coordinates of C are (40, 50).

The coordinates of D are (40, 0).

Step 5

Input these coordinates into profit inequality found in step 2 $(0.33(x) + 0.21(y) = \text{profit})$:

For A $0.33(0) + 0.21(70) = 14.70$

For B $0.33(20) + 0.21(70) = 21.30$

For C $0.33(40) + 0.21(50) = 23.70$

For D $0.33(40) + 0.21(0) = 13.20$

Therefore the maximum possible profit is £23.70.

For this the manager will need to sell 40 cheeseburgers and 50 chicken burgers.

EXERCISE 4

SKILLS

CRITICAL
THINKING
REASONING
ANALYSIS

For questions 1–2 describe the shaded region.

1 ▶

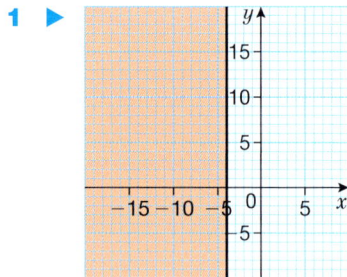

2 ▶

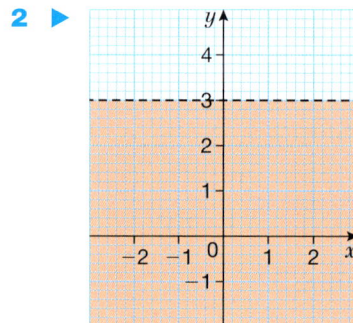

For questions 3–8, define the region labelled R.

3 ▶

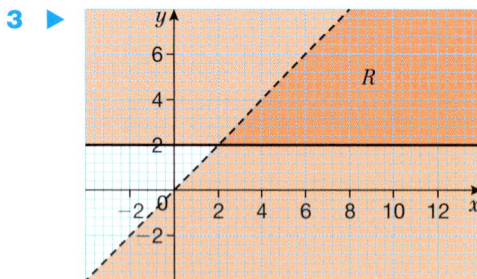

4 ▶

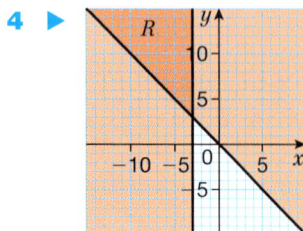

5 ▶

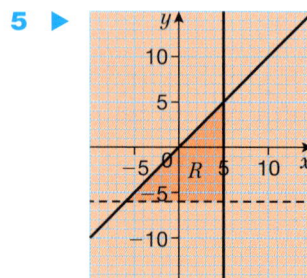

6 ▶

7 ▶

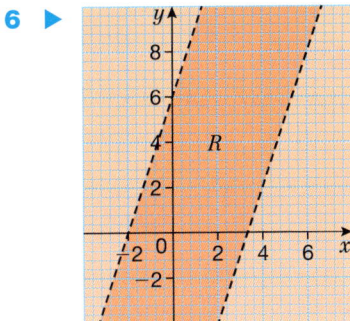

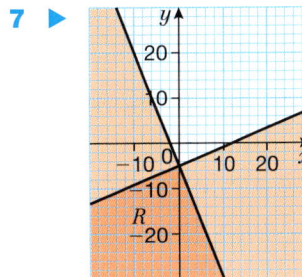

For questions 8–11, represent the region R defined by each set of inequalities, by drawing lines and shading.

8 ▶ $y \geqslant 2x, x + 2y \leqslant 4, y + 2x > 1$

9 ▶ $2y > x, y + 2x \leqslant 4, y > 2x + 2$

10 ▶ $x \geqslant 0, y \geqslant 0, y < \dfrac{x}{2} + 4, y \leqslant 6 - 2x$

11 ▶ $x > 0, y \geqslant 0, 3x + 4y \leqslant 12, 5x + 2y \leqslant 10$

12 ▶ Li is buying some chickens and lambs for his farm. He buys c chickens at Y120 each. He buys l lambs at Y200 each. He wants at least 10 animals in total. He wants more lambs than chickens. He has a maximum of Y1800 to spend.

     a Write down three inequalities involving c and l.

     b Li can sell the produce of each chicken for Y150 and the produce of each lamb for Y450. How many of each should he buy to maximise his profit? Use a graphical approach.

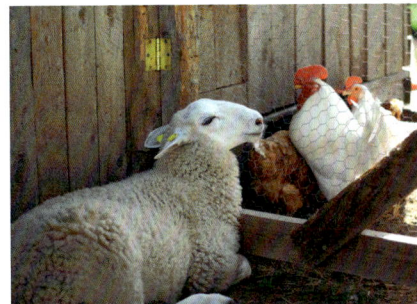

13 ▶ Tala is a semi-professional photographer in her spare time. As a wedding photographer she can earn 10 Jordanian Dinars (JOD) an hour. As a studio photographer she can earn 8 JOD an hour. She wants to spend at least 6 hours as a studio photographer. She can only work for a maximum of 20 hours a week. Find her maximum possible weekly earnings.

Q14 HINT

Use the information given in the question to set up linear inequalities.

14 ▶ A firm is planning to produce two types of light fittings, type A and type B. Market research suggests that, each week, at least 50 type A light fittings should be produced.

The number of type A light fittings should be between 20% and 40% of the total number of light fittings produced.

Each type A light fitting requires 3 light bulbs and each type B light fitting requires 2 light bulbs. The firm can only buy 200 light bulbs each week.

The profit on each type A light fitting is £15. The profit on each type B light fitting is £12.

The firm wants to maximise its weekly profit.

Formulate this situation as a linear programming problem and find the maximum profit.

DIVIDE A POLYNOMIAL BY $x \pm p$

KEY POINTS

A quotient in mathematics is the result of the division of two numbers.

EXAMPLE 11

Divide $x^3 + 2x^2 - 17x + 6$ by $(x - 3)$

SKILLS

ADAPTIVE LEARNING

Step 1:

$$\begin{array}{r} x^2 \\ x - 3\overline{)x^3 + 2x^2 - 17x + 6} \\ x^3 - 3x^2 \\ \hline 5x^2 - 17x \end{array}$$

Start by dividing the first term of the polynomial by x, so that $x^3 \div x = x^2$

Next multiply $(x - 3)$ by x^2, so that $x^2 \times (x - 3) = x^3 - 3x^2$

Now subtract, so that $(x^3 + 2x^2) - (x^3 - 3x^2) = 5x^2$

Then copy $-17x$

Step 2:

$$\begin{array}{r} x^2 + 5x \\ x - 3\overline{)x^3 + 2x^2 - 17x + 6} \\ x^3 - 3x^2 \\ \hline 5x^2 - 17x \\ 5x^2 - 15x \\ \hline -2x + 6 \end{array}$$

Repeat the method. Divide $5x^2$ by x, so that $5x^2 \div x = 5x$

Multiply $(x - 3)$ by $5x$, so that $5x \times (x - 3) = 5x^2 - 15x$

Subtract, so that $(5x^2 - 17x) - (5x^2 - 15x) = -2x$

Copy 6

Step 3:

$$\begin{array}{r} x^2 + 5x - 2 \\ x - 3\overline{)x^3 + 2x^2 - 17x + 6} \\ x^3 - 3x^2 \\ \hline 5x^2 - 17x \\ 5x^2 - 15x \\ \hline -2x + 6 \\ -2x + 6 \\ \hline 0 \end{array}$$

Repeat the method. Divide $-2x$ by x, so that $-2x \div x = -2$

Multiply $(x - 3)$ by -2, so that $-2 \times (x - 3) = -2x + 6$

Subtract, so that $(-2x + 6) - (-2x + 6) = 0$

No numbers left to copy, so you have finished.
The **remainder** is 0

So $(x^3 + 2x^2 - 17x + 6) \div (x - 3) = x^2 + 5x - 2$ $x^2 + 5x - 2$ is called the **quotient**.

EXAMPLE 12

Divide $-3x^4 + 8x^3 - 8x^2 + 13x - 10$ by $(x - 2)$.

Step 1:

$$\begin{array}{r} -3x^3 \\ x - 2\overline{)-3x^4 + 8x^3 - 8x^2 + 13x - 10} \\ -3x^4 + 6x^3 \\ \hline 2x^3 - 8x^2 \end{array}$$

Start by dividing the first term of the polynomial by x, so that $-3x^4 \div x = -3x^3$

Next multiply $(x - 2)$ by $-3x^3$, so that $-3x^3 \times (x - 2) = -3x^4 + 6x^3$

Now subtract, so that $(-3x^4 + 8x^3) - (-3x^4 + 6x^3) = 2x^3$

Finally copy $-8x^2$

Step 2:

$$\begin{array}{r} -3x^3 + 2x^2 \\ x-2)\overline{-3x^4 + 8x^3 - 8x^2 + 13x - 10}\\ -3x^4 + 6x^3 \\ \hline 2x^3 - 8x^2 \\ 2x^3 - 4x^2 \\ \hline -4x^2 + 13x \end{array}$$

Repeat the method. Divide $2x^3$ by x, so that $2x^3 \div x = 2x^2$

Multiply $(x-2)$ by $2x^2$, so that $2x^2 \times (x-2) = 2x^3 - 4x^2$

Subtract, so that $(2x^3 - 8x^2) - (2x^3 - 4x^2) = -4x^2$

Copy $13x$

Step 3:

$$\begin{array}{r} -3x^3 + 2x^2 - 4x \\ x-2)\overline{-3x^4 + 8x^3 - 8x^2 + 13x - 10}\\ -3x^4 + 6x^3 \\ \hline 2x^3 - 8x^2 \\ 2x^3 - 4x^2 \\ \hline -4x^2 + 13x\\ -4x^2 + 8x\\ \hline 5x - 10 \end{array}$$

Divide $-4x^2$ by x, so that $-4x^2 \div x = -4x$

Multiply $(x-2)$ by $-4x$, so that $-4x \times (x-2) = -4x^2 + 8x$

Subtract, so that $(-4x^2 + 13x) - (-4x^2 + 8x) = -5x$

Copy -10

Step 4:

$$\begin{array}{r} -3x^3 + 2x^2 - 4x + 5\\ x-2)\overline{-3x^4 + 8x^3 - 8x^2 + 13x - 10}\\ -3x^4 + 6x^3 \\ \hline 2x^3 - 8x^2 \\ 2x^3 - 4x^2 \\ \hline -4x^2 + 13x\\ -4x^2 + 8x\\ \hline 5x - 10\\ 5x - 10\\ \hline 0 \end{array}$$

Repeat the method. Divide $5x$ by x, so that $5x \div x = 5$

Multiply $(x-2)$ by 5, so that $5 \times (x-2) = 5x - 10$

Subtract, so that $(5x - 10) - (5x - 10) = 0$

So $(-3x^4 + 8x^3 - 8x^2 + 13x - 10) \div (x-2) = -3x^3 + 2x^2 - 4x + 5$

The **quotient** is $-3x^3 + 2x^2 - 4x + 5$. The **remainder** is 0.

EXERCISE 5

SKILLS

ADAPTIVE LEARNING

1 ▶ Divide

a $x^3 + 2x^2 - 23x - 60$ by $x + 4$
b $x^3 + 2x^2 - 21x + 18$ by $x - 3$
c $x^3 + 6x^2 + 8x + 3$ by $x + 1$
d $x^3 + 3x^2 - 18x - 40$ by $x - 4$
e $x^3 - x^2 + x + 14$ by $x + 2$
f $x^3 - 5x^2 + 8x - 4$ by $x - 2$
g $x^3 - x^2 + x - 1$ by $x - 1$
h $x^3 + 5x^2 + 2x + 1$ by $x + 5$

2 ▶ Divide

a $-2x^3 - 5x^2 + 3x + 10$ by $x + 2$
b $4x^3 + 20x^2 - 8x - 96$ by $x + 3$
c $6x^3 + 27x^2 + 14x + 8$ by $x + 4$
d $3x^3 - 10x^2 - 10x + 8$ by $x - 4$

    e $-3x^3 + 15x^2 + 108x - 540$ by $x - 6$ **f** $-5x^3 - 27x^2 + 23x + 30$ by $x + 6$

    g $2x^3 - 3x^2 - 3x + 2$ by $x - 2$

3 ▶ Divide

    a $2x^3 + 5x^2 - 5x + 1$ by $(2x - 1)$ **b** $6x^3 - 7x^2 - 29x - 12$ by $(3x + 4)$

    c $3x^3 - 10x^2 - 27x + 10$ by $(3x - 1)$ **d** $2x^3 - 3x^2 - 11x + 6$ by $(2x - 1)$

    e $6x^3 + x^2 - 7x + 2$ by $(3x - 1)$ **f** $2x^3 + 7x^2 + 7x + 2$ by $(2x + 1)$

FACTORISE A POLYNOMIAL BY USING THE FACTOR THEOREM

You can factorise a polynomial by using the **factor theorem**:

If f(x) is a polynomial and f(p) = 0, then $x - p$ is a factor of f(x).

EXAMPLE 13

SKILLS

ADAPTIVE
LEARNING

Show that $(x - 2)$ is a factor of $x^3 + x^2 - 4x - 4$ by

a Algebraic division   **b** The factor theorem.

a
$$
\begin{array}{r}
x^2 + 3x + 2 \\
x - 2 \overline{) x^3 + x^2 - 4x - 4} \\
\underline{x^3 - 2x^2} \\
3x^2 - 4x \\
\underline{3x^2 - 6x} \\
2x - 4 \\
\underline{2x - 4} \\
0
\end{array}
$$

    Divide $x^3 + x^2 - 4x - 4$ by $(x - 2)$

    The remainder is 0, so $(x - 2)$ is a factor of $x^3 + x^2 - 4x - 4$

b   f(x) = $x^3 + x^2 - 4x - 4$ Write the polynomial as a function

     f(2) = $2^3 + 2^2 - 4 \times 2 - 4$ Substitute $x = 2$

        = $8 + 4 - 8 - 4 = 0$

     So $(x - 2)$ is a factor of $x^3 + x^2 - 4x - 4$ Use the factor theorem:
If f(p) = 0, then $(x - p)$ is a factor of f(x). Here $p = 2$, so $(x - 2)$ is a factor of $x^3 + x^2 - 4x - 4$

EXAMPLE 14

Factorise $2x^3 + x^2 - 18x - 9$.

f(x) = $2x^3 + x^2 - 18x - 9$ Write the polynomial as a function

f(-1) = $2(-1)^3 + (-1)^2 - 18(-1) - 9 = 8$ Try values of x that are a factor of 9, e.g. $-1, 1, 3, \ldots$ until you find f(p) = 0. Here f(3) = 0

  f(1) = $2(1)^3 + (1)^2 - 18(1) - 9 = -24$

  f(2) = $2(2)^3 + (2)^2 - 18(2) - 9 = -25$

  f(3) = $2(3)^2 + (3)^2 - 18(3) - 9 = 0$

So $(x - 3)$ is a factor of $2x^3 + x^2 - 18x - 9$ Use the factor theorem: If f(p) = 0, then $(x - p)$ is a factor of f(x). Here $p = 3$

$$\begin{array}{r} 2x^2 + 7x + 3 \\ x - 3\overline{\smash{\big)}\,2x^3 + x^2 - 18x - 9} \\ 2x^3 - 6x \\ \hline 7x^2 - 18x \\ 7x^2 - 21x \\ \hline 3x - 9 \\ 3x - 9 \\ \hline 0 \end{array}$$

Divide $2x^3 + x^2 - 18x - 9$ by $(x - 3)$

You can check your division here: $(x - 3)$ is a factor of $2x^3 + x^2 - 18x - 9$, so the remainder must be 0

$$2x^3 + x^2 - 18x - 9 = (x - 3)(2x^2 + 7x + 3)$$

$2x^2 + 7x + 3$ can also be factorised

$$= (x - 3)(2x + 1)(x + 3)$$

EXAMPLE 15

Given that $(x + 1)$ is a factor of $4x^4 - 3x^2 + a$, find the value of a.

$$f(x) = 4x^4 - 3x^2 + a$$

Write the polynomial as a function

$$f(-1) = 0$$

Use the factor theorem the other way around: $(x - p)$ is a factor of $f(x)$, so $f(p) = 0$. Here $p = -1$

$$4(-1)^4 - 3(-1)^2 + a = 0$$

$$4 - 3 + a = 0$$

Substitute $x = -1$ and solve the equation for a. Note that $(-1)^4 = (-1)^2 = +1$

$$a = -1$$

EXAMPLE 16

Show that if $(x - p)$ is a factor of $f(x)$ then $f(p) = 0$.

If $(x - p)$ is a factor of $f(x)$ then

Write the polynomial as a function

$$f(x) = (x - p) \times g(x)$$

where $g(x)$ is a polynomial. So

$$f(p) = (p - p) \times g(p)$$

$$= 0 \times g(p)$$

$$= 0$$

Remember that $0 \times$ anything $= 0$

So $f(p) = 0$ as required.

EXERCISE 6

SKILLS

ANALYSIS

1 ▶ Use the factor theorem to show that

    a $(x + 2)$ is a factor of $2x^3 - 3x^2 - 12x + 4$

    b $(x - 1)$ is a factor of $2x^4 - 3x^3 - x^2 + 2$

    c $(x + 3)$ is a factor of $2x^4 + 5x^3 - 8x^2 - 17x - 6$

    d $(x - 2)$ is a factor of $x^3 - 5x^2 + 2x + 8$

    e $(x + 4)$ is a factor of $x^7 + 10x^6 + 27x^5 - 57x^3 - 30x^2 + 29x + 20$.

2 ▶ Show that $x^4 - 3x^2 + 2x + 4$ is exactly **divisible** by $(x + 1)$ but not by $(x - 2)$.

3 ▶ Show that $(x - 2)$ is a factor of $x^3 - 3x^2 - 2x + 8$ and factorise.

4 ▶ Show that $(x - 3)$ is a factor of $x^3 - 2x^2 - 5x + 6$ and factorise.

5 ▶ Show that $(x + 4)$ is a factor of $2x^3 + 3x^2 - 18x + 8$ and factorise.

6 ▶ Given that $(x - 2)$ is a factor of $3x^3 - x^2 - 12x + a$ find the value of a.

7 ▶ Given that $(3x + 2)$ is a factor of $3x^3 + bx^2 - 3x - 2$

    a find the value of b **b** **hence** factorise completely.

Q8 HINT

Solve simultaneous equations.

8 ▶ Given that $(x - 1)$ and $(2x - 1)$ are factors of $px^3 + qx^2 + 9x - 2$, find the value of p and q.

9 ▶ Given that $(x + 2)$ and $(x - 2)$ are factors of $ax^3 + bx^2 - 12x + 4$,

    a find the value of a and b **b** factorise f(x) completely.

USING THE REMAINDER THEOREM, FIND THE REMAINDER WHEN A POLYNOMIAL IS DIVIDED BY $(ax - b)$

By using the remainder theorem, you can find the remainder when a polynomial is divided by $(ax - b)$. If a polynomial f(x) is divided by $(ax - b)$ then the remainder is $f\left(\dfrac{b}{a}\right)$

KEY POINTS

A *remainder* in mathematics is what is left over in a division problem.

EXAMPLE 17

Find the remainder when $x^3 - 20x + 3$ is divided by $(x - 4)$ using

SKILLS

  a Algebraic division   **b** The remainder theorem.

ADAPTIVE LEARNING

a
$$x - 4 \overline{)\begin{array}{l} x^2 + 4x - 4 \\ x^3 + 0x^2 - 20x + 3 \end{array}}$$

Divide $x^3 - 20x + 3$ by $(x - 4)$

$\underline{x^3 - 4x^2}$

Remember to use $0x^2$

$4x^2 - 20x$
$\underline{4x^2 - 16x}$
$-4x + 3$
$\underline{-4x + 16}$
-13

The remainder is -13.

b f$(x) = x^3 - 20x + 3$

Write the polynomial as a function

f$(4) = 4^3 - 20 \times 4 + 3$

$= 64 - 80 + 3$

$= -13$

The remainder is -13.

Use the remainder theorem: If f(x) is divided by $(ax - b)$, then the remainder is $f\left(\dfrac{b}{a}\right)$. Compare $(x - 4)$ to $(ax - b)$: Here $a = 1$, $b = 4$, and the remainder is $f\left(\dfrac{4}{1}\right) = f(4)$. So substitute $x = 4$

EXAMPLE 18   When $8x^4 - 4x^3 + ax^2 - 1$ is divided by $(2x + 1)$ the remainder is 3. Find the value of a.

$f(x) = 8x^4 - 4x^3 + ax^2 - 1$

$f\left(-\dfrac{1}{2}\right) = 3$

$8\left(-\dfrac{1}{2}\right)^4 - 4\left(-\dfrac{1}{2}\right)^3 + a\left(-\dfrac{1}{2}\right)^2 - 1 = 3$

$8\left(\dfrac{1}{16}\right) - 4\left(-\dfrac{1}{8}\right) + a\left(\dfrac{1}{4}\right) - 1 = 3$

$\dfrac{1}{2} + \dfrac{1}{2} + \dfrac{1}{4}a - 1 = 3$

$\dfrac{1}{4}a = 3$

$a = 12$

> Use the remainder theorem: If $f(x)$ is divided by $(ax - b)$, then the remainder if $f\left(\dfrac{b}{a}\right)$. Compare $(2x + 1)$ to $(ax - b)$: here $a = 2$, $b = -1$, and the remainder is 3.
> So substitute $x = -\dfrac{1}{2}$, use the fact that the remainder is 3, and solve the equation for a

EXERCISE 7

SKILLS

ANALYSIS
REASONING

1 ▶ In each of these questions, find the remainder using the remainder theorem.

     a $4x^3 - 5x + 4$ divided by $(2x - 1)$ **b** $4x^3 - 5x^2 + 7x + 1$ divided by $(x - 2)$

     c $6x^3 + 7x^2 - 15x + 4$ divided by $(x - 1)$ **d** $2x^5 - 32x^3 + x - 10$ divided by $(x - 4)$

2 ▶ In each of these questions, find the remainder using algebraic division.

     a $x^3 + 3x^2 + 3x + 1$ divided by $(x + 2)$ **b** $x^3 + 2x^2 - x - 1$ divided by $(x - 1)$

     c $3x^3 - x^2 - x - 1$ divided by $(x - 4)$

3 ▶ $f(x) = 3x^3 - 5x^2 - 58x + 40$. Find the remainder when $f(x)$ is divided by $(x - 4)$.

4 ▶ When $5 + 6x + bx^2 - x^3$ is divided by $(x - 1)$ the remainder is 17. Find b.

5 ▶ The expression $3x^3 + px^2 - 3x + 4$ is divided by $(x + 4)$. State the remainder of this expression in terms of p.

6 ▶ When $16x^3 - bx^2 + 30x - 8$ is divided by $(2x - 1)$ the remainder is 1. Find b.

7 ▶ When $ax^3 - bx + 5$ is divided by $(x - 2)$ the remainder is 5 and when it is divided by $(x + 1)$ the remainder is 6. Find the values of a and b.

8 ▶ When $ax^3 - x^2 + bx + 2$ is divided by $(x + 3)$ the remainder is -73 and when it is divided by $(x - 2)$ the remainder is 22.

     a   Find the values of a and b.

     b   Find the remainder when the expression is divided by $(3x + 1)$.

9 ▶ The expression $2x^3 - x^2 + ax + b$ gives a remainder of 14 when divided by $(x - 2)$ and a remainder of -86 when divided by $(x + 3)$. Find the values of a and b.

10 ▶ The expression $3x^3 + 2x^2 - px + q$ is divisible by $(x - 1)$ but leaves a remainder of 10 when divided by $(x + 1)$. Find the values of p and q.

EXAM PRACTICE: CHAPTER 3

1 ▶ Solve these simultaneous equations: [4]

$x + y = 2$

$4y^2 - x^2 = 11$

2 ▶ Solve these simultaneous equations, giving your answers as Cartesian coordinates: [3]

$y - 3x + 2 = 0$

$y^2 - x = 6x^2$

3 ▶ The line $y = x + 2$ meets the curve $x^2 + 4y^2 - 2x = 35$ at the points p and q.

Find the coordinates of p and the coordinates of q. [3]

4 ▶ Find the set of values of x for which: [3]

  a $4x - 5 > 15 - x$

  b $x(x - 4) > 12$

5 ▶ Find the set of values of x for which:

  a $(2x - 7)(x + 1) < 0$ [2]

  b $3(x - 2) - 8 + 2x < 0$ [2]

  c   Both $(2x - 7)(x + 1) < 0$ and $3(x - 2) - 8 + 2x < 0$ [3]

6 ▶ Find the set of values of x for which:

$2x^2 - 5x - 12 > 0$ [3]

7 ▶ Solve these simultaneous equations, giving your answers as Cartesian coordinates: [4]

$x - 6y - 1 = 0$

$x = \dfrac{1}{y} + 4y$

8 ▶ Find the set of values of x for which:

  a $2p^2 + 9p > 5$ [2]

  b $n(n + 9) < 2(n - 5)$ [3]

9 ▶ $f(x) = 2x^3 - 7x^2 - 10x + 24$ [4]

  a   Show that $(x + 2)$ is a factor of $f(x)$.

  b   Hence factorise $f(x)$.

10 ▶ $f(x) = x^3 + 8x^2 + 17x + 16$ [4]

  a   Show that $f(x) \div (x + 5)$ has a remainder of 6.

  b   Find the quotient of $f(x) \div (x + 5)$.

11 ▶ $f(x) = -3x^3 + 13x^2 - 6x + 8$ [4]

  a   Show that $(x - 4)$ is a factor of $f(x)$.

  b   Hence factorise $f(x)$ completely.

12 ▶ Factorise completely $2x^3 - 7x^2 - 5x + 4$ [3]

13 $f(x) = x^4 + 5x^3 + px + q$

p and q are integers.   [4]

   a The remainder when f(x) is divided by ($x - 2$) is equal to the remainder when
      f(x) is divided by ($x + 1$). Find the value of p.

   b Given that ($x + 3$) is a factor of f(x), find the value of q.

14 $f(x) = x^3 - 2x + 21$ [4]

   a Show that ($x + 3$) is a factor of f(x).

   b Hence factorise f(x) = 0.

15 $f(x) = px^3 + 6x^2 + 12x + q$.   [4]

Given that the remainder when f(x) is divided by ($x - 1$) is equal to the remainder when
f(x) is divided by ($2x + 1$),

Find the value of p.

16 $f(x) = x^3 - x^2 - 7x + a$, where a is a constant.

Given that f(4) = 0,

   a find the value of a.   [1]

   b factorise f(x) as the product of a linear factor and a quadratic factor.   [2]

17 **a** Factorise completely g(x) = $2x^3 - x^2 - 4x + 3$ [4]

   b Solve g(x) = 0.   [1]

18 Illustrate, on a graph, the region that is represented by $x \leqslant \dfrac{y}{2} + 3$, $y > 3x - 4$ and
$2x + y > -4$.   [5]

19 A company buys two types of diary to send to its customers, a desk top diary and a pocket
diary. They will need to place a minimum order of 200 desk top and 80 pocket diaries.

They need at least twice as many pocket diaries as desk top diaries.

They will need a total of at least 400 diaries.

Each desk top diary costs $6 and each pocket diary costs $3.

The company wishes to minimize the cost of buying these diaries.

   a Write down the inequalities of this problem.   [5]

   b Represent these graphically.   [4]

CHAPTER SUMMARY: CHAPTER 3

■ When you multiply or divide both sides of an inequality by a negative number you need to reverse the inequality sign

■ The steps for solving a quadratic inequality are:

■ Solve the corresponding quadratic equation

■ Sketch the graph of the quadratic function

■ Use the sketch to find the required set of values

■ If f(x) is a polynomial and f(a) = 0, then ($x - a$) is a factor of f(x)

This is known as the *factor* theorem

■ If f(x) is a polynomial and f$\left(\dfrac{b}{a}\right)$ = 0 then ($ax - b$) is a factor of f(x)

This is also known as the factor theorem

■ If a polynomial f(x) is divided by ($ax - b$) then the remainder is f$\left(\dfrac{b}{a}\right)$

This is known as the *remainder* theorem

CHAPTER 4

4 SKETCHING POLYNOMIALS

Graphs are a vital tool for physicists. They help explain relationships between physical things, for example the volume of gas is inversely proportional to the pressure acting on it. If this relationship is modelled as a graph it produces the graph $y = \dfrac{k}{x}$. You will learn about this graph, and others, in this chapter.

An inflated balloon also obeys the equation above. If it is placed in a sealed chamber and the air pressure is doubled, it shrinks to half its original volume. If the pressure is decreased to one-tenth of the original, the balloon will expand to ten times its original volume – if it does not burst first.

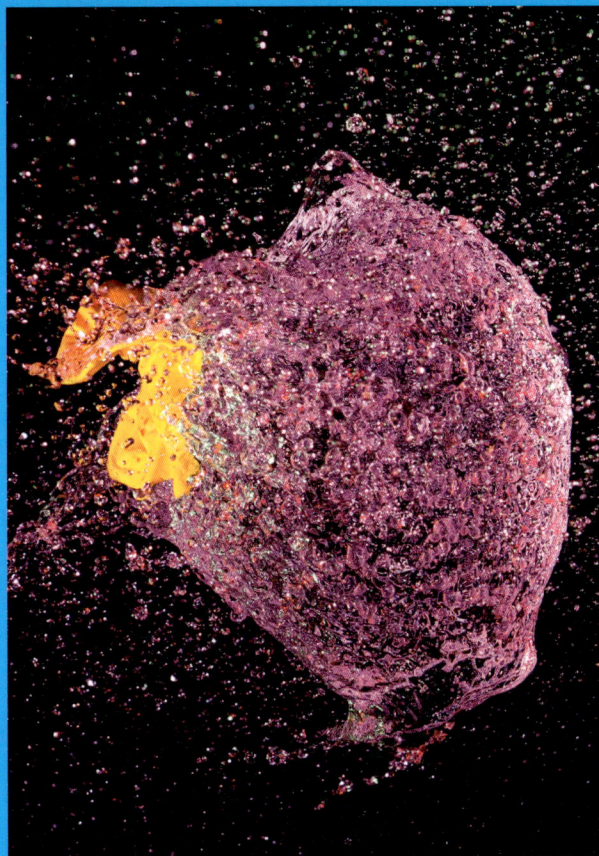

LEARNING OBJECTIVES

- Sketch cubic curves of the form $y = ax^3 + bx^2 + cx + d$ or $y = (x + a)(x + b)(x + c)$

- Sketch and **interpret** graphs of cubic functions of the form $y = x^3$

- Sketch the **reciprocal function** $y = \dfrac{k}{x}$ where k is a constant

- Sketch curves of functions to show points of intersection and solutions to equations

- Apply **transformations** to more complicated curves

STARTER ACTIVITIES

Sketch these curves.

1 ▶
a $y = x^2$
b $y = x^2 + 1$
c $y = 2x^2$
d $y = 2(x^2 + 1)$
e $y = (x + 1)^2$

f $y = 4x^2$
g $y = x^2 - 4$
h $y = \dfrac{1}{2}x^2$
i $y = \dfrac{1}{2}x^2 - 2$
j $y = \sqrt{x}$

k $y = \dfrac{1}{x}$
l $y = x^3$
m $y = x^3 + 1$

SKETCH CUBIC CURVES OF THE FORM $y = ax^3 + bx^2 + cx + d$ OR $y = (x + a)(x + b)(x + c)$

You need to be able to sketch equations of the form

$y = ax^3 + bx^2 + cx + d$ or $y = (x + a)(x + b)(x + c)$

This involves finding the points where the curve crosses the x- and y-axes.

These types of curves are known as *cubic* curves and the general shape is as follows:

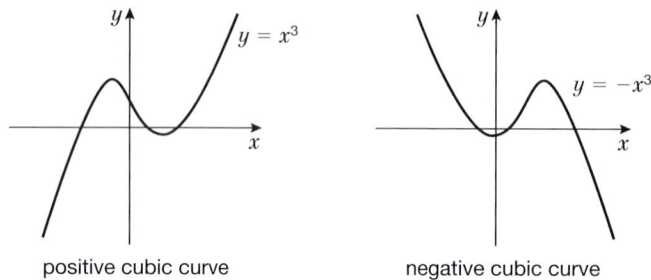

positive cubic curve　　　　　negative cubic curve

$y = -x^3$ is a reflection in the x-axis, as all the y values are now negative

EXAMPLE 1　Sketch the curve with the equation $y = (x - 2)(x - 1)(x + 1)$.

Put $y = 0$ and solve for x to find the roots of the equation (where the curve crosses the x-axis)

If $y = 0$

$0 = (x - 2)(x - 1)(x + 1)$

So $x = 2, 1$ or -1

$(-1, 0)$ $(1, 0)$ and $(2, 0)$

Put $x = 0$ to find out where the curve crosses the y-axis

If $x = 0$, $y = (0 - 2)(0 - 1)(0 + 1)$

So $y = 2$

$(0, 2)$

Now plot these coordinates on a Cartesian graph.

$y = (x - 2)(x - 1)(x + 1)$ crosses the y-axis at $(0, -2)$ and the x-axis at $(-1, 0)$ $(1, 0)$ $(2, 0)$.

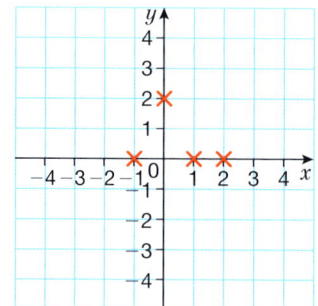

Next draw a curve through all these points.

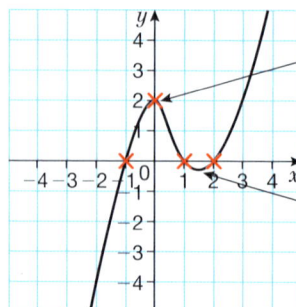

This is called the maximum point. The gradient changes from positive to 0 to negative.

This is called a minimum point. The gradient changes from negative to 0 to positive.

Note: You will learn more about maximum and minimum points in Chapter 9.

EXAMPLE 2

Sketch the curve of $y = (x - 2)(1 - x)(1 + x)$ and show the points where it crosses the coordinate axes.

Put $y = 0$ and solve for x to find the roots of the equation (where the curve crosses the x-axis).

If $y = 0$, $0 = (x - 2)(1 - x)(1 + x)$

So $x = 2, 1$ or $- 1$

$(-1, 0)$ $(1, 0)$ and $(2, 0)$

Put $x = 0$ to find out where the curve crosses the y-axis.

If $x = 0$, $y = (0 - 2)(1 - 0)(1 + 0)$

So $y = -2$

$(0, -2)$

Now plot these coordinates on a Cartesian graph.

The curve crosses the y-axis at $(0, -2)$ and the x-axis at $(-1, 0)$ $(1, 0)$ $(2, 0)$.

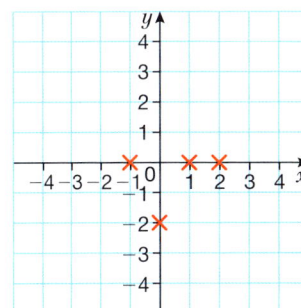

Now draw the curve through all these points.

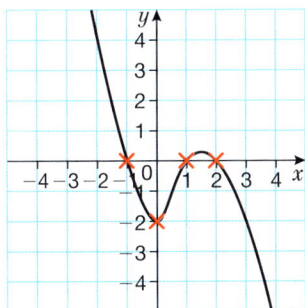

EXAMPLE 3

Sketch these curves.

a $y = (x - 1)^2(x + 1)$ **b** $y = x^3 - 2x^2 - 3x$

---

a $y = (x - 1)^2(x + 1)$

If $y = 0$

$0 = (x - 1)^2(x + 1)$

So $x = 1$ or $x = -1$

Points are $(-1, 0)$ and $(1, 0)$.

If $x = 0$

$y = (0 - 1)^2(0 + 1)$

So $y = 1$

Point is $(0, 1)$.

Plot the points and sketch the curve.

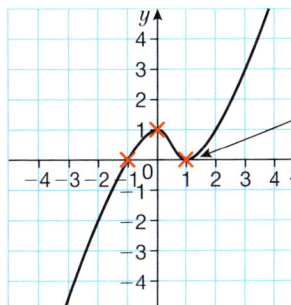

Repeated root from $(x - 1)^2$

b $y = x^3 - 2x^2 - 3x$

$y = x(x^2 - 2x - 3)$ Factorise

$y = x(x - 3)(x + 1)$

If $y = 0$

$0 = x(x - 3)(x + 1)$

So $x = 0, 3$ or -1

Points are $(0, 0)$, $(3, 0)$ and $(-1, 0)$.

If $x = 0$

$y = 0(0 - 3)^2(0 + 1)$

So $y = 0$

Point is $(0, 0)$.

Plot the points and sketch the curve

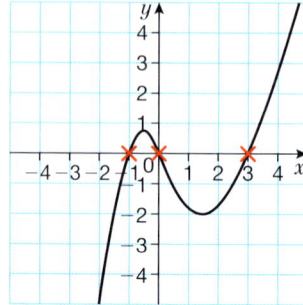

EXERCISE 1

SKILLS

ADAPTIVE LEARNING

1 ▶ Sketch these curves and indicate clearly the points of intersection with the axes.

a $y = (x + 3)(x - 2)(x + 1)$ **b** $y = (x + 1)(x - 2)(x - 3)$ **c** $y = (x + 4)(x - 3)(x + 2)$

d $y = x(x - 1)(x + 1)$ **e** $y = 3x(x - 1)(2x + 1)$ **f** $y = x(2x + 1)(x - 3)$

g $y = 4x(2x - 1)(x + 2)$ **h** $y = (x + 1)^2(3 + x)$ **i** $y = (x - 2)^2(x - 4)$

j $y = (x + 2)^2(5 + x)$ **k** $y = x^2(3 + x)$ **l** $y = (x - 4)^2(x + 5)$

2 ▶ Sketch these functions and indicate the points of intersection with the axes.

a $y = x^3 + x^2 - 2x$ **b** $y = x^3 + 5x^2 + 4x$ **c** $y = x - x^3$

d $y = 3x + 2x^2 - x^3$ **e** $y = 12x^3 - 3x$ **f** $y = x^3 - 9x$

g $y = x^3 - 9x^2$

SKETCH AND INTERPRET GRAPHS OF CUBIC FUNCTIONS OF THE FORM $y = x^3$

Below is a sketch of the graph $y = x^3$

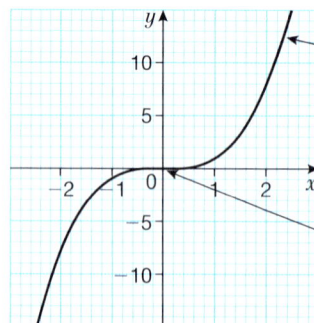

Notice that as x increases, y increases rapidly

The curve is flat at $(0, 0)$. This point is called a point of inflexion. The gradient is positive just before $(0, 0)$ and positive just after $(0, 0)$.

EXAMPLE 4 ▶ Sketch the curves of these equations and show their relative positions to $y = x^3$.

a $y = -x^3$ **b** $y = (x + 1)^3$ **c** $y = (3 - x)^3$

HINT
You do not need to plot any points. It is quicker to realise that the curve $y = -x^3$ is a reflection of the curve $y = x^3$.

a

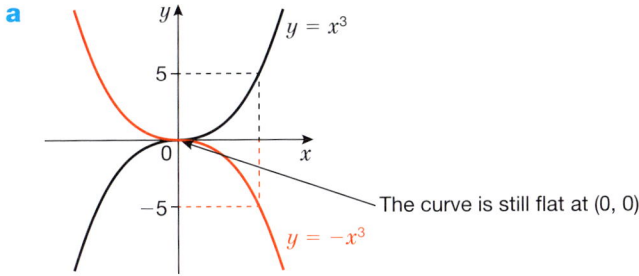

The curve is still flat at (0, 0)

$y = -x^3$

b

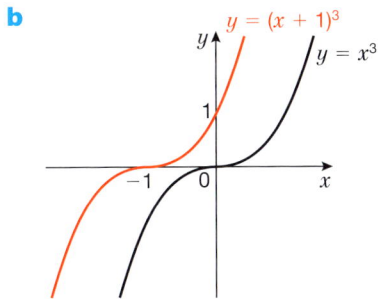

$y = (x + 1)^3$

$y = x^3$

HINT
You do not need to plot any points. Instead realise that this is a **translation** of the curve $y = x^3$.
When a value 'a' is added to a cubic, inside the brackets, it creates a horizontal **shift** of '$-a$'.

When $x = 0$: $y = (0 + 1)^3$, so that $y = 1$

c

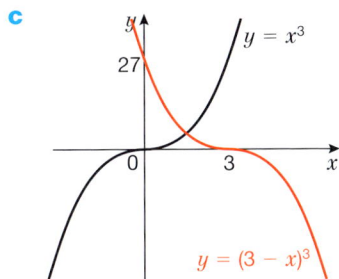

$y = x^3$

Reflected in the x-axis

HINT
$y = (3 - x)^3 \Rightarrow y = -(x - 3)^3$.

Horizontal **shift**, 3 to the right

$y = (3 - x)^3$

When $x = 0$: $y = (3 - 0)^3$, so that $y = 27$

EXERCISE 2

SKILLS

ADAPTIVE
LEARNING

Sketch these curves and show their relative positions in relation to $y = x^3$

a $y = (x - 2)^3$ **b** $y = (2 - x)^3$ **c** $y = (x - 3)^3$ **d** $y = (x + 4)^3$

e $y = -(x - 2)^3$ **f** $y = -(x - 4)^3$ **g** $y = \left(x + \dfrac{1}{2}\right)^3$ **h** $y = (1 - x)^3$

SKETCH THE RECIPROCAL FUNCTION $y = \dfrac{k}{x}$ WHERE k IS A CONSTANT

The curves with the equations $y = \dfrac{k}{x}$ fall into two categories.

Type 1: $y = \dfrac{k}{x}$ where $k > 0$

The curve does not cross the axes.
The curve tends towards the x-axis when x is large and positive or large and negative.
The curve tends towards the y-axis when x is large and positive or large and negative.

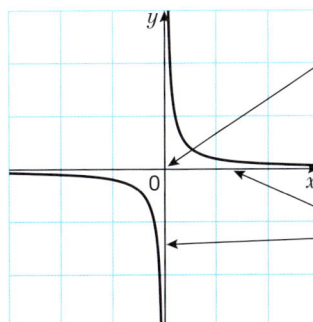

When $x = 0$, y is undefined.
When $y = 0$, x is undefined.
$x \to +\infty, y \to 0$
$-x \to +\infty, y \to 0$
$y \to +\infty, x \to 0$
$-y \to +\infty, x \to 0$

These are the horizontal and vertical asymptotes (where the graph never reaches the x- and y-axes).

Type 2: $y = \dfrac{k}{x}$ where $k < 0$

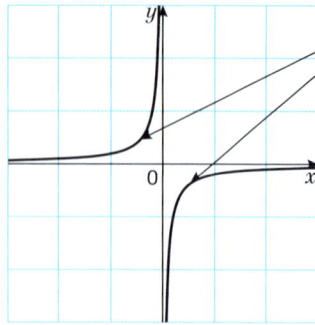

The curves behave in the same way as in Type 1, but are confined to two different quadrants

EXAMPLE 5

a Sketch the graph $y = \dfrac{3}{x}$.

b Sketch the graph $y = -\dfrac{1}{x}$.

a Sketch the graph of the function $y = \dfrac{3}{x}$.

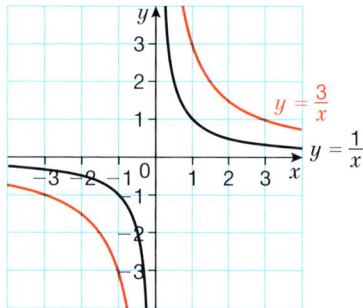

HINT

The curve will be the same as $y = \dfrac{1}{x}$, but further out from the origin. Its asymptotes are, however, the same.

b Sketch the graph of the function $y = -\dfrac{1}{x}$.

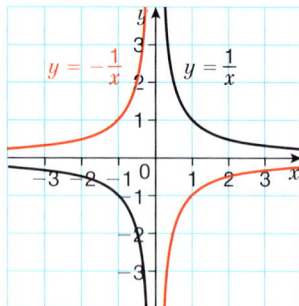

HINT

The curve will be the same as $y = \dfrac{1}{x}$, but reflected in the x-axis.

EXERCISE 3

SKILLS

INTERPRETATION

Sketch these pairs of equations on the same axes.

a $y = \dfrac{1}{x}, y = \dfrac{3}{x}$

b $y = \dfrac{4}{x}, y = \dfrac{8}{x}$

c $y = \dfrac{3}{x}, y = -\dfrac{3}{x}$

d $y = -\dfrac{4}{x}, y = -\dfrac{6}{x}$

e $y = \dfrac{8}{x}, y = -\dfrac{7}{x}$

f $xy = 6, xy = -5$

SKETCH CURVES OF DIFFERENT FUNCTIONS TO SHOW POINTS OF INTERSECTION AND SOLUTIONS TO EQUATIONS

EXAMPLE 6

a On the same diagram sketch the curves with the equations $y = x(x - 3)$ and $y = x^2(1 - x)$.

b Find the coordinates of the points of intersection.

a

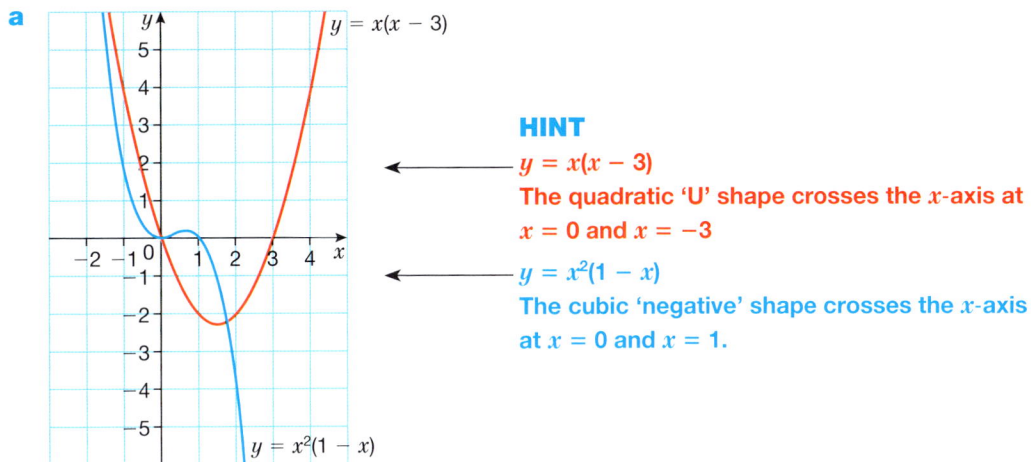

HINT

$y = x(x - 3)$
The quadratic 'U' shape crosses the x-axis at $x = 0$ and $x = -3$

$y = x^2(1 - x)$
The cubic 'negative' shape crosses the x-axis at $x = 0$ and $x = 1$.

b $y = x(x - 3)$ and $y = x^2(1 - x)$

The coordinates of the points of intersection are the points where the two functions have the same value.

$x(x - 3) = x^2(1 - x)$

$x^2 - 3x = x^2 - x^3$ Expand brackets

$x^3 - 3x = 0$ Collect like terms and equate to 0

$x(x^2 - 3) = 0$ Factorise

$x = 0$ or $x = \pm\sqrt{3}$

You can use the equation $y = x(x - 3)$ to find the y-coordinates:

If $x = -\sqrt{3}$,

$y = -\sqrt{3}(-\sqrt{3} - 3)$

$y = 3 + 3\sqrt{3}$

If $x = 0$,

$y = 0(0 - 3)$

$y = 0$

If $x = \sqrt{3}$,

$y = \sqrt{3}(\sqrt{3} - 3)$

$y = 3 - 3\sqrt{3}$

The coordinates of the points of intersection are $(-\sqrt{3}, 3 + 3\sqrt{3})$, $(0, 0)$ and $(\sqrt{3}, 3 - \sqrt{3})$.

EXAMPLE 7 **a** On the same diagram sketch the curves with equations $y = x^2(x - 1)$ and $y = \dfrac{2}{x}$.

b Explain why your sketch shows there are two roots to the equation $x^2(x - 1) = \dfrac{2}{x}$.

a

HINT

$y = x^2(x - 1)$

The cubic 'positive' shape crosses the x-axis at $x = 0$ and $x = 1$.

$y = \dfrac{2}{x}$

The reciprocal 'positive' shape does not cross any axes.

b From the sketch there are only two points of intersection of the curves. This means there are only two values of x where

$$x^2(x - 1) = \dfrac{2}{x}$$

So this equation has two roots.

Note: You would not be expected to solve this equation.

EXERCISE 4

SKILLS

PROBLEM
SOLVING

1 ▶ Consider the pairs of equations, **a–f**, below. In each case

   i sketch the two curves on the same axes

   ii state the number of points of intersection, if any

   iii write down a suitable equation which would give the x-coordinates of these points. You do not need to solve the equation.

   a $y = x^2$, $y = x^3$ **b** $y = x(x + 2)$, $y = -\dfrac{3}{x}$

   c $y = x^2(1 - x)$, $y = -\dfrac{2}{x}$ **d** $y = x(x - 4)$, $y = (x - 2)^3$

   e $y = -x^3$, $y = -\dfrac{2}{x}$ **f** $y = -x^3$, $y = x^2$

2 ▶ **a** On the same axes sketch the curves given by $y = x^2(x - 4)$ and $y = x(4 - x)$.

   b Find the coordinates of the points of intersection.

3 ▶ **a** On the same axes sketch the curves given by $y = (x - 1)^3$ and $y = x^2 - 1$.

   b Find the coordinates of the points of intersection.

4 ▶ On the same axes sketch $y = \dfrac{2}{x}$ and $y = -x(x - 1)^2$ and use your sketch to explain why there is no solution to $\dfrac{2}{x} = -x(x - 1)^2$.

5 ▶ Sketch the curves of $y = 1 - 4x^2$ and $y = x(x - 2)^2$ and use your sketch to explain how many solutions there are to the equation $1 - 4x^2 = x(x - 2)^2$.

6 ▶ Sketch the curves $y = x^3 - 2x^2 - x + 2$ and the line $y = 14x + 2$ and find the points of intersection.

APPLY TRANSFORMATIONS TO CURVES

Applying transformations to curves is beyond the scope of the specification and won't be examined. However this exercise can be set as an extension activity. Polynomial curves can be transformed in *four* basic ways. This is explained in more detail below.

NAME	f(x)	DESCRIPTION
Horizontal translation of $-a$	$f(x + a)$	The value of a is subtracted from all the x-coordinates, but the y-coordinates stay unchanged. In other words the curve moves a units to the left.
Vertical translation of $+a$	$f(x) + a$	The value of a is added to all the y-coordinates, but the x-coordinates stay unchanged. In other words the curve moves a units up.
Horizontal **stretch** of scale factor $\frac{1}{a}$	$f(ax)$	All the x coordinates are multiplied by $\frac{1}{a}$, but the y-coordinates stay unchanged. In other words the curve is squashed in a horizontal direction.
Vertical stretch of scale factor a	$af(x)$	All the y-coordinates are multiplied by a, but the x-coordinates stay unchanged. In other words the curve is stretched in a vertical direction.

EXAMPLE 8

Sketch these functions.

a $f(x) = x^2$

b $g(x) = (x + 3)^2$

c $h(x) = x^2 + 3$

$f(x) = x^2$ is a standard curve:

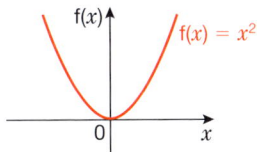

$g(x) = (x + 3)^2$ is the same moved 3 units to the left:

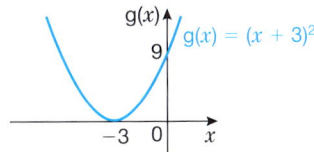

$h(x) = x^2 + 3$ is the same curve, moved 3 units up:

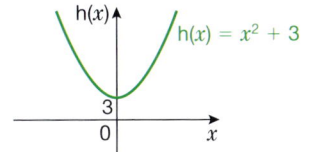

EXAMPLE 9

Sketch the graph of $y = (x - 2)^2 + 3$

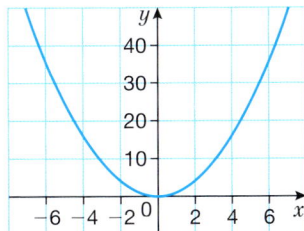

Step 1: Sketch the graph of $f(x) = x^2$

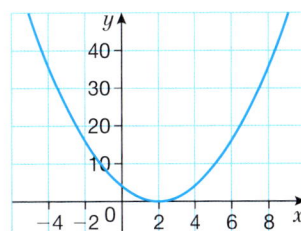

Step 2: Sketch the graph of $f(x) = (x - 2)^2$ Horizontal translation of $+2$

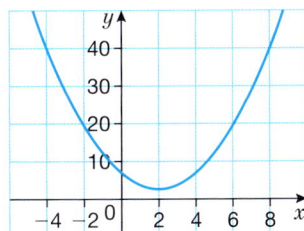

Step 3: Sketch the graph of $f(x) = (x - 2)^2 + 3$ Vertical translation of $+3$

EXAMPLE 10

Sketch the graph of $y = \dfrac{2}{x + 5} - 3$

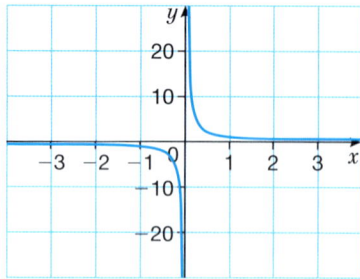

Step 1: Start with the graph $y = \dfrac{1}{x}$

Or:

$f(x) = \dfrac{1}{x}$

and

Asymptotes are: $x = 0$ and $y = 0$

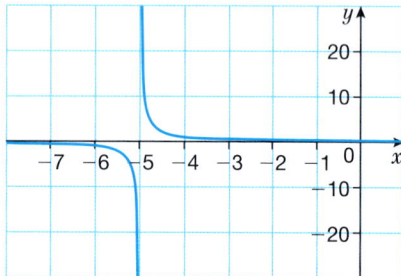

Step 2: $y = \dfrac{1}{x + 5}$

Horizontal shift of -5

Or:

$f(x + 5)$

and

Asymptotes are: $x = -5$ and $y = 0$

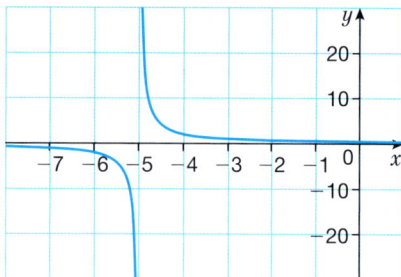

Step 3: $y = \dfrac{2}{x + 5}$

Vertical stretch, scale factor 2

Or:

$2f(x + 5)$

and

Asymptotes are: $x = -5$ and $y = 0$

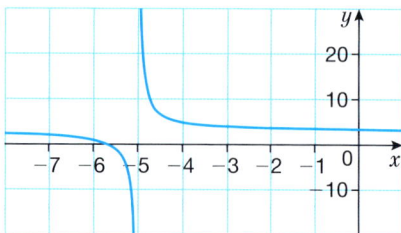

Step 4: $y = \dfrac{2}{x + 5} + 3$

Vertical translation of $+3$

Or:

$2f(x + 5) + 3$

and

Asymptotes are: $x = -5$ and $y = 3$

EXERCISE 5

SKILLS

INTERPRETATION

Sketch these curves.

a $y = 3x^2 - 4$

b $y = \dfrac{3}{x} - 2$

c $y = 3(3x + 1)^2$

d $y = \dfrac{2}{x - 2}$

e $y = \dfrac{1}{x - 1} + 3$

f $y = \dfrac{1}{x - 2} - 1$

g $y = \dfrac{3}{2 - x} - 5$

h $y = 3x^2 + 2$

EXAM PRACTICE: CHAPTER 4

1 The curve C has equation $y = \dfrac{3}{x}$ and the line l has equation $y = 2x + 5$

   a Sketch the graphs of C and l, indicating clearly the coordinates of any intersections with the axes.   **[4]**

   b Find the coordinates of the points of intersection of C and l.   **[1]**

2 The curve C has the equation $y = (x + \tfrac{1}{2})(x - 2)(x + 1)$.

   Sketch the curve, indicating where the curve crosses the x-axis.   **[3]**

3   **a** Sketch the graphs of $y = x(x + 2)(3 - x)$ and $y = -\dfrac{2}{x}$, showing clearly the coordinates of all the points where the curves cross the coordinate axes.   **[4]**

   b Using your sketch, state the number of real solutions to the equation

      $x(x + 2)(3 - x) = -\dfrac{2}{x}$ and give a reason for your answer.   **[1]**

4 Sketch the graphs of $y = x(4 - x)$ and $y = x^2(6 - x)$ showing clearly the coordinates of the points of intersection.   **[3]**

5   **a** Factorise completely $x^3 - 3x$.   **[1]**

   b Sketch the curve C with equation $y = x^3 - 3x$.   **[2]**

6 The diagram below shows a sketch of $y = \dfrac{1}{x}$.

   Copy the diagram. On the same diagram sketch the graph $y = \dfrac{2}{x + 1} + 3$ **[2]**

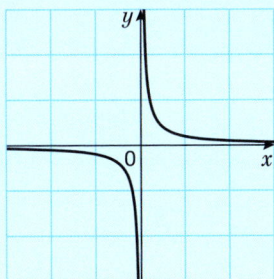

7 The diagram below shows a sketch of the curve with equation

   $y = \mathrm{f}(x)$ where $\mathrm{f}(x) = \dfrac{1}{(x - 2)}$.

   Copy the diagram. On the same diagram sketch the curve with equation $y = \mathrm{f}(x - 1)$ and state the equations of the asymptotes of this curve.   **[3]**

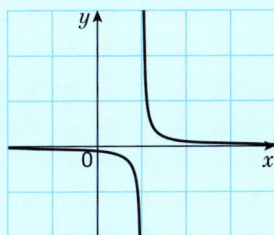

8 **a** $x^3 - 4x^2 + x + 6 = (x + 1)(ax^2 - bx + 6)$. Find a and b by factorising. **[3]**

  b Hence sketch the curve of $y = x^3 - 4x^2 + x + 6$. **[2]**

9 Sketch these curves on the same axes.

  a $y = x^3$

  b $y = -\left(x - \dfrac{1}{3}\right)^3$

  c $y = -2\left(x - \dfrac{1}{3}\right)^3$ **[4]**

10 The diagram below shows a sketch of a curve $y = f(x)$.

  a On the same axes sketch the curves with the equations

   i $y = f(x + 3)$ **[2]**

   ii $y = -f(-x)$ **[2]**

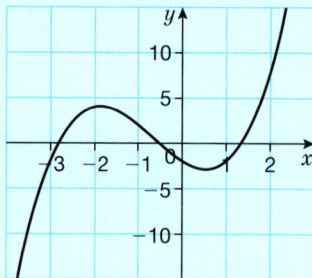

11 **a** On the same axes sketch the curves given by $y = \dfrac{1}{x}$ and $y = -x(x - 2)^2$. **[4]**

  b Explain how your sketch shows that there are no solutions to the equation
    $1 + x^2(x - 2)^2 = 0$. **[1]**

CHAPTER SUMMARY: CHAPTER 4

■ You need to know the shapes of these basic curves

$y = x^2$

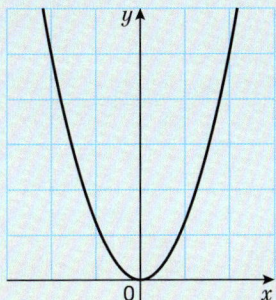

$y = x^3$

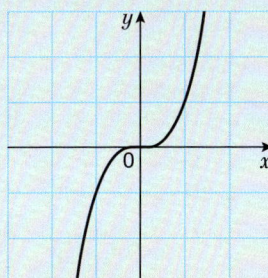

$y = (x - a)(x - b)(x - c)$

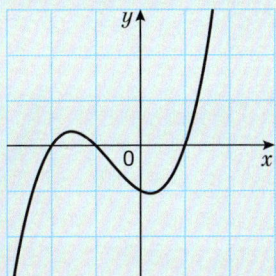

$y = \dfrac{1}{x}$

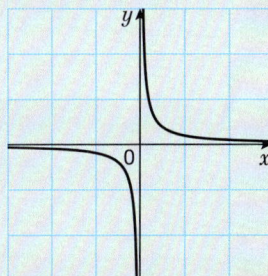

■ You also need to know the basic rules of transformations

NAME	f(x)	DESCRIPTION
Horizontal translation of $-a$	$f(x + a)$	The value of a is subtracted from all the x-coordinates, but the y-coordinates stay unchanged. In other words the curve moves **a** units to the left.
Vertical translation of $+a$	$f(x) + a$	The value of a is added to all the y-coordinates, but the x-coordinates stay unchanged. In other words the curve moves **a** units up.
Horizontal stretch of scale factor $\dfrac{1}{a}$	$f(ax)$	All the x-coordinates are multiplied by $\dfrac{1}{a}$, but the y-coordinates stay unchanged. In other words the curve is squashed in a horizontal direction.
Vertical stretch of scale factor a	$af(x)$	All the y-coordinates are multiplied by a, but the x-coordinates stay unchanged. In other words the curve is stretched in a vertical direction.

CHAPTER 5

5 SEQUENCES AND SERIES

A **recurrence relationship** is a **sequence** where the next **term** of the sequence is derived from the preceding terms. The best-known is the Fibonacci sequence, named after the Italian mathematician who wanted to find out how fast rabbits could breed.

Each term is found by adding up the two previous terms. The sequence is: 0, 1, 1, 2, 3, 5, 8, 13, 21, 34, …

The sequence is found throughout nature, from leaves to pineapple scales. Natural growth often follows this pattern, for example in animal cells, grains and even **beehives**.

Fibonacci introduced the sequence to Europe in 1202, but it was known to the Arabs and the Indians before that.

LEARNING OBJECTIVES

- Identify an **arithmetic sequence**
- Find the **common difference**, first term and nth term of an arithmetic **series**
- Find the sum of an arithmetic series and be able to use $\sum$ **(sigma) notation**
- Identify a **geometric sequence**
- Find the **common ratio**, first term and nth term of the sequence
- Find the sum of a **geometric series**
- Find the sum to infinity of a convergent geometric series

STARTER ACTIVITIES

The two key concepts in this chapter are sequences and series. In the English language these terms are interchangeable. In mathematics, however, the definition of a sequence and a series differ greatly, therefore it is important to know the difference.

A sequence is a list of numbers: $a_1, a_2, a_3, \ldots$

A series is the expression you get when you insert '*addition*' symbols: $a_1 + a_2 + a_3 + \ldots$

In a sequence the order in which the numbers are listed is important, for instance:

1, 2, 3, 4, 5, …   is one sequence, and

2, 1, 4, 3, 6, 5, …   is an entirely different sequence.

A series is a sum of numbers. For example,

$1 + 3 + 5 + 7 + 9 + \ldots$

or

$1 + \frac{1}{2} + \frac{1}{4} + \frac{1}{8} + \frac{1}{16} + \ldots$

IDENTIFY AN ARITHMETIC SEQUENCE

Consider these three common sequences

2, 5, 8, 11, …

0, 5, 10, 15, …

5, 2, −1, −4, …

To get to the next term, you add a fixed value to the previous term. Hence the difference between the terms is fixed. Note that you can also subtract a **common difference** to obtain a sequence.

A sequence that increases or decreases by a constant amount each time is a called an **arithmetic sequence**.

Here are some examples of arithmetic sequences

3, 7, 11, 15, 19,   … because you add 4 each time

2, 7, 12, 17, 22,   … because you add 5 each time

17, 14, 11, 8,   … because you subtract 3 each time

$a, a + d, a + 2d, a + 3d,$ … because you add d each time

KEY POINTS

- A recurrence relationship is a sequence where there is a relationship between two consecutive terms.

- A recurrence relationship of the form $U_{k+1} = U_k + c$, $k \geqslant 1$, $c \in \mathbb{R}$ is called an arithmetic sequence

EXAMPLE 1

Find the **a** 10th, **b** nth and **c** 50th terms of the arithmetic sequence 3, 7, 11, 15, 19, …

SKILLS

ADAPTIVE
LEARNING
PROBLEM
SOLVING

a   First term = 3   The sequence goes up in fours, starting at 3. The first term is $3 + 0 \times 4$

    Second term = 3 + 4   The second term is $3 + 1 \times 4$

    Third term = 3 + 4 + 4   The third term is $3 + 2 \times 4$

    Fourth term = 3 + 4 + 4 + 4   The fourth term is $3 + 3 \times 4$

    Therefore the 10th term is $3 + 9 \times 4 = 3 + 36 = 39$

b   The nth term is:

    $3 + (n - 1) \times 4 = 4n - 1$ nth term = first term + $(n - 1) \times$ difference

c   The 50th term is $3 + (50 - 1) \times 4 = 3 + 196 = 199$

EXAMPLE 2

A tree that is 6 metres tall is planted in a garden. If it grows 1.5 metres a year

a   how tall will it be after it has been in the garden for 8 years?

b   after how many years will it be 24 metres tall?

a $6 + 8 \times 1.5$ It starts at 6 metres and it has 8 years' growth at 1.5 metres a year

    $= 6 + 12$

    $= 18$ metres

b $24 - 6 = 18$ metres   Find out how much it has grown in total

So number of years $= \dfrac{18}{1.5} = 12$ years.   It grows 1.5 metres a year

EXAMPLE 3   Find the number of terms in the arithmetic sequence 7, 11, 15, ..., 143

The sequence goes up in fours.   Work out how to get from one term to the next

It goes from 7 to 143, a difference of 136.   Work out the difference between the last number and the first number

$\dfrac{136}{4} = 34$ jumps

There is one more term than the number of jumps, so 34 jumps means 35 terms.

EXERCISE 1

SKILLS

ADAPTIVE
LEARNING
PROBLEM
SOLVING

1 ▶ Which of these sequences are arithmetic?

   a 9, 11, 12, 14
   b 8, 10, 12, 14, 16
   c $\dfrac{1}{3}, \dfrac{1}{2}, \dfrac{2}{3}$

   d 16, 8, 4, 2, 1
   e 7, 10, 13, 16, 19
   f 2.5, 4, 5.5, 7

   g $-3, -6, -8, -10, -12$
   h $2y, 4y, 6y, 8y$
   i $4 + d, 6 + 2d, 8 + 3d, 10 + 3d$

2 ▶ Find the 10th term in each arithmetic progression.

   a 3, 5, 7, 9
   b 7, 7.5, 8, 8.5
   c 69, 73, 77, 81

   d $x, 2x, 3x, 4x$
   e $4 + a, 6 + 2a, 8 + 3a$

3 ▶ Nadine puts \$4000 into her account.
Every month after that, she pays in another \$200.

How much money in total will she have
invested at the start of

   a the 10th month?

   b the nth month?

Note: At the start of the 6th month she will have
only made 5 payments.

4 ▶ Calculate the number of terms in these arithmetic sequences

   a 5, 9, 13, ... 133
   b 11, 14, 17, ... 59
   c 136, 125, 114, ... -84

   d 671, 663.5, 656, ... 581
   e $y, 3y, 5y, ... 35y$
   f $m, m + p, m + 2p, ... m + (n - 1)p$

FIND THE COMMON DIFFERENCE, FIRST TERM AND nth TERM OF AN ARITHMETIC SERIES

Arithmetic *series* are formed by adding together terms of an arithmetic sequence, $u_1 + u_2 + u_3 \ldots + u_n$

In an arithmetic series, the next term is found by adding (or subtracting) a constant number.

This number is called the common difference and is often represented by d.

The first term is often represented by a.

All arithmetic series can be written in the form:

$$a \quad + \quad (a + d) \quad + \quad (a + 2d) \quad + \quad (a + 3d) \quad + \quad (a + 4d) \quad + \ldots$$

First term   Second term   Third term   Fourth term   Fifth term

Look at the relationship between the number of the term and coefficient of d. You should be able to see that the coefficient of d is one less than the number of the term.

You can use this fact to produce a formula for the nth term of an arithmetic series:

KEY POINTS   The nth term of an arithmetic series $u_n = a + (n - 1)d$, where a is the first term and d is the common difference. Please note that this formula is not given in the exam.

EXAMPLE 4

SKILLS

PROBLEM SOLVING

Find **i** the 20th and **ii** the 50th terms of these series.

a $4 + 7 + 10 + 13 + \ldots$ **b** $100 + 93 + 86 + 79 + \ldots$

---

a $a = 4$ and $d = 3$ $d = 7 - 4$

     i   20th term   Use the formula $u_n = a + (n - 1)d$ with $n = 20$

        $u_{20} = 4 + (20 - 1) \times 3$

            $= 4 + 19 \times 3$

            $= 61$

     ii   50th term   Use the formula $u_n = a + (n - 1)d$ with $n = 50$

        $u_{50} = 4 + (50 - 1) \times 3$

            $= 4 + 49 \times 3$

            $= 151$

b $a = 100$ and $d = -7$ $d = 93 - 100 = -7$

     i   20th term

        $u_{20} = 100 + (20 - 1) \times (-7)$

            $= 100 + 19 \times (-7)$

            $= -33$

     ii   50th term

        $u_{50} = 100 + (50 - 1) \times (-7)$

            $= 100 + 49 \times (-7)$

            $= -243$

EXAMPLE 5

For the arithmetic series $5 + 9 + 13 + 17 + 21 + ... + 805$:

a Find the number of terms in the series.   **b** Which term of the series would be 129?

---

a The series is $5 + 9 + 13 + 17 + 21 + ... + 805$

With $a = 5$ and $d = 4$

$805 = 5 + (n - 1) \times 4$

$805 = 5 + 4n - 4$

$805 = 4n + 1$

$804 = 4n$

$n = 201$

There are 201 terms in this series.

> The nth term $u_n = a + (n - 1)d$, so replace u_n with 805 and solve for n

b $129 = 5 + (n - 1)d$

$129 = 4n + 1$

$128 = 4n$

$n = 32$

The 32nd term is 129.

> The nth term $u_n = a + (n - 1)d$, so replace u_n with 129 and solve for n

---

EXAMPLE 6

Given that the 3rd term of an arithmetic series is 20 and the 7th term is 12

a find the first term   **b** find the 20th term.

Note: These are very popular questions and involve setting up and solving simultaneous equations.

---

a 3rd term is 20 so $a + 2d = 20$ (1)

7th term is 12 so $a + 6d = 12$ (2)

Subtracting (1) from (2):

$4d = -8$

$d = -2$

The common difference is -2.

$a + 2 \times (-2) = 20$

$a - 4 = 20$

$a = 24$

The first term is 24.

> Use that the nth term is $u_n = a + (n - 1)d$, with $n = 3$ and $n = 7$

> Substitute $d = -2$ back into equation (1)

b The 20th term is:

$u_{20} = a + 19d$

$= 24 + 19 \times (-2)$

$= 24 - 38$

$= -14$

The 20th term is -14.

EXERCISE 2

1 ▶ Find **i** the 20th term and **ii** the nth term of these arithmetic series.

a $4 + 7 + 10 + 13 + ...$

b $17 + 20 + 23 + 26 + ...$

c $102 + 98 + 94 + 90 + ...$

d $16 + 10 + 4 + (-2) + ...$

e $\dfrac{6}{5} + \dfrac{23}{15} + \dfrac{28}{15} + \dfrac{11}{15} + ...$

f $q + 3q + 5q + 7q + ...$

g $5k + k + (-3k) + (-7k) + ...$

2 ▶ Find the number of terms in these arithmetic series.

a $5 + 8 + 11 + ... + 62$

b $-14 + (-8) + (-2) + ... + 700$

c $120 + 117 + 114 + ... + 24$

d $x + 5x + 9x + ... + 201x$

e $0.25 + 1.75 + 3.25 + ... + 39.25$

f $2100 + 2089.5 + 2079 + ... + 1669.5$

3 ▶ The 1st term of an arithmetic series is 6 and the 4th term is 18.
Find the common difference.

4 ▶ The 3rd term of an arithmetic series is 12 and the 10th term is -93.

a Find the first term and the common difference.

b Find the term in which the series turns negative.

5 ▶ The 20th term of an arithmetic series is 18.82 and the 35th term is 15.52.
Find the 5th term.

6 ▶ The first three terms of an arithmetic series are $5p$, 20 and $3p$.
Find the value of p and hence the values of the three terms.

7 ▶ For which values of n would the expressions -8, n^2 and $17n$ form the first three terms of an arithmetic series?

FIND THE SUM OF AN ARITHMETIC SERIES AND BE ABLE TO USE $\sum$ NOTATION

When the famous mathematician Gauss was ten, his teacher, Bütner, set his pupils the 100 term sum

$$81297 + 81495 + 81693 + ... + 100899.$$

He had hardly finished giving his students the problem when Gauss threw his slate on the table with a single, correct, number on it.

The formula he proved for the sum of the arithmetic series is

Karl Friedrich Gauß.

KEY POINTS

The formula for the sum of an arithmetic series is

$$S_n = \frac{n}{2}[2a + (n - 1)d] \qquad \text{or} \qquad S_n = \frac{n}{2}(a + L)$$

where a is the first term, d is the common difference, n is the number of terms and L is the last term in the series.

EXAMPLE 7

Find the sum of the first 100 odd numbers.

$S_n = 1 + 3 + 5 + 7 + ...$ $\qquad$ Use $S_n = \dfrac{n}{2}[2a + (n - 1)d]$

$\quad = \dfrac{100}{2}[2 \times 1 + (100 - 1)2]$

$\quad = 50(2 + 198)$

$\quad = 50 \times 200$

$\quad = 10\,000$

Alternatively, find L and use $S_n = \dfrac{n}{2}(a + L)$

Note: This is a very useful formula that is worth remembering.

$L = a + (n - 1)d$

$\quad = 1 + 99 \times 2$

$\quad = 199$

$S_n = \dfrac{n}{2}(a + L)$

$\quad = \dfrac{100}{2}(1 + 199)$

$\quad = 10\,000$

EXAMPLE 8

Find the minimum number of terms required for the sum $4 + 9 + 14 + 19 + \ldots$ to exceed 2000.

$4 + 9 + 14 + 19 + \ldots > 2000$

> Always establish what you are given in a question. As you are adding on positive terms, it is easier to solve the equality $S_n = 2000$

Using $S_n = \dfrac{n}{2}[2a + (n - 1)d]$

> You know $a = 4$, $d = 5$ and $S_n = 2000$, you need to find n

$2000 = \dfrac{n}{2}[2 \times 4 + (n - 1) \times 5]$

$4000 = n[2 \times 4 + (n - 1)5]$

$4000 = n(8 + 5n - 5)$

$4000 = n(5n + 3)$

$4000 = 5n^2 + 3n$

$5n^2 + 3n - 4000 = 0$

$n = \dfrac{-3 \pm \sqrt{9 + 80\,000}}{10}$

> Solve using the quadratic formula

$n = 28.0$ or $n = -28.6$

28 terms are needed

> Accept positive answer

EXAMPLE 9

Robert starts his new job on a salary of £15 000. He is promised a salary increase of £1000 each year, at the end of every year, until he reaches his maximum salary of £25 000. Find his total **earnings** (since appointed) after

a 8 years   **b** 14 years.

a Total earnings = £15 000 + £16 000 + ...   For 8 years

$\quad a = 15\,000$, $d = 1000$ and $n = 8$ Write down what you know

$\quad S_8 = \dfrac{8}{2}[30\,000 + 7 \times 1000]$ Use $S_n = \dfrac{n}{2}[2a + (n - 1)d]$

$\quad S_8 = £148\,000$

b   Total earnings = £15 000 + £16 000 + ... + 25 000 + 25 000 + 25 000 + 25 000

> This time there are 10 years of increases, taking him to the end of his 11th year, and 3 years of the same salary

$a = 15\,000$, $d = 1000$ and $n = 11$ For the first 11 years

$S_{11} = \dfrac{11}{2}[30\,000 + 10 \times 1000]$ Use $S_n = \dfrac{n}{2}[2a + (n-1)d]$

$S_{11} = £220\,000$

After that 3 years at £25 000 so add another £75 000

Total earnings = £220 000 + £75 000 = £295 000

EXAMPLE 10

Show that the sum of the first n natural numbers is $\dfrac{1}{2}n(n+1)$.

This is an arithmetic series with $a = 1$, $d = 1$, $n = n$ In the sequence of natural numbers, the first term is 1, the difference between terms is 1 and the number of terms in the sequence is n

$S_n = \dfrac{n}{2}[2 \times 1 + (n-1) \times 1]$

$S_n = \dfrac{n}{2}[2 + n - 1]$ Use $S_n = \dfrac{n}{2}[2a + (n-1)d]$

$S_n = \dfrac{n}{2}(n+1)$

$S_n = \dfrac{1}{2}n(n+1)$

You can use $\sum$ to mean 'the sum of'.

For example:

$\displaystyle\sum_{n=1}^{10} 2n$ means the sum of $2n$ from $n = 1$ to $n = 10$

$\displaystyle\sum_{n=1}^{10} 2n = 2 + 4 + 6 + 8 + 10 + 12 + 14 + 16 + 18 + 20$

$\displaystyle\sum_{n=1}^{10} U_n = U_1 + U_2 + U_3 + U_4 + U_5 + U_6 + U_7 + U_8 + U_9 + U_{10}$

$\displaystyle\sum_{r=0}^{10} (2 + 3r)$ means the sum of $2 + 3r$ from $r = 0$ to $r = 10$

$\qquad = 2 + 5 + 8 + ... + 32$

$\displaystyle\sum_{r=5}^{15} (10 - 2r)$ means the sum of $10 - 2r$ from $r = 5$ to $r = 15$

$\qquad = 0 + (-2) + (-4) + ... + (-20)$

EXAMPLE 11

Calculate $\displaystyle\sum_{r=1}^{20} 4r + 1$

$\displaystyle\sum_{r=1}^{20} 4r + 1$ Substitute $r = 1, 2, ...$ to find the terms in the series

$= 5 + 9 + 13 + ... + 81$ This is an arithmetic series

$a = 5$, $d = 4$ and $n = 20$

$S_{20} = \dfrac{20}{2}[2 \times 5 + (20 - 1) \times 4]$ Use $S_n = \dfrac{n}{2}[2a + (n-1)d]$

$\qquad = 10 \times (10 + 19 \times 4)$

$\qquad = 10 \times 86$

$\qquad = 860$

EXERCISE 3

SKILLS

CRITICAL
THINKING
PROBLEM
SOLVING

1 ▶ Find the sum of these series.

   a $4 + 7 + 10 + 13 + \dots$ (20 terms)   b $3 + 5 + 7 + 9 + \dots$ (30 terms)

   c $150 + 145 + 140 + 135 + \dots$ (10 terms)   d $-15 + (-12.5) + (-10) + \dots$ (50 terms)

   e $(x + 1) + (2x + 1) + (3x + 1) + \dots + (21x + 1)$

2 ▶ Find how many terms of these series are needed to make the given sum.

   a $6 + 16 + 26 + \dots$, sum $= 12\,550$

   b $7 + 11 + 15 + 19 + \dots$, sum $= 900$

   c $-20 + (-17) + (-11) + (-8) + \dots$, sum $= 848$

   d $29 + 24 + 19 + 14 + \dots$, sum $= -247\,491$

3 ▶ Find the sum of the first 30 odd numbers.

4 ▶ Ali starts work on an annual salary of $20\,000. His contract will give him an increase of $120 every 6 months. If he keeps working for 15 years, how much will Ali earn in total over the 15 years?

5 ▶ Find the sum of the natural numbers up to 200.

6 ▶ Kumar earns €35\,000 a year. He gets an increase of €123 every year on his salary. He works for 20 years and then retires. His pension entitles him to 5% of his final year's salary as a monthly allowance. What is his monthly pension allowance?

7 ▶ Find the sum of the even numbers from 26 to 126.

8 ▶ A jogger is training for a 5 km run.
She starts training with 200 m and increases her run by 50 m a day.
How many days does it take her to reach 5 km?

9 ▶ Show that the sum of the first $2n$ natural numbers is $n(2n + 1)$

10 ▶ The sum of the interior angles of a triangle is 180°, a quadrilateral 360° and a pentagon 540° Assuming the pattern continues, find the sum of the interior angles of a dodecagon (12-sided shape).

11 ▶ Rewrite these series using sigma $\sum$ notation.

   a $3 + 5 + 7 + \dots + 21$ b $9 + 17 + 25 + 23 + \dots + 97$

   c $36 + 32 + 28 + \dots + 0$ d The multiples of 4 less than 75

12 ▶ Prove that the formula of an arithmetic series is: $S_n = \dfrac{n}{2}(a + L)$.

13 ▶ Calculate

   a $\sum\limits_{r=1}^{15}(4r - 1)$ b $\sum\limits_{r=1}^{21}3(r - 1)$ c $\sum\limits_{r=1}^{12}(3 - 6r)$ d $\sum\limits_{r=1}^{7}(15r + 13)$

Q14 HINT
You will need to solve a quadratic inequality.

14 ▶ For what value of n does $\sum\limits_{r=1}^{n}(2r + 3)$ first exceed 100?

15 ▶ What is the smallest value of n such that $\sum\limits_{r=1}^{n}(100 - 6r) < 0$?

IDENTIFY A GEOMETRIC SEQUENCE

Consider the sequence

3, 9, 27, 81 …

The pattern here is that each term is multiplied by 3.

Consider another sequence

3, −6, 12, −24…

The pattern here is that each term is multiplied by −2.

Sequences like these are known as **geometric sequences**.

These sequences are called geometric sequences.

1, 2, 4, 8, 16, …

100, 25, 6.25, 1.5625, …

2, −6, 18, −54, 162, …

To get from one term to the next you multiply by the same number each time. This number is called the **common ratio**, and often represented by r.

KEY POINTS

Common ratio $r = \dfrac{u_2}{u_1}$, where u_1 and u_2 are the first two elements

EXAMPLE 12

Find the common ratios in these geometric sequences.

a 2, 10, 50, 250, …

b 90, −30, 10, $-\dfrac{10}{3}$, …

a Common ratio $= \dfrac{10}{2} = 5$

b Common ratio $= -\dfrac{30}{90} = -\dfrac{1}{3}$ The common ratio can be any non-zero number

EXERCISE 4

SKILLS

REASONING

1 ▶ Which of these are geometric sequences? For the ones that are, find the common ratio.

a 2, 10, 50, 250, …

b 3, 6, 18, 34, …

c 211, 105.5, 52.75, …

d 4, 7, 9, 12, …

e 7, −7, 7, −7, …

f 9, 9, 9, 9, …

g 120, −30, 7.5, −1.875, …

h 61, 59, 57, 55, …

2 ▶ Find the next three terms of these geometric sequences.

a 113, −339, 1017, …

b 20, 80, 320, …

c $\dfrac{2}{9}, \dfrac{2}{3}, 2, …$

d 3, 15, 75, …

e 1, −0.25, 0.0625, …

f $1, x, x^2, …$

3 ▶ If 4, p and 16 are the first three terms of geometric sequence, and p>0, find

a the exact value of p.

b the exact value of the 5th term.

FIND THE COMMON RATIO, FIRST TERM AND nth TERM OF A GEOMETRIC SEQUENCE

You can define a geometric sequence using the first term a and the common ratio r.

$$a, \qquad ar, \qquad ar^2, \qquad ar^3, \qquad ..., \qquad ar^{n-1}$$

First term   Second term   Third term   Fourth term nth term

Sometimes a geometric sequence is called a geometric progression.

HINT

Look at the relationship between the position of the term in the sequence and the index of the term. You should be able to see that the index of r is one less than its position in the sequence. So the nth term of a geometric sequence $u_n = ar^{n-1}$.

EXAMPLE 13

Find **i** the 10th term and **ii** the nth term in these geometric sequences.

a 3, 6, 12, 24, ...   **b** 40, −20, 10, −5, ...

a 3, 6, 12, 24, ...

  i $a = 3, r = \dfrac{6}{3} = 2$ and $n = 10$

    10th term $= 3 \times (2)^9$ Use ar^{n-1}

              $= 3 \times 512$

              $= 1536$

  ii $a = 3, r = 2$ and $n = n$

    nth term $= 3 \times (2)^{n-1}$ Use ar^{n-1}

b 40, −20, 10, −5

  i $a = 40, r = \dfrac{-20}{40} = -\dfrac{1}{2}$ and $n = 10$.

    10th term $= 40 \times \left(-\dfrac{1}{2}\right)^9$ Use ar^{n-1}

             $= -\dfrac{5}{64}$

  ii $40 \times \left(-\dfrac{1}{2}\right)^{n-1}$

    $= 5 \times 8 \times \left(-\dfrac{1}{2}\right)^{n-1}$

    $= 5 \times 2^3 \times (-1)^{n-1} \times \left(\dfrac{1}{2}\right)^{n-1}$

    $= 5 \times (-1)^{n-1} \times 2^3 \times (2^{-1})^{n-1}$ Use law of indices $\dfrac{1}{x^m} = x^{-m}$ and $(x^m)^n = x^{m \times n}$

    $= 5 \times (-1)^{n-1} \times 2^3 \times 2^{-n+1}$

    $= 5 \times (-1)^{n-1} \times 2^{3-n+1}$

    $= 5 \times (-1)^{n-1} \times 2^{4-n}$

EXAMPLE 14

The second term of a geometric sequence is 4, and the 4th term is 8. The common ratio of the sequence is greater than 0. Find the exact values of

a the common ratio   **b** the first term   **c** the 10th term.

a 2nd term $= 4$, $ar = 4$ (1)

4th term $= 8$, $ar^3 = 8$ (2)   using nth term$= ar^{n-1}$ with $n = 2$ and 4

(2) $\div$ (1) gives:

$r^2 = \dfrac{8}{4} = 2$

$r = \sqrt{2}$ So the common ratio is $\sqrt{2}$

b Substitute the common ratio back into (1) to find: $a\sqrt{2} = 4$

$a = \dfrac{4}{\sqrt{2}}$ To rationalise $\dfrac{4}{\sqrt{2}}$, multiply top and bottom by $\sqrt{2}$

$= \dfrac{4\sqrt{2}}{2}$

$= 2\sqrt{2}$ So the first term is $2\sqrt{2}$

c The 10th term is:

$ar^9 = 2\sqrt{2} \times (\sqrt{2})^9$ Substitute the values of a and r back into ar^{n-1} with $n = 10$

$= 2 \times (\sqrt{2})^{10}$ Use $(\sqrt{2})^{10} = (2^{\frac{1}{2}})^{10} = 2^{\frac{1}{2} \times 10} = 2^5$

$= 2 \times 2^5$

$= 2^6$

$= 64$

EXAMPLE 15   The numbers 3, x and $x + 6$ form the first three terms of a positive geometric sequence.

Find

    a the possible values of x **b** the 10th term of the sequence.

---

a The sequence is a geometric sequence only if $\dfrac{U_2}{U_1} = \dfrac{U_3}{U_2}$

$\dfrac{x}{3} = \dfrac{x + 6}{x}$ Cross multiply

$x^2 = 3(x + 6)$

$x^2 = 3x + 18$

$x^2 - 3x - 18 = 0$ Factorise

$(x - 6)(x + 3) = 0$

The solutions are $x = 6$, $x = -3$, but this is a positive sequence so the only answer is $x = 6$.

b The 10th term is ar^9. Here $a = 3$ and $r = \dfrac{U_2}{U_1} = \dfrac{6}{3} = 2$.   Use the formula for the nth term $u_n = ar^{n-1}$ with $n = 10$, $a = 3$, $r = 2$

$ar^9 = 3 \times 2^9 = 3 \times 512 = 1536$

1 ▶ Find the 5th, 7th and nth term of each sequence:

    a 3, 6, 12, ...   **b** 160, 80, 40, ...   **c** 2, (−6), 18, ...   **d** (−1), (−2), (−4), ...

2 ▶ Find the common ratio and the first term in the geometric sequence where:

    a The 2nd term is 6 and the 4th term is 24.

    b The 3rd term is 60 and the 6th term is −480.

    c The 3rd term is −7.5 and the 6th term is 0.9375.

    d The 4th term is 4 and the 7th term is 32.

3 ▶ The nth term of a geometric sequence is $3(5^{n-1})$

    a Find the first term.   **b** Find the 5th term.

4 ▶ Given that the first term of a geometric sequence is 8 and the third term is 2, find the possible values of for the 6th term.

5 ▶ The expressions $p - 6$, $2p$ and p^2 form the first three terms of a geometric sequence. Find the possible values of the first term.

Q5 HINT
Calculate different
expressions for
the common ratio.
Then form and
solve an equation
in p.

FIND THE SUM OF A GEOMETRIC SERIES

The general rule for the sum of a geometric series is:

$$S_n = \frac{a(r^n - 1)}{r - 1} \text{ or } S_n = \frac{a(1 - r^n)}{1 - r}$$

Note: You will not be asked to prove these formulae.

EXAMPLE 16

Find the sum of these series.

  a $2 + 6 + 18 + 54 + ...$ (for 10 terms)   **b** $1024 - 512 + 256 - 128 + ... + 1$

a The series is $2 + 6 + 18 + 54 + ...$ (for 10 terms)

    So $a = 2$, $r = \dfrac{6}{2} = 3$, $n = 10$

    So $S_{10} = \dfrac{2(3^{10} - 1)}{3 - 1} = 59\,048$

b The series is $1024 - 512 + 256 - 128 + ... + 1$

    So $a = 1024$, $r = -\dfrac{512}{1024} = -\dfrac{1}{2}$, and nth term is 1.   Solve $ar^{n-1} = 1$ to find n

    $1024 \times \left(-\dfrac{1}{2}\right)^{n-1} = 1$

             $1024 = (-2)^{n-1}$

    1024 is positive so $(-2)^{n-1}$ must be positive, and equal to 2^{n-1}

        $2^{n-1} = 1024$

    $(n - 1)\lg 2 = \lg (1024)$

        $n - 1 = \dfrac{\lg (1024)}{\lg (2)} = 10$

           $n = 11$ If you noticed that $1024 = 2^{10}$ you could have solved this without using logarithms

So:

$$S_{11} = \frac{1024\left[1 - \left(-\frac{1}{2}\right)^{11}\right]}{1 - \left(-\frac{1}{2}\right)}$$

$$= \frac{1024 \times \left(1 + \frac{1}{2048}\right)}{1 + \frac{1}{2}}$$

$$= \frac{\left(\frac{2049}{2}\right)}{\left(\frac{3}{2}\right)} = 683$$

EXAMPLE 17

An investor invests £2000 on January 1st each year in a **savings account** that guarantees him 4% per annum for life. If interest is calculated on the 31st of December each year, how much will be in the account at the end of the 10th year?

End of year 1, amount $= 2000 \times 1.04$

Start of year 2, amount $= 2000 \times 1.04 + 2000$

End of year 2, amount $= (2000 \times 1.04 + 2000) \times 1.04$

$= 2000 \times 1.04^2 + 2000 \times 1.04$

Start of year 3,

amount $= (2000 \times 1.04^2 + 2000 \times 1.04 + 2000) \times 1.04$

$= 2000 \times 1.04^3 + 2000 \times 1.04^2 + 2000 \times 1.04$

So by end of year 10,

amount $= 2000 \times 1.04^{10} + 2000 \times 1.04^9 + ... + 2000 \times 1.04$

$= 2000 \times (1.04^{10} + 1.04^9 + ... + 1.04)$

$= 2000 \times \frac{1.04 \times (1.04^{10} - 1)}{1.04 - 1}$

$= 2000 \times 12.486... = £24\,972.70$

> A rate of 4% means $\times 1.04$
>
> Every new year he invests £2000
>
> At the end of every year the total amount in the account is multiplied by 1.04
>
> Look at the values for the end of year 3 and extend this for 10 years
>
> This is a geometric series. Substitute $a = 1.04$, $r = 1.04$, $n = 10$ in $S = \frac{a \times (r^n - 1)}{r - 1}$

EXAMPLE 18

Find the least value of n such that the sum of $1 + 2 + 4 + 8 + ...$ to n terms would exceed $2\,000\,000$.

Sum to n terms is $S_n = 1 \times \frac{2^n - 1}{2 - 1} = 2^n - 1$

If this is to exceed $2\,000\,000$ then:

$2^n - 1 > 2\,000\,000$

$2^n > 2\,000\,001$

$n \lg(2) > \lg(2\,000\,001)$

$n > \frac{\lg(2\,000\,001)}{\lg(2)}$

$n > 20.9$

It needs 21 terms to exceed $2\,000\,000$

> Substitute $a = 1$, $r = 2$ into $S_n = \frac{a \times (r^n - 1)}{r - 1}$
>
> Use laws of logarithms: $\lg(a^n) = n \lg a$
>
> Round up to the nearest **integer**

HINT
$\log_2 2 = 1$

Alternative method: $2^n - 1 > 2\,000\,000$

$2^n > 2\,000\,001$

$n \log_2 2 > \log_2 2\,000\,001$

$n > \log_2 2\,000\,001$

$n > 20.9$

It needs 21 terms to exceed 2 000 000

EXAMPLE 19

Find $\displaystyle\sum_{r=1}^{10}(3 \times 2^r)$

$S_{10} = \displaystyle\sum_{r=1}^{10}(3 \times 2^r)$

$= 3 \times 2^1 + 3 \times 2^2 + 3 \times 2^3 + \ldots + 3 \times 2^{10}$

The quantity in parentheses is a geometric series with $a = 2$, $r = 2$, $n = 10$

$= 3[2^1 + 2^2 + 2^3 + \ldots + 2^{10}]$

$= 3 \times 2\left(\dfrac{2^{10} - 1}{2 - 1}\right)$

Use $S_n = \dfrac{a \times (r^n - 1)}{r - 1}$

So $S_{10} = 6138$

EXERCISE 6

SKILLS

CRITICAL THINKING

1 ▶ Find the sum of these geometric series:

   a $1 + 3 + 9 + 27 + \ldots$ (7 terms)
   b $50 + (-25) + 12.5 + (-6.25) + \ldots$ (10 terms)

   c $4 + 12 + 36 + \ldots$ (15 terms)
   d $320 + 80 + 20 + 5 + \ldots$ (6 terms)

   e $\displaystyle\sum_{r=1}^{7} 5^r$
   f $\displaystyle\sum_{r=1}^{10}(2 \times 2^r)$

   g $\displaystyle\sum_{r=1}^{11} 6 \times \left(\dfrac{1}{0.75}\right)^r$
   h $\displaystyle\sum_{r=1}^{6} 3(-7)^r$

2 ▶ **Legend** has it that the inventor of chess was asked to name his reward for the invention by the ruling king of the time. He asked for 1 grain of rice on the first square of the chess board, 2 grains of rice of the second square, 4 grains of rice on the third square and so on until all the 64 squares were covered in rice. How many grains of rice could the inventor claim?

3 ▶ A savings scheme is offering a rate of interest of 3.5% **per annum** for the lifetime of the plan. Ji Won wants to save up to $20 000. She works out that she can afford to save $500 every year. How many years will it be until she has saved up $20 000?

4 ▶ The rate of tax in India operates on a flat rate system. If you earn more than 50 000 rupees then you pay a flat rate of tax of 20%. If you earn less than 50 000 rupees then you pay a flat tax rate of 15%. You earn 3750 rupees in the first month, and for each month after that your salary increases by 3% of the previous month's salary. How much tax would you pay that year?

5 ▶ You are offered a job that lasts for 5 weeks and you can choose your salary. You have two options:

   a You get paid $100 a day for the first day, $200 for the second day, $300 for the third day and so on. Each day your salary increases by $100.

b You get paid 1 cent for the first day, 2 cents for the second day, 4 cents for the third day and so on. Each day you are paid double of what you were paid for the previous day. Which salary would you choose?

6 ▶ Abishek is sponsored to cycle from Cape Town to Durban (1600 kilometres away) over a number of days. Abishek cycles 15 km on day 1 and increases his distance by 15% each day. How long will it take him to complete the challenge?

7 ▶ Find the lowest value of n for which the sum $3 + 6 + 12 + \ldots + n$ exceeds 1.5 million.

8 ▶ The first and last terms of a geometric series are 2 and 2048 respectively. The sum of the series is 2730. Find the number of terms and the common ratio.

FIND THE SUM TO INFINITY OF A CONVERGENT GEOMETRIC SERIES

Consider the series $S = 3 + 1.5 + 0.75 + 0.375 + 0.1875 + \ldots$

No matter how many terms of the series you take, the sum never exceeds a certain number.

This number is called the limit of the sum, or more often, the sum to infinity.

You can find out what this limit is.

As $a = 3$ and $r = \frac{1}{2}$, then $S = \frac{1(1 - r^n)}{1 - r} = \frac{3\left(1 - \left(\frac{1}{2}\right)^n\right)}{1 - \frac{1}{2}} = 6\left(1 - \left(\frac{1}{2}\right)^n\right)$

If you replace n with certain values to find the sum you find that:

when $n = 3$, $S_3 = 5.25$

when $n = 5$, $S_5 = 5.8125$

when $n = 10$, $S_{10} = 5.9994$

when $n = 20$, $S_{20} = 5.999994$

You can see that as n gets larger, S becomes closer and closer to 6.

You say that this **infinite series** is convergent, and has a sum to infinity of 6. Convergent means that the series tends towards a specific value as more terms are added.

Not all series converge. The reason that this one does is that the terms of the sequence are getting smaller.

This happens because $-1 < r < 1$. The sum to infinity of a geometric series exists only if $-1 < r < 1$.

$$S_n = \frac{a(1 - r^n)}{1 - r}$$

HINT

You can write 'the sum to infinity' as S_∞.

If $-1 < r < 1$, $r^n \to 0$ as $n \to \infty$, so that:

$$S_\infty = \frac{a(1 - 0)}{1 - r} = \frac{a}{1 - r}$$

HINT

$|r| < 1$ means all numbers whose actual size, irrespective of sign, is less than 1.

KEY POINTS ▶ The sum to infinity of a geometric series is $\dfrac{a}{1 - r}$ if $|r| < 1$

EXAMPLE 20

SKILLS

CRITICAL THINKING

Find the sum to infinity of these series.

a $40 + 10 + 2.5 + 0.625 + \ldots$

b $1 + \dfrac{1}{p} + \dfrac{1}{p^2} + \dfrac{1}{p^3} + \ldots$, where p is a positive number.

a $40 + 10 + 2.5 + 0.625 + \ldots$

In this series $a = 40$, $r = \dfrac{10}{40} = \dfrac{1}{4}$ Always write down the values of a and r, using $\dfrac{U_2}{U_1}$ for r

$-1 < r < 1$, so S_∞ exists:

$S_\infty = \dfrac{a}{1-r} = \dfrac{40}{1 - \frac{1}{4}} = \dfrac{40}{\frac{3}{4}} = \dfrac{160}{3}$ Substitute $a = 40$, $r = \dfrac{10}{40} = \dfrac{1}{4}$ into $S_\infty = \dfrac{a}{1-r}$

b $1 + \dfrac{1}{p} + \dfrac{1}{p^2} + \dfrac{1}{p^3} + \ldots$

In this series $a = 1$, $r = \dfrac{U_2}{U_1} = \dfrac{\left(\frac{1}{p}\right)}{1} = \dfrac{1}{p}$

S will exist if $\left|\dfrac{1}{p}\right| < 1$, so S_∞ exists only if $p > 1$

If $p > 1$, $S_\infty = \dfrac{1}{1 - \frac{1}{p}} = \dfrac{p}{p-1}$ Multiply top and bottom by p

EXAMPLE 21

The sum of the first 4 terms of a geometric series is 15 and the sum to infinity is 16.

a Find the possible values of r.

b Given that the terms are all positive, find the first term in the series.

a $S_4 = 15$ Use the formula $S_n = \dfrac{a(1-r^n)}{1-r}$, with $n = 4$

$\dfrac{a(1-r^4)}{1-r} = 15$ (1)

$\dfrac{a}{1-r} = 16$ (2)   Solve the two equations simultaneously

$16(1-r^4) = 15$

$16 - 16r^4 = 15$

$16r^4 = 1$

$r^4 = \dfrac{1}{16}$

$r = \pm\dfrac{1}{2}$

b As all terms are positive, r is $+\dfrac{1}{2}$

Substitute $r = \dfrac{1}{2}$ back into equation (2) to find a:

$\dfrac{a}{1 - \frac{1}{2}} = 16$

$16\left(1 - \dfrac{1}{2}\right) = a$

$a = 8$

The first term in the series is 8.

EXERCISE 7

SKILLS

CRITICAL THINKING

1 ▶ Find the sum to infinity, if it exists, of these series.

     a $1 + 0.1 + 0.01 + 0.001 + \ldots$ **b** $2 + 6 + 10 + 14 + \ldots$

     c $0.4 + 0.8 + 1.2 + \ldots$ **d** $1 - 2y + 4y^2 - 8y^3 + \ldots$

2 ▶ The first three terms of a geometric series are $4 + 2 + 1$

     a   What is the common ratio of this series?

     b   Find the sum to infinity.

3 ▶ The first three terms of a geometric series are $100 + 90 + 81$

     a   What is the common ratio of this series?

     b   Find the sum to infinity.

4 ▶ Find $\sum\limits_{r=1}^{\infty} 3(0.5)^r$

5 ▶ Find the sum to infinity of the geometric series having a second term of -9 and a fifth term of $\dfrac{1}{3}$

6 ▶ A ball is dropped vertically from a height of 6 metres. Suppose the ball **rebounds** $\dfrac{2}{3}$ of the height from which it falls. Find the total distance of travelled by the ball.

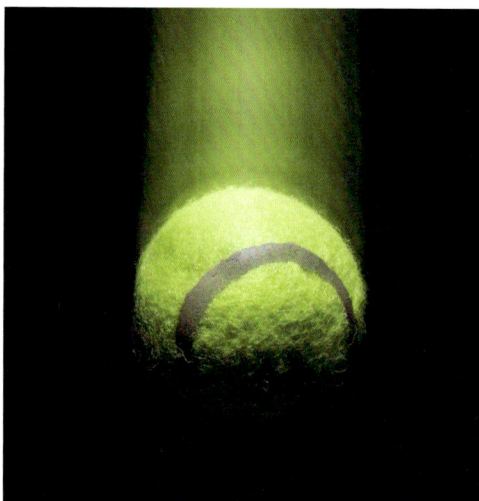

7 ▶ The lengths of the radii of circles form a geometric series. The radius of the first circle is 15 cm. The radius decreases by $\dfrac{4}{5}$ of the length of the previous circle. Determine the total area of all the circles in the series. Give your answer in terms of π.

8 ▶ A factory contributes £1 million into a small city. It is estimated that 75% of that money is re-spent back into the community. Economists assume that the money is re-spent again and again at a rate of 75%. Find an approximation for the total money re-spent from this original £1 million.

9 ▶ The sum of the first three terms of a geometric series is 9 and its sum to infinity is 8. What can you deduce about the common ratio and why? Find the first term and common ratio.

EXAM PRACTICE: CHAPTER 5

1 The third and fifth terms of an arithmetic series are 67 and 121.

   a Find the common difference. [2]

   b Find the first term. [2]

   c Find the sum of the first 25 terms of the series. [2]

2 The first three terms of an arithmetic series are 1, $(2q - 5)$ and 8.6

   a Find the value of q. [2]

   b Find the 16th term of the series. [4]

3 Calculate $\displaystyle\sum_{r=3}^{20} (5r - 1)$ [3]

4 The fifth and twentieth terms of an arithmetic series are 18 and 63.

   a Find the first term and common difference. [4]

   b Given that the sum of the n terms of the series is 270, find the value of n.

5 The third and eighth terms of an arithmetic series are 72 and 37 respectively.

   a Find the first term and common difference of the series [3]

   b Find the sum of the first 25 terms of the series. [3]

6 A geometric series has a common ratio of -2 and the first term of 3.

   a Find the sum of the first ten terms of the series [2]

   b Show that the sum of the first eight positive terms of the series is 65 535. [4]

7 Evaluate $\displaystyle\sum_{r=3}^{12} r^2$ [3]

8 The second and fourth terms of a geometric series are 30 and 2.7 respectively. Given that the common ratio, r, of the series is positive

   a find the common ratio [4]

   b show that the first term is 100 [1]

   c find the sum to infinity, correct to 3 significant figures [2]

9 The second term of a geometric series is 80 and the fifth term is 5.12

   a Show that the common ratio of the series is 0.4

   Calculate:

   b the first term of the series. [2]

   c the sum to infinity of the series, giving your answer as an exact fraction. [2]

   d the difference between the sum to infinity of the series and the sum of the first 14 terms of the series, giving your answer in the form $a \times 10^n$ where $1 \le a \le 10$ and n is an integer.

10 A geometric series is $a + ar + ar^2 + \dots$

Prove that the sum of the first n terms of this series is given by $S_n = \dfrac{a(1 - r^n)}{1 - r}$. **[4]**

11 The first three terms of a geometric series are $(p + 4)$, p and $(2p - 15)$ respectively, where p is a positive constant.

  a Show that $p^2 - 7p - 60 = 0$ **[3]**

  b Hence show that $p = 12$ **[1]**

  c Find the common ratio. **[2]**

  d Find the sum to infinity. **[2]**

CHAPTER SUMMARY: CHAPTER 5

■ All arithmetic series can be written in the form:

$$a \quad + \quad (a + d) \quad + \quad (a + 2d) \quad + \quad (a + 3d) \quad + \quad ... \quad + (a + (n - 1)d) \quad + \quad ...$$

First term   Second term   Third term   Fourth term nth term

■ The nth term of an arithmetic sequence is $a + (n - 1)d$, where a is the first term and d is the common difference

■ The sum of an arithmetic series is:

$$S_n = \frac{n}{2}[2a + (n - 1)d] \text{ or } S_n = (a + L)$$

where a is the first term, d is the common difference, n is the number of terms and L is the last term in the sequence

■ You can use the symbol $\sum$ to indicate 'sum of'. The symbol $\sum$ is used to write a series in a quick and concise way. For example, $\sum_{r=1}^{500}(2r + 50) = 52 + 54 + 56 + ... + 1050$

■ In a geometric sequence you can get from one term to another by multiplying by a constant called the common ratio

■ The formula for the nth term is ar^{n-1} where a is the first term and r is the common ratio

■ The formula for the sum of the n terms of a geometric series is

$$S_n = \frac{a(1 - r^n)}{1 - r} \text{ or } S_n = \frac{a(r^n - 1)}{r - 1}$$

■ The sum to infinity exists if $-1 < r < 1$ and $S_\infty = \frac{a}{1 - r}$

CHAPTER 6

6 THE BINOMIAL SERIES

The **binomial series** has a long history that stretches round the entire world.

Both the ancient Greeks and the ancient Hindus were fascinated by the different ways in which you can select objects from a group. **The binomial theorem** itself was first proved by Persian mathematician Al-Karaji in the 11th century, who also described its **triangular pattern**. Another Persian, Omar Khayyam, took the formula to higher powers. The binomial **expansion** of small degrees was known in the 13th century to Yang Hui of China.

In 1544, the German mathematician Michael Stifel introduced the term 'binomial coefficient' and showed how to express $(1 + a)^n$ and $(1 + a)^{n-1}$ using **Pascal's triangle**. Sir Isaac Newton of England wrote down **the generalised binomial theorem**, valid for any **rational exponent**.

▲ Sir Isaac Newton (1642–1727)

LEARNING OBJECTIVES

- Use $\binom{n}{r}$ to work out the coefficients in the binomial expansion

- Use the binomial expansion to expand $(1 + x)^n$

- Determine the range of values for which x is true and valid for the expansion

STARTER ACTIVITIES

Consider these mathematical statements.

$(a + b)^0 = 1$

$(a + b)^1 = 1a + 1b$

$(a + b)^2 = 1a^2 + 2ab + 1b^2$

$(a + b)^3 = 1a^3 + 3a^2b + 3ab^2 + 1b^3$

$(a + b)^4 = 1a^4 + 4a^3b + 6a^2b^2 + 4ab^3 + 1b^4$

There is a pattern in the coefficients. Can you **spot** it?

The coefficients form a pattern known as **Pascal's triangle**:

KEY POINTS

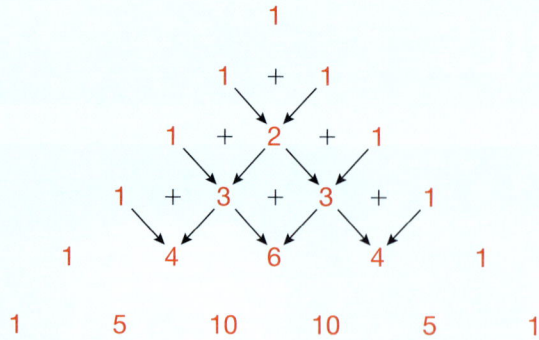

Note: To get from one line to another you add the **adjacent** numbers, as shown in the diagram.

EXAMPLE 1

By using Pascal's triangle find the **expansion** of

a $(2x + y)^3$ b $(3a - 2b)^5$

a $(2x + y)^3$ is in the form $(a + b)^n$ with $a = 2x$, $b = y$ and $n = 3$ so use

$(a + b)^3 = a^3 + 3a^2b + 3ab^2 + b^3$ and substitute in for a and b

> These numbers have come from the triangle in the key point above

$(2x + y)^3 = (2x)^3 + 3(2x)^2(y) + 3(2x)(y)^2 + (y)^3$

$= 8x^3 + 12x^2y + 6xy^2 + y^3$ Simplify

HINT

Watch out for negative powers.

b $(3a - 2b)^4$ is in the form $(a + b)^n$ with $a = 3a$, $b = -2b$ and $n = 4$ so use

$(a + b)^4 = a^4 + 4a^3b + 6a^2b^2 + 4ab^3 + b^4$ and substitute in for a and b

$(3a - 2b)^4 = (3a)^4 + 4(3a)^3(-2b) + 6(3a)^2(-2b)^2 + 4(3a)(-2b)^3 + (-2b)^4$

$= 81a^4 - 216a^3b + 216a^2b^2 - 96ab^3 + 16b^4$ Simplify

EXERCISE 1

1 ▶ Expand these expressions using Pascal's triangle.

a $(3 + x)^3$ b $(5 + 2x)^3$ c $(2 + x)^4$

2 ▶ Find the **coefficient** of x^3 in these expansions.

a $(5 + x)^7$ b $(6 + 3x)^5$

USE $\binom{n}{r}$ TO WORK OUT THE COEFFICIENTS IN THE BINOMIAL EXPANSION

For a binomial expression with a large power, e.g. $(1 + x)^{32}$, Pascal's triangle contains a huge number of rows. A better method is to use the binomial theorem. This enables you to expand $(a + b)^n$ into increasing powers of b and decreasing powers of a. You will look at expanding expressions of the form $(a + b)^2$, $(a + b)^3$, ... , $(a + b)^{32}$, ... when the power is a positive whole number.

KEY POINTS

$\binom{n}{r}$ is sometimes written as ^nC_r where n is a positive integer. This can be evaluated on most calculators. ^nC_r is often pronounced 'n choose r'.

KEY POINTS

The binomial expansion, **when n is a positive integer**, is a formula for

$(a + b)^n = (a + b) \times \dots \times (a + b)$ (n times)

$(a + b)^n = {}^nC_0 a^n + {}^nC_1 a^{n-1} b^1 + {}^nC_2 a^{n-2} b^2 + \dots + {}^nC_{n-1} a^1 b^{n-1} + {}^nC_n b^n$

or

$(a + b)^n = \binom{n}{0} a^n + \binom{n}{1} a^{n-1} b^1 + \binom{n}{2} a^{n-2} b^2 + \dots + \binom{n}{n-1} a^1 b^{n-1} + \binom{n}{n} b^n$

$$C_r^n = \frac{n!}{(n - r)!r!}$$

$$C_1^n = \frac{n!}{(n - 1)!1!}$$

EXAMPLE 2

Use the binomial theorem to find the expansion of $(2x + y)^4$

$(2x + y)^4 = \binom{4}{0}(2x)^4 + \binom{4}{1}(2x)^3(y) + \binom{4}{2}(2x)^2(y)^2 + \binom{4}{3}(2x)^1(y)^3 + \binom{4}{4}(y)^4$ $n = 4$, $a = 2x$ and $b = y$

$= (2x)^4 + (4)(2x)^3(y) + (6)(2x)^2(y)^2 + (4)(2x)^1(y)^3 + (y)^4$

$\binom{n}{r} = \frac{n!}{(n-r)!r!}$ so $\binom{4}{0} = \frac{4!}{4!0!} = 1$, $\binom{4}{1} = \frac{4!}{3!1!} = 4$, $\binom{4}{2} = \frac{4!}{2!2!} = 6$, $\binom{4}{3} = \frac{4!}{1!3!} = 4$, $\binom{4}{4} = \frac{4!}{0!4!} = 1$

$= 16x^4 + 32x^3y + 24x^2y^2 + 8xy^3 + y^4$

EXAMPLE 3

Use the binomial theorem to find the expansion of $(3 - 2x)^5$

$(3 - 2x)^5 = \binom{5}{0}(3)^5 + \binom{5}{1}(3)^4(-2x) + \binom{5}{2}(3)^3(-2x)^2 + \binom{5}{3}(3)^2(-2x)^3 + \binom{5}{4}(3)(-2x)^4 + \binom{5}{5}(-2x)^5$

$n = 5$, $a = 3$ and $b = -2x$

$= (3)^5 + (5)(3)^4(-2x) + (10)(3)^3(-2x)^2 + (10)(3)^2(-2x)^3 + (5)(3)(-2x)^4 + (-2x)^5$

$\binom{n}{r} = \frac{n!}{(n-r)!r!}$ so $\binom{5}{0} = \frac{5!}{5!0!} = 1$, $\binom{5}{1} = \frac{5!}{4!1!} = 5$, $\binom{5}{2} = \frac{5!}{3!2!} = 10$,

$\binom{5}{3} = \frac{5!}{3!2!} = 10$, $\binom{5}{4} = \frac{5!}{4!1!} = 5$, $\binom{5}{5} = \frac{5!}{5!0!} = 1$

$= 243 - 810x + 1080x^2 - 720x^3 + 240x^4 - 32x^5$

EXERCISE 2

1 ▶ Expand these expressions using the binomial expansion.

  a $(3x + y)^3$ **b** $(m - n)^4$ **c** $(1 + 3x)^3$ **d** $\left(1 + \frac{1}{4}y\right)^4$ **e** $(3y + 4x)^3$

2 ▶ Find the term in x^4 of these expansions.

  a $(3x + 6)^6$ **b** $(4 + 5x)^7$ **c** $(1 + x)^{21}$ **d** $(1 - x)^{30}$

3 ▶ Using the binomial theorem, or otherwise, find the first four terms of these expressions in ascending powers of x, y or b.

  a $(3x + 1)^4$ **b** $\left(1 - \frac{1}{4}y\right)^7$ **c** $(7 - b)^3$ **d** $(3x^2 + 2)^{10}$

4 ▶ The coefficient of x^2 in the binomial expansion of $\left(1 + \frac{2}{5}x\right)^n$, where n is a positive integer, is 1.6

  a Find the value of n.

  b Use your value of n to find the coefficient of the x^4 in the expansion.

USE THE BINOMIAL EXPANSION TO EXPAND $(1 + x)^n$

There is a shortened version of the expansion when one of the terms is 1.

$1^n = 1$, where n is any number, and can therefore be ignored.

The coefficients give values from Pascal's triangle. $^nC_1$ cancels to n, $^nC_2$ cancels to $\dfrac{n(n-1)}{2!}$ and so on.

KEY POINTS

$$(1 + x)^n = \binom{n}{0}1^n + \binom{n}{1}1^{n-1}x^1 + \binom{n}{2}1^{n-2}x^2 + \ldots + \binom{n}{r}1^{n-r}x^r + \ldots + \binom{n}{n}x^n$$

Using the expression for **the binomial coefficients**

$$(1 + x)^n = 1 + nx + \frac{n(n-1)}{2!}x^2 + \frac{n(n-1)(n-2)}{3!}x^3 + \ldots$$

For example, if $n = 4$

$$(1 + x)^4 = 1 + 4x + 6x^2 + 4x^3 + x^4$$

EXAMPLE 4   Find the first four terms in the binomial expansion of

    a $(1 + 3x)^6$ **b** $(1 - 2x)^3$

a $(1 + 3x)^6 = 1 + 6(3x) + \dfrac{6(5)}{2!}(3x)^2 + \dfrac{6(5)(4)}{3!}(3x)^3 + \ldots$

                $= 1 + 6(3)x + 15(3x)^2 + 20(3x)^3$ Substitute in $n = 6$ and $x = 3x$

                $= 1 + 18x + 135x^2 + 540x^3$ Simplify

HINT

It is **very** important to put brackets around the expressions including x parts.

b $(1 - 2x)^3 = 1 + (3)(-2x) + (3)(2)\dfrac{(-2x)^2}{2} + (3)(2)(1)\dfrac{(-2x)^3}{6}$ Substitute in $n = 3$ and $x = -2x$

                $= 1 - 6x + 12x^2 - 8x^3$ Simplify

EXAMPLE 5   Find the coefficient of

    a x^3 **b** x^5

in the binomial expansion of $\left(1 - \dfrac{1}{2}x\right)^6$

a $\left(1 - \dfrac{1}{2}x\right)^6 = \binom{6}{3}\left(-\dfrac{1}{2}x\right)^3$

              $= -\dfrac{5}{2}x^3$

so the coefficient of x^3 is $-\dfrac{5}{2}$

HINT

You do not need the entire expansion, just the required terms.

b $\left(1 - \dfrac{1}{2}x\right)^6 = \binom{6}{5}\left(-\dfrac{1}{2}x\right)^5$

              $= -\dfrac{3}{16}x^5$

so the coefficient of x^5 is $-\dfrac{3}{16}$

$^6C_3 = \binom{6}{3} = \dfrac{6!}{3!3!}$

EXERCISE 3

1 ▶ Use the binomial expansion to find the first four terms of these series, in ascending powers of x.

    a $(1 + x)^9$ **b** $(1 - 3y)^5$ **c** $(1 + 4x)^7$ **d** $\left(1 + \dfrac{x}{2}\right)^9$

    e $(1 - 3x)^7$ **f** $\left(1 - \dfrac{1}{3}x\right)^6$ **g** $\left(1 - \dfrac{x}{4}\right)^6$

2 ▶ When $(1 - 5x)^q$ is expanded the coefficient of $-x$ is 40. Given than $q > 0$, find

    a the constant q **b** the coefficient of x^2 **c** the coefficient of x^3.

3 ▶ **a** Find the first four terms of $(1 - x)^8$.

    b By substituting a suitable value of x into your answer for part **a**, obtain an estimate for 0.99^8

4 ▶ **a** Find the first four terms of $(1 + x)^6$.

    b By substituting a suitable value of x into your answer, obtain an estimate for 1.02^6, giving your answer to 4 decimal places.

5 ▶ Find the coefficient of x^3 in these expressions

    a $(1 - x)^6$ **b** $(1 + x)^9$ **c** $(1 + 2x)^7$

6 ▶ When $\left(1 - \dfrac{2}{3}x\right)^p$ is expanded, the coefficient of x is -4. Given than $q > 0$, find

    a the constant p **b** the coefficient of x^2 **c** the coefficient of x^3.

DETERMINE THE RANGE OF VALUES FOR WHICH x IS TRUE AND VALID FOR AN EXPANSION

The binomial expansion is shown below. When n is a positive integer, the expansion is **finite** and exact. This is not the case when n is negative or a fraction. When n is not a positive integer the series will be infinite. In this case the expansion $(1 + x)^n$ will be valid only in the range $-1 < x < 1$. This can also be written using the **modulus** function as $|x| < 1$

$$(1 + x)^n = 1 + nx + \frac{n(n-1)}{2!}x^2 + \frac{n(n-1)(n-2)}{3!}x^3 + \dots$$

EXAMPLE 6   Use the binomial expansion to find the first four terms of $\dfrac{1}{1 + 2x}$

$$\frac{1}{1 + 2x} = (1 + 2x)^{-1} \qquad\qquad \text{Rewrite } \frac{1}{1 + 2x} \text{ in index form}$$

$$= 1 + (-1)(2x) + \frac{(-1)(-2)}{2}(2x)^2 + \frac{(-1)(-2)(-3)}{6}(2x)^3 + \dots$$

Use the formula $(1 + x)^n = 1 + nx + \dfrac{n(n-1)}{2!}x^2 + \dfrac{n(n-1)(n-2)}{3!}x^3$ with $n = -1$ and $x = 2x$

$$= 1 - 2x + 4x^2 - 8x^3 + \dots$$

The expansion is infinite, but the first four terms can be used as an **approximation** for $\dfrac{1}{1 + 2x}$

provided that $|2x| < 1$. The approximation works well for $2x$ close to 0, but not as well if $2x$ is close to 1, and not at all if $2x$ is larger than 1.

KEY POINTS   When n is not a positive integer none of the $(n - r)$ terms in the coefficients will be equal to zero and so the series will continue and be infinite. In this case the expansion of $(1 + x)^n$ will only be valid for values of x in the range $-1 < x < 1$. This is sometimes written using the modulus function as $|x| < 1$.

EXAMPLE 7

Use the binomial expansion to find the first three terms of

a $\sqrt[3]{1 - 2x}$ **b** $\dfrac{1}{(1 + 4x)^3}$

and state the range of values of x for which the expressions are valid.

---

a $\sqrt[3]{1 - 2x} = (1 - 2x)^{\left(\frac{1}{3}\right)}$ Rewrite in index form

$$= 1 + \left(\frac{1}{3}\right)(-2x) + \left(\frac{1}{3}\right)\left(-\frac{2}{3}\right)\frac{(-2x)^2}{2} + \left(\frac{1}{3}\right)\left(-\frac{2}{3}\right)\left(-\frac{5}{3}\right)\frac{(-2x)^3}{6}$$

> Use $(1 + x)^n = 1 + nx + \dfrac{n(n-1)}{2!}x^2 + \dfrac{n(n-1)(n-2)}{3!}x^3$ with $n = \dfrac{1}{3}$, $x = -2x$

$$= 1 - \frac{2}{3}x - \frac{4}{9}x^2 - \frac{40}{81}x^3 + \ldots$$

The range of validity is given by $|2x| < 1$, so that $|x| < \dfrac{1}{2}$ In this case the 'x' term is $2x$

b $\dfrac{1}{(1 + 4x)^3} = (1 + 4x)^{-3}$ Rewrite in index form

$$= 1 + (-3)(4x) + (-3)(-4)\frac{(4x)^2}{2} + (-3)(-4)(-5)\frac{(4x)^3}{6}$$

> Use $(1 + x)^n = 1 + nx + \dfrac{n(n-1)}{2!}x^2 + \dfrac{n(n-1)(n-2)}{3!}x^3$ with $n = -3$, $x = 4x$

$$= 1 - 12x + 96x^2 - 640x^3 + \ldots$$

The range of validity is given by $|4x| < 1$, so that $|x| < \dfrac{1}{4}$ In this case the 'x' term is $4x$

EXAMPLE 8

Find the binomial expansion of $\sqrt{1 - 2x}$ and by using $x = 0.01$, find and estimate of $\sqrt{2}$.

$\sqrt{1 - 2x} = (1 - 2x)^{\frac{1}{2}}$ Rewrite in index form

$$= 1 + \left(\frac{1}{2}\right)(-2x) + \left(\frac{1}{2}\right)\left(-\frac{1}{2}\right)\frac{(-2x)^2}{2} + \left(\frac{1}{2}\right)\left(-\frac{1}{2}\right)\left(-\frac{3}{2}\right)\frac{(-2x)^3}{6}$$

> Use $(1 + x)^n = 1 + nx + \dfrac{n(n-1)}{2!}x^2 + \dfrac{n(n-1)(n-2)}{3!}x^3$, in this case with $n = \dfrac{1}{2}$ and $x = 2x$

$$= 1 - x - \frac{1}{2}x^2 - \frac{1}{2}x^3$$

$\sqrt{0.98} = 1 - 0.01 - 0.00005 - 0.0000005$ Substitute $x = 0.01$

$\sqrt{\dfrac{98}{100}} = 0.9899495$ Rewrite 0.98 as a fraction

$\dfrac{7\sqrt{2}}{10} = 0.9899495$ Calculate the square root of the numerator and denominator separately

$\sqrt{2} = \dfrac{9.899495 \times 10}{7}$ Multiply by 10 and divide by 7

$\qquad = 1.414213571$

EXERCISE 4

1 ▶ Expand these expressions up to and including x^3, and state the values of x for which the expansion is valid where appropriate.

a $(1 + 2x)^{-3}$ b $\dfrac{1}{(1 - 3x)}$ c $\dfrac{1}{\sqrt{4 + 6x}}$

2 ▶ Find the coefficient of the x^3 term, and state the values of x for which the expansion is valid.

a $\dfrac{1}{1 + x}$ b $\sqrt{1 + 2x}$ c $\dfrac{1}{(1 - 3x)}$ d $\sqrt[3]{1 - x}$

3 ▶ a Expand $(1 + 3x)^{-1}$, $|x| < \dfrac{1}{3}$ in ascending powers of x up to and including the term in x^3.

b Hence, or otherwise, find an expression for $\dfrac{1 - x}{1 + 3x}$, $|x| < \dfrac{1}{3}$ in ascending powers of x up to and including the term in x^3.

4 ▶ In the expansion of $(1 + bx)^{-\frac{1}{2}}$ the coefficient of x^2 is 24. Find the possible values of the constant b and the coefficient of x^3.

5 ▶ a Find the binomial expansion of $\sqrt[3]{(1 + 6x)}$ in ascending powers of x up to and including the term in x^3.

b By substituting $x = 0.004$ find an approximation to $\sqrt[3]{2}$. By comparing it to the exact value, comment on the accuracy of your approximation.

6 ▶ Find the coefficient of the x^3 in $\dfrac{1 + 3x}{(1 + 2x)^3}$.

EXAM PRACTICE: CHAPTER 6

1 Find the first 4 terms of the binomial expansion, in ascending powers of x, of $\left(1 + \frac{x}{4}\right)^7$ giving each term in its simplest form. **[5]**

2 **a** Write down in ascending powers of x, up to and including x^3, the expansion of $(3 + ax)^5$ where a is a non-zero constant. **[3]**
b Given that the coefficient of x^2 is double the coefficient of x, find the value of a. **[4]**

3 The coefficient of x^2 in the expansion of $\left(1 - \frac{x}{2}\right)^n$, where n is a positive integer, is 9. Find the value of n. **[3]**

4 Show that $\sqrt{\dfrac{1+x}{1-x}} \approx 1 + x + \frac{1}{2}x^2$, $|x| < 1$. **[7]**

5 $f(x) = \dfrac{1}{\sqrt{4+x}}$
a Use the binomial expansion to expand $f(x)$ in ascending powers of x up to and including x^3. **[4]**
b State for what values of x the expansion is valid. **[1]**

6 **a** Find in ascending powers of x, up to and including x^3, the expansion of $(1 + 3x)^{\frac{1}{2}}$. **[3]**
b By substituting $x = 0.01$ in the expansion, find an approximation to $\sqrt{103}$. **[4]**
c By comparing to the exact value, comment on the accuracy. **[2]**

7 Find the coefficient of the x^3 term of $\dfrac{1 + 3x}{1 + x}$. **[3]**

8 $f(x) = \sqrt{1 - 8x}$
a Use the binomial expansion to expand $f(x)$ in ascending powers of x up to and including x^3. **[4]**
b State for which values of x the expansion is valid. **[1]**
c By substituting $x = 0.01$ obtain an approximation to $\sqrt{23}$. **[4]**

9 $f(x) = (1 - 3x)^{\frac{3}{2}}$
a Use the binomial expansion to expand $f(x)$ in ascending powers of x up to and including x^3. **[4]**
b By substituting a suitable value of x, find an approximation to $97^{\frac{3}{2}}$. **[4]**

10 **a** Expand $\dfrac{5}{\sqrt{1 - 2x}}$ in ascending powers of x up to and including x^3 and simplify each term fully. **[5]**
b State for which values of x the expansion is valid. **[1]**

11 $f(x) = \dfrac{4}{\sqrt{1 + \frac{2}{3}x}}$, $-\dfrac{3}{2} < x < \dfrac{3}{2}$
a Expand $f(x)$ in ascending powers of x up to and including x^2 and simplify each term fully. **[5]**
b Given that $f\left(\frac{1}{10}\right) = \sqrt{15}$. Obtain an approximation of $\sqrt{15}$, giving your answer as a fully simplified fraction. **[4]**

12 **a** Expand $\dfrac{2}{\sqrt{1 + 2x}}$ in ascending powers of x up to and including x^3 and simplify each term fully. **[4]**
b State for which the values of x the expansion is valid. **[2]**

CHAPTER SUMMARY: CHAPTER 6

■ The binomial expansion $(1 + x)^n = 1 + nx + \dfrac{n(n-1)}{2!}x^2 + \dfrac{n(n-1)(n-2)}{3!}x^3 + \ldots$

can be used to give an exact expression if n is a positive integer. It can also be used to give an approximation for any **rational** number

■ The expansion of $(1 + x)^n = 1 + nx + \dfrac{n(n-1)}{2!}x^2 + \dfrac{n(n-1)(n-2)}{3!}x^3 + \ldots$

where n is negative or a fraction, is only valid if $|x| < 1$

■ The first four terms of $(1 + 3x)^6$ are

$1 + 6(3x) + \dfrac{6(5)}{2!}(3x)^2 + \dfrac{6(5)(4)}{3!}(3x)^3 + \ldots = 1 + 18x + 135x^2 + 540x^3$

The expansion is finite and exact

■ The first four terms of $(1 - 2x)^{\frac{1}{3}}$ are

$1 + \left(\dfrac{1}{3}\right)(-2x) + \left(\dfrac{1}{3}\right)\left(-\dfrac{2}{3}\right)\dfrac{(-2x)^2}{2} + \left(\dfrac{1}{3}\right)\left(-\dfrac{2}{3}\right)\left(-\dfrac{5}{3}\right)\dfrac{(-2x)^3}{6} = 1 - \dfrac{2}{3}x - \dfrac{4}{9}x^2 - \dfrac{40}{81}x^3$

The expansion is infinite and approximate

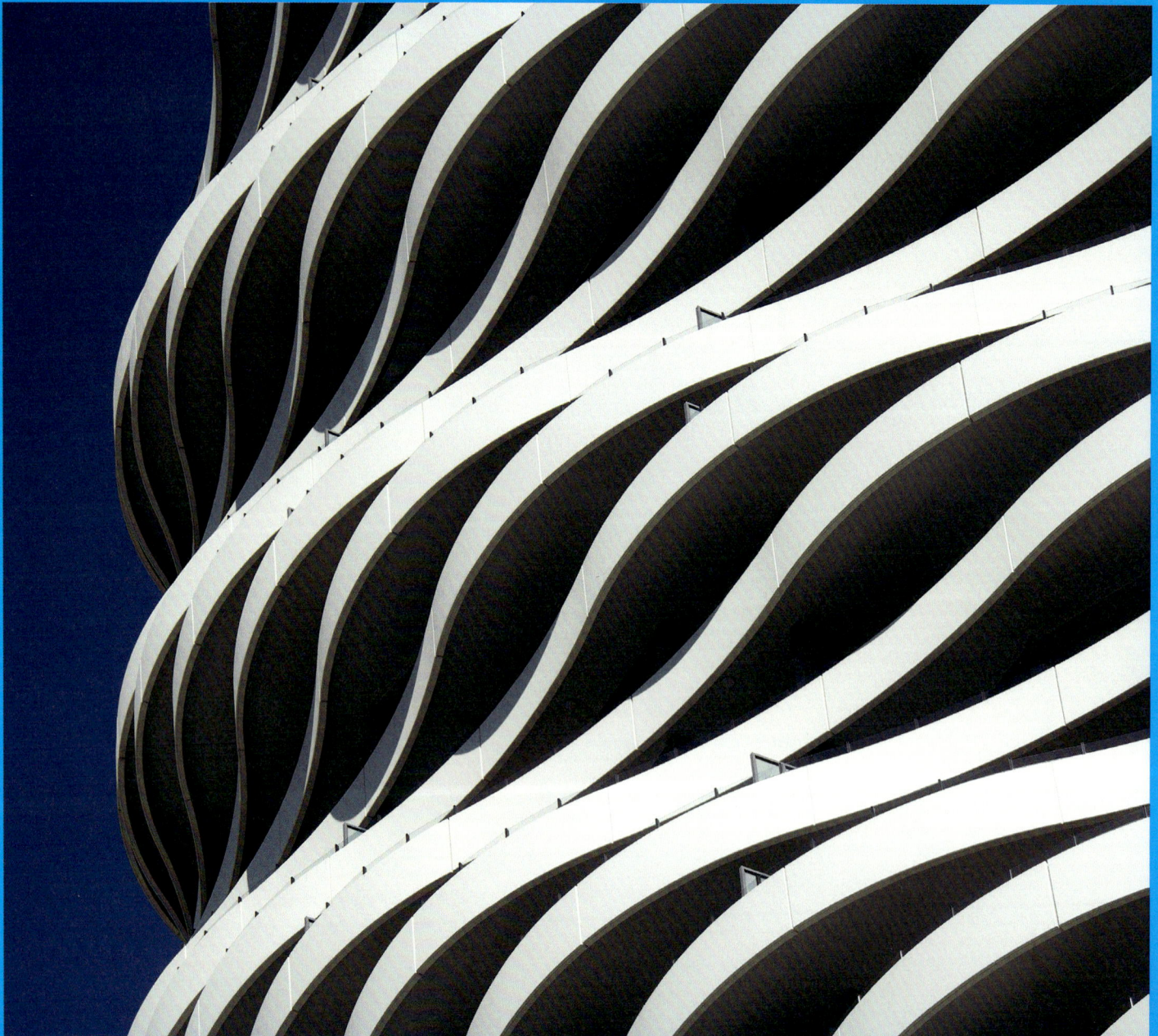

CHAPTER 7

7 SCALAR AND VECTOR QUANTITIES

In the United States, there are around 5000 aeroplanes in the sky at any given time. How do the pilots and air traffic control ensure that these aircraft move around the skies without colliding? They use **vectors** to keep the aircraft on specific flight paths. Vectoring is used to aid navigation and to guide aircraft into their final position so that they can land safely.

Without the use of vectors, commercial aviation would hardly have developed at all.

LEARNING OBJECTIVES

- Use vector notation and draw vector diagrams
- Perform simple vector arithmetic and understand the definition of a unit vector
- Use vectors to describe the position of a point in two dimensions
- Write down and use the **Cartesian** components of a vector in two dimensions
- Use vectors to demonstrate simple properties of geometrical figures

STARTER ACTIVITIES

A quantity that has both **size** (magnitude) and **direction** is a **vector**.
A quantity that just has *size* is a scalar.

A scalar quantity can be described by using a single number (its magnitude or size).

A vector quantity has both **magnitude** and direction.

For example

Scalar: The distance from P to Q is 100 metres.
(Distance is a scalar.)

Vector: From P to Q you go 100 metres north.
(This is called the **displacement** from P to Q. Displacement is a vector.)

Scalar: A ship is sailing at 12 km h^{-1}.
(Speed is a scalar.)

Vector: A ship is sailing at 12 km h^{-1}, on a **bearing** of 060°.
(This is called the velocity of the ship. Velocity is a vector.)

The diagram below shows the displacement vector from P to Q where Q is 500 m **due north** of P.

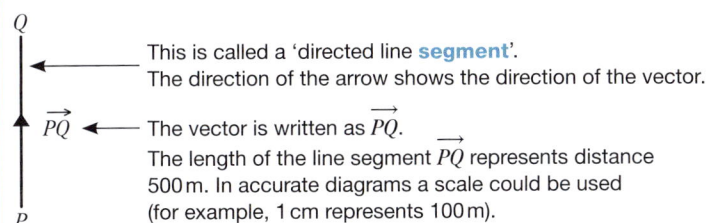

This is called a 'directed line **segment**'.
The direction of the arrow shows the direction of the vector.

The vector is written as $\overrightarrow{PQ}$.

The length of the line segment $\overrightarrow{PQ}$ represents distance 500 m. In accurate diagrams a scale could be used (for example, 1 cm represents 100 m).

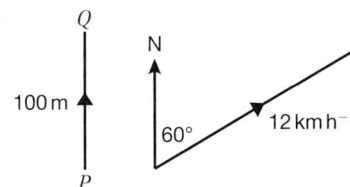

Sometimes, instead of using the end points P and Q, a small (lower case) letter is used. In print, the small letter will be in **bold type**. In writing you should underline the small letter to show it is a vector: <u>a</u> or **a**

VECTOR NOTATION AND HOW TO DRAW VECTOR DIAGRAMS

You need to be able to write down vectors and draw vector diagrams.

Vectors that are equal have both the same magnitude and the same direction.

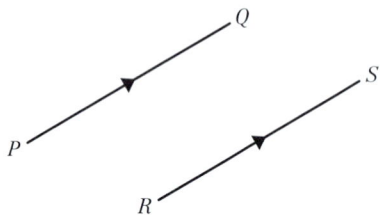

Here $\overrightarrow{PQ} = \overrightarrow{RS}$

HINT
Think of displacement vectors. If you travel from P to Q, then from Q to R, the resultant journey is P to R: $\overrightarrow{PQ} + \overrightarrow{QR} = \overrightarrow{PR}$.

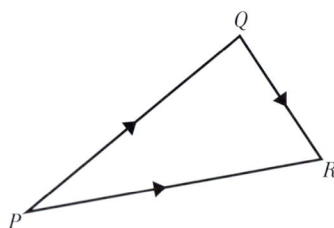

Two vectors are added using the 'triangle law'

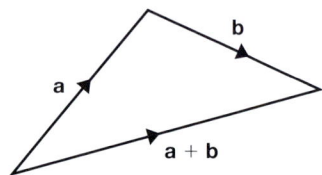

When you add the vectors **a** and **b**, the resultant vector **a** + **b** goes from 'the start of **a** to the finish of **b**'. This is sometimes called the triangle law for vector addition

EXAMPLE 1

The diagram shows the vectors **a**, **b** and **c**. Draw another diagram to illustrate the vector **a** + **b** + **c**

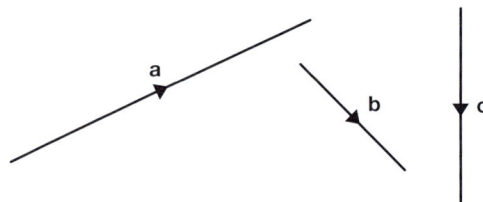

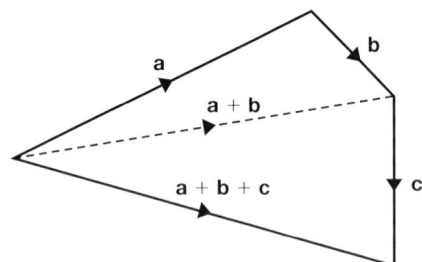

First use the triangle law for **a** + **b**. Then use it again for (**a** + **b**) + **c**
The resultant goes from the start of **a** to the finish of **c**

HINT
If you travel from P to Q, then back from Q to P, you are back where you started, so your displacement is zero.

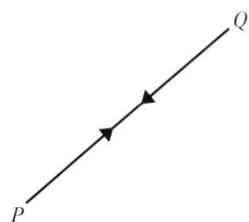

Adding the vectors $\overrightarrow{PQ}$ and $\overrightarrow{QP}$ gives the zero vector **0**: $\overrightarrow{PQ} + \overrightarrow{QP} = \mathbf{0}$

The zero displacement vector is **0**. It is printed in bold type, or underlined in written work.

You can also write $\overrightarrow{PQ} = -\overrightarrow{QP}$. So $\overrightarrow{PQ} + \overrightarrow{QP} = \mathbf{0}$ or $\overrightarrow{PQ} - \overrightarrow{PQ} = \mathbf{0}$

The **modulus**, or magnitude, of a vector is written in single vertical bars.

The modulus of the vector **a** is written as |**a**|.

The modulus of the vector $\overrightarrow{PQ}$ is written as $\left|\overrightarrow{PQ}\right|$.

EXAMPLE 2

The vector **a** is directed due east and |**a**| = 12.
The vector **b** is directed due south and |**b**| = 5.
Find |**a** + **b**|.

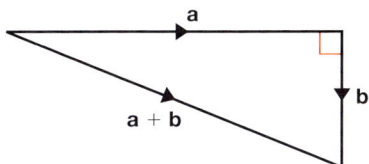

Use the triangle law for adding the vectors **a** and **b**

$|\mathbf{a} + \mathbf{b}|^2 = 12^2 + 5^2 = 169$ Use Pythagoras' theorem

$|\mathbf{a} + \mathbf{b}| = 13$

EXAMPLE 3

In the diagram, $\overrightarrow{QP} = \mathbf{a}$, $\overrightarrow{QR} = \mathbf{b}$, $\overrightarrow{QS} = \mathbf{c}$ and $\overrightarrow{RT} = \mathbf{d}$.
Find in terms of **a**, **b**, **c** and **d**.

a $\overrightarrow{PS}$

b $\overrightarrow{RP}$

c $\overrightarrow{PT}$

d $\overrightarrow{TS}$

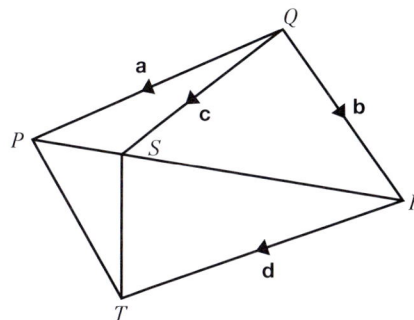

a $\overrightarrow{PS} = \overrightarrow{PQ} + \overrightarrow{QS} = -\mathbf{a} + \mathbf{c} = \mathbf{c} - \mathbf{a}$ Add vectors using the triangle $\triangle PQS$

b $\overrightarrow{RP} = \overrightarrow{RQ} + \overrightarrow{QP} = -\mathbf{b} + \mathbf{a} = \mathbf{a} - \mathbf{b}$ Add vectors using $\triangle RQP$

c $\overrightarrow{PT} = \overrightarrow{PR} + \overrightarrow{RT} = (\mathbf{b} - \mathbf{a}) + \mathbf{d} = \mathbf{b} + \mathbf{d} - \mathbf{a}$

Add vectors using $\triangle PRT$ and use
$\overrightarrow{PR} = -\overrightarrow{RP} = -(\mathbf{a} - \mathbf{b}) = (\mathbf{b} - \mathbf{a})$

d $\overrightarrow{TS} = \overrightarrow{TR} + \overrightarrow{RS} = -\mathbf{d} + (\overrightarrow{RQ} + \overrightarrow{QS})$

So $\overrightarrow{TS} = -\mathbf{d} + (-\mathbf{b} + \mathbf{c}) = \mathbf{c} - \mathbf{b} - \mathbf{d}$ Add vectors using $\triangle TRS$ and also $\triangle RQS$

EXERCISE 1

SKILLS

PROBLEM
SOLVING
REASONING

1 ▶ Given vector **a** (as seen in the diagram), draw the vectors

 a 4**a**

 b −2**a**

 c $\frac{1}{4}\mathbf{a}$

 d $-\frac{1}{3}\mathbf{a}$

2 ▶ The vectors **a** and **b** are shown in the diagram. Draw

 a **a** + **b**   **b** 2**a** − **b**   **c** **a** − 2**b**

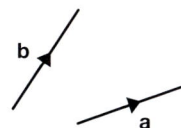

3 ▶ The vector **a** is directed due east and |**a**| = 32.

The vector **b** is directed due north east and |**b**| = 6.

Find |**a** + **b**|.

4 ▶ The vector **a** is directed south west and |**a**| = 16.

The vector **b** is directed south east and |**b**| = 20.

Find |**a** + **b**|.

5 ▶ In the diagram $\overrightarrow{NP}$ = **a**, $\overrightarrow{PQ}$ = **b**, $\overrightarrow{QM}$ = **c** and $\overrightarrow{NO}$ = **d**

Find in terms of **a**, **b**, **c**, **d**

a $\overrightarrow{NQ}$ **b** $\overrightarrow{MN}$

c $\overrightarrow{OQ}$ **d** $\overrightarrow{PO}$

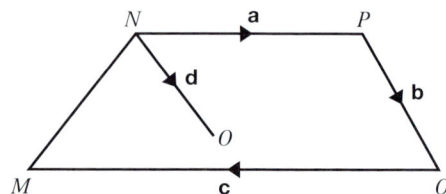

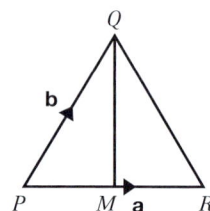

6 ▶ In the diagram $\overrightarrow{PR}$ = **a** and $\overrightarrow{PQ}$ = **b**. *M* is the **midpoint** of $\overrightarrow{PR}$.

In terms of **a** and **b** find

a $\overrightarrow{PM}$

b $\overrightarrow{MQ}$

c $\overrightarrow{QM}$

7 ▶ In the diagram $\overrightarrow{QP}$ = **a**, $\overrightarrow{QR}$ = **b** and $\overrightarrow{QS}$ = **c**.

Given that $\overrightarrow{PR}$ = $\overrightarrow{RS}$, prove that −**a** + 2**b** = **c**.

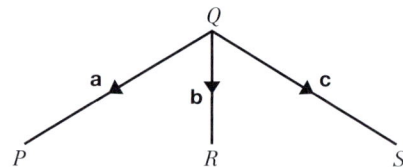

PERFORM SIMPLE VECTOR ARITHMETIC AND UNDERSTAND THE DEFINITION OF A UNIT VECTOR

KEY POINTS   A unit vector is a vector with a magnitude of 1. Two important unit vectors are commonly used: these are the vectors in the direction of the x and y. The unit vector in the direction of the x-axis is **i** and the unit vector in the direction of the y-axis is **j**.

EXAMPLE 4   The diagram shows the vector **a**.

Draw diagrams to illustrate the vectors 3**a** and −2**a**.

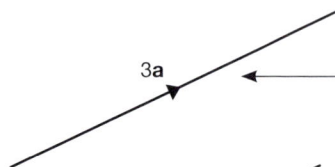

The vector 3**a** is **a** + **a** + **a**, so it is in the same direction as **a** with 3 times its magnitude. The vector **a** has been multiplied by the scalar 3 (a scalar multiple).

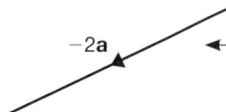

The vector −2**a** is −**a** − **a**, so it is in the opposite direction as **a** with 2 times its magnitude.

Any vector **parallel** to the vector **a** may be written as λ**a**, where λ is a non-zero scalar.

EXAMPLE 5 Show that the vectors 6**a** + 8**b** and 9**a** + 12**b** are parallel.

9**a** + 12**b**

$= \dfrac{3}{2}(6\mathbf{a} + 8\mathbf{b})$ $\lambda = \dfrac{3}{2}$

So the vectors are parallel.

Subtracting a vector is equivalent to 'adding a negative vector', so **a** − **b** is defined to
be **a** + (−**b**).

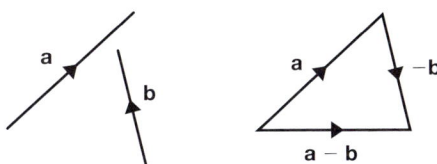

HINT
To subtract **b**, you reverse
the direction of **b**, then add.

A unit vector is a vector with modulus 1.

EXAMPLE 6 The vector **a** has magnitude 20 units. Write down a unit vector that is parallel to **a**.

The unit vector is $\dfrac{\mathbf{a}}{20}$ or $\dfrac{1}{20}\mathbf{a}$ Divide **a** by its magnitude. In general, the unit vector is $\dfrac{\mathbf{a}}{|\mathbf{a}|}$

If λ**a** + μ**b** = α**a** + β**b** and the non-zero vectors **a** and **b** are not parallel, then $\alpha = \lambda$ and $\beta = \mu$.

The above result can be shown as follows:

λ**a** + μ**b** = α**a** + β**b** can be written as $(\lambda - \alpha)$**a** = $(\beta - \mu)$**b**, but two vectors cannot be equal unless
they are parallel or zero.

Since the vectors **a** and **b** are not parallel or zero, $(\lambda - \alpha) = 0$ and $(\beta - \mu) = 0$, so $\alpha = \lambda$ and $\beta = \mu$.

EXAMPLE 7 Given that 5**a** − 4**b** = $(2s + t)$**a** + $(s - t)$**b**, where the non-zero vectors **a** and **b** are not parallel, find
the values of the scalars s, t.

$2s + t = 5$ Equate the coefficients of **a** and **b**

$s - t = -4$

$3s = 1$ Solve simultaneously by adding the equations

$s = \dfrac{1}{3}$

$t = s + 4 = 4\dfrac{1}{3}$

So $s = \dfrac{1}{3}$ and $t = 4\dfrac{1}{3}$

EXAMPLE 8

In the diagram, $\overrightarrow{PQ} = 3\mathbf{a}$, $\overrightarrow{QR} = \mathbf{b}$, $\overrightarrow{SR} = 4\mathbf{a}$ and $\overrightarrow{PX} = k\overrightarrow{PR}$. Find, in terms of $\mathbf{a}$, $\mathbf{b}$ and k:

a $\overrightarrow{PS}$

b $\overrightarrow{PX}$

c $\overrightarrow{SQ}$

d $\overrightarrow{SX}$

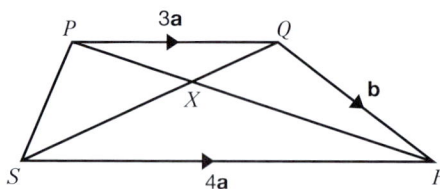

HINT

It is useful to check that the result is correct in special cases. For example, if $k = 1$, $\overrightarrow{SX} = 4\mathbf{a}$. This is correct because if $k = 1$, X and R are the same point and $\overrightarrow{SR} = 4\mathbf{a}$.

a $\overrightarrow{PS} = \overrightarrow{PR} + \overrightarrow{RS} = \overrightarrow{PQ} + \overrightarrow{QR} + \overrightarrow{RS} = 3\mathbf{a} + \mathbf{b} - 4\mathbf{a} = \mathbf{b} - \mathbf{a}$ Use the triangle law

b $\overrightarrow{PR} = \overrightarrow{PQ} + \overrightarrow{QR} = 3\mathbf{a} + \mathbf{b}$

  $\overrightarrow{PX} = k\overrightarrow{PR} = k(3\mathbf{a} + \mathbf{b})$

c $\overrightarrow{SQ} = \overrightarrow{SR} + \overrightarrow{RQ} = 4\mathbf{a} + (-\mathbf{b}) = 4\mathbf{a} - \mathbf{b}$

d $\overrightarrow{SX} = \overrightarrow{SP} + \overrightarrow{PX} = -\overrightarrow{PS} + \overrightarrow{PX} = -(\mathbf{b} - \mathbf{a}) + k(3\mathbf{a} + \mathbf{b}) = (3k + 1)\mathbf{a} + (k - 1)\mathbf{b}$

EXERCISE 2

SKILLS

REASONING
CRITICAL
THINKING

1 ▶ In the triangle ABC, $\overrightarrow{AB} = 2\mathbf{a}$, $\overrightarrow{BC} = \mathbf{b}$. The midpoint of $\overrightarrow{AC}$ is M.

Find in terms of $\mathbf{a}$ and $\mathbf{b}$

a $\overrightarrow{AC}$ b $\overrightarrow{AM}$ c $\overrightarrow{CM}$

2 ▶ The diagram shows a **parallelogram** $ABCD$.

E is a point on BC such that $BE:EC = 1:3$

Write expressions for these vectors.

a $\overrightarrow{DC}$ b $\overrightarrow{CD}$ c $\overrightarrow{AC}$

d $\overrightarrow{AE}$ e $\overrightarrow{DE}$

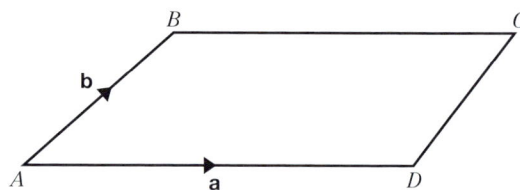

3 ▶ In each part, determine if the given vector is parallel to $2\mathbf{a} + 3\mathbf{b}$.

a $6\mathbf{a} + 9\mathbf{b}$ b $24\mathbf{a} + 7\mathbf{b}$ c $\mathbf{a} + \frac{3}{2}\mathbf{b}$ d $6\mathbf{b} + 14\mathbf{a}$

4 ▶ The non-zero vectors $\mathbf{a}$ and $\mathbf{b}$ are not parallel. In each part find the value of λ and μ:

a $\mathbf{a} + 4\mathbf{b} = 2\lambda\mathbf{a} - \mu\mathbf{b}$ b $(\lambda + 2)\mathbf{a} + (\mu - 3)\mathbf{b} = 0$

c $5\lambda\mathbf{a} - 4\mathbf{b} - 2\mathbf{a} + \mu\mathbf{b} = 0$ d $(1 + \lambda)\mathbf{a} + 3\lambda\mathbf{b} = \mu\mathbf{a} + 4\mu\mathbf{b}$

e $(3\mu + 5)\mathbf{a} + \mathbf{b} = 2\mu + (\lambda - 3)\mathbf{b}$ f $6\mathbf{a} - 5\mathbf{b} = (2\lambda + \mu)\mathbf{a} + (\lambda - \mu)\mathbf{b}$

g $10\mathbf{a} - 8\mathbf{b} = (4\lambda + 2\mu)\mathbf{a} + (\lambda - \mu)\mathbf{b}$

5 ▶ In the triangle PQR, $\overrightarrow{PQ} = \mathbf{a}$, $\overrightarrow{PR} = \mathbf{b}$.

M is the midpoint of $\overrightarrow{PQ}$ and N lies on $\overrightarrow{PR}$ such that $\overrightarrow{PN}:\overrightarrow{PR} = 1:4$.

Find in terms of $\mathbf{a}$ and $\mathbf{b}$.

a $\overrightarrow{PM}$ b $\overrightarrow{QR}$ c $\overrightarrow{PN}$

d $\overrightarrow{RN}$ e $\overrightarrow{QN}$

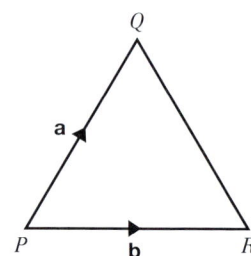

6 ▶ $ABCDEF$ is a regular **hexagon** with centre O.

$\overrightarrow{OA} = \mathbf{a}$ and $\overrightarrow{AB} = \mathbf{b}$

Find expressions, in terms of $\mathbf{a}$ and $\mathbf{b}$, for

   a $\overrightarrow{OB}$

   b $\overrightarrow{AC}$

   c $\overrightarrow{EC}$

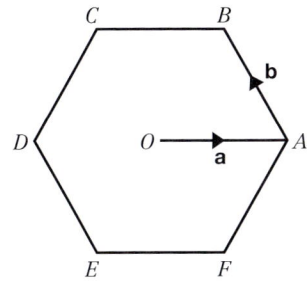

7 ▶ The diagram shows two sets of parallel lines.

Vector $\overrightarrow{PQ} = 2\mathbf{a}$ and vector $\overrightarrow{PS} = 3\mathbf{b}$.

$\overrightarrow{PR} = 3\overrightarrow{PQ}$ and $\overrightarrow{PU} = 2\overrightarrow{PS}$

   a   Write the vector $\overrightarrow{PV}$ in terms of $\mathbf{a}$ and $\mathbf{b}$.

   b   Write the vector $\overrightarrow{RU}$ in terms of $\mathbf{a}$ and $\mathbf{b}$.

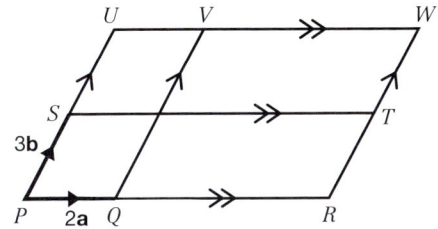

USE VECTORS TO DESCRIBE THE POSITION OF A POINT IN TWO DIMENSIONS

The position vector of a point A is the vector $\overrightarrow{OA}$, where O is the origin.

$\overrightarrow{OA}$ is usually written as vector $\mathbf{a}$

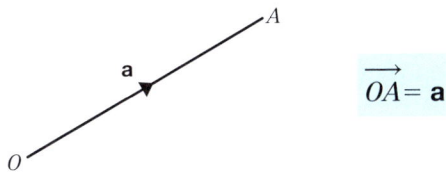

$$\boxed{\overrightarrow{OA} = \mathbf{a}}$$

$\overrightarrow{AB} = \mathbf{b} - \mathbf{a}$, where $\mathbf{a}$ and $\mathbf{b}$ are the position vectors of A and B respectively.

HINT

Use the triangle law to give

$\overrightarrow{AB} = \overrightarrow{AO} + \overrightarrow{OB}$

     $= -\mathbf{a} + \mathbf{b}$

So $\overrightarrow{AB} = \mathbf{b} - \mathbf{a}$.

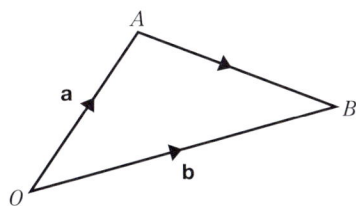

EXAMPLE 9

In the diagram the points A and B have position vectors **a** and **b** respectively (referred to the origin O). The point P divides AB in the ratio $1:2$.

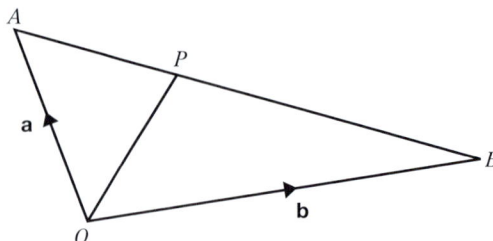

Find the position vector of P.

$$\overrightarrow{AB} = \mathbf{b} - \mathbf{a}$$

$$\overrightarrow{OP} = \overrightarrow{OA} + \overrightarrow{AP}$$ $\qquad$ $\overrightarrow{OP}$ is the position vector of P

$$\overrightarrow{AP} = \frac{1}{3}(\mathbf{b} - \mathbf{a})$$ $\qquad$ Use the $1:2$ ratio ($\overrightarrow{AP}$ is one third of $\overrightarrow{AB}$)

$$\overrightarrow{OP} = \mathbf{a} + \frac{1}{3}(\mathbf{b} - \mathbf{a}) = \frac{2}{3}\mathbf{a} + \frac{1}{3}\mathbf{b}$$

EXERCISE 3

SKILLS

ANALYSIS

1 ▶ The points A and B have position vectors **a** and **b** respectively (referred to the origin O). The point P divides AB in the ratio $1:5$.
Find, in terms of **a** and **b**, the position vector of P.

2 ▶ The points A, B and C have position vectors **a**, **b** and **c** respectively (referred to the origin O). The point P is the midpoint of AB.
Find, in terms of **a**, **b** and **c**, the vector $\overrightarrow{PC}$.

3 ▶ $OABCDE$ is a regular hexagon. The points A and B have position vectors **a** and **b** respectively, referred to the origin O.
Find, in terms of **a** and **b**, the position vectors of C, D and E.

USE VECTORS TO DEMONSTRATE SIMPLE PROPERTIES OF GEOMETRICAL FIGURES

EXAMPLE 10

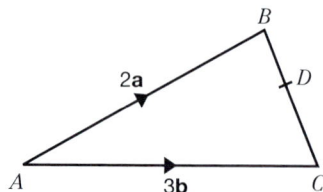

ABC is a triangle
AB is $2\mathbf{a}$
AC is $3\mathbf{b}$

a Find BC in terms of **a** and **b**

$$BC = BA + AC$$
$$BC = -2\mathbf{a} + 3\mathbf{b}$$

D is a point on the line BC such that $BD:DC = 2:3$

b Show that AD is parallel to the vector $\mathbf{a} + \mathbf{b}$

First you need to find AD in terms of $\mathbf{a}$ and $\mathbf{b}$.

$AD = AB + BD$

$AD = AB + \dfrac{2}{5}BC$

$AD = 2\mathbf{a} + \dfrac{2}{5}(-2\mathbf{a} + 3\mathbf{b})$

$AD = 2\mathbf{a} + -\dfrac{4}{5}\mathbf{a} + \dfrac{6}{5}\mathbf{b}$ By expanding the brackets

$AD = \dfrac{6}{5}\mathbf{a} + \dfrac{6}{5}\mathbf{b}$

Factorise to find if parallel.

$AD = \dfrac{6}{5}(\mathbf{a} + \mathbf{b})$

Therefore line AD is parallel to vector $\mathbf{a} + \mathbf{b}$ because AD is a multiple of vector $\mathbf{a} + \mathbf{b}$

EXAMPLE 11

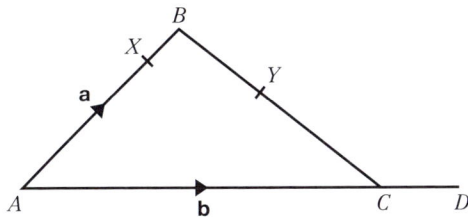

In the diagram $AB = \mathbf{a}$ is and $AC = \mathbf{b}$

The point X divides AB in the ratio

$$AX:AB = 4:1$$

The point Y divides BC in the ratio

$$BY:YC = 2:3$$

The point D on AC is such that

$$AC:CD = 5:3$$

a Show that $\overrightarrow{XY} = \dfrac{2}{5}\mathbf{b} - \dfrac{1}{5}\mathbf{a}$

$\overrightarrow{XY} = XB + BY$

$\overrightarrow{XB} = \dfrac{1}{5}\mathbf{a}$

$\overrightarrow{BC} = -\mathbf{a} + \mathbf{b}$

Therefore:

$\overrightarrow{XY} = \dfrac{1}{5}\mathbf{a} + \dfrac{2}{5}(-\mathbf{a} + \mathbf{b})$ Due to the ratio $2:3$

$\quad = \dfrac{1}{5}\mathbf{a} - \dfrac{2}{5}\mathbf{a} + \dfrac{2}{5}\mathbf{b}$

$\quad = -\dfrac{1}{5}\mathbf{a} + \dfrac{2}{5}\mathbf{b}$

$\quad = \dfrac{2}{5}\mathbf{b} - \dfrac{1}{5}\mathbf{a}$

HINT

Co-linear means all the points are on the same line.

b Show that X, Y and D are co-linear

If two points are parallel and come from the same point then they are co-linear.

$XD = XA + AD$

$XD = XA + AC + CD$

$XD = -\dfrac{4}{5}\mathbf{a} + (\mathbf{b} + \dfrac{3}{5}\mathbf{b})$

$XD = -\dfrac{4}{5}\mathbf{a} + 1\dfrac{3}{5}\mathbf{b}$

$XD = -\dfrac{4}{5}\mathbf{a} + \dfrac{8}{5}\mathbf{b}$

$XY = -\dfrac{1}{5}\mathbf{a} + \dfrac{2}{5}\mathbf{b}$

Therefore XD is $4(XY)$ which shows XD is parallel to XY

Since XD and XY share a point and are parallel then they must be on the same straight line and co-linear

EXERCISE 4

1 ▶

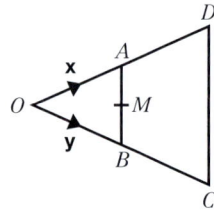

In triangle OAB the midpoint on AB is M.

$$\overrightarrow{OA} = \mathbf{x} \quad \overrightarrow{OB} = \mathbf{y} \quad \overrightarrow{OD} = 2\mathbf{x} \text{ and } \overrightarrow{OC} = 2\mathbf{y}$$

a Express $\overrightarrow{AB}$, $\overrightarrow{OM}$ and $\overrightarrow{DC}$ in terms of **x** and **y**

b Show that AB and DC are parallel.

2 ▶

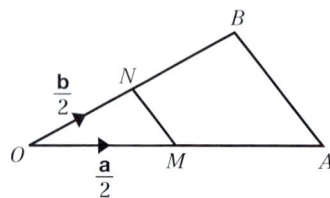

N is the midpoint of $\overrightarrow{OB}$

M is the midpoint of $\overrightarrow{OA}$

$$\overrightarrow{OA} = \mathbf{a} \quad \overrightarrow{OB} = \mathbf{b}$$

Show MN is parallel to AB

3 ▶

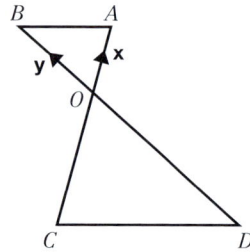

The ratio of $OA:OC = 1:2$ and $OB:OD = 1:2$

a Find AB, OC, OD and DC

b Show that AB is parallel to DC

4 ▶

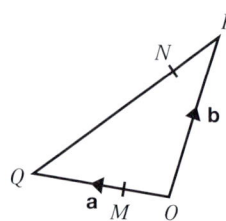

$OM:MQ = 1:2$

$$PN = \frac{1}{3}PQ$$

Show that OP and MN are parallel

5 ▶

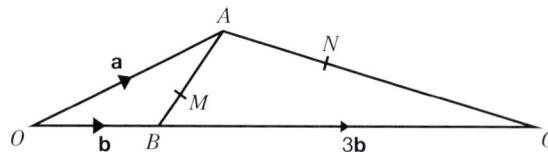

The diagram shows $OABCMN$.

$$\overrightarrow{OA} = \mathbf{a}, \ \overrightarrow{OB} = \mathbf{b}, \ \overrightarrow{BC} = 3\mathbf{b}$$

$AM:MB = 2:1$

$AN:NC = 1:2$

a Find $\overrightarrow{AB}$ in terms of **a** and **b**

b Find $\overrightarrow{OM}$ in terms of **a** and **b**

c Show that OMN are co-linear

6 ▶

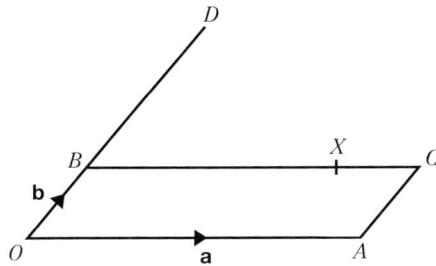

$OACB$ is a parallelogram

OA is **a**

OB is **b**

OB to OD is in the ratio $1:3$

XC is $\dfrac{1}{3}BC$

a   Show that $AD = 3\mathbf{b} - \mathbf{a}$

b   Show that A, X, D are co-linear

7 ▶

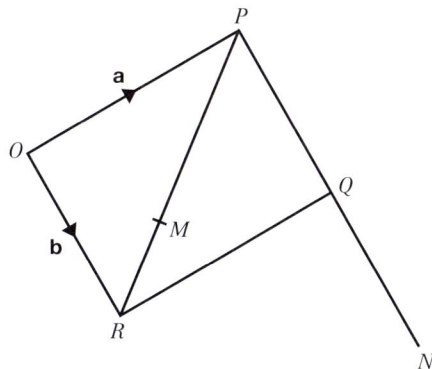

$OP = \mathbf{a} \quad OR = \mathbf{b}$

N is the point such that $\overrightarrow{PQ} = \overrightarrow{QN}$

The point M divides PR in the ratio $2:1$

a   Show that $\overrightarrow{OM} = \dfrac{1}{3}\mathbf{a} + \dfrac{2}{3}\mathbf{b}$

b   Prove that OMN is a straight line

WRITE DOWN AND USE CARTESIAN COMPONENTS OF A VECTOR IN TWO DIMENSIONS

The vectors **i** and **j** are unit vectors parallel to the x-axis and the y-axis, and in the direction of x increasing and y increasing, respectively.

EXAMPLE 12 ▶

The points A and B in the diagrams have coordinates $(3, 4)$ and $(11, 2)$ respectively. Find, in terms of **i** and **j** :

a   The position vector of A.

b   The position vector of B.

c   The vector $\overrightarrow{AB}$.

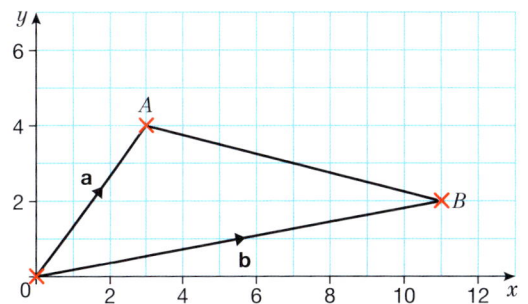

HINT

Column vector notation is easy to read and avoids the need to write out lengthy expressions with **i** and **j** terms.

a $\mathbf{a} = \overrightarrow{OA} = 3\mathbf{i} + 4\mathbf{j}$

b $\mathbf{b} = \overrightarrow{OB} = 11\mathbf{i} + 2\mathbf{j}$

c $\overrightarrow{AB} = \mathbf{b} - \mathbf{a} = (11\mathbf{i} + 2\mathbf{j}) - (3\mathbf{i} + 4\mathbf{j})$

         $= 8\mathbf{i} - 2\mathbf{j}$

(**i** goes one unit 'across', **j** goes one unit 'up')

You can see from the diagram that the vector $\overrightarrow{AB}$ goes 8 units 'across' and 2 units 'down'

You can write a vector with Cartesian components $x\mathbf{i} + y\mathbf{j}$ as a **column vector**: $\begin{pmatrix} x \\ y \end{pmatrix}$.

EXAMPLE 13

Given that $\mathbf{a} = 2\mathbf{i} + 5\mathbf{j}$, $\mathbf{b} = 12\mathbf{i} - 10\mathbf{j}$ and $\mathbf{c} = -3\mathbf{i} + 9\mathbf{j}$, find $\mathbf{a} + \mathbf{b} + \mathbf{c}$ using **column vector** notation in your working.

$$\mathbf{a} + \mathbf{b} + \mathbf{c} = \begin{pmatrix} 2 \\ 5 \end{pmatrix} + \begin{pmatrix} 12 \\ -10 \end{pmatrix} + \begin{pmatrix} -3 \\ 9 \end{pmatrix} = \begin{pmatrix} 11 \\ 4 \end{pmatrix}$$

Add the numbers in the top line to get 11, the x component, and the bottom line to get 4, the y component. This is $11\mathbf{i} + 4\mathbf{j}$.

The modulus or magnitude of $x\mathbf{i} + y\mathbf{j}$ is $\sqrt{x^2 + y^2}$.

EXAMPLE 14

The vector $\mathbf{a}$ is equal to $5\mathbf{i} - 12\mathbf{j}$. Find $|\mathbf{a}|$, and find a unit vector in the same direction as $\mathbf{a}$.

$$|\mathbf{a}| = \sqrt{5^2 + (-12)^2} = \sqrt{169} = 13$$

A unit vector in the same direction of $\mathbf{a}$ is $\dfrac{\mathbf{a}}{|\mathbf{a}|}$.

$$\frac{\mathbf{a}}{|\mathbf{a}|} = \frac{5\mathbf{i} - 12\mathbf{j}}{13} = \frac{5}{13}\mathbf{i} - \frac{12}{13}\mathbf{j}$$

You can also express this as $\dfrac{1}{13}\begin{pmatrix} 5 \\ -12 \end{pmatrix}$.

HINT

From Pythagoras' theorem, the magnitude of $x\mathbf{i} + y\mathbf{j}$, represented by the hypotenuse, is $\sqrt{x^2 + y^2}$.

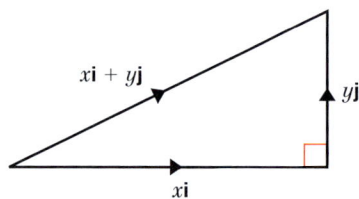

EXAMPLE 15

Given that $\mathbf{a} = 5\mathbf{i} + \mathbf{j}$ and $\mathbf{b} = -2\mathbf{i} - 4\mathbf{j}$, find the exact value of $|2\mathbf{a} + \mathbf{b}|$.

$$2\mathbf{a} + \mathbf{b} = 2\begin{pmatrix} 5 \\ 1 \end{pmatrix} + \begin{pmatrix} -2 \\ -4 \end{pmatrix} = \begin{pmatrix} 10 \\ 2 \end{pmatrix} + \begin{pmatrix} -2 \\ -4 \end{pmatrix} = \begin{pmatrix} 8 \\ -2 \end{pmatrix}$$

$$|2\mathbf{a} + \mathbf{b}| = \sqrt{8^2 + (-2)^2} = \sqrt{68} = \sqrt{4}\sqrt{17} = 2\sqrt{17}$$

EXERCISE 5

SKILLS

INTERPRETATION

1 ▶ Given that $\mathbf{a} = 3\mathbf{i} + 4\mathbf{j}$ and $\mathbf{b} = -2\mathbf{i} + 2\mathbf{j}$, find

    a $2\mathbf{a}$ b $-3\mathbf{b}$ c $\mathbf{a} + \mathbf{b}$ d $4\mathbf{b} - 5\mathbf{a}$

2 ▶ Given that $\mathbf{a} = 4\mathbf{i} + 4\mathbf{j}$, $\mathbf{b} = 2\mathbf{i} + 6\mathbf{j}$ and $\mathbf{c} = 3\mathbf{i} + 4\mathbf{j}$, find

    a $\mathbf{a} + \mathbf{b} + \mathbf{c}$ b $|\mathbf{a} + \mathbf{b}|$ c $2\mathbf{b} - \mathbf{c}$

    d $|2\mathbf{b} - \mathbf{c}|$ e $2\mathbf{b} + 2\mathbf{c} - 3\mathbf{a}$

3 ▶ The points A, B and C have coordinates $(4, -2)$, $(6, 4)$ and $(22, 6)$. Find

    a the position vectors of A, B and C b $\overrightarrow{AB}$ c $\overrightarrow{AC}$

    d $|\overrightarrow{OC}|$ e $|\overrightarrow{AB}|$ f $|\overrightarrow{AC}|$

4 ▶ P, Q and R are points with position vectors $2\mathbf{i} - 3\mathbf{j}$, $\mathbf{i} + 2\mathbf{j}$ and $4\mathbf{i} - 2\mathbf{j}$. Find in terms of $\mathbf{i}$ and $\mathbf{j}$

   a $\overrightarrow{PQ}$ b $\overrightarrow{QR}$ c $\overrightarrow{RP}$

5 ▶ If the coordinates of A are $(3, 4)$ and $AB = 2\mathbf{i} + 2\mathbf{j}$, find the position vector of B.

6 ▶ Given that $\mathbf{a} = 6\mathbf{i} + 3\mathbf{j}$, $\mathbf{b} = 6\mathbf{i} - 8\mathbf{j}$ and $\mathbf{c} = -5\mathbf{i} + 14\mathbf{j}$, find the unit vector in the direction of $\mathbf{a}$, $\mathbf{b}$ and $\mathbf{c}$.

7 ▶ Given that $2\mathbf{e} - 3\mathbf{f} = \begin{pmatrix} 5 \\ 15 \end{pmatrix}$, where $\mathbf{e} = \begin{pmatrix} 4 \\ m \end{pmatrix}$ and $\mathbf{f} = \begin{pmatrix} n \\ -3 \end{pmatrix}$, find the constants m and n.

8 ▶ If $\mathbf{r} = \begin{pmatrix} 4 \\ -1 \end{pmatrix}$, $\mathbf{s} = \begin{pmatrix} 3 \\ 7 \end{pmatrix}$ and $p\mathbf{r} + q\mathbf{s} = \begin{pmatrix} 7 \\ 37 \end{pmatrix}$, find the constants p and q.

9 ▶ Given that $\mathbf{a} = \begin{pmatrix} 2 \\ 3 \end{pmatrix}$ and $\mathbf{b} = \begin{pmatrix} 2 \\ -6 \end{pmatrix}$, find

   a $\mathbf{a} + 3\mathbf{b}$ b $|\mathbf{a} + 3\mathbf{b}|$ c $4\mathbf{a} + 2\mathbf{b}$ d $|4\mathbf{a} + 2\mathbf{b}|$

EXAM PRACTICE: CHAPTER 7

1 Relative to a fixed origin O, the point A has position vector $5\mathbf{i} - 6\mathbf{j}$.

The point B is such that $\overrightarrow{AB} = \mathbf{i} + 11\mathbf{j}$.

Show that the triangle OAB is isosceles. **[4]**

2 In the diagram below, $\overrightarrow{BA} = \mathbf{a}$ and $\overrightarrow{BC} = \mathbf{b}$. DE is such that $DA : DE = 1 : 5$ and AX is such that $AX : XC = 3 : 2$.

Prove BX and XE are co-linear

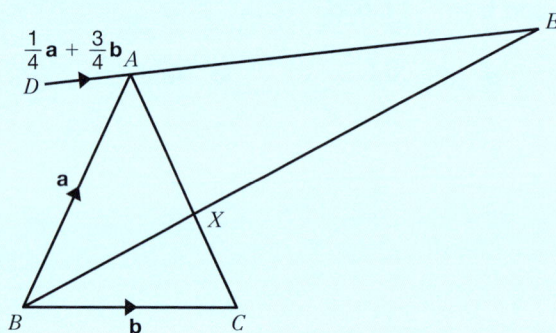

[5]

3 If the vectors $4\mathbf{i} - 6\mathbf{j}$ and $m\mathbf{i} - 2\mathbf{j}$ are parallel, state the value of m. **[2]**

4 The vectors of A and B are $3\mathbf{i} - 2\mathbf{j}$ and $t\mathbf{i} + \mathbf{j}$. Find the value of t if OAB is a straight line. **[3]**

5 Given that $\mathbf{p} = \mathbf{i} + 3\mathbf{j}$ and $\mathbf{q} = 4\mathbf{i} - 2\mathbf{j}$

  a Find the values of m and n such that $m\mathbf{p} + n\mathbf{q} = -5\mathbf{i} + 13\mathbf{j}$ **[3]**

  b Find the value of o such that $o\mathbf{p} + \mathbf{q}$ is parallel to vector $\mathbf{j}$ **[2]**

  c Find the value of λ such that $\mathbf{p} + \lambda\,\mathbf{q}$ is parallel to vector $3\mathbf{i} - \mathbf{j}$ **[3]**

6 Zaynab, Asaad and Alistair enter a running competition. They all take different routes, which are described by these vectors, where $\mathbf{s} = \begin{pmatrix} 2 \\ 2 \end{pmatrix}$, $\mathbf{t} = \begin{pmatrix} 4 \\ 6 \end{pmatrix}$ and the units are km.

Zaynab: $\mathbf{s} + 2\mathbf{t}$

Asaad: $2\mathbf{s} + \mathbf{t}$

Alistair: $5\mathbf{s} - \mathbf{t}$

a Express each journey as a column vector. [3]

b They all take 6 hours to complete their routes.

   i Find the length of each journey in km. [2]

   ii Find the average speed of each runner. [1]

7 $OPQR$ is a parallelogram. M is the midpoint of the diagonal OQ.

$\overrightarrow{OP} = 2\mathbf{a}$ and $\overrightarrow{OR} = 2\mathbf{b}$

a Express $\overrightarrow{OM}$ in terms of $\mathbf{a}$ and $\mathbf{b}$. [2]

b Use vectors to show that M is the midpoint of PR. [2]

8 The diagram below shows a regular hexagon.   [5]

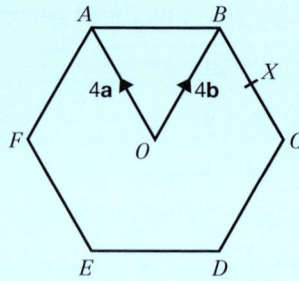

$\overrightarrow{OA} = 4\mathbf{a}$ $\overrightarrow{OB} = 4\mathbf{b}$

Express in terms of **a** and/or **b**

a $\overrightarrow{AB}$ **b** $\overrightarrow{EF}$

X is the midpoint of BC.

c Express $\overrightarrow{EX}$ in terms of **a** and/or **b**.

Y is the point on AB extended such that $AB:BY = 3:2$

d Prove that E, X and Y lie on the same straight line.

9 Show that the triangle whose vertices have position vectors $2\mathbf{i} + 6\mathbf{j}$, $8\mathbf{i} + 2\mathbf{j}$ and
$11\mathbf{i} + 13\mathbf{j}$ is an isosceles triangle.   [3]

10 $\mathbf{a} = \begin{pmatrix} 3 \\ -6 \end{pmatrix}$, $\mathbf{b} = \begin{pmatrix} 4 \\ -2 \end{pmatrix}$

Find $\mathbf{b} - 2\mathbf{a}$.   [2]

11 OAB is a triangle. M is the midpoint of OA. N is the midpoint of OB.

$\overrightarrow{OM} = \mathbf{a}$ and $\overrightarrow{ON} = \mathbf{b}$. Show that AB is parallel to MN.   [3]

12

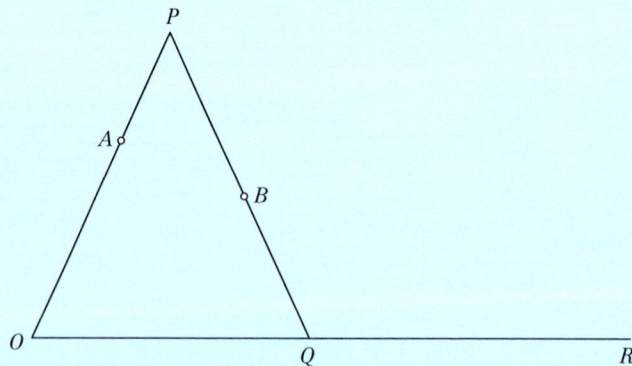

OPQ is a triangle. A is the point on OP such that $OA:AP = 2:1$
R is the point such that Q is the midpoint of OR.
B is the midpoint of PQ
$\overrightarrow{OP} = 6a$ $\overrightarrow{OQ} = 4b$
Show that ABR is a straight line.

CHAPTER SUMMARY: CHAPTER 7

The velocity of a skier moving down a ski slope has direction and magnitude

- Vectors that are equal have both the same magnitude and the same direction
- Two vectors can be added using the 'triangle law'

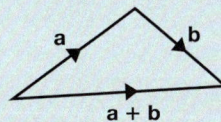

- The *modulus* of the vector is another way of saying its *magnitude*. The words are interchangeable
  - The modulus of vector **a** is written as $|\mathbf{a}|$
  - The modulus of vector $\overrightarrow{PQ}$ is written as $|\overrightarrow{PQ}|$
  - The modulus of $x\mathbf{i} + y\mathbf{j}$ is $\sqrt{x^2 + y^2}$
- The vector $-\mathbf{a}$ has the same magnitude as the vector **a** but in the opposite direction
- If vector **a** is parallel to vector **b**, $\mathbf{a} = \lambda\mathbf{b}$ where λ is a **scalar**
- $\mathbf{a} - \mathbf{b}$ is the same as $\mathbf{a} + (-\mathbf{b})$
- A unit vector is a vector that has a modulus (or magnitude) of 1 unit
- If $\lambda\mathbf{a} + \mu\mathbf{b} = \alpha\mathbf{a} + \beta\mathbf{b}$ and the non-zero vectors **a** and **b** are not parallel, then $\lambda = \alpha$ and $\mu = \beta$
- The position vector of point A is the vector $\overrightarrow{OA}$, where O is the origin
- $\overrightarrow{OA}$ is usually written as vector **a**
- $\overrightarrow{AB} = \mathbf{b} - \mathbf{a}$, where **a** and **b** are the position vectors of A and B respectively

CHAPTER 8

8 RECTANGULAR CARTESIAN COORDINATES

Straight line graphs are an excellent tool for showing **linear growth** or a **linear relationship** between two variables. Scientists and engineers use them on a daily basis.

One example of this is the linear relationship between the flow of water and water level. In May 2006, the Sichuan earthquake in China caused **landslides** that blocked several rivers, creating natural dams. Lakes formed behind these dams and the largest of these was Lake Tangjiashan. This filled with water at a rate that was about five times the rate at which water could drain from it. As a result, the water level grew to the point where it threatened to flood an area that is home to over one million people.

Scientists used the methods you will cover in this chapter to predict when the lake would overflow. This gave time for towns and villages to be evacuated, saving many lives.

LEARNING OBJECTIVES

- Use the equation of the straight line $y = mx + c$ and $ax + by + c = 0$
- Work out the **gradient** of a straight line
- Find the equation of a straight line
- Understand the relationships between the gradients of parallel and perpendicular lines
- Find the distance between two points on a straight line
- Find the coordinates of a point that divides a straight line in a given ratio

STARTER ACTIVITIES

1 ▶ Write out the gradient and *y*-intercept of these lines.

a $y = 2x + 5$ **b** $10x - 5y = 15$ **c** $y = \frac{1}{3}x$ **d** $y = 6$ **e** $y = \frac{2}{3}x + 9$

WORK OUT THE GRADIENT OF A STRAIGHT LINE

KEY POINTS

You can work out the gradient (m) of a straight line joining the point with coordinates (x_1, y_1) to the point with coordinates (x_2, y_2) by using the formula

$$m = \frac{y_2 - y_1}{x_2 - x_1}$$

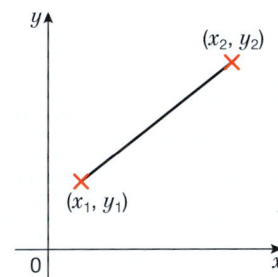

EXAMPLE 1

Work out the gradient of the line joining these pairs of points.

a $(-2, 7)$ and $(4, 5)$　　　　　　　**b** $(2d, -5d)$ and $(6d, 3d)$

a $(x_1, y_1) = (-2, 7)$ and $(x_2, y_2) = (4, 5)$

So, $m = \dfrac{5 - 7}{4 - (-2)}$

$= \dfrac{-2}{6} = -\dfrac{1}{3}$

The gradient of the line is $-\dfrac{1}{3}$

> Use $m = \dfrac{y_2 - y_1}{x_2 - x_1}$

b $(x_1, y_1) = (2d, -5d)$ and $(x_2, y_2) = (6d, 3d)$

$m = \dfrac{3d - (-5d)}{6d - 2d}$

$= \dfrac{8d}{4d} = 2$

> Use $m = \dfrac{y_2 - y_1}{x_2 - x_1}$

The gradient of the line is 2.

EXAMPLE 2

The line joining $(2, -5)$ to $(4, a)$ has gradient -1. Work out the value of a.

$m = -1$, $(x_1, y_1) = (2, -5)$ and $(x_2, y_2) = (4, a)$

$m = \dfrac{a - (-5)}{4 - 2} = -1$

> Use $m = \dfrac{y_2 - y_1}{x_2 - x_1}$

So　$\dfrac{a + 5}{2} = -1$,

$a + 5 = -2$

and　　　$a = -7$

EXERCISE 1

1 ▶ Work out the gradient of the lines joining these points.

　　a $(4, 3)$ and $(6, 4)$　　　　　　　　**b** $(-3, 2)$ and $(-4, -2)$

　　c $\left(\dfrac{1}{3}, \dfrac{2}{3}\right)$ and $\left(\dfrac{4}{5}, \dfrac{1}{2}\right)$　　　　**d** $(2c, 4c)$ and $(5c, 6c)$

2 ▶ The line joining $(2, -4)$ to $(5, d)$ has a gradient of 3. Work out the value of d.

3 ▶ The line joining $(3, -6)$ to $(6, a)$ has a gradient of 3. Find a.

4 ▶ The line joining $(a, 3)$ to $(2, 1)$ has a gradient of $-\dfrac{1}{3}$. Find a.

5 ▶ The line joining $(-10a, 6)$ to $(17, -4)$ has a gradient of $-\dfrac{1}{5}$. Find a.

6 ▶ The line joining $(3a, a)$ to $(-27, -7)$ has a gradient of $\dfrac{23}{25}$. Find a.

7 ▶ The **quadrilateral** A, B, C, D has coordinates $(-6, 1)$, $(-4, 4)$, $(2, 0)$ and $(0, -3)$.

　　a Find the gradients of the lines AB, BC, CD and DA.

　　b What do these gradients tell us about the quadrilateral?

FIND THE EQUATION OF A STRAIGHT LINE

You can find the equation of a straight line with gradient m that passes through the point with coordinates (x_1, y_1) by using the formula $y - y_1 = m(x - x_1)$

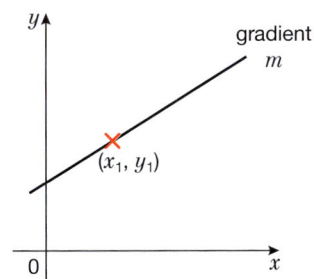

EXAMPLE 3 Find the equation of the line with gradient $-\frac{1}{2}$ that passes through the point $(4, -6)$.

$m = -\frac{1}{2}$, $(x_1, y_1) = (4, -6)$

$y - (-6) = -\frac{1}{2}(x - 4)$ Use $y - y_1 = m(x - x_1)$

$y + 6 = -\frac{1}{2}(x - 4)$

$y + 6 = -\frac{1}{2}x + 2$

$y = -\frac{1}{2}x - 4$

EXAMPLE 4 Find the equation of the line with gradient 5 that passes through the point $(3, 2)$.

The gradient is 5, so

$\frac{y - 2}{x - 3} = 5$ (x, y) is *any* point on the line.

$y - 2 = 5(x - 3)$ Use $y - y_1 = m(x - x_1)$

$y - 2 = 5x - 15$

$y = 5x - 13$

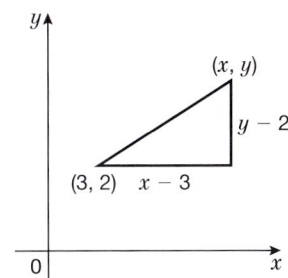

EXAMPLE 5 A line l is parallel to the line $y = 2x + 3$ and passes through the point $(1, 2)$.
Find the equation of the line l.

Parallel lines have the same gradient so line l has gradient 2.

$2 = 2 \times 1 + c$ To find c, substitute $m = 2$, $x = 1$ and $y = 2$ into $y = mx + c$

$c = 0$

So line l has equation

$y = 2x$

KEY POINTS Parallel lines have the same gradient.

EXERCISE 2

SKILLS

CRITICAL
THINKING

1 ▶ Find the equation of the line with gradient m that passes through the point (x_1, y_1) when

   a $m = 3$ and $(x_1, y_1) = (2, 6)$ **b** $m = -6$ and $(x_1, y_1) = (3, 6)$

   c $m = \dfrac{1}{2}$ and $(x_1, y_1) = (-6, -10)$

2 ▶ Find the equation of the line that passes through the points $(4, 13)$ and $(-15, 6)$.
Write your answer in the form $ax + by + c = 0$

3 ▶ Find the equation of the line that passes through the points $(22, 9)$ and $(6, 8)$.
Write your answer in the form $y = mx + c$

4 ▶ Find the equation of the line that passes through the points $(18, 6)$ and $(4, 12)$.
Write your answer in the form $y = mx + c$

5 ▶ A line is parallel to the line $y = -\dfrac{2}{5}x - 3$ and intercepts the y-axis at $(0, -4)$.

   Calculate the equation of the line and write your answer in the form $ax + by + c = 0$.

6 ▶ A line is parallel to the line $2x - 3y + 7 = 0$ and passes through the point $(0, 3)$.
Write down the equation of the line.

7 ▶ The line $y = 6x - 18$ meets the x-axis at the point P. Calculate the coordinates of P.

8 ▶ The line $y = \dfrac{2}{3}x + 7$ meets the y-axis at point the B. The point C has coordinates $(6, 3)$.

   Find the equation of the line joining B and C.

UNDERSTAND THE RELATIONSHIP BETWEEN PERPENDICULAR LINES

If a line has a gradient of m, a line perpendicular to it has a gradient of $-\dfrac{1}{m}$.

You can also say that if two lines are perpendicular, the product of their gradients is -1.

EXAMPLE 6

Work out the gradient of the lines that are perpendicular to the lines with these gradients.

   a 3 **b** $\dfrac{1}{2}$ **c** $-\dfrac{2}{5}$

   a Gradient $m = 3$ so the gradient of the perpendicular line is $-\dfrac{1}{3}$.   Gradient $= -\dfrac{1}{m}$

   b Gradient $m = \dfrac{1}{2}$ so the gradient of the perpendicular line is -2. $-\dfrac{1}{2} \times -2 = -1$

   c Gradient $m = -\dfrac{2}{5}$. so the gradient of the perpendicular line is $\dfrac{5}{2}$. $-\dfrac{1}{2} \times -2 = -1$

EXAMPLE 7

Show that the line $y = 3x + 4$ is perpendicular to the line $x + 3y - 3 = 0$.

The gradient of the line $y = 3x + 4$ is 3.   Compare $y = 3x + 4$ with $y = mx + c$ to find m

$$x + 3y - 3 = 0$$ Rearrange into the form $y = mx + c$

$$3y = -x + 3$$

$$y = -\frac{1}{3}x + 1$$

The gradient of this line is $-\frac{1}{3}$.

The products of the two gradients is $3 \times -\frac{1}{3} = -1$.

The lines are perpendicular because the product of their gradients is -1.

EXAMPLE 8

Work out whether these pairs of lines are parallel, perpendicular, or neither.

a $y = -2x + 9$ and $y = -2x - 3$

b $3x - y - 2 = 0$ and $x + 3y - 6 = 0$

c $y = \frac{1}{2}x$ and $2x - y + 4 = 0$

a $y = -2x + 9$ has gradient -2 This is of the form $y = mx + c$, so $m = -2$

$y = -2x - 3$ has gradient -2

Since the gradients are equal the two lines are parallel.

b $3x - y - 2 = 0$

so, $y = 3x - 2$ Rearrange the equation

Therefore the gradient of this line is 3.

$x + 3y - 6 = 0$

So, $y = -\frac{1}{3}x + 2$

Therefore the gradient of this line is $-\frac{1}{3}$

Since $3 \times \frac{1}{3} = -1$ the lines are perpendicular.

c $y = \frac{1}{2}x$ is already in the form $y = mx + c$

So, the gradient is $\frac{1}{2}$.

$2x - y + 4 = 0$

So, $y = 2x + 4$

Therefore the gradient of this line is 2.

These two lines are neither parallel nor perpendicular.

EXAMPLE 9 Find an equation of the line that passes through the point $(3, -1)$ and is perpendicular to the line $y = 2x - 4$.

The line $y = 2x - 4$ has gradient $m = 2$.

So the gradient of the perpendicular line is $-\frac{1}{2}$.

$m = -\frac{1}{2}, (x_1, y_1) = (3, -1)$

Use the rule $-\frac{1}{m}$ with $m = 2$

Use $y - y_1 = m(x - x_1)$

$y - (-1) = -\frac{1}{2}(x - 3)$

$y + 1 = -\frac{1}{2}x + \frac{3}{2}$

$y = -\frac{1}{2}x + \frac{1}{2}$

EXERCISE 3

SKILLS

REASONING

1 ▶ Work out if these pairs of lines are parallel, perpendicular or neither.

a $y = 4x + 2$

$y = -\frac{1}{4}x - 7$

b $y = \frac{3}{4}x + 3$

$y = \frac{3}{4}x - 5$

c $y = 5x - 3$

$5x - y = -4$

d $5x - y - 1 = 0$

$y = -\frac{1}{5}x + 2$

e $y = -\frac{3}{2}x + 6$

$3x + 2y - 3 = 0$

f $5x - y + 5 = 0$

$2x + 5y - 6 = 0$

2 ▶ Find the equation of the line that passes through $(-3, 8)$ and is perpendicular to the line $y = 5x + 2$.

3 ▶ Find the equation of the line

a perpendicular to the line $y = -2x + 3$ and passing through $(1, 1)$

b perpendicular to the line $y = 4x - 4$ and passing through $(-2, 6)$

c perpendicular to the line $2x + y - 9 = 0$ and passing through $(3, 2)$

d perpendicular to the line $4x - 6y = -7$ and passing through $(-3, 4)$.

4 ▶ Find the equation of a line passing through the point $(3, -4)$ that is perpendicular to the line $8x + 6y = 15$. Write your answer in the form $ax + by + c = 0$.

5 ▶ Find the equation of a line passing through the point $(6, 3)$ and perpendicular to the line $4x - 5y = -10$. Write your answer in the form $ax + by + c = 0$.

6 ▶ Find the equation of a line that passes through $(5, 6)$ and is perpendicular to the line whose equation is $y = \frac{2}{3}x + 5$

7 ▶ Find the equation of a line that passes through $(7, -3)$ and is perpendicular to $4x + 3y = 12$.

8 ▶ The vertices of a quadrilateral $PQRS$ have coordinates $P(-1, 5)$, $Q(7, 1)$, $R(5, -3)$, $S(-3, 1)$. Show that the quadrilateral is a rectangle.

FIND THE DISTANCE BETWEEN TWO POINTS ON A LINE

You can find the distance d between two points (x_1, y_1) and (x_2, y_2) that lie on a straight line using the formula:

$$d = \sqrt{(x_2 - x_1)^2 + (y_2 - y_1)^2}$$

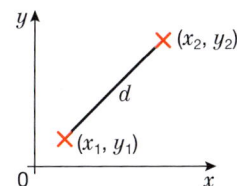

EXAMPLE 10 Find the distance between these pairs of points.

a $(2, 3)$ and $(5, 7)$ **b** $(4a, a)$ and $(-3a, 2a)$ **c** $(2\sqrt{2}, -5\sqrt{2})$ and $(4\sqrt{2}, \sqrt{2})$

a
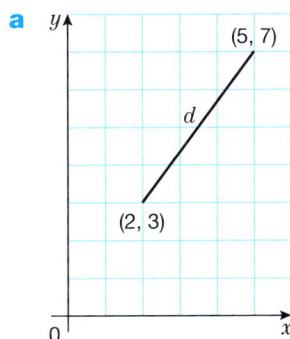

Draw a sketch

Let $(x_1, y_1) = (2, 3)$ and $(x_2, y_2) = (5, 7)$

$d = \sqrt{(5 - 2)^2 + (7 - 3)^2}$ Use $d = \sqrt{(x_2 - x_1)^2 + (y_2 - y_1)^2}$

$\quad = \sqrt{3^2 + 4^2}$

$\quad = \sqrt{25} = 5$ Take the positive square root because d is a length

b Let $(x_1, y_1) = (4a, a)$ and $(x_2, y_2) = (-3a, 2a)$

$d = \sqrt{(-3a - 4a)^2 + (2a - a)^2}$

$\quad = \sqrt{(-7a)^2 + a^2}$

$\quad = \sqrt{49a^2 + a^2}$

$\quad = \sqrt{50a^2}$

So $d = 5\sqrt{2}a$

c $(x_1, y_1) = (2\sqrt{2}, -5\sqrt{2})$ and $(x_2, y_2) = (4\sqrt{2}, \sqrt{2})$

$d = \sqrt{(4\sqrt{2} - 2\sqrt{2})^2 + (\sqrt{2} - (-5\sqrt{2}))^2}$

$\quad = \sqrt{(2\sqrt{2})^2 + (6\sqrt{2})^2}$

$\quad = \sqrt{8 + 72}$

$\quad = \sqrt{80}$

So $d = 4\sqrt{5}$

EXERCISE 4

SKILLS

REASONING

1 ▶ Find the distance between these points, leaving your answer in surd form where appropriate.

a $(1, 2)$ and $(7, 10)$ **b** $(3, -7)$ and $(8, 5)$

c $(-2, 2)$ and $(1, 6)$ **d** $(5, 2)$ and $(1, 6)$

e $(-1, -5)$ and $(5, 5)$ **f** $(-4a, 0)$ and $(3a, -2a)$

g $(-7b, 5b)$ and $(2b, -5b)$ **h** $(-2c, 2c)$ and $(-3c, 5c)$

FIND THE COORDINATES OF A POINT THAT DIVIDES A LINE IN A GIVEN RATIO

Consider a line between points $A(x_1, y_1)$ and $B(x_2, y_2)$, divided by the point $P(x_p, y_p)$ in a ratio of $m:n$.

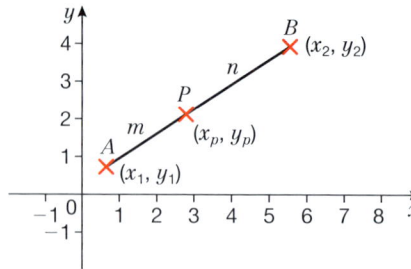

HINT

If $m = n$ then the coordinate P is the midpoint of A and B.

Using **similar triangles**, you can derive these formulae:

$$x_p = \frac{nx_1 + mx_2}{m + n} \text{ and } y_p = \frac{ny_1 + my_2}{m + n}$$

EXAMPLE 11

Find the coordinates of the point which divides $A(0, 6):B(4, 10)$ in the ratio $3:1$.

$$x_p = \frac{(1)(0) + (3)(4)}{3 + 1} = 3 \qquad \text{Use } x_p = \frac{nx_1 + mx_2}{m + n}$$

$$y_p = \frac{(1)(6) + (3)(10)}{3 + 1} = 9 \qquad \text{Use } y_p = \frac{ny_1 + my_2}{m + n}$$

Therefore the coordinates are $(3, 9)$

EXAMPLE 12

A line between points $A(-1, 3)$ and $B(5, 7)$ is divided by point P such that $AP:PB = 1:4$. Find the coordinates of point P.

$$x_p = \frac{4(-1) + (1)(5)}{1 + 4} \qquad \text{Use } x_p = \frac{nx_1 + mx_2}{m + n}$$

$$= \frac{1}{5}$$

$$y_p = \frac{4(3) + 1(7)}{1 + 4} \qquad \text{Use } y_p = \frac{ny_1 + my_2}{m + n}$$

$$= \frac{19}{5}$$

Therefore the coordinates of P are $\left(\frac{1}{5}, \frac{19}{5}\right)$

EXERCISE 5

SKILLS

INTERPRETATION

1 ▶ Find the coordinates of the points which divide AB in the given ratios.

    a $A(1, 5):B(-2, 8)$ in the ratio $1:2$.   **b** $A(3, -7):B(-2, 8)$ in the ratio $3:2$.

    c $A(-2, 5):B(5, 2)$ in the ratio $4:3$.   **d** $A(4, 2):B(6, 8)$ in the ratio $2:2$.

2 ▶ Find the coordinates of the point which divides the line segment from $(-2, 1)$ to $(2, 3)$ in the ratio $3:4$.

3 ▶ Find the coordinates of the point that divides the line segment MN with coordinates $M(-4, 0)$ and $N(0, 4)$ in the ratio $3:1$.

EXAM PRACTICE: CHAPTER 8

1 A is a point with coordinates (2, 4) and B is a point with coordinates $(-1, 0)$.
The line L has the equation $3y = 4 - 2x$. Is the line L parallel to AB?
Show your working clearly.   **[2]**

2 The straight line L_1 passes through the points $(-3, 0)$ and $(9, 10)$.
Find an equation for L_1 in the form $ax + by + c = 0$, where a, b and c are integers.   **[2]**

3 The equation of a line is given as $4x - 5y - 8 = 0$.
Point $A(7, 4)$ and $B(2, 0)$ lie on the line.

  a Find the length of AB, leaving your answer in surd form.   **[3]**

  The point C has coordinates $(2, t)$, where $t > 0$, and $AC = AB$.

  b Find the value of t.   **[1]**

  c Find the area of triangle ABC.   **[2]**

4 Find the equation of the line L_1 which is perpendicular to the line
$y = 2x + 8$ at the point (1, 10).
Give your answer in the form $ax + by + c = 0$.   **[3]**

5 Find the equation of the line which is perpendicular to the line
$y = 5x + 8$ at the point (5, 33).   **[2]**

6 Find the equation of the line which is perpendicular to the line
$y = -\dfrac{1}{3}x + 8$ at the point (9, 5).   **[3]**

7 A is the point (0, 1) and B is the point (10, 6).

  a Find the coordinates of the midpoint of AB.   **[2]**

  The equation of the straight line through A and B is $y = \dfrac{1}{2}x + 1$.

  b Write down the equation of another straight line that is parallel to AB and passes
through the point (0, 5).   **[1]**

8 Show that the coordinates (1, 7), (4, 2), $(-1, -1)$, $(-4, 4)$ form a square.   **[2]**

9 Find the area of rectangle $ABCD$ with vertices
$A(-3, 0)$, $B(3, 2)$, $C(4, -1)$, and $D(-2, -3)$.   **[2]**

10 Quadrilateral $ABCD$ has vertices $A(-3, 0)$, $B(2, 4)$, $C(3, 1)$, and $D(-4, -3)$.
Calculate the perimeter of the quadrilateral.   **[2]**

11 The line l_1 passes through the points $A(-1, 2)$ and $B(11, 8)$.

    a Find an equation for l_1.   **[2]**

    The line l_2 passes through the point $C(10, 0)$ and is perpendicular to l_1.
    The lines l_1 and l_2 intersect at the point D.

    b Calculate the coordinates of D.   **[2]**

    c Calculate the length AD.   **[2]**

    d Hence, or otherwise, calculate the area of the triangle ACD.   **[1]**

12 Given the points $A(-1, 2)$ and $B(7, 8)$, determine the coordinates of point P that divides AB in the ratio $1:3$.   **[3]**

13 Determine the midpoint between $(-7, -2)$ and $(4, 5)$.   **[2]**

14 The points $A(-5, 5)$ and $B(9, -2)$ lie on the line L.

    a Find an equation for L in the form $ax + by + c = 0$.   **[2]**

    b Show that the distance between A and B is $7\sqrt{5}$.   **[2]**

15 Quadrilateral $DEFG$ has vertices $D(5, 1)$, $E(2, 4)$, $F(-4, 4)$ and $G(-1, 1)$.   **[4]**

    a Find the equation of the line of DE.

    b Calculate the area of $DEFG$.

CHAPTER SUMMARY: CHAPTER 8

- The general form of the equation of the straight line is $y = mx + c$ where m is the gradient and c is the y-intercept or constant

  Another form of this equation is $ax + by + c = 0$ where a, b, c are integers

- The formula for calculating the gradient is $m = \dfrac{y_2 - y_1}{x_2 - x_1}$

- You can find the equation of the line with gradient m that passes through the point with coordinates (x_1, y_1) by using $y - y_1 = m(x - x_1)$

- Two lines with the same gradient are parallel

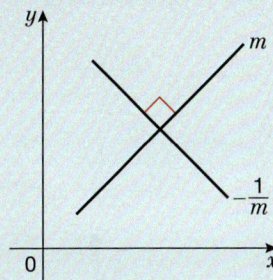

- If a line has a gradient of m, a line perpendicular to it has a gradient of $-\dfrac{1}{m}$

- You can also say that if two lines are perpendicular, the product of their gradients is -1

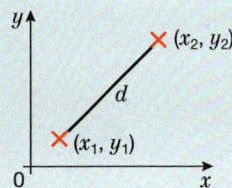

- You can find the distance d between (x_1, y_1) and (x_2, y_2) using the formula:

  $d = \sqrt{(x_2 - x_1)^2 + (y_2 - y_1)^2}$

- The coordinates of the point (x_p, y_p) dividing the line joining the points (x_1, y_1) and (x_2, y_2) in the ratio $m:n$ are given by $x_p = \dfrac{nx_1 + mx_2}{m + n}$ and $y_p = \dfrac{ny_1 + my_2}{m + n}$

CHAPTER 9

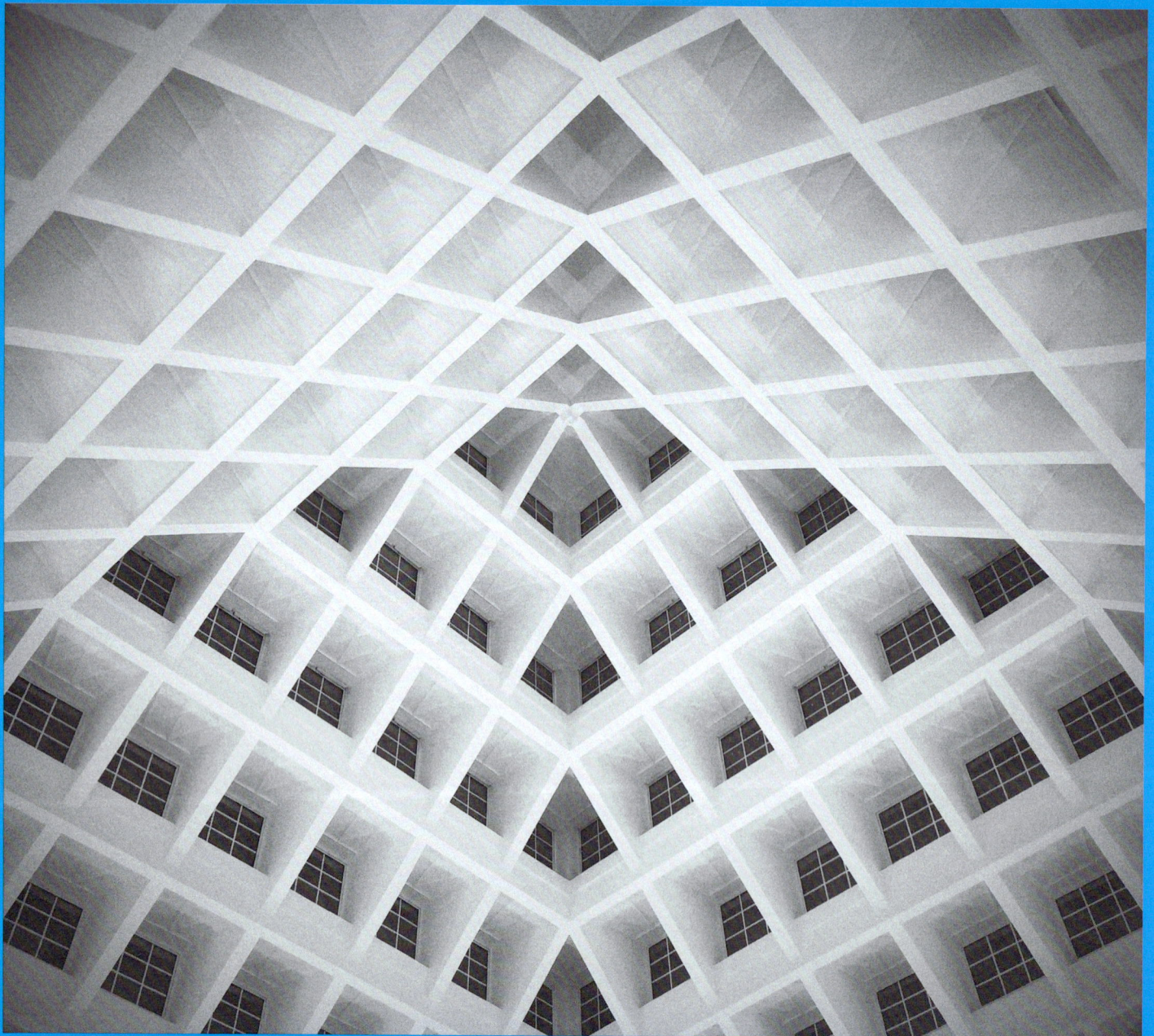

9 DIFFERENTIATION

In the time of Sir Isaac Newton and Gottfried Leibniz, the founders of **calculus**, one of the biggest problems was poor navigation at sea. Shipwrecks occurred because the captain did not know the actual position of his ship. This was mainly due to a poor understanding of how the earth, planets and stars moved in relation to each other. Calculus (differentiation and integration) was developed to improve this understanding and help improve navigation at sea.

Differentiation is used to solve many real life problems. For example, it is used to determine maximum and minimum values, which you will learn about in this chapter. This technique is very useful for companies to determine costs, and for engineers and architects to calculate the amount of building material required.

LEARNING OBJECTIVES

- Find the gradient function of a curve and differentiate a function that has multiple powers of x
- Differentiate e^{ax}, $\sin ax$ and $\cos ax$
- Use the **chain rule** to differentiate more complicated functions
- Use the **product rule** to differentiate more complicated functions
- Use the **quotient rule** to differentiate more complicated functions
- Find the equation of the **tangent** and **normal** to the curve $y = f(x)$
- Find the stationary points of a curve and calculate if they are minimum or maximum points
- Apply what you have learned about turning points to solve problems

STARTER ACTIVITIES

1 ▶ Simplify

a $a^6 \times a^7$ | **b** $\dfrac{a^7}{a^{-3}}$ | **c** $\dfrac{a^{-5}}{a^9}$ | **d** $a^{-4} \times a^{-2}$

e $(a^2)^{-1}$ | **f** $(a^2)^{-3}$ | **g** $(a^{-2})^{-4}$ | **h** $\left(a^{\frac{1}{2}}\right)^5$

i $(a^3)^{-\frac{1}{2}}$ | **j** $(a^6)^{\frac{1}{3}}$ | **k** $(a^9)^{-\frac{1}{3}}$ | **l** $(a^{-12})^{-\frac{1}{4}}$

m $\left(\dfrac{a}{b}\right)^2$ | **n** $(a^2 \times b^{-4})^3$ | **o** $\left(a^3 b^{\frac{1}{2}}\right)^4$ | **p** $(a^2 b^{-2})^{-2}$

q $\left(\dfrac{a^2}{b^3}\right)^4$ | **r** $(m^{-1} n^3)^{-2}$ | **s** $\left(\dfrac{a^6}{b^{10}}\right)^{\frac{1}{2}}$ | **t** $\left(\dfrac{a^2}{m^4}\right)^{-\frac{1}{2}}$

u $\left(\dfrac{a^8 b^2}{c^6}\right)^{-\frac{1}{2}}$ | **v** $\left(\dfrac{m^2}{x}\right)^{-1}$ | **w** $\left(\dfrac{x^2 y}{z^3}\right)^{-4}$ | **x** $\left[(a^3 b^{-8})^{-\frac{1}{3}}\right]^2$

FIND THE GRADIENT FUNCTION OF A CURVE AND DIFFERENTIATE A FUNCTION THAT HAS MULTIPLE POWERS OF x

On a straight line graph, the **gradient** is constant, the same everywhere along the line: it has a fixed value.

However, on a curved graph the gradient is always changing. The gradient depends on where you are along the x-axis. The different gradients can be shown by tangents, lines that touch the curve in one place only.

KEY POINTS

Differentiation is the process by which you produce an equation to calculate the gradient at a specific point.

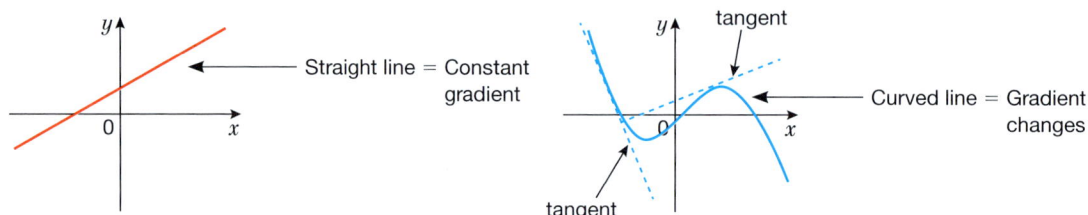

Straight line = Constant gradient

Curved line = Gradient changes

As a general rule, if;

$f(x) = ax^n$ | This is the formula for the curve. i.e. the function

then…

$f'(x) = nax^{n-1}$. | This is the gradient function for f(x), the formula that gives the gradient at any point.
It is also known as the **derivative**, or 'derived functon'

KEY POINTS

A function can be written as f(x) or as an equation in the form $y = ax^2 + bx + c$.

The notation for the gradient function is: $f'(x)$ or $\dfrac{dy}{dx}$.

EXAMPLE 1

Find the **derived function** when f(x) equals

a x^6 **b** $x^{\frac{1}{2}}$ **c** x^{-2} **d** $\dfrac{x}{x^5}$ **e** $x^2 \times x^3$

---

a $6x^5$ The power 6 is reduced to the power 5 and the 6 multiplies the new expression

b $f(x) = x^{\frac{1}{2}}$ The power $\dfrac{1}{2}$ is reduced to $\dfrac{1}{2} - 1 = -\dfrac{1}{2}$, and the $\dfrac{1}{2}$ multiplies the new expression

$f'(x) = \dfrac{1}{2}x^{-\frac{1}{2}}$

$= \dfrac{1}{2\sqrt{x}}$ This is then written in an alternative form

c $f(x) = x^{-2}$

$f'(x) = -2x^{-3}$ The power -2 is reduced to -3 and the -2 multplies the new expression

$= -\dfrac{2}{x^3}$ This is also rewritten in an alternative form using knowledge of negative powers

d Let $f(x) = \dfrac{x}{x^5}$

$\qquad = x^{-4}$ Simplify using rules of powers to give one simple power, i.e. subtract $1 - 5 = -4$

So $f'(x) = -4x^{-5}$ Reduce the power -4 to give -5, then multiply the new expression by -4

$\qquad = -\dfrac{4}{x^5}$

e Let $f(x) = x^2 \times x^3$ Add the powers this time to give $2 + 3 = 5$

$\qquad = x^5$

So $f'(x) = 5x^4$ Reduce the power 5 to 4 and multiply the new expression by 5

EXAMPLE 2

Use standard results to differentiate

a $x^3 + x^2 - x^{\frac{1}{2}}$ **b** $2x^{-3}$ **c** $\dfrac{1}{3}x^{\frac{1}{2}} + 4x^2$

a $y = x^3 + x^2 - x^{\frac{1}{2}}$

So $\dfrac{dy}{dx} = 3x^2 + 2x - \dfrac{1}{2}x^{-\frac{1}{2}}$ Differentiate each term as you come to it. First x^3, then x^2, then $x^{\frac{1}{2}}$

$\qquad\qquad = 3x^2 + 2x - \dfrac{1}{2\sqrt{x}}$

b $y = 2x^{-3}$

So $\dfrac{dy}{dx} = -6x^{-4}$ Differentiate x^{-3}, then multiply the new expression by 2

$\qquad\quad = -\dfrac{6}{x^4}$

c $y = \dfrac{1}{3}x^{\frac{1}{2}} + 4x^2$

So $\dfrac{dy}{dx} = \dfrac{1}{3} \times \dfrac{1}{2}x^{-\frac{1}{2}} + 8x$ Take each term as you come to it, and treat each term as a multiple

$\qquad\quad = \dfrac{1}{6} \times x^{-\frac{1}{2}} + 8x$

$\qquad\quad = \dfrac{1}{6\sqrt{x}} + 8x$

EXAMPLE 3

Let $f(x) = 4x^2 - 8x + 3$

a Find the gradient of $y = f(x)$ at the point $\left(\dfrac{1}{2}, 0\right)$.

b Find the coordinates of the point on the graph of $y = f(x)$ where the gradient is 8.

c Find the gradient of $y = f(x)$ at the points where the curve meets the line $y = 4x - 5$.

a   As $f(x) = 4x^2 - 8x + 3$

$\qquad f'(x) = (4 \times 2)x - 8 + 0$

$\qquad f'(x) = 8x - 8 + 0$ First find $f'(x)$, the derived function

So $f'\left(\dfrac{1}{2}\right) = -4$ Then substitute the x-coordinate value to obtain the gradient

b $f'(x) = 8x - 8 = 8$ Put the gradient function equal to 8

so $x = 2$ Then solve the equation you have obtained to give the value of x

and $y = f(2) = 3$ Substitute this value for x into $f(x)$ to give the value of y

The point where the gradient is 8 is $(2, 3)$.   Interpret your answer in words

c $4x^2 - 8x + 3 = 4x - 5$

$4x^2 - 12x + 8 = 0$

Put $f(x) = 4x - 5$, then rearrange and collect terms to give a quadratic equation

$x^2 - 3x + 2 = 0$

Divide by the common factor 4

$(x - 2)(x - 1) = 0$

So $x = 1$ or $x = 2$

Solve the quadratic equation by factorising

At $x = 1$ the gradient is 0.

At $x = 2$ the gradient is 8, as in part b.

Substitute the values of x into $f'(x) = 8x - 8$ to give the gradients at the specified points

---

EXAMPLE 4 Use standard results to differentiate.

a $\dfrac{1}{4\sqrt{x}}$

b $x^3(3x + 1)$

c $\dfrac{x - 2}{x^2}$

---

a Let $y = \dfrac{1}{4\sqrt{x}}$

$= \dfrac{1}{4}x^{-\frac{1}{2}}$

Express the 4 in the denominator as a multiplier of $\dfrac{1}{4}$ and express the x term as power $-\dfrac{1}{2}$

Therefore $\dfrac{dy}{dx} = -\dfrac{1}{8}x^{-\frac{3}{2}}$

Differentiate by reducing the power of x and multiplying $\dfrac{1}{4}$ by $-\dfrac{1}{2}$

b Let $y = x^3(3x + 1)$

$= 3x^4 + x^3$

Multiply out the brackets to give a polynomial function

Therefore $\dfrac{dy}{dx} = 12x^3 + 3x^2$

Differentiate each term

$= 3x^2(4x + 1)$

Factorise

c Let $y = \dfrac{x - 2}{x^2}$

$= \dfrac{1}{x} - \dfrac{2}{x^2}$

Express the single fraction as two separate fractions, and simplify $\dfrac{x}{x^2}$ to $\dfrac{1}{x}$

$= x^{-1} - 2x^{-2}$

Therefore $\dfrac{dy}{dx} = -x^{-2} + 4x^{-3}$

Then express the rational expressions as negative powers of x, and differentiate

$= \dfrac{-(x - 4)}{x^3}$

EXERCISE 1

SKILLS

REASONING

1 ▶ Find $f'(x)$, given that $f(x)$ equals

a x^8

b x^3

c $x^{\frac{1}{2}}$

d $x^{\frac{3}{2}}$

e x^{-3}

f $\sqrt{x}$

g $\sqrt[3]{x}$

h x^{-4}

i $\dfrac{1}{x^2}$

j $\dfrac{1}{\sqrt[3]{x}}$

k $\dfrac{x^3}{x^2}$

l $x^3 \times x^6$

m $x^{-4} \times x^{\frac{1}{2}}$

2 ▶ Differentiate

    a $3x^2$ **b** $7x^4$ **c** $3x^{-2}$

    d $\dfrac{3}{x}$ **e** $5x^5$ **f** $3\sqrt{x}$

    g $\dfrac{3}{\sqrt{x}}$ **h** $\dfrac{5}{\sqrt[3]{x}}$

3 ▶ Differentiate

    a $y = x^5 + x^{-2}$ **b** $y = \dfrac{1}{2}x^{-2} + 4x^2$ **c** $y = x^{\frac{1}{8}} + 3x^{-2} + 9x^{\frac{1}{3}}$

4 ▶ Find $\dfrac{dy}{dx}$ when

    a $y = x^6 + x^2 + 2x$ **b** $y = x^3 + 3$ **c** $y = 6x^3 - 5x^2 + 3x^{-2} + 6x + 3$

5 ▶ Find $f'(x)$ when

    a $f(x) = 3x + \dfrac{2}{3}x^{\frac{1}{3}}$ **b** $f(x) = 3x^{\frac{1}{6}} + 2x^{\frac{3}{4}}$ **c** $f(x) = 3 - 8x^{-1} + x^{-\frac{2}{3}}$

6 ▶ Find the gradient of the curve at point A for

    a $f(x) = x^4 + 3x^2 + 6x + 3$ and $A = (0, 0)$

    b $f(x) = 3x^2 + 2x^{-1}$ and $A = (2, 13)$

    c $f(x) = 4x^2 + 3x^{-1} + x^{\frac{1}{2}} + 157$ and $A = (4, 223.75)$

7 ▶ Differentiate

    a $\dfrac{1}{3}x^3(x - 2)$ **b** $3\sqrt{x} + \dfrac{1}{2x}$ **c** $\dfrac{2x + 3}{x}$

    d $\dfrac{3x^2 - 6}{x}$ **e** $x(x^2 - x + 2)$ **f** $(3x - 2)\left(4x + \dfrac{1}{x}\right)$

USE THE CHAIN RULE TO DIFFERENTIATE MORE COMPLICATED FUNCTIONS

Consider the function $y = (1 + x)^{10}$.

One way of calculating $\dfrac{dy}{dx}$ is to use the binomial expansion, but this is a very long and inefficient way of calculating it.

Another way is to use the **chain rule**.

EXAMPLE 5   Differentiate $y = (3x^4 + x)^5$

Let $u = 3x^4 + x$ Using the chain rule $\dfrac{dy}{dx} = \dfrac{dy}{du} \times \dfrac{du}{dx}$

$\dfrac{du}{dx} = 12x^3 + 1$

$y = u^5$

$\dfrac{dy}{du} = 5u^4$

$\dfrac{dy}{dx} = \dfrac{dy}{du} \times \dfrac{du}{dx}$

$\quad = 5u^4 \times 12x^3 + 1$

$\quad = 5(3x^4 + x)^4(12x^3 + 1)$ Substitute $u = 3x^4 + x$ back into the equation

EXAMPLE 6   Differentiate: $y = \sqrt{5x^2 + 1}$

Let $u = 5x^2 + 1$ Using the chain rule $\dfrac{dy}{dx} = \dfrac{dy}{du} \times \dfrac{du}{dx}$

$\dfrac{du}{dx} = 10x$

$y = \sqrt{u}$

$y = u^{\frac{1}{2}}$ Using the rules of indices

$\dfrac{dy}{du} = \dfrac{1}{2}u^{-\frac{1}{2}}$

$\dfrac{dy}{dx} = \dfrac{dy}{du} \times \dfrac{du}{dx}$

$\quad = \dfrac{1}{2}u^{-\frac{1}{2}} \times 10x$

$\quad = 5xu^{-\frac{1}{2}}$

$\quad = 5x(5x^2 + 1)^{-\frac{1}{2}}$ $u = 5x^2 + 1$ back into the equation.

$\quad = \dfrac{5x}{\sqrt{5x^2 + 1}}$

EXAMPLE 7   Given that $y = (x^2 - 7x)^4$

Calculate $\dfrac{dy}{dx}$ using the chain rule.

$y = (x^2 - 7x)^4$

$\dfrac{dy}{dx} = \dfrac{dy}{du} \times \dfrac{du}{dx}$

let $u = x^2 - 7x$ $\dfrac{du}{dx} = 2x - 7$ Differentiate u in terms of x

$y = u^4$ $\dfrac{dy}{du} = 4u^3$ Differentiate y in terms of u

$\dfrac{dy}{dx} = 4u^3(2x - 7)$ Substitute expressions for $\dfrac{dy}{du}$ and $\dfrac{du}{dx}$ into $\dfrac{dy}{dx} = \dfrac{dy}{du} \times \dfrac{du}{dx}$

$\dfrac{dy}{dx} = 4(x^2 - 7x)^3(2x - 7)$ Substitute in $u = x^2 - 7x$

EXAMPLE 8   Differentiate

$y = \sin(2x^2 + 3)$

$y = \sin(2x^2 + 3)$

Let $u = 2x^2 + 3$ so $\dfrac{du}{dx} = 4x$

$y = \sin u$ so $\dfrac{dy}{du} = \cos u$

$\dfrac{dy}{dx} = \cos u \times 4x$

$\dfrac{dy}{dx} = 4x \cos(2x^2 + 3)$ Substitute $u = 2x^2 + 3$ back into the equation

---

EXERCISE 2

SKILLS

CRITICAL
THINKING
PROBLEM
SOLVING

1 ▶ Differentiate

    a $(3x + 1)^4$ **b** $(2x - 4)^6$ **c** $(1 + x^2)^3$ **d** $(1 - 5x)^7$ **e** $(2 + 3x)^{-1}$

    f $(6x + 2)^{\frac{1}{2}}$ **g** $\left(\dfrac{2x^4 + 6}{2}\right)^7$ **h** $\sqrt{7 - x}$ **i** $4(2 - 7x)^4$ **j** $6(7 - 3x)^{-3}$

2 ▶ Differentiate

    a $6(2x + 1)^2$ **b** $10(1 + x)^2$ **c** $3(2 + x)^{-1}$ **d** $\sqrt{x + 1}$

3 ▶ Differentiate

    a $\sin(2x + 1)$ **b** $\cos(2x^2 + 3)$ **c** $\cos(x + 1)$ **d** $2\sin(2x + 1)$

4 ▶ Given that $y = \dfrac{1}{(3x - 2)^3}$ find the value of $\dfrac{dy}{dx}$ at the point $(1, 1)$.

5 ▶ Find an equation for the tangent to each curve at the point on the curve with the given x-coordinate.

    a $y = (4x - 6)^4$ at $x = 2$ **b** $y = \sin(2x + 6)$ at $x = -3$ radians

DIFFERENTIATE e^{ax}, $\sin ax$ AND $\cos ax$

In Chapter 10 you will learn about radians. Radians are just an alternative way of measuring angles.
The conversion between radians and degrees is:

π radians = 180 degrees

These rules apply when radians are used.

KEY POINTS

If $y = \sin ax$ then $\dfrac{dy}{dx} = a\cos ax$

If $y = a\cos x$ then $\dfrac{dy}{dx} = -a\sin ax$

HINT
Please see examples below for extra help on some of these questions.

You will also need to differentiate the exponential function you met in Chapter 1.

This function, e^x, is very special, as the gradient of the curve is the same as the value of the function itself.

KEY POINTS

In other words, if $y = e^x$ then $\dfrac{dy}{dx} = e^x$

It follows that if $y = e^{ax}$ then $\dfrac{dy}{dx} = ae^{ax}$

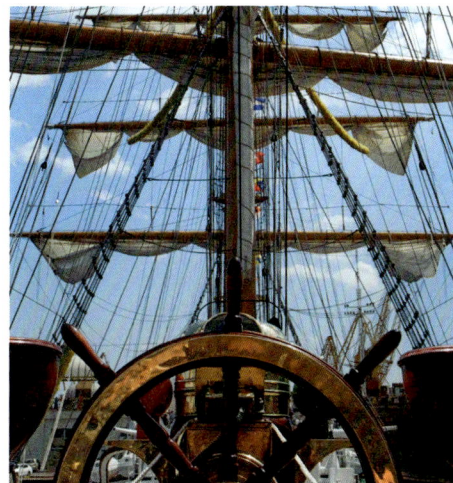

EXAMPLE 9   Differentiate

a $y = \sin 4x$ **b** $y = 2 \sin 5x$ **c** $y = 4 \cos x$

d $y = e^{\frac{1}{2}x}$ **e** $y = 3e^{2x}$

---

a $y = \sin 4x$

Using the chain rule $= \dfrac{dy}{dx} = \dfrac{dy}{du} \times \dfrac{dy}{dx}$

Let $u = 4x$

$\dfrac{du}{dx} = 4$

$y = \sin u$

$\dfrac{dy}{du} = \cos u$

Therefore

$\dfrac{dy}{dx} = \dfrac{dy}{du} \times \dfrac{du}{dx}$

$\dfrac{dy}{dx} = \cos u \times 4$

$\dfrac{dy}{dx} = 4 \cos u$

$\dfrac{dy}{dx} = 4 \cos 4x$ as $u = 4x$

b $y = 2 \sin 5x$

Using the chain rule $= \dfrac{dy}{dx} = \dfrac{dy}{du} \times \dfrac{dy}{dx}$

Let $u = 5x$

$\dfrac{du}{dx} = 5$

$y = 2 \sin u$

$\dfrac{dy}{du} = 2 \cos u$

Therefore

$\dfrac{dy}{dx} = \dfrac{dy}{du} \times \dfrac{du}{dx}$

$\dfrac{dy}{dx} = 2 \cos u \times 5$

$\dfrac{dy}{dx} = 10 \cos u$

$\dfrac{dy}{dx} = 10 \cos 5x$ as $u = 5x$

c $y = 4\cos x$

Using the chain rule $= \dfrac{dy}{dx} = \dfrac{dy}{du} \times \dfrac{du}{dx}$

Let $u = x$

$\dfrac{du}{dx} = 1$

$y = 4\cos u$

$\dfrac{dy}{du} = -4\sin u$

Therefore

$\dfrac{dy}{dx} = \dfrac{dy}{du} \times \dfrac{du}{dx}$

$\dfrac{dy}{dx} = -4\sin u \times 1$

$\dfrac{dy}{dx} = -4\sin u$

$\dfrac{dy}{dx} = -4\sin x$ as $u = x$

d $y = e^{\frac{1}{2}x}$

$\dfrac{dy}{dx} = \dfrac{1}{2}e^{\frac{1}{2}x}$ If $y = e^{ax}$ then $\dfrac{dy}{dx} = ae^{ax}$ with $a = \dfrac{1}{2}$

e $y = 3e^{2x}$

$\dfrac{dy}{dx} = 6e^{2x}$ If $y = ke^{ax}$ then $\dfrac{dy}{dx} = kae^{ax}$ with $a = 2$ and $k = 3$

EXERCISE 3

SKILLS

ANALYSIS
REASONING

1 ▶ Differentiate

    a $\sin 3x$ **b** $-\cos x$ **c** $-3\sin 2x$

    d e^{2x} **e** $3\sin x - 2\cos 3x$ **f** $2e^{2x} + 4x$

2 ▶ Find $\dfrac{dy}{dx}$ **when**

    a $y = \sin 6x$ **b** $y = 3\cos\dfrac{1}{2}x$

    c $y = \dfrac{1}{2}\sin 8x + 3\cos 8x + 54$ **d** $y = 3e^{4x}$

    e $y = -\dfrac{1}{2}e^{3x} + 3e^{5x} - 48x$

3 ▶ Find the gradient of the curve with the equation $y = 3e^{-x}$ at the point (0, 3).

4 ▶ Find the gradient of the curve with the equation $y = 3\sin x$ at the point $\left(\dfrac{\pi}{3}, \dfrac{3\sqrt{3}}{2}\right)$.

5 ▶ Find the gradient of the curve with the equation $y = 5\cos 2x$ at the point $\left(\dfrac{\pi}{4}, 0\right)$.

USE THE PRODUCT RULE TO DIFFERENTIATE MORE COMPLICATED FUNCTIONS

KEY POINTS

You need to be able to differentiate functions that are multiplied together, using the product rule.

If $y = uv$

$$\frac{dy}{dx} = u\frac{dv}{dx} + v\frac{du}{dx}$$

EXAMPLE 10

Given that $f(x) = x(2x + 1)^3$ find $f'(x)$.

$f(x) = x(2x + 1)^3$	Apply the product rule
let $u = x$ so $\dfrac{du}{dx} = 1$	
let $v = (2x + 1)^3$ so $\dfrac{dv}{dx} = 3(2x + 1)^2(2)$	Use the chain rule
$\qquad\qquad\qquad\quad = 6(2x + 1)^2$	
$\dfrac{dy}{dx} = (x)(6(2x + 1)^2) + (2x + 1)^3(1)$	Use $\dfrac{dy}{dx} = u\dfrac{dv}{dx} + v\dfrac{du}{dx}$
$\quad = 6x(2x + 1)^2 + (2x + 1)^3$	
$\quad = (2x + 1)^2(6x + (2x + 1))$	$(2x + 1)^2$ is a common factor to both terms, so factorise
$\quad = (2x + 1)^2(8x + 1)$	You can also now simplify the part in brackets

EXAMPLE 11

Given that $f(x) = x^2\sqrt{3x - 1}$, find $f'(x)$.

$f(x) = x^2\sqrt{3x - 1}$	Apply the product rule
let $u = x^2$ so $\dfrac{du}{dx} = 2x$	
let $v = (3x - 1)^{\frac{1}{2}}$ so $\dfrac{dv}{dx} = \dfrac{1}{2}(3x - 1)^{-\frac{1}{2}}(3)$	Use the chain rule
$\qquad\qquad\qquad\qquad = \dfrac{3}{2}(3x - 1)^{-\frac{1}{2}}$	
$\dfrac{dy}{dx} = (x^2)(\dfrac{3}{2}(3x - 1)^{-\frac{1}{2}}) + (3x - 1)^{\frac{1}{2}}(2x)$	Use $\dfrac{dy}{dx} = u\dfrac{dv}{dx} + v\dfrac{du}{dx}$
$\quad = \dfrac{3x^2}{2}(3x - 1)^{-\frac{1}{2}} + 2x(3x - 1)^{\frac{1}{2}}$	
$\quad = \dfrac{3x^2}{2\sqrt{3x - 1}} + 2x\sqrt{3x - 1}$	

EXAMPLE 12

Differentiate

a $y = e^x\sin x$ **b** $y = xe^{x^2}$

a $y = e^x\sin x$	Apply the product rule
Let $u = e^x$ so $\dfrac{du}{dx} = e^x$	
Let $v = \sin x$ so $\dfrac{dv}{dx} = \cos x$	

$$\frac{dy}{dx} = e^x(\cos x) + \sin x(e^x)$$

$$\frac{dy}{dx} = e^x(\cos x + \sin x)$$

Use $\dfrac{dy}{dx} = u\dfrac{dv}{dx} + v\dfrac{du}{dx}$

HINT

You will also need to use the chain rule to differentiate e^{x^2}.

b $y = xe^{x^2}$

Let $u = x$ so $\dfrac{du}{dx} = 1$

Let $v = e^{x^2}$ so $\dfrac{dv}{dx} = 2xe^{x^2}$

$$\frac{dy}{dx} = x(2xe^{x^2}) + e^{x^2}(1)$$

$$= 2x^2e^{x^2} + e^{x^2}$$

$$= e^{x^2}(2x^2 + 1)$$

Apply the product rule

Use $\dfrac{dy}{dx} = u\dfrac{dv}{dx} + v\dfrac{du}{dx}$

EXERCISE 4

SKILLS

CRITICAL THINKING
PROBLEM SOLVING

1 ▶ Use the **product rule** to differentiate

   a $x(1 + 4x)^4$ **b** $2x(1 + 3x^2)^2$ **c** $x\sqrt{x - 2}$

   d $2x^4(5 + x)^3$ **e** $4x^2(5x - 2)^{-1}$ **f** $x^3\sqrt{3x + 1}$

2 ▶ Use the product rule to differentiate

   a xe^{3x} **b** $(x^2 - 4)e^{-2x}$ **c** $2xe^{-3x}$

   d $(4x)e^{x^3}$ **e** $(6x + 1)e^{x^2}$ **f** $(5x + 2)e^{-x^2}$

3 ▶ Use the product rule to differentiate

   a $x\cos x$ **b** $\cos^2 x\sin x$ **c** $4x\sin 6x$

   d $e^x(\cos x)$ **e** $e^x(\sin x)$

4 ▶ Find the value of $\dfrac{dy}{dx}$ at the point on the curve

   a $x^2(4x - 3)^3$ where $x = 2$

   b $4x(2x - 2)^{\frac{1}{2}}$ where $x = 3$

   c $(2x + 1)(x + 3)^2$ where $x = 4$.

5 ▶ Find the equation of the tangent to the curve at the point given by the x-coordinate
   $f(x) = x^2(4x - 1)^{\frac{1}{2}}$ where $x = 1$.

USE THE QUOTIENT RULE TO DIFFERENTIATE MORE COMPLICATED FUNCTIONS

KEY POINTS

You need to be able to differentiate functions using the quotient rule:

If $y = \dfrac{u}{v}$ where u and v are functions of x then $\dfrac{dy}{dx} = \dfrac{v\dfrac{du}{dx} - u\dfrac{dv}{dx}}{v^2}$.

EXAMPLE 13

Given that $y = \dfrac{x^2}{2x + 5}$ find $\dfrac{dy}{dx}$

$y = \dfrac{x^2}{2x + 5}$	Apply the quotient rule
Let $u = x^2$ so $\dfrac{du}{dx} = 2x$	Differentiate
Let $v = 2x + 5$ so $\dfrac{dv}{dx} = 2$	Differentiate
$\dfrac{dy}{dx} = \dfrac{(2x + 5)(2x) - (x^2)(2)}{(2x + 5)^2}$	Substitute each component into $\dfrac{dy}{dx} = \dfrac{v\dfrac{du}{dx} - u\dfrac{dv}{dx}}{v^2}$
$= \dfrac{4x^2 + 10x - 2x^2}{(2x + 5)^2}$	Simplify/work out parts of the numerator
$= \dfrac{2x(x + 5)}{(2x + 5)^2}$	Group together like terms

EXAMPLE 14

Differentiate

a $y = \dfrac{e^{2x+3}}{x}$ **b** $y = \dfrac{e^x}{\sin x}$

a $y = \dfrac{e^{2x+3}}{x}$	Apply the quotient rule
Let $u = e^{2x+3}$ so $\dfrac{du}{dx} = 2e^{2x+3}$	
Let $v = x$ so $\dfrac{dv}{dx} = 1$	
Therefore	
$\dfrac{dy}{dx} = \dfrac{x(2e^{2x+3}) - e^{2x+3}(1)}{x^2}$	Substitute in each component into $\dfrac{dy}{dx} = \dfrac{v\dfrac{du}{dx} - u\dfrac{dv}{dx}}{v^2}$
$= \dfrac{2xe^{2x+3} - e^{2x+3}}{x^2}$	Simplify

$$= \frac{e^{2x+3}(2x-1)}{x^2}$$

b $y = \frac{e^x}{\sin x}$ · · · Apply the quotient rule

Let $u = e^x$ · · so $\frac{du}{dx} = e^x$

Let $v = \sin x$ · · so $\frac{dv}{dx} = \cos x$

$\frac{dy}{dx} = \frac{\sin x(e^x) - e^x(\cos x)}{(\sin x)^2}$ · · · Substitute in each component into $\frac{dy}{dx} = \frac{v\frac{du}{dx} - u\frac{dv}{dx}}{v^2}$

$= \frac{e^x(\sin x - \cos x)}{\sin^2 x}$ · · · Simplify

EXERCISE 5

SKILLS

CRITICAL THINKING
PROBLEM SOLVING

1 ▶ Use the **quotient rule** to differentiate

a $\frac{6x}{x-1}$ · · · · · · · · **b** $\frac{3x}{6x+3}$ · · · · · · · · **c** $\frac{3x^2}{(2x-3)^3}$

d $\frac{6x^2}{(x+2)^2}$ · · · · · · · · **e** $\frac{\sqrt{x+3}}{4x^2}$ · · · · · · · · **f** $\frac{x+6}{\sqrt{4x+3}}$

2 ▶ Use the quotient rule to differentiate

a $\frac{x}{e^{3x}}$ · · · · · · **b** $\frac{e^{x^2}}{x+1}$ · · · · · · **c** $\frac{e^{x^2}}{x}$ · · · · · · **d** $\frac{e^{3x}}{1-e^{3x}}$

3 ▶ Use the quotient rule to differentiate

a $\frac{\cos x}{x}$ · · · · · · **b** $\frac{e^x}{\sin x}$ · · · · · · **c** $\frac{3x^2+1}{\cos x}$ · · · · · · **d** $\frac{2x-1}{\sin x}$

HINT

Please see the example below for extra help on this question.

4 ▶ Find the equation of the tangent to each curve at the point given by the x-coordinate.

a $y = \frac{3x^2+1}{(x+1)^2}$ at $x = 3$ · · · · · · **b** $y = \frac{\sin x}{x}$ at $x = \pi$

FIND THE EQUATION OF THE TANGENT AND NORMAL TO THE CURVE $y = f(x)$

A tangent to a curve is a straight line that touches the curve at one point only. As a result the gradient of the tangent is the same as the gradient of the curve at the point where it touches the curve.

The 'normal' is a straight line perpendicular to the tangent at the point where it touches the curve.

You can use differentiation to find the tangent to a curve at a particular point.

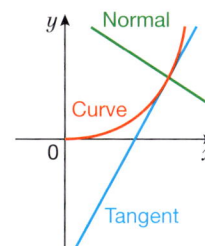

EXAMPLE 15 · · · Find the equation of the tangent to the curve $y = x^3 - 3x^2 + 2x - 1$ at the point (3, 5).

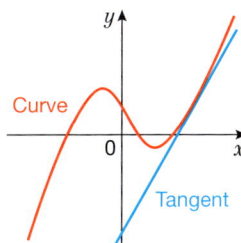

$$y = x^3 - 3x^2 + 2x - 1$$

$$\frac{dy}{dx} = 3x^2 - 6x + 2$$ Differentiate to get the gradient function

$$f(3) = 3(3)^2 - 6(3) + 2$$ Substitute the x value in to find the gradient

$$f(3) = 11$$

The gradient at (3, 5) is 11

$$y - y_1 = m(x - x_1)$$ Use the equation for a straight line

$$y - 5 = 11(x - 3)$$ Substitute in the values of the coordinates and the gradient

$$y - 5 = 11x - 33$$ Expand brackets

$$y = 11x - 28$$

EXAMPLE 16   Find the equation of the normal to the curve with the equation $y = 3\cos 2x$ at the point $\left(\frac{\pi}{4}, 0\right)$.

$$y = 3\cos 2x$$

$$f'(x) = 3(-\sin 2x) \times 2$$

$$= -6\sin 2x$$

$$f'\left(\frac{\pi}{4}\right) = -6\sin\frac{2\pi}{4}$$

$$= -6$$ Substitute the x value in to find the gradient

The gradient of the tangent at $\left(\frac{\pi}{4}, 0\right)$ is -6.

So the gradient of the normal is $\frac{1}{6}$.   Product of the gradients of perpendicular lines is -1

$$y - y_1 = m(x - x_1)$$ Use the formula for a straight line

$$y - 0 = \frac{1}{6}\left(x - \frac{\pi}{4}\right)$$ Substitute values of the coordinates and the gradient in

$$y = \frac{1}{6}x - \frac{\pi}{24}$$ This is the equation of the normal at $\left(\frac{\pi}{4}, 0\right)$

EXERCISE 6

SKILLS

INTERPRETATION

1 ▶ Find the equations of the tangent and normal of these equations at the given coordinates.

     a $y = x^2 - 8x + 11$ at (3, −4)

     b $y = \frac{1}{2}x^2 - x^{-3} + 4x + 2$ at $\left(1, \frac{11}{2}\right)$

     c $y = \sqrt{x} - \frac{3}{x^2}$ at (1, −2)

     d $y = e^{2x}$ at $(1, e^2)$

     e $y = e^{-3x}$ at $\left(1, \frac{1}{e^2}\right)$

FIND THE STATIONARY POINTS OF A CURVE AND CALCULATE WHETHER THEY ARE MINIMUM OR MAXIMUM STATIONARY POINTS

A point where the gradient of f(x) stops increasing and starts decreasing is called a **maximum point**.

A point where the gradient of f(x) stops decreasing and starts increasing is called a **minimum point**.

These are known as **turning points**, and occur where f$'($x$) = 0$.

To find the coordinates of these points, you need to

• Differentiate f(x) to find the gradient function.

• Solve f$'($x$) = 0$ (as this represents the gradient being 0)

• Substitute the value(s) of x into the original equation to find the corresponding y-coordinate

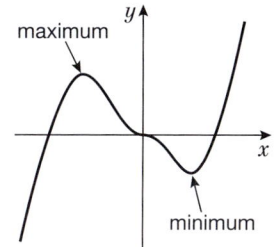

You can also find out whether stationary points are maximum or minimum points by finding the value of f$''($x$)$ $\left(\text{i.e. } \dfrac{\mathrm{d}^2 y}{\mathrm{d}x^2}\right)$ at the stationary point.

This is because f$''($x$)$ measures the change in gradient.

You obtain f$''($x$)$ by differentiating f(x) twice.

If $\dfrac{\mathrm{d}y}{\mathrm{d}x} = 0$ and $\dfrac{\mathrm{d}^2 y}{\mathrm{d}x^2} < 0$, the point is a maximum.

If $\dfrac{\mathrm{d}y}{\mathrm{d}x} = 0$ and $\dfrac{\mathrm{d}^2 y}{\mathrm{d}x^2} > 0$, the point is a minimum.

EXAMPLE 17 Find the coordinates of the turning point on the curve $y = x^4 - 32x$, and state whether it is a maximum or minimum.

$y = x^4 - 32x$

$\dfrac{\mathrm{d}y}{\mathrm{d}x} = 4x^3 - 32$ Differentiate to find the derivative function

$4x^3 - 32 = 0$ Set the derivative function equal to 0

$4x^3 = 32$ Simplify

$x = 2$

$y = x^4 - 32x$

$y = (2)^4 - 32(2)$ To find the value of y at $x = 2$ substitute $x = 2$ into the original equation

$y = -48$

The stationary point is at $(2, -48)$

$\dfrac{\mathrm{d}y}{\mathrm{d}x} = 4x^3 - 32$

$\dfrac{\mathrm{d}^2 y}{\mathrm{d}x^2} = 12x^2$ Differentiate again

$= 12(2)^2$ Substitute in $x = 2$

$= 48$

So the stationary point is a minimum.   Positive number = minimum point and negative number = maximum point

EXAMPLE 18

Find the stationary points on the curve

$$f(x) = 2x^3 - 15x^2 + 24x + 6$$

and state whether they are minimum or maximum points.

$f(x) = 2x^3 - 15x^2 + 24x + 6$	
$f'(x) = 6x^2 - 30x + 24$	Differentiate to find the derivative function
$6x^2 - 30x + 24 = 0$	Set the derivative function equal to 0
$6(x^2 - 5x + 4) = 0$	Factorise
$6(x - 4)(x - 1) = 0$	Factorise again
$x = 1$ or $x = 4$	Write the solutions

Substituting into the original formula will give these coordinates as stationary points.

(1, 17) and (4, −10)

$f'(x) = 6x^2 - 30x + 24$

$f''(x) = 12x - 30$	Differentiate again

HINT

'Minima' and 'maxima' are the plural forms of 'minimum' and 'maximum'.

$f''(1) = 12(1) - 30$ and $f''(4) = 12(4) - 30$

Substitute in $x = 1$	Substitute in $x = 4$
$= -18$	$= 18$

So (1, 17) is a maximum and (4, −10) is a minimum

Note: This is an extension activity and will not be in the exam.

Consider the curve $f(x) = 6x - x^2$ below. The gradient of the tangent at any point is given by $f'(x) = 6 - 2x$.

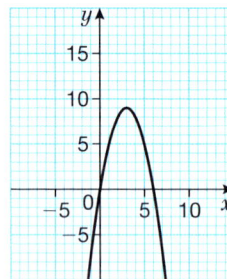

At the point $f'(1)$ the gradient is 4. When the tangent has a positive gradient, the graph is going up and the function is increasing.

At the point $f'(4)$ the gradient is −2. When the tangent has a negative gradient the graph is going down the curve and the function is decreasing.

At the point $f'(3)$ the gradient is 0 and it is a stationary point.

KEY POINT

$f'(x_0) > 0 \Rightarrow$ f is increasing at $x = x_0$

$f'(x_0) < 0 \Rightarrow$ f is decreasing at $x = x_0$

$f'(x_0) = 0 \Rightarrow$ f is stationary at $x = x_0$

EXERCISE 7

SKILLS

DECISION MAKING

1 ▶ Find the values of x for which $\dfrac{dy}{dx} = 0$

    a $y = x^2 + 12x$

    b $y = 5x^2 + 3x - 2$

    c $y = 4x^2 - 3x - 2$

    d $y = 2x + \dfrac{18}{x}$

2 ▶ Find the x-coordinates of the points where the gradient is zero. Establish whether these points are maximum or minimum points.

    a $y = 6x^2 + 2x$

    b $y = 10 + 7x - 6x^2$

    c $y = 10 - 2x + 4x^2$

    d $y = x^3 - x^2 - x + 1$

    e $y = x + \dfrac{1}{x}$

    f $y = x^2 + \dfrac{54}{x}$

APPLY WHAT YOU HAVE LEARNT ABOUT TURNING POINTS TO SOLVE PROBLEMS

Whenever you see a question asking about the maximum value or minimum value of a quantity, you are likely to use differentiation at some point. Most questions will involve creating a formula, for example for volume or area, and then calculating the maximum value of it.

EXAMPLE 19

a A large tank (shown) is to be made from $54\,\text{m}^2$ of sheet metal. It has no top.

Show that the volume of the tank is given by $V = 18x - \dfrac{2}{3}x^3$

b Calculate the values of x that will give the largest volume possible, and calculate what this volume is.

c Justify that the value of V you have found is a maximum.

---

a **Step 1**

Try to make formulae using the information you have.

    $V = x^2y$ Formula for volume

  $SA = 2x^2 + 3xy$ Formula for the surface area (no top)

Step 2

Find a way to remove a constant, in this case y. You can rewrite the surface area formula in terms of y.

$2x^2 + 3xy = 54$ so $54 - 2x^2 = 3xy$ and $y = \dfrac{54 - 2x^2}{3x}$

Step 3

Substitute the surface area formula into the volume formula, to replace y.

$V = x^2y$ so $V = x^2\left(\dfrac{54 - 2x^2}{3x}\right)$ and $V = \dfrac{54x^2 - 2x^4}{3x}$

$V = 18x - \dfrac{2}{3}x^3$ Simplify

b $\dfrac{dV}{dx} = 18 - 2x^2$ Differentiate to find the derivative function

$18 - 2x^2 = 0$ Set the derivative function equal to 0 (since you are looking for the maximum)

$$2x^2 = 18$$

$$x = \pm 3$$

There is a maximum at $x = +3$ (since a length cannot be negative)

$$V = 18(3) - \frac{2}{3}(3)^3$$

Substitute $x = 3$ into the formula for volume

$$= 36\,\text{m}^2$$

c $\dfrac{d^2V}{dx^2} = -4x$

When $x = 3$, $\dfrac{d^2V}{dx^2} = -4 \times 3 = -12$

This is negative, so $V = 36$ is the maximum value of V.

EXAMPLE 20

The diagram shows a minor sector OMN of a circle with centre O and radius r cm. The perimeter of the sector is 100 cm and the area of the sector is A cm².

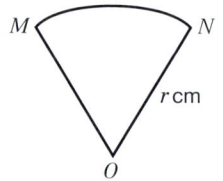

a Show that $A = 50r - r^2$

Given that r varies, find

b The value of r for which A is a maximum and show that A is a maximum.

c The value of $\angle MON$ for this maximum area.

d The maximum area of the sector OMN.

---

a Let the perimeter of the sector be P, so

$$P = 2r + r\theta$$

This is the sum of two radii ($2r$) and an arc length MN ($r\theta$)

$$\theta = \frac{100 - 2r}{r} \quad \text{equation (1)}$$

Rearrange and substitute $P = 100$

Let the area of the sector be A, so

$$A = \frac{1}{2}r^2\theta \qquad \text{(equation 2)}$$

Substitute equation 1 into equation 2

The area formula is in terms of two variables r and θ, so you need to substitute for θ so that the formula is in terms of one variable, r

$$A = \frac{1}{2}r^2\left(\frac{100 - 2r}{r}\right)$$

$$= 50r - r^2$$

b $\dfrac{dA}{dr} = 50 - 2r$

When $\dfrac{dA}{dr} = 0$, $r = 25$

Also $\dfrac{d^2A}{dr^2} = -2$, which is negative

Use the method which you learned to find stationary values: put the first derivative equal to zero, then check the sign of the second derivative

So the area is a maximum when $r = 25$.

c $\theta = \dfrac{100 - 50}{25}$

Substitute $r = 25$ into $\theta = \dfrac{100 - 2r}{r}$

$$= 2$$

So angle $M\hat{O}N = 2$ radians

d The maximum value of the area is

$$50 \times 25 - 25^2 = 625\,\text{cm}^2$$

Use $A = 50r - r^2$

1 ▶ A rectangular field is fenced on three sides. A house forms the fourth side of the rectangle. Given that the total length of the fence is 80 m, show that the area, A, of the field is given by the formula $A = y(80 - 2y)$, where y is the perpendicular distance from the house to the end of the field.

Given that the area is a maximum for this length of fence, find the dimensions of the enclosed field and the area which is enclosed.

2 ▶ A closed cylinder has a total surface area equal to 600π. Show that the volume, $V\,\text{cm}^3$, of this cylinder is given by the formula $V = 300\pi r - \pi r^3$, where $r\,\text{cm}$ is the radius of the cylinder.

Find the maximum volume of such a cylinder.

3 ▶ A shape consists of a rectangular base with a semi-circular top, as shown. Given that the perimeter of the shape is 40 cm, show that its area is given by the formula

$A = 40r - 2r^2 - \dfrac{\pi r^2}{2}$ where $r\,\text{cm}$ is the radius of the semicircle.

Find and justify the maximum value for this area.

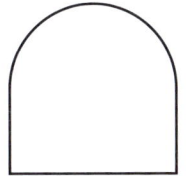

4 ▶ A wire of length 2 m is bent into the shape shown, made up of a rectangle and a semi-circle.

   a Find an expression for y in terms of x.

   b Show that the area is given by $A = \dfrac{x}{8}(8 - 4x - \pi x)$

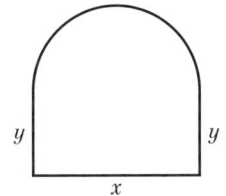

5 ▶ The shape shown is a wire frame in the form of a large rectangle split by parallel lengths of wire into 12 smaller equal-sized rectangles.

The total length of wire used to complete the whole frame is 1512 mm and the width of one of the smaller rectangles is x mm. Show that the area of the whole shape is $A\,\text{mm}^2$,

where $A = 1296x - \dfrac{108\,x^2}{7}$

Find and justify the maximum area which can be enclosed in this way.

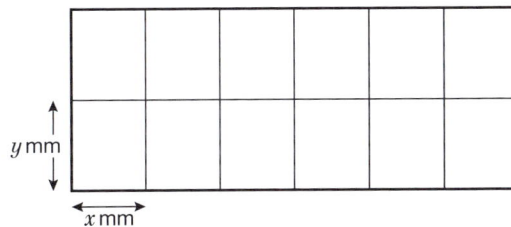

EXAM PRACTICE: CHAPTER 9

1 $f(x) = x^3 + 3x \qquad x > 0$

    a Differentiate to find $f'(x)$.   [2]

    b Given that $f'(x) = 15$, find the value of x.   [1]

2 Given that $y = 5x - 7 + \dfrac{2\sqrt{x} + 3}{x} \qquad x > 0$ find $\dfrac{dy}{dx}$ [3]

3 $f(x) = \dfrac{(3 - 4\sqrt{x})(3 - 4\sqrt{x})}{x^{\frac{1}{2}}} \qquad x > 0$

    a Show that $f(x) = 9x^{-\frac{1}{2}} + Px^{\frac{1}{2}} + Q$, where P and Q are constants to be found.   [2]

    b Find $f'(x)$.   [4]

    c Evaluate $f'(9)$.   [1]

4 A curve C has equation $y = 2x^3 + kx^2 + 7$

    a Find $\dfrac{dy}{dx}$ [2]

    b The point P, where $x = -2$, lies on C.
       The tangent to C at the point P is parallel to the line with equation $y = \dfrac{17}{2}x + 5$
       Find the value of k.   [2]

    c Find the value of the y-coordinate of P.   [1]

5 The curve C has equation $y = x^3 - 2x^2 - x + 9 \qquad x > 0$

    a The point P has x-coordinate 2. If the x-coordinate lies on the curve, find the value of the y-coordinate.   [1]

    b Find the equation of the tangent to C at P. The point Q also lies on C.   [2]

    c Given that the tangent to C at Q is perpendicular to the tangent to C at P, find the x-coordinate of Q, giving your answer in surd form.   [3]

6 A curve has equation $y = \dfrac{x^2 - 5x - 24}{x}$

    a Find $\dfrac{dy}{dx}$ in its simplest form.   [4]

    b Find an equation of the tangent at the point $x = 2$.   [3]

7 Find $\dfrac{dy}{dx}$ if $y = 3\sin 5x + 4\cos 3x$ [3]

8 Find $\dfrac{dy}{dx}$ if $y = \cos\left(\dfrac{x}{2}\right)$ [2]

9 $f(x) = e^{2x} + 3x^2 + 4\sin 4x$. Find $f'(x)$ [3]

10 Find the gradient of the curve $y = 2e^{-2x}$ at point (0, 2). [3]

11 Find the gradient of the curve with equation $y = 4\cos 2x$ at the point where $x = \dfrac{\pi}{4}$. [3]

12 $f(x) = \dfrac{x + k}{x - 2k}$

Find $f'(x)$. [3]

13 $f(x) = x^2 + 3 + \dfrac{4}{(x - 2)}$

Find the equation of the normal to the curve $y = f(x)$ at the point where $x = 3$. [3]

14 Differentiate $y = 6e^{2x^3}$ [3]

15 Differentiate $y = 3\sin^2 2x$ [4]

Q16 HINT

$x \in \mathbb{R}$ means x
is a real number.
It can be positive,
negative or
zero, including
integers, rational
numbers.

16 The function $g(x) = \dfrac{e^x}{(e^x - 2)^2}$ $x \in \mathbb{R}, x \neq \ln 2$

Find $g'(x)$. [4]

17 Differentiate with respect to x, $\dfrac{\sin 4x}{x^3}$, giving your answer in its simplest form. [3]

18 Differentiate $x^2 \cos 3x$ with respect to x. [3]

19 Given $f(x) = (3x^2 - 1)(x^2 + 5x + 2)$, find the derivative of $f(x)$. [3]

20 Find the equation of the tangent to the curve $f(x) = x\sin x$ where $x = \dfrac{3}{2}\pi$. [5]

21 A curve has the equation $y + 10 = 12x^{\frac{1}{2}} - x^{\frac{3}{2}}$ [4]

    a Find the coordinates of the turning point.

    b Determine the nature of the turning point.

22 $y = x^2 - kx^{\frac{1}{2}}$ [4]

    a Show that $\dfrac{dy}{dx} = 2x - \dfrac{1}{2}kx^{-\frac{1}{2}}$

    b Given that y is decreasing at $x = 4$, find the possible set of values for k

Note: This is an extension activity and will not be in the exam.

23 A sector OMN of a circle has area 100 cm². [5]

a Show that the perimeter of this sector is given by the formula $P = 2r + \dfrac{200}{r}$.

b Find the minimum value for the perimeter of such a sector.

CHAPTER SUMMARY: CHAPTER 9

■ You should know, and be able to use, these standard formulae:

Function	Derivative
x^n	nx^{n-1}
$\sin ax$	$a\cos ax$
$\cos ax$	$-a\sin x$
e^{ax}	ae^{ax}

■ You also need to know these rules

■ Chain rule:

$$\frac{dy}{dx} = \frac{dy}{du} \times \frac{du}{dx}$$

■ Product rule:

If $y = uv$ then $\dfrac{dy}{dx} = u\dfrac{dv}{dx} + v\dfrac{du}{dx}$

■ Quotient rule:

If $y = \dfrac{u}{v}$ then $\dfrac{dy}{dx} = \dfrac{v\dfrac{du}{dx} - u\dfrac{dv}{dx}}{v^2}$

■ A turning point is a point where $\dfrac{dy}{dx} = 0$

If $\dfrac{dy}{dx} = 0$ and $\dfrac{d^2y}{dx^2} > 0$ then the point is a minimum

If $\dfrac{dy}{dx} = 0$ and $\dfrac{d^2y}{dx^2} < 0$ then the point is a maximum

CHAPTER 10

10 INTEGRATION

Integration has many uses but it is especially important in **kinematics**. Integration helps engineers understand the relationship between displacement, velocity and **acceleration**.

You already know how to find the area of common shapes, but how do you find the area under a curve? Integration helps you solve this problem and you'll learn about it in this chapter. You will also take this a step further to calculate the **volume** of solids which have curved surfaces.

LEARNING OBJECTIVES

- Use integration to reverse the process of differentiation
- Understand how calculus is related to problems involving kinematics
- Use integration to find areas
- Use Integration to find the **volume of revolution**
- Relate rates of change to each other

STARTER ACTIVITIES

Copy and complete the table below.

f(x)	**i** GRADIENT FUNCTION f'(x)	**ii** f'(2)	**iii** f'(−1)	**iv** f'(0)
a $y = (x + 3)(x - 6)$				
b $y = \dfrac{x^2 + x^3}{x}$				
c $y = x(x^5 - 7x)$				
d $y = \dfrac{x^2 \times x^3}{x}$				
e $y = \dfrac{1}{4}x + 2$				
f $y = \dfrac{(x^2 + 3x)(1 - x)}{x}$				

INTEGRATION AS THE REVERSE OF DIFFERENTIATION

The indefinite integral of x^n is denoted by $\int x^n \, dx$

c is the constant of integration and it is important in indefinite integrals because the derivative only tells you about the change that occurred. If you integrate the derivative, you will calculate the entire change that occurred over the range of integration. However, it doesn't tell you where you started, hence c is a generic 'starting point'

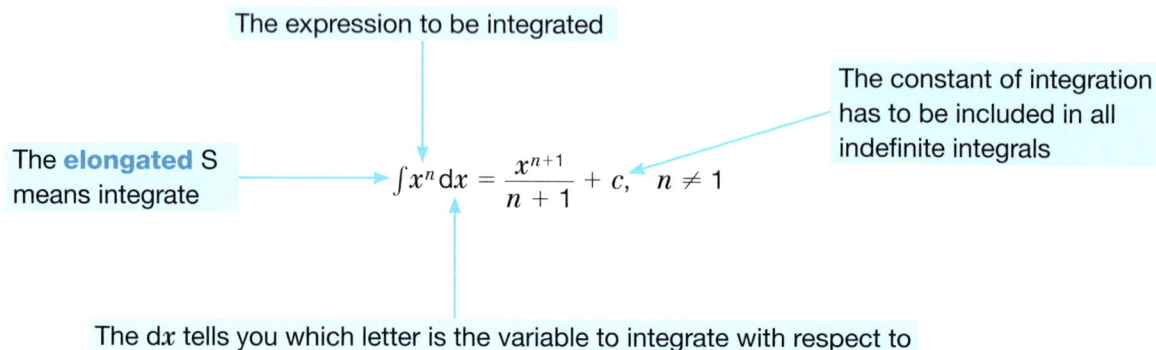

The expression to be integrated

The constant of integration has to be included in all indefinite integrals

The **elongated** S means integrate

$$\int x^n \, dx = \frac{x^{n+1}}{n+1} + c, \quad n \neq 1$$

The dx tells you which letter is the variable to integrate with respect to

The rules for integration you need for this course are

KEY POINTS

$$\int x^n \, dx = \frac{x^{n+1}}{n+1} + c, \quad (n \neq 1)$$

This is the one you will most commonly meet

KEY POINTS

$$\int e^{ax} \, dx = \frac{1}{a} e^{ax} + c$$

This arises from the equation showing the unusual character of e: $\int e^x \, dx = e^x + c$

KEY POINTS

$$\int \sin x \, dx = -\cos x + c$$

Notice the minus sign

KEY POINTS

$$\int \sin ax \, dx = -\frac{1}{a} \cos ax + c$$

KEY POINTS

$$\int \cos x \, dx = \sin x + c$$

No minus sign

KEY POINTS

$$\int \cos ax \, dx = \frac{1}{a} \sin ax + c$$

EXAMPLE 1

Integrate

a $\int 2x^3 \, dx$

b $\int 3x^{\frac{1}{2}} \, dx$

c $\dfrac{dy}{dx} = 6x + 2x^{-3} - 3x^{\frac{1}{2}}$

d $f'(x) = \frac{1}{2} x^{-\frac{1}{2}} - \frac{1}{2} x^{-\frac{3}{2}}$

e $\int (x^{\frac{1}{2}} + 2x^3) \, dx$

f $\int (3x^2 + px^{-2} + q^2) \, dx$

a $\int 2x^3 \, dx$

$$= \frac{2x^4}{4} + c$$

Increase the power by one, and divide by the new power

$$= \frac{1}{2} x^4 + c$$

b $\int 3x^{\frac{1}{2}} dx$

$$= \frac{3x^{\frac{3}{2}}}{\frac{3}{2}} + c$$ Increase the power by one, and divide by the new power

$$= 2x^{\frac{3}{2}} + c$$

c $\frac{dy}{dx} = 6x + 2x^{-3} - 3x^{\frac{1}{2}}$

$$y = \frac{6}{2}x^2 + \frac{2}{-2}x^{-2} - \frac{3}{\frac{3}{2}}x^{\frac{3}{2}} + c$$ Integrate each part separately

$$= 3x^2 - x^{-2} - 2x^{\frac{3}{2}} + c$$ Simplify

$$= 3x^2 - \frac{1}{x^2} - 2\sqrt{x^3} + c$$

d $f'(x) = \frac{1}{2}x^{-\frac{1}{2}} - \frac{1}{2}x^{-\frac{3}{2}}$

$$f(x) = \frac{\frac{1}{2}x^{\frac{1}{2}}}{\frac{1}{2}} - \frac{\frac{1}{2}x^{-\frac{1}{2}}}{-\frac{1}{2}} + c$$ Integrate each part separately

$$= x^{\frac{1}{2}} + x^{-\frac{1}{2}} + c$$ Simplify if possible

$$= \sqrt{x} + \frac{1}{\sqrt{x}} + c$$

e $\int (x^{\frac{1}{2}} + 2x^3) dx$ Integrate each part separately

$$= \frac{2}{3}x^{\frac{3}{2}} + \frac{2}{4}x^4 + c$$ Simplify

$$= \frac{2}{3}\sqrt{x^3} + \frac{1}{2}x^4 + c$$

f $\int (3x^2 + px^{-2} + q^2) dx$ Integrate each part separately

$$= \frac{3}{3}x^3 + \frac{p}{-1}x^{-1} + q^2 x + c$$ Simplify

$$= x^3 - \frac{p}{x} + q^2 x + c$$

HINT

p and q^2 should be treated as if they were just numbers.

EXAMPLE 2   Find $\int (2\cos x + 3e^{-x} - \sin 2x) dx$

$$\int (2\cos x + 3e^{-x} - \sin 2x) dx = \int 2\cos x \, dx + \int 3e^{-x} dx - \int \sin 2x \, dx$$ Integrate each term separately using standard integration rules.

$$= 2\sin x - 3e^{-x} + \frac{1}{2}\cos 2x + c$$

EXERCISE 1

SKILLS

REASONING
INTERPRETATION

1 ▶ Integrate with respect to x

  a $\int (x^3 + 3x)\,dx$

  b $\int (4x^3 - 2x)\,dx$

  c $\int (3x^{-2} + 4)\,dx$

  d $\int (5x^{\frac{1}{2}} - 3x^2)\,dx$

  e $\int (30x^2 - x^{-3})\,dx$

  f $\int (x^2 + x^{-\frac{1}{2}} - x^{\frac{3}{2}} + 4)\,dx$

  g $\int (4x^2 - 3x^{-4} + r)\,dx$

  h $\int (px^4 + 2t + 3x^{-2})\,dx$

  i $\int \left(\dfrac{3 - x^3}{4x^2}\right)\,dx$

2 ▶ Integrate with respect to x

  a $\int (2x + 3)x^2\,dx$

  b $\int \left(\dfrac{2x^2 + 3}{x^2}\right)\,dx$

  c $\int (2x + 3)^2\,dx$

  d $\int \left(\dfrac{2x + 3}{\sqrt{x}}\right)\,dx$

  e $\int \left(\dfrac{1}{4x^3} - \dfrac{3}{x^2}\right)\,dx$

  f $\int (x^{\frac{5}{3}} + x^{-\frac{7}{4}})\,dx$

3 ▶ Integrate with respect to x

  a $2\cos x$

  b $2\sin 3x$

  c $4e^x$

  d $3e^{4x}$

  e $3e^{-x}$

  f $5e^{-3x}$

  g $\sin\dfrac{1}{2}x$

  h $5\cos 3x$

  i $4\sin 3x$

4 ▶ Integrate with respect to x

  a $2(\cos x - \sin x + 3x)$

  b $7e^x + 3\sin x - 2x^{-2}$

  c $e^x + \sin x + 2\cos x$

  d $3x^2 + 2\sin 2x + 3e^{4x}$

  e $4(\cos x + e^x + x^2)$

UNDERSTAND HOW CALCULUS IS RELATED TO PROBLEMS INVOLVING KINEMATICS

KEY POINTS

You need to understand how displacement (s), velocity (v) and **acceleration** (a) can relate to calculus. The relationship between these variables in calculus is:

$$v = \frac{ds}{dt} \quad \text{and} \quad a = \frac{dv}{dt} \qquad \left(\text{or } a = \frac{d^2 s}{dt^2}.\right. \text{ This is known as a } \textit{second derivative}.)$$

These can also be written as

$$s = \int v\,dt \quad \text{and} \quad v = \int a\,dt$$

EXAMPLE 3

The velocity, $v\,\text{m\,s}^{-1}$, of a ball after t seconds, is given by $v = 8 + 10t - t^2$. ($t \geq 0$)

a Find the acceleration after t seconds.

b Calculate t when the acceleration is zero.

c Hence, or otherwise, find the maximum velocity.

a $a = \dfrac{dv}{dt} = 10 - 2t$ | Integrate the function for v to find a

b $a = 10 - 2t$

  $0 = 10 - 2t$ | Substitute $a = 0$

  $2t = 10$

  $t = 5\,\text{seconds}$ | Solve

c   The maximum velocity occurs when $\dfrac{\mathrm{d}v}{\mathrm{d}t} = 0$ and $t = 5$.

Therefore, $v_{\text{max}} = 8 + 50 - 25 = 33\,\text{m}\,\text{s}^{-1}$.

EXAMPLE 4

The velocity, $v\,\text{m}\,\text{s}^{-1}$, of a particle after t seconds is given by

$v = 12t - 8t^3 \quad (t \geqslant 0)$

Given that the initial displacement is $10\,\text{m}$, find

a   an expression for s in terms of t b   the displacement when $t = 2$.

a $s = \int v\,\mathrm{d}t$

$= \int (12t - 8t^3)\,\mathrm{d}t$

$= 6t^2 - 2t^4 + c$

$10 = 6(0)^2 - 2(0)^4 + c$ To find c substitute initial conditions
$t = 0$ and $s = 10$ into $v = 12t - 8t^3$

$c = 10$

Thus, $s = 6t^2 - 2t^4 + 10$

b   When $t = 2$

$s = 6(2)^2 - 2(2)^4 + 10$ Substitute $t = 2$ into $s = 6t^2 - 2t^4 + 10$

$s = 2\,\text{m}$

EXERCISE 2

SKILLS

PROBLEM
SOLVING
CRITICAL
THINKING

1 ▶ The displacement, s metres, of a particle after t seconds is given by $s = 250 + 10t^2$.
   Find an expression for the velocity.

2 ▶ The displacement, s metres, of a particle after t seconds is given by $s = 60 + 48t - 16t^2$.
   Find an expression for the velocity.

3 ▶ The displacement, s metres, of a particle after t seconds is given by $s = 25 + 30t - 5t^2$
   a   Find an expression for the velocity.
   b   Work out the velocity after 3 seconds. Clearly state your units.

4 ▶ The velocity, $v\,\text{m}\,\text{s}^{-1}$, of a particle after t seconds is given by $v = 160 - 32t$.
   a   Find an expression for the acceleration.
   b   At $t = 0$ the particle's displacement is $384\,\text{m}$ from its starting point.
      Find
      i   an expression for this displacement
      ii   the time when the particle's displacement is $0\,\text{m}$ from its starting point.

5 ▶ The velocity, $v\,\text{m}\,\text{s}^{-1}$, of a particle after t seconds is given by $v = 24 + 6t - t^2$
   a   Find an expression for its acceleration.
   b   Calculate its acceleration after 2 seconds.
   c   When $s = 0$, $t = 0$. Find the displacement when $t = 2$.

USE INTEGRATION TO FIND AREAS

The definite integral is defined as

$$\int_a^b f'(x)\,dx = [f(x)]_a^b = f(b) - f(a)$$

a and *b* are called the 'limits' of the integral

provided f′ is the derived function of f throughout the **interval** (a, b).

In particular if you wish to find the area between a curve, the x-axis and the lines $x = a$ and $x = b$ you use

$$\text{Area} = \int_a^b y\,dx$$

where $y = f(x)$ is the equation of the curve.

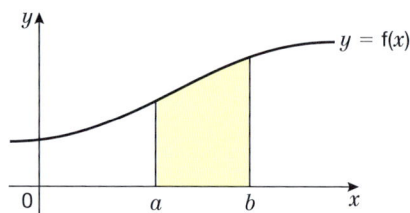

EXAMPLE 5

Find the area of the region R bounded by the curve with equation $y = (4 - x)(x + 2)$ and the positive x- and y-axes.

When $x = 0$, $y = 8$

When $y = 0$, $x = 4$ or -2

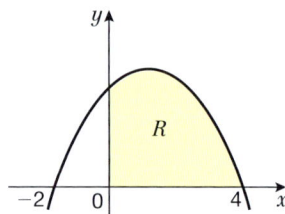

The area of R is given by

A sketch of the curve will often help in this type of question

$$A = \int_0^4 (4 - x)(x + 2)\,dx$$

So $\quad A = \int_0^4 (8 + 2x - x^2)\,dx$

Expand the brackets to leave the function in a form that you can integrate

$$A = \left[8x + x^2 - \frac{1}{3}x^3\right]_0^4$$

Integrate

$$= \left(8(4) + 4^2 - \frac{4^3}{3}\right) - \left(8(0) + 0^2 - \frac{0^3}{3}\right)$$

Substitute in limits of 4 and 0

$$= \left(32 + 16 - \frac{64}{3}\right) - (0)$$

So the area is $26\frac{2}{3}$ square units

EXAMPLE 6

The region R is enclosed by the curve with equation $y = x^2 + \dfrac{4}{x^2}$, $x > 0$, the x-axis and the lines $x = 1$ and $x = 3$. Find the area of R.

$\text{Area} = \int_1^3 \left(x^2 + \dfrac{4}{x^2} \right) dx$

This curve is not one you would be expected to sketch but the limits of the integral are simply $x = 1$ and $x = 3$, so you can write down an expression for the area without referring to a sketch

$$= \int_1^3 (x^2 + 4x^{-2})\, dx$$ Write the expression in a form suitable for integrating

$$= \left[\dfrac{1}{3}x^3 - 4x^{-1} \right]_1^3$$ Integrate

$$= \left[\dfrac{1}{3}x^3 - \dfrac{4}{x} \right]_1^3$$ Simplify

$$= \left(\dfrac{1}{3}(3)^3 - \dfrac{4}{3} \right) - \left(\dfrac{1}{3}(1)^3 - \dfrac{4}{1} \right)$$ Substitute in the limits 3 and 1

$$= \left(9 - \dfrac{4}{3} \right) - \left(\dfrac{1}{3} - 4 \right)$$ Simplify

$$= 13 - \dfrac{5}{3}$$

$$= 11\dfrac{1}{3}$$

You may be able to use a **graphical calculator** to check your answer, but you must show your working.

In the examples thus far, the area that was calculated was above the x-axis.
If the area between the curve and the x-axis lies below the x-axis, then $\int y\, dx$ will give a negative answer.

EXAMPLE 7

Find the area of the finite region bounded by the curve $y = x(x - 3)$ and the x-axis.

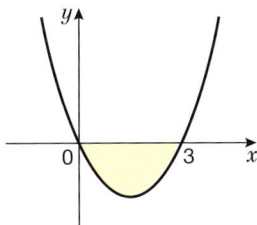

First draw a sketch. The solutions to $y = x(x - 3)$ are $x = 0$ and $x = 3$. So the curve crosses the x-axis −
(0, 0) and (3, 0)

In this case you can see that the region is *below* the x-axis

$\text{Area} = \int_0^3 x(x - 3)\, dx$

$$= \int_0^3 (x^2 - 3x)\, dx$$ Multiply out the brackets

$$= \left[\dfrac{1}{3}x^3 - \dfrac{3}{2}x^2 \right]_0^3$$ Integrate and use square brackets

$$= \left(\dfrac{1}{3}(3)^3 - \dfrac{3}{2}(3)^2 \right) - \left(\dfrac{1}{3}(0)^3 - \dfrac{3}{2}(0)^2 \right)$$ Substitute in the limits

$$= \left(9 - \frac{27}{2}\right) - 0$$

Work out each part

$$= -\frac{9}{2}$$

The minus sign indicates that the area is below the x-axis

Thus, the area is $\frac{9}{2}$ square units.

EXAMPLE 8   Find the area between the curve $y = x(x + 1)(x - 1)$ and the x-axis.

First let's try this in the same way as in the previous examples.

Start with a sketch.

You can see this time that part of the curve is above the x-axis and part is below

Resultant area $= \int_{-1}^{1} x(x + 1)(x - 1)\,dx$

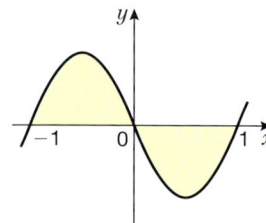

$$= \int_{-1}^{1} (x^3 - x)\,dx$$

Expand the brackets

$$= \left[\frac{1}{4}x^4 - \frac{1}{2}x^2\right]_{-1}^{1}$$

Integrate and use square brackets

$$= \left(\frac{1}{4}(1)^4 - \frac{1}{2}(1)^2\right) - \left(\frac{1}{4}(-1)^4 - \frac{1}{2}(-1)^2\right)$$

Use the limits

$$= \left(-\frac{1}{4}\right) - \left(-\frac{1}{4}\right)$$

$$= 0$$

From the sketch you can see that this is clearly not the correct answer and this method will not work. As a result, you must approach this type of question differently. You need to integrate each section separately and then combine them as positive values.

Area $= \int_{-1}^{1} x(x + 1)(x - 1)\,dx = \int_{-1}^{0} x(x + 1)(x - 1)\,dx - \int_{0}^{1} x(x + 1)(x - 1)\,dx$

Area above the x-axis   Area below the x-axis

Area above the x-axis $= \int_{-1}^{0} x(x + 1)(x - 1)\,dx$

Use the limits -1 and 0 as the curve lies above the x-axis in this region

$$= \int_{-1}^{0} (x^3 - x)\,dx$$

Expand the brackets

$$= \left[\frac{1}{4}x^4 - \frac{1}{2}x^2\right]_{-1}^{0}$$

Integrate

$$= \left(\frac{1}{4}(0)^4 - \frac{1}{2}(0)^2\right) - \left(\frac{1}{4}(-1)^4 - \frac{1}{2}(-1)^2\right)$$

Use the limits

$$= 0 - \left(-\frac{1}{4}\right)$$

$$= \frac{1}{4}$$

So the area above the x-axis is $\frac{1}{4}$ square unit.

Area below the x-axis $= \int_0^1 x(x+1)(x-1)\,dx$

$$= \int_0^1 (x^3 - x)\,dx$$ Expand the brackets

$$= \left[\frac{1}{4}x^4 - \frac{1}{2}x^2\right]_0^1$$ Integrate

$$= \left(\frac{1}{4}(1)^4 - \frac{1}{2}(1)^2\right) - \left(\frac{1}{4}(0)^4 - \frac{1}{2}(0)^2\right)$$ Use the limits

$$= -\frac{1}{4} - 0$$

$$= -\frac{1}{4}$$ The minus sign indicates that the area is beneath the x-axis

So the area below the x-axis is $\frac{1}{4}$ square units.

The total area of the curve between $x = -1$ and $x = 1$ is $\frac{1}{4} + \frac{1}{4} = \frac{1}{2}$ square units.

Sometimes you may need to find the area between a curve and a line, or between two curves.

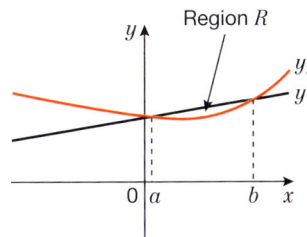

KEY POINTS

The area between a line (y_1) and a curve (y_2) is given by:

Area $= \int_a^b y_1\,dx - \int_a^b y_2\,dx$

EXAMPLE 9

Below is a diagram showing the line $y = x$ and the curve $y = x(4-x)$.
Find the area bounded by the line and the curve.

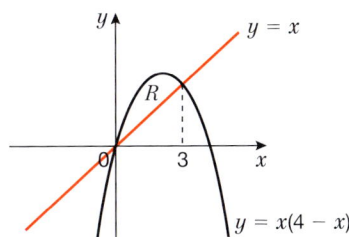

$x = x(4-x)$ Equate the equation of the line and the equation of the curve to find the x-values where the line crosses the curve

$x = 4x - x^2$ Expand the bracket

$x^2 - 3x = 0$

$x(x-3) = 0$

$x = 0$ or $x = 3$

Area $= \int_0^3 (x(4 - x)\,\mathrm{d}x - \int_0^3 x\,\mathrm{d}x$ | Use $\int_a^b y_1\,\mathrm{d}x - \int_a^b y_2\,\mathrm{d}x$ to find the area

$= \int_0^3 (3x - x^2)\,\mathrm{d}x$

$= \left[\dfrac{3}{2}x^2 - \dfrac{1}{3}x^3 \right]_0^3$

$= \left(\dfrac{3}{2}(3)^2 - \dfrac{1}{3}(3)^3 \right) - \left(\dfrac{3}{2}(0)^2 - \dfrac{1}{3}(0)^3 \right)$

$= \left(\dfrac{27}{2} - 9 \right) - 0$

$= \dfrac{9}{2}$ square units

EXERCISE 3

SKILLS

DECISION
MAKING
CRITICAL
THINKING

1 ▶ Sketch these curves and find the area of the finite region bounded by the curves and the x-axis.

   a $y = x(x - 2)$ **b** $y = (x + 2)(x - 3)$

   c $y = -(x + 4)(x - 1)$ **d** $y = x(x - 2)(x - 5)$

2 ▶ Find the area between the curve with equation $y = f(x)$, the x-axis and the lines $x = a$ and $x = b$ in each case.

   a $f(x) = 4x^2 - 2x + 2$ $a = 0, b = 3$ **b** $f(x) = 3x - x^2$ $a = -1, b = 2$

   c $f(x) = x^3 - 4x$ $a = 1, b = 2$ **d** $f(x) = \dfrac{4x^4 - x}{2x}$ $a = -1, b = 2$

   e $f(x) = 8x^{-3} + \sqrt{x}$ $a = 1, b = 4$

3 ▶ Find the area of the region between the curves or lines represented by these equations.

   a $y = x^2$ and $y = 2x$ | Some of these will give a negative area as the graph falls below the x-axis. You can address this by translating both equations so the area between them stays constant, but both will give a positive value when integrating to find the areas.

   b $y = x^2$ and $y = 4$

   c $y = x(2 - x)$ and $y = x$

   d $y = x^2 - 2$ and $y = \dfrac{1}{2}x^2$

   e $y = x^2 - 1$ and $y = x + 1$ e.g. $y = x^2 - 5$ and $y = x + 2$

                                             Translate both by $+5$ along the y axis so that equations are now

                                             $y = x^2$ and $y = x + 7$

4 ▶ Evaluate

   a $\displaystyle\int_1^2 3x^2\,\mathrm{d}x$ **b** $\displaystyle\int_1^2 \dfrac{1}{x^2}\,\mathrm{d}x$

   c $\displaystyle\int_4^9 \dfrac{1}{x^{\frac{1}{2}}}\,\mathrm{d}x$ **d** $\displaystyle\int_0^4 (x^3 - 2x - 3x^{\frac{1}{2}})\,\mathrm{d}x$

5 ▶ Find the area enclosed by the curve $y = x^2 - x - 1$ and the line $y = 5$.

6 ▶ Find the area between $y = 1 + 4x^{-2}$ and the x-axis from $x = 1$ to $x = 2$.

7 ▶ The diagram shows the curve $y = x^2$ and the line $y = 9$, with the enclosed region shaded.

   a Find the points of intersection A and B.

   b Find the area of the shaded region.

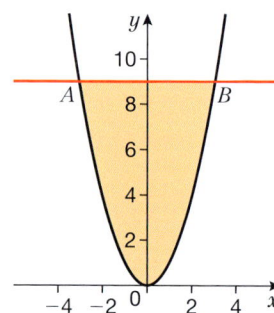

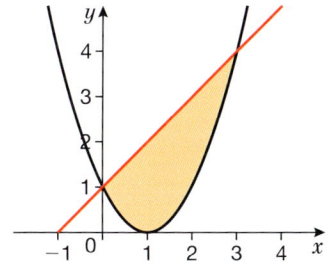

8 ▶ The diagram shows the curve $y = x^2 - 2x + 1$ and the line $y = x + 1$, with the enclosed region shaded.

    a Find the points of intersection of the curve and the line.

    b Find the area of the shaded region.

9 ▶ The diagram shows the curve $y = x^2 + 3x$.

    Find the area of the shaded region between $x = -1$ and $x = 2$.

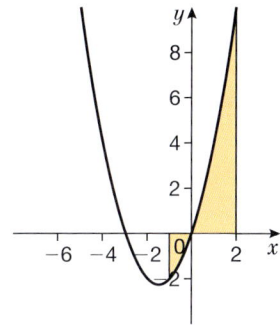

10 ▶ The diagram shows the finite region R, bounded by the curve with equation $y = x(4 + x)$, the line $y = 12$ and the y-axis.

    a Find the coordinates of point A.

    b Show that the area of the shaded region is $13\frac{1}{3}$ units.

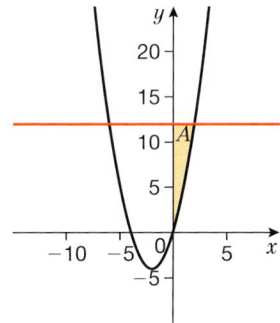

11 ▶ Show that the area between the curve $y = 4x - x^2$ and the x-axis from $x = 0$ to $x = 5$ is 13

USE INTEGRATION TO FIND A VOLUME OF REVOLUTION

You can also use integration to find volumes.

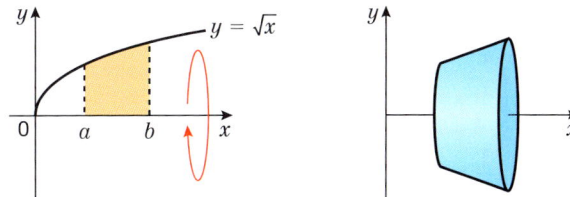

KEY POINTS ▶ The volume of revolution of a solid rotated 2π **radians** around the x-axis between $x = a$ and $x = b$ is given by: Volume $= \pi\int_a^b y^2\,dx$

EXAMPLE 10 Find the volume of revolution formed by rotating the area enclosed by the curve $y = x + x^2$, the x-axis and the coordinates $x = 1$, $x = 3$.

First sketch the curve.

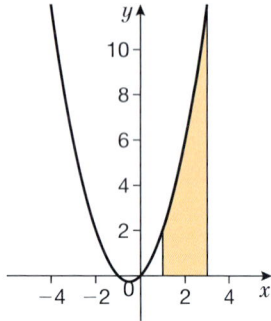

$V = \pi \int_{1}^{3} (x + x^2)^2 \, dx$ Use $V = \pi \int_{a}^{b} y^2 \, dx$

$= \pi \int_{1}^{3} (x^2 + 2x^3 + x^4) \, dx$ Expand

$= \pi \left[\frac{1}{3}x^3 + \frac{1}{2}x^4 + \frac{1}{5}x^5 \right]_{1}^{3}$ Integrate

$= \pi \left[\left(\frac{1}{3}(3)^3 + \frac{1}{2}(3)^4 + \frac{1}{5}(3)^5 \right) - \left(\frac{1}{3}(1)^3 + \frac{1}{2}(1)^4 + \frac{1}{5}(1)^5 \right) \right]$ Substitute in the limits

$= \pi \left[\frac{981}{10} - \frac{31}{30} \right]$ Simplify

$= \frac{1456}{15} \pi$ cubic units

EXAMPLE 11 The region R is bounded by the curve with the equation $y = x^2 - 1$, the x-axis and the lines $x = 1$ and $x = -1$.

a Find the area of R

b Find the volume of the solid formed when the region R is rotated through 2π radians about the x-axis.

a Area $= \int_{-1}^{1} (x^2 - 1) \, dx$

$= \left[\frac{x^3}{3} - x \right]_{-1}^{1}$

$= \left(\frac{1}{3} - 1 \right) - \left(\frac{-1}{3} + 1 \right)$

$= -\frac{4}{3}$

b $V = \pi \int_{\pi}^{b} y^2 \, dx$

$= \pi \int_{-1}^{1} (x^2 - 1)^2 \, dx$

$= \pi \int_{-1}^{1} (x^4 - 2x^2 + 1) \, dx$

$= \pi \left[\frac{x^5}{5} - \frac{2x^3}{3} + x \right]_{-1}^{1}$

$$= \pi \left\{ \left(\frac{1}{5} - \frac{2}{3} + 1 \right) - \left(-\frac{1}{5} + \frac{2}{3} - 1 \right) \right\}$$

$$= \frac{16\pi}{15}$$

EXAMPLE 12

The region R is bounded by the curve with the equation $y = \sin 2x$, the x-axis and the lines $x = 0$ and $x = \frac{\pi}{2}$.

  a Find the area of R.

  b Find the volume of the solid formed when the region R is rotated through 2π radians about the x-axis.

  a Area $= \int_0^{\frac{\pi}{2}} \sin 2x \, dx$

$$= \left[-\frac{1}{2} \cos 2x \right]_0^{\frac{\pi}{2}}$$

$$= \left(\left(-\frac{1}{2} \right)(-1) \right) - \left(\left(-\frac{1}{2} \right)(1) \right)$$

$$= 1$$

  b Volume $= \pi \int_0^{\frac{\pi}{2}} \sin^2 2x \, dx$

Use $\cos 2A = 1 - 2\sin^2 A$
Rearrange to give $\sin^2 A = \ldots$

$$= \left(\frac{1}{2} \right) \pi \int_0^{\frac{\pi}{2}} \frac{1}{2} (1 - \cos 4x) \, dx$$

Note that $2 \times 2x$ gives $4x$ in the cos term

$$= \left(\frac{1}{2} \right) \pi \left[x - \frac{1}{4} \sin 4x \right]_0^{\frac{\pi}{2}}$$

$$= \left(\frac{1}{2} \right) \pi \left(\frac{\pi}{2} - 0 \right) - (0)$$

Multiply out and integrate

$$= \frac{\pi^2}{4}$$

EXERCISE 4

SKILLS

PROBLEM SOLVING INTERPRETATION

1 ▶ Find the volume of the solid formed by rotating the area enclosed by the curve $y = x^2$, the x-axis and the line $x = 2$.

2 ▶ Find the volume of the solid formed by rotating the area enclosed by the curve $y = x^3$, the x-axis and the line $x = 2$.

3 ▶ Find the volume of the solid formed by rotating the area enclosed by the curve $y = x^3 + 1$, the x-axis, the line $x = 1$ and the line $x = 2$.

4 ▶ The region R is bounded by the curve with equation $y = f(x)$, the x-axis and the lines $x = a$ and $x = b$. In each part find the exact value of:

  i the area of R,

  ii the volume of the solid of revolution formed by rotating R through 2π radians about the x-axis.

    a $f(x) = \dfrac{2}{1 + x}$; $a = 0, b = 1$

    b $f(x) = x\sqrt{4 - x^2}$; $a = 0, b = 2$

RELATE RATES OF CHANGE TO EACH OTHER

Differential equations arise from many problems in mechanics, physics, chemistry, biology and economics. As their name suggests, these equations involve differential coefficients and so equations of the form

$$\frac{dy}{dx} = 3y, \quad \frac{ds}{dt} = 2 + 6t, \quad \frac{d^2y}{dt^2} = -25y \quad \frac{dP}{dt} = 10 - 4P$$

are differential equations (x, y, t, s and P are variables).

KEY POINTS

You can set up simple differential equations from information given in context. This may involve using connected rates of change, or ideas of proportion.

EXAMPLE 13

The image shows a right circular cylindrical metal rod which is expanding as it is heated. After t seconds the radius of the rod is x cm and the length of the rod is $5x$ cm.

$$\frac{dA}{dt} = 0.032 \, \text{cm}^2 \, \text{s}^{-1} \text{ and } \frac{dA}{dx} = 2\pi x$$

Find $\frac{dx}{dt}$ when the radius of the rod is 2 cm, giving your answer to 3 significant figures.

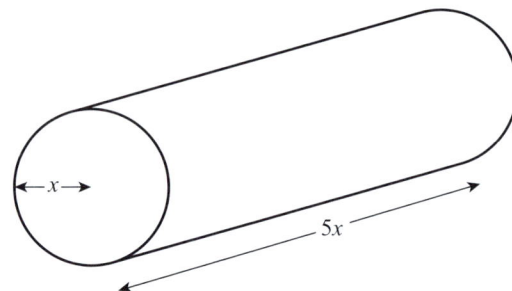

$$\frac{dx}{dt} = \frac{dA}{dt} \times \frac{dx}{dA}$$

$\frac{dA}{dx}$ is given in the question but we need to use the reciprocal to create an equation using the chain rule to eliminate dA.

$$\frac{dx}{dt} = 0.032 \times \frac{1}{2\pi x}$$

Use the reciprocal of $\frac{dA}{dx}$

$$\frac{dx}{dt} = \frac{0.016}{\pi x}$$

When $x = 2$ cm

$$\frac{dx}{dt} = \frac{0.016}{2\pi}$$

Substitute $x = 2$ into $\frac{dx}{dt}$

$$\frac{dx}{dt} = 0.00255 \, \text{cm s}^{-1}$$

EXAMPLE 14

A vase with a circular cross-section is shown. Fluid is flowing into the vase.

When the depth of the water is h cm, the volume of water $V \, \text{cm}^3$ is given by

$$V = 4\pi h(h + 4), \qquad 0 \leqslant h \leqslant 25$$

Water flows into the vase at a constant rate of $80\pi \, \text{cm}^3\text{s}^{-1}$ and

$$\frac{dV}{dt} = 80\pi \text{ and } \frac{dV}{dh} = 8\pi h + 16\pi$$

HINT

Find $\frac{dh}{dt}$.

Find the rate of change of the depth of the water, in cm s^{-1}, when $h = 6$

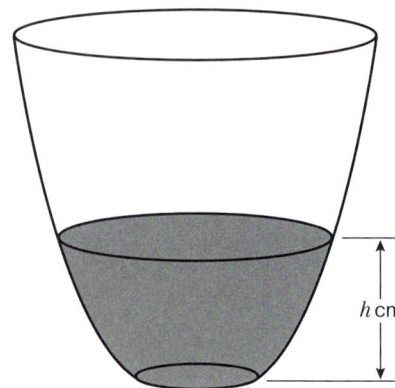

$$\frac{dh}{dt} = \frac{dV}{dt} \times \frac{dh}{dV}$$

$\frac{dV}{dh}$ is given in the question but we need to use the reciprocal to create an equation using the chain rule to eliminate dV.

$$\frac{dh}{dt} = 80\pi \times \frac{1}{8\pi h + 16\pi}$$

Use the reciprocal of $\frac{dV}{dh}$

When $h = 6$

$$\frac{dh}{dt} = 80\pi \times \frac{1}{8\pi(6) + 16\pi}$$

Substitute $h = 6$ into $\frac{dh}{dx}$

$$\frac{dh}{dt} = \frac{80\pi}{64\pi}$$

$$\frac{dh}{dt} = 1.25 \, \text{cm s}^{-1}$$

You can relate one rate of change to another. This is useful when a situation involves more than two variables.

EXAMPLE 15

Given that the area of a circle, A, is related to its radius r by the formula $A = \pi r^2$, and the rate of change of its radius in cm is given by $\frac{dr}{dt} = 5$, find $\frac{dA}{dt}$ when $r = 3$.

$$A = \pi r^2$$

$$\frac{dA}{dr} = 2\pi r$$

As A is a function of r differentiate to find $\frac{dA}{dr}$

Using $\frac{dA}{dt} = \frac{dA}{dr} \times \frac{dr}{dt}$

$$\frac{dA}{dt} = 2\pi r \times 5$$

Substitute in values of $\frac{dA}{dr}$ and $\frac{dr}{dt}$

$$= 30\pi$$

when $r = 3$

EXAMPLE 16

The volume of a **hemisphere** $V \, \text{cm}^3$ is related to its radius $r \, \text{cm}$ by the formula $V = \frac{2}{3}\pi r^3$ and the total surface area $S \, \text{cm}^2$ is given by the formula $S = \pi r^2 + 2\pi r^2 = 3\pi r^2$. Given that the rate of increase in volume, in $\text{cm}^3 \text{s}^{-1}$, $\frac{dV}{dt} = 6$, find the rate of increase of surface area $\frac{dS}{dt}$.

$$V = \frac{2}{3}\pi r^3 \text{ and } S = 3\pi r^2$$

This is area of circular base plus area of curved surface.

$$\frac{dV}{dr} = 2\pi r^2 \text{ and } \frac{dS}{dr} = 6\pi r$$

As V and S are functions of r, find $\frac{dV}{dr}$ and $\frac{dS}{dr}$

Now $\frac{dS}{dt} = \frac{dS}{dr} \times \frac{dr}{dV} \times \frac{dV}{dt}$

Use an extended chain rule together with the property that $\frac{dr}{dV} = 1 \div \frac{dV}{dr}$

$$= 6\pi r \times \frac{1}{2\pi r^2} \times 6$$

$$= \frac{18}{r}$$

You can use this formula for finding approximations.

$$\delta y \approx \frac{dy}{dx} \times \delta x$$

This formula shows an approximate relationship between a small change in the variable, x, δx and the equivalent small change in the variable y, δy.

EXAMPLE 17

Given that $y = 4x^3$, find the approximate percentage change in y for a 1% change in x.

HINT

δx is 1% of x
so $\delta x = \frac{x}{100}$

$\delta y \approx \frac{12x^3}{100}$.

$$y = 4x^3$$

so $\dfrac{dy}{dx} = 12x^2$ Differentiate

$$\delta y \approx 12x^2 \times \frac{x}{100}$$ Substitute into $\delta y \approx \dfrac{dy}{dx} \times \delta x$

The percentage change in y will be $\dfrac{\delta y}{y} \times 100$

Percentage change $= \dfrac{12x^3}{4x^3 \times 100} \times 100$ Substitute $\delta y \approx \dfrac{12x^3}{100}$

$= 3\%$

EXERCISE 5

SKILLS

INTERPRETATION
REASONING

1 ▶ Given that $V = \dfrac{1}{3}\pi r^3$ and that $\dfrac{dV}{dt} = 8$ find $\dfrac{dr}{dt}$ when $r = 3$.

2 ▶ Given that $V = \dfrac{1}{4}\pi r^2$ and that $\dfrac{dr}{dt} = 6$ find $\dfrac{dV}{dt}$ when $r = 2$.

3 ▶ Given that $y = xe^x$ and that $\dfrac{dx}{dt} = 5$ find $\dfrac{dy}{dt}$ when $x = 2$.

4 ▶ Given that $r = 1 + 3\cos\theta$ and that $\dfrac{d\theta}{dt} = 3$, find $\dfrac{dr}{dt}$ when $\theta = \dfrac{\pi}{6}$.

5 ▶ If $y = 3x^2$, find the approximate percentage change in y due to a change of 1% in the value of x.

6 ▶ If $y = 9x^3$, find the approximate percentage change in y due to a change of 1% in the value of x.

7 ▶ In a study of the water loss of picked leaves, the mass M grams of a single leaf was measured at times t days after the leaf was picked. It was found that the rate of loss of mass was proportional to the mass M of the leaf.
Write down a differential equation for the rate of change of mass of the leaf.

8 ▶ A curve C has equation $y = f(x)$, $y > 0$. At any point P on the curve, the gradient of C is proportional to the product of the x and the y coordinates of P. The point A with coordinates (4, 2) is on C and the gradient of C at A is $\dfrac{1}{2}$.

Show that $\dfrac{dy}{dx} = \dfrac{xy}{16}$.

Note: These are extension activities and will not be in the exam.

9 ▶ At time t seconds the surface area of a cube is A cm² and the volume is V cm³.

The surface area of the cube is expanding at a constant rate of 2 cm² s⁻¹.

Show that $\dfrac{\mathrm{d}V}{\mathrm{d}t} = \dfrac{1}{2}V^{\frac{1}{3}}$.

10 ▶ An inverted conical funnel is full of salt. The salt is allowed to leave by a small hole in the vertex. It leaves at a constant rate of 6 cm³ s⁻¹.

Given that the angle of the cone between the slanting edge and the vertical is $30°$, show that the volume of the salt is $\dfrac{1}{9}\pi h^3$, where h is the height of salt at time t seconds.

Show that the rate of change of the height of the salt in the funnel is inversely proportional to h^2. Write down the differential equation relating h and t.

EXAM PRACTICE: CHAPTER 10

1 $\dfrac{dy}{dx} = (x^2 + 3)^2$ and the point C with coordinates $(3, 20)$ lies on the curve C.

Find the equation of the curve in the form $y = f(x)$.   [3]

2 The gradient function of a curve is $f'(x) = -x^3 + 2x^{-2} - \dfrac{5}{2}x^{-3}$.

Find the equation of the curve given that it passes through the point $(1, 7)$.   [3]

3 Given that $y = 5x^3 - 5x^{-2}$, $x \neq 0$, find $\int y\,dx$ [2]

4 $\dfrac{dy}{dx} = \dfrac{x + 9}{\sqrt{x}}$. Find y.   [3]

5 Integrate $5e^x - 4\cos x + 2x^3$ [4]

6 The diagram shows a sketch of the curve $y = 10 + 8x + x^2 - x^3$. The x-coordinate of point A is 2. The region R, shown shaded, is bounded by the curve, the y-axis and the line from O to A, where O is the origin.
Find the exact value of the shaded region R.

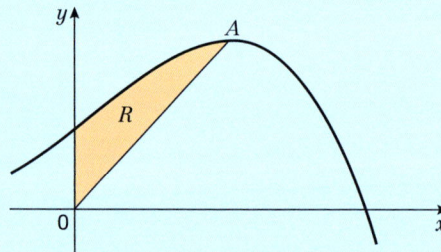

[5]

7 The line $y = 10 - x$ intersects the curve with equation $y = 10x - x^2 - 8$ at A and B.

  a Find the coordinates of A and B.   [2]

  b Calculate the exact value of the region bounded by the curve and line.   [4]

8 The diagram shows the curve $y = 4 + 3x - x^2$

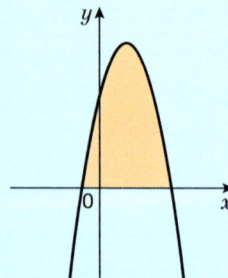

  a Find the coordinates where the curve crosses the x-axis.   [2]

  b Find the exact area of the shaded region.   [3]

9 Find $\displaystyle\int_{2}^{5} (2x + 3\sqrt{x})\,dx$ [3]

10 The diagram shows the curve C with the equation $y = x(x + 4)(x - 2)$. The graph intersects the x-axis at $x = 0$, $x = -4$ and $x = 2$. The finite region, shown shaded in the diagram, is bounded by the curve C and the x-axis. Find the total area of the finite region shown shaded in the diagram.

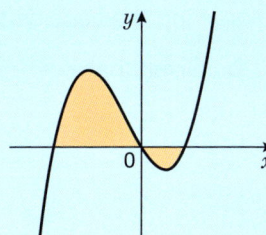

[4]

11 The diagram shows a sketch of the curve $y = x^2 - 3x + 2$. Find the sum of the areas. [4]

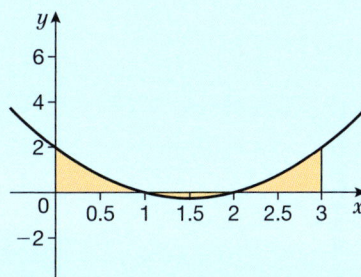

12 Find the area bounded by the line $y = -x - 11$ and the curve $y = 9 - x^2$ shown in the diagram.

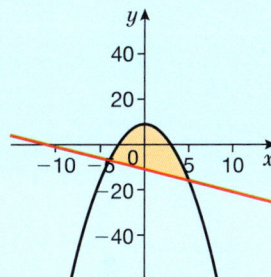

[4]

13 Find the volume of the solid formed when the area enclosed by the curve $y = x^3$, the x-axis and the line $x = 2$ performs one revolution about the x-axis. [5]

14 Find the volume of the solid formed when the area enclosed by the curve $y = x^3 + 1$, the x-axis and the line $x = 1$ performs one revolution about the x-axis. [5]

15 Find the volume of the solid formed when the area enclosed by the curve $y = x^2 + 3$ and the lines $x = 1$ and $x = 2$ performs one revolution about the x-axis. [5]

16 A particle Q is moving along the x-axis. At time t seconds, the velocity of Q is $(-3t^3 + 2t + 8)$ms^{-1} in the direction of x increasing. At time $t = 0$, Q is at the point where $x = 4$. Find the distance of P from O when $t = 1$. [3]

17 A particle P moves along the x-axis so that, at time t seconds, the displacement of P from O is x metres and the velocity of P is $v\,\text{ms}^{-1}$, where

$$v = \frac{1}{2}t^3 + 6t$$

a Find the acceleration of P when $t = 3$. **[3]**

b Given that $x = -5$ when $t = 0$, find the distance OP when $t = 3$, to the nearest metre. **[2]**

CHAPTER SUMMARY: CHAPTER 10

■ You should know, and be able to use, these standard integral formulae

FUNCTION	INTEGRAL
x^n	$\dfrac{1}{n+1}x^{n-1}, n \neq -1$
$\sin ax$	$-\dfrac{1}{a}\cos ax + c$
$\cos ax$	$\dfrac{1}{a}\sin ax + c$
e^{ax}	$\dfrac{1}{a}e^{ax} + c$

■ You should also know how to calculate areas and volumes:

  ■ Area between a curve and x-axis $= \int\limits_{a}^{b} y\,dx, y \geqslant 0$

  ■ Area between a curve and y-axis $= \int\limits_{c}^{d} x\,dy, x \geqslant 0$

■ Volume of revolution about the x-axis $= \pi\int\limits_{a}^{b} y^2\,dx$

■ Volume of revolution about the y-axis $= \pi\int\limits_{c}^{d} x^2\,dy$

CHAPTER 11

11 TRIGONOMETRY

Hummingbirds are tiny, colourful birds with beautiful feathers. They are admired for the sound of their wings, which flap up to 80 times per second, and for their song.

Sound is vibrations. These can by analysed as a combination of sine waves (sine is a trigonometric function – you can see a sine wave on page 191): any sound can be created with the right combination. When physicists or engineers investigate sound, they are actually investigating sine waves. Without their mathematical understanding of these waves, their analysis of sound would be very limited.

LEARNING OBJECTIVES

- Measure angles in radians
- Calculate arc length in a circle using radians
- Calculate the area of a **sector** using radians
- Understand the basic trigonometrical ratios and sine, cosine and tangent graphs
- Use **sine** and **cosine rules**
- Use sine and cosine rules to solve problems in 3D
- Use trigonometry identities and formulae to solve problems
- Solve trigonometric equations
- Use trigonometric formulae to solve equations

STARTER ACTIVITIES

Q1 HINT

This is a way of remembering how to compute the sine, cosine, and tangent of an angle. In other words, what are the standard formulae for sine, cosine and tangent?

1 ▶ Write down the meaning of SOHCAHTOA.

2 ▶ An aeroplane climbs at an angle of 15 degrees with the ground. What is the distance it has travelled (to the nearest hundred metres) when it has attained an altitude of 400 metres?

3 ▶ The angle of elevation to the top of a tree is 20°. How far away are you from the tree, if the tree's height is 15 m? Round your answer to 3 significant figures.

MEASURE ANGLES IN RADIANS

Radians are an alternative to degrees. Some calculations involving circles are easier when radians are used, as opposed to degrees.

KEY POINTS

• A radian is the angle **subtended** at the centre of a circle by an arc whose length is equal to that of the radius of the circle.

• 1 radian $= \dfrac{180°}{\pi}$.

HINT

The symbol for radians is ^{c}, so θ^c means that θ is in radians. If there is no symbol with an angle you should assume that it is in radians, unless the context makes it clear that it is in degrees.

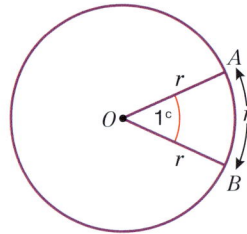

EXAMPLE 1   Convert these angles into degrees.

a $\dfrac{7\pi}{8}^c$

b $\dfrac{4\pi}{15}^c$

a $\dfrac{7\pi}{8}^c$

$\quad = \dfrac{7}{8} \times 180°$ Remember that π rad $= 180°$

$\quad = 157.5°$ Check using your calculator

b $\dfrac{4\pi}{15}^c$

$\quad = \dfrac{4}{15} \times 180°$

$\quad = 48°$

EXAMPLE 2   Convert these angles into radians.

a 150°

b 110°

HINT

Your calculator will give the decimal answer 1.91986

These answers, in terms of π, are exact.

a $150° = 150° \times \dfrac{\pi}{180°}^c$ Since $180° = \pi$ rad, $1° = \dfrac{\pi}{180°}$ rad

$\quad = \dfrac{5\pi}{6}^c$

b $110° = 110° \times \dfrac{\pi}{180°}^c$

$\quad = \dfrac{11}{18}\pi^c$

1 ▶ Convert these angles (in radians) to degrees.

a $\frac{1}{10}\pi$ b $\frac{1}{20}\pi$ c $\frac{5}{12}\pi$ d $\frac{1}{2}\pi$ e π

f 3π g 5π h $\frac{7}{9}\pi$ i $\frac{5}{4}\pi$ j $\frac{3\pi}{2}$

2 ▶ Use your calculator to convert these to degrees.

a 0.57^c b 1^c c 2^c d 1.37^c

e $\sqrt{2}^c$ f 3.14^c g 4.49^c

3 ▶ Use your calculator to write down the value of these trigonometric functions.

a $\sin\left(\frac{1^c}{4}\right)$ b $\tan\sqrt{2}^c$ c $\cos 0.56^c$

d $\cos 3.2^c$ e $\sin 3.2^c$ f $\tan 3.2^c$

4 ▶ Convert these angles to radians, giving your answer as multiples of π.

a $8°$ b $10°$ c $22.5°$ d $30°$

e $112.5°$ f $120°$ g $135°$ h $240°$

i $270°$ j $315°$ k $330°$

5 ▶ Use your calculator to convert these angles to radians, giving your answer to 3 significant figures.

a $50°$ b $75°$ c $100°$

d $120°$ e $235°$ f $325°$

CALCULATE ARC LENGTH AND THE AREA OF A CIRCLE USING RADIANS

The formula for the length of an arc is simpler in radians than in degrees.

• To find the arc length l of a circle use the formula $l = r\theta$, where r is the radius of the circle and θ is the angle, in radians, contained by the sector.

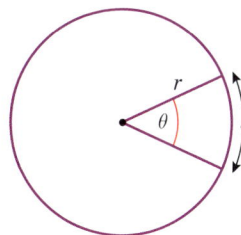

Show that the length of an arc is $l = r\theta$.

The circle has centre O and radius r. The arc AB has length l.
The length of the arc is proportional to the angle around O.

So $\frac{l}{2\pi r} = \frac{\theta}{2\pi}$ which means $l = r\theta$

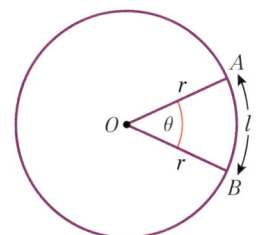

HINT

$\frac{\text{Length of arc}}{\text{Circumference}} = \frac{\text{Angle } AOB}{\text{Total angle around } O}$, with both angles in radians.

EXAMPLE 4

Find the length of the arc of a circle of radius 5.2 cm, given that the arc subtends an angle of 0.8^c at the centre of the circle.

Arc length $= 5.2 \times 0.8$ Use $l = r\theta$ with $r = 5.2$ and $\theta = 0.8^c$

$= 4.16$ cm

EXAMPLE 5

An arc AB of a circle, with centre O and radius r cm, subtends an angle of θ radians at O. The **perimeter** of the sector AOB is P cm. Express r in terms of P and θ.

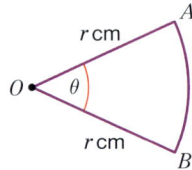

Draw a diagram to display the data

HINT

The perimeter is given by the arc AB, by OA and by OB. The length of the arc AB is $r\theta$.

$P = r\theta + 2r$

$= r(\theta + 2)$

$r = \dfrac{P}{2 + \theta}$

EXAMPLE 6

The border of a garden pond consists of a straight edge AB of length 2.4 m, and a curved part C, as shown in the diagram below. The curved part is an arc of a circle, centre O and radius 2 m. Find the length of C.

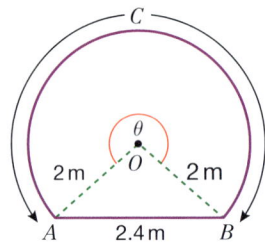

C subtends the reflex angle θ at O, so the length of C is 2θ measured in metres, because the radius is 2 m

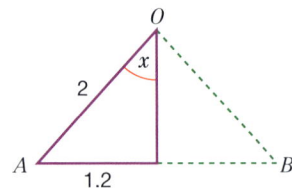

You can use the isosceles triangle AOB to find the angle AOB inside the triangle

(Use your calculator in radian mode)

$\sin x = \dfrac{1.2}{2}$, so $x = 0.6435^c$

The acute angle AOB is $2x$ rad $= 2(0.6435)$ Use $\theta +$ the acute angle AOB is $2\pi^c$

$= 1.287^c$

So $\theta = (2\pi - 1.287)$ rad $= 4.996^c$

So the length of C is $2\theta = 9.99$ m (3 s.f.)

The formula for the area of a sector is also simpler with radians.

KEY POINTS

- To find the area A of a sector of a circle use the formula $A = \dfrac{1}{2}r^2\theta$, where r is the radius of the circle and θ is the angle, in radians, contained by the sector.

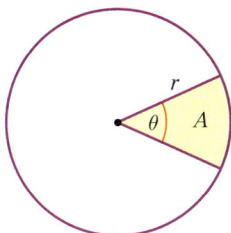

EXAMPLE 7

Show that the area of the sector of a circle with radius r is $A = \dfrac{1}{2}r^2\theta$

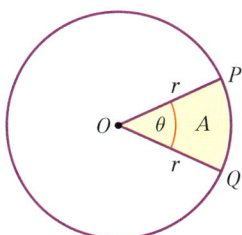

The circle has centre O and radius r.

The sector POQ has area A.

The area of the sector is proportional to the angle around O, so

$\dfrac{A}{\pi r^2} = \dfrac{\theta}{2\pi}$ | $\dfrac{\text{Area of sector}}{\text{Area of circle}} = \dfrac{\text{Angle } POQ}{\text{Total angle around } O}$

$A = \dfrac{1}{2}r^2\theta$ | Rearrange

EXAMPLE 8

A **plot** of land is in the shape of a sector of a circle of radius 55 m. The length of fencing that is erected along the edge of the plot to enclose the land is 176 m. Calculate the area of the plot of land.

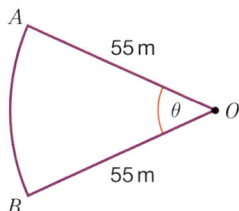

Draw a diagram to include all the data and let the angle of the sector be θ.

Arc $AB = 176 - (55 + 55) = 66$ m | As the perimeter is given, first find length of arc AB

$66 = 55\theta$ | Use formula for arc length, $l = r\theta$, where θ is in radians

So $\theta = 1.2$ rad.

Area of plot $= \dfrac{1}{2}(55)^2(1.2)$ | Use the formula for area of a sector, $A = \dfrac{1}{2}r^2\theta$

$= 1815$ m^2

1 ▶ An arc AB of a circle, centre O and radius r cm, subtends an angle θ radians at O.
The length of AB is l cm.

  a Find l when

    i $r = 8$, $\theta = 0.45$ **ii** $r = 5.5$, $\theta = \dfrac{3}{2}\pi$ **iii** $r = 22$, $\theta = 0.7$

  b Find r when

    i $l = 10$, $\theta = 0.5$ **ii** $l = 2.34$, $\theta = 0.7$ **iii** $l = 2.5$, $\theta = \dfrac{5}{12}\pi$

  c Find θ when

    i $l = 10$, $r = 8.4$ **ii** $l = 5.5$, $r = 5.625$ **iii** $l = \sqrt{12}$, $r = \sqrt{2}$

  d Find the area of the sector contained by angle θ when these statements are true.

    i $r = 8$, $\theta = 0.43$ **ii** $r = 3.5$, $\theta = \dfrac{3\pi}{2}$ **iii** $r = 22$, $\theta = 0.7$

2 ▶ Find the area of the sector and the arc length of these (angles given in radians).

  a

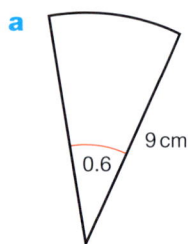

9 cm
0.6

  b

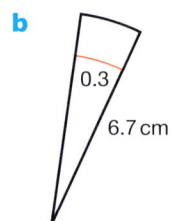

0.3
6.7 cm

  c

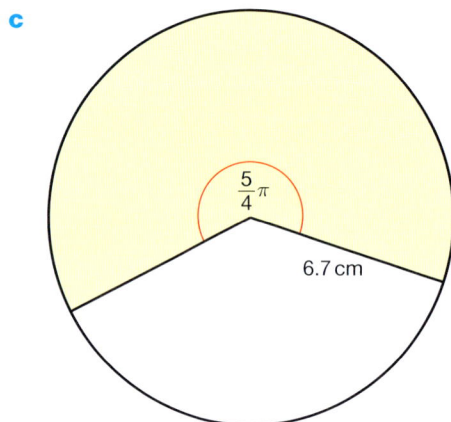

$\dfrac{5}{4}\pi$

6.7 cm

3 ▶ Find the area the shaded area (angles given in radians).

  a

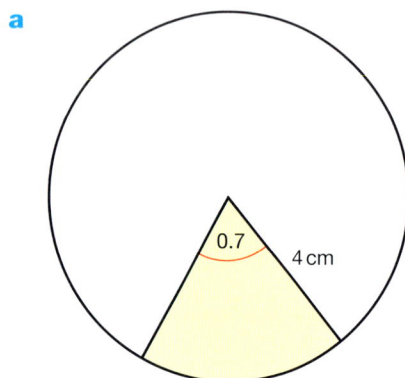

0.7
4 cm

  b

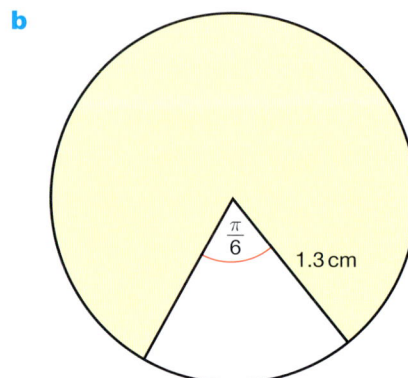

$\dfrac{\pi}{6}$
1.3 cm

4 ▶ Find the area of the shaded region in this diagram.

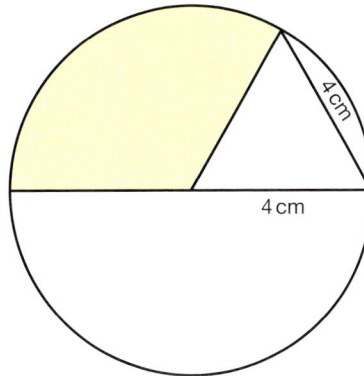

4 cm

4 cm

5 ▶ The area of sector OAB is 250 cm². The radius is 11 cm.

    a Find θ.

    b Find the length of the arc.

A

B

θ 11 cm

O

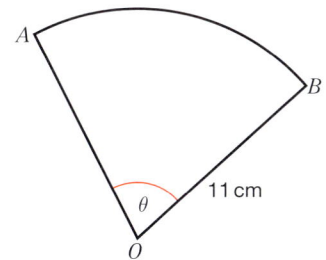

6 ▶ A sector of a circle has radius 6 cm and angle 2.2ᶜ. Calculate the area and perimeter.

7 ▶ Referring to the diagram, find

    a the perimeter of the shaded region

    b the area of the shaded region.

2 cm

0.6ᶜ

4 cm

2 cm

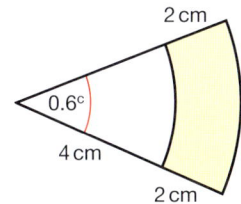

8 ▶ In the diagram, AB is the diameter of a circle with centre O and radius 4 cm. The point C is on the circle such that $\angle COB$ is $\frac{2}{3}\pi$. Find

    a the perimeter of the shaded region

    b the area of the shaded region.

C

$\frac{2}{3}\pi$

A O 4 cm B

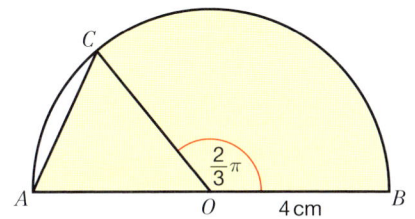

9 ▶ The arc AB of a circle with centre O and radius r is such that, $\angle AOB = 0.25$ᶜ. Given that the perimeter of the minor sector AOB is 45 cm,

    a calculate r

    b show that the area of the minor sector AOB is 50 cm²

    c find the area of the segment enclosed by the chord AB and the minor arc AB.

10 ▶ In the diagram, BC is the arc of a circle with centre O and radius 7 cm. The angle subtended by the arc is 1.9ᶜ. The points A and D are such that $OA = OD = 3$cm. Calculate the area of the shaded region.

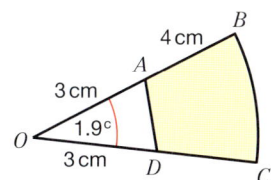

B

4 cm

A

3 cm

O 1.9ᶜ

3 cm D C

11▶ In the diagram, OAB is a sector of a circle with centre O and radius R cm. $\angle AOB = 2\theta$ radians. A circle with centre C and radius r cm touches the arc AB at T, and touches OA and OB at D and E respectively, as shown.

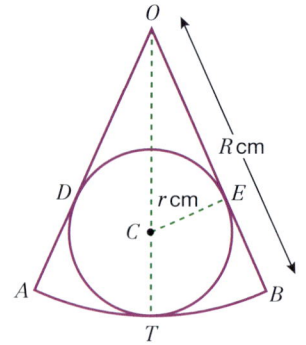

   a Write down, in terms of R and r, the length of OC.

   b Using $\angle OCE$, show that $R\sin\theta = r(1 + \sin\theta)$.

   c Given that $\sin\theta = \dfrac{3}{4}$ and that the perimeter of the sector OAB is 21 cm, find r, giving your answer to 3 significant figures.

12▶ The diagram shows a triangular plot of land. The sides AB, BC and CA have lengths 12 m, 14 m and 10 m respectively. The lawn is a sector of a circle with centre A and radius 6 m.

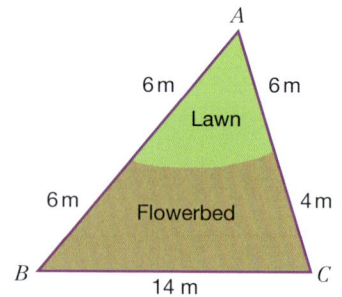

   a Show that $\angle BAC = 1.37$ radians.

   b Calculate the area of the flowerbed.

13▶ There is a straight path of length 70 m from the point A to the point B. The points are joined by a railway track in the form of an arc of the circle whose centre is C and whose radius is 44 m, as shown in the diagram.

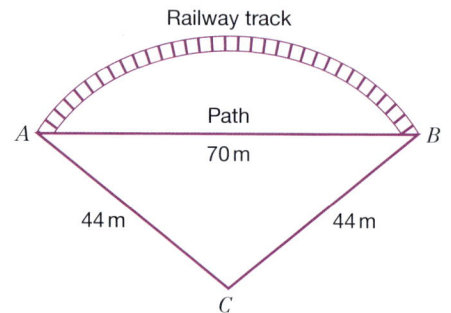

   a Show that the size, to 2 decimal places, of $\angle ABC$ is 1.84 radians.

   b Calculate

     i the length of the railway track

     ii the shortest distance from C to the path

     iii the area of the region bounded by the railway track and the path.

UNDERSTAND THE BASIC TRIGONOMETRICAL RATIOS AND SINE, COSINE AND TANGENT GRAPHS

You need to memorise the exact values of certain trigonometrical ratios and you need to be able to find the exact values of some trigonometrical ratios.

You can find the trigonometrical ratios of angles 30°, 45° and 60° exactly. Consider an equilateral triangle ABC of side 2 units. If you drop a perpendicular from A to meet BC at D, then $BD = DC = 1$ unit, the angle BAD is 30°, and the angle ABD is 60°.

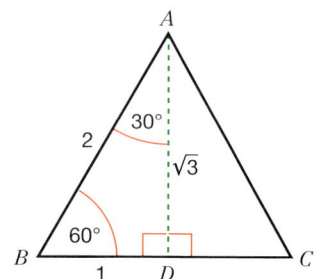

Using Pythagoras' theorem in the triangle ABD

$$AD^2 = 2^2 - 1^2 = 3$$

So $AD = \sqrt{3}$ units.

Using the triangle ABD, $\sin 30° = \dfrac{1}{2}$, $\cos 30° = \dfrac{\sqrt{3}}{2}$, $\tan 30° = \dfrac{1}{\sqrt{3}} = \dfrac{\sqrt{3}}{3}$

and $\qquad\qquad \sin 60° = \dfrac{\sqrt{3}}{2}$, $\cos 60° = \dfrac{1}{2}$, $\tan 60° = \sqrt{3}$

If you now consider an isosceles right-angled triangle PQR, in which $PQ = QR = 1$ unit, then the ratios for 45° can be found.

Using Pythagoras' theorem

$PR^2 = 1^2 + 1^2 = 2$

So $PR = \sqrt{2}$ units.

Then $\sin 45° = \cos 45° = \dfrac{1}{\sqrt{2}} = \dfrac{\sqrt{2}}{2}$ and $\tan 45° = 1$.

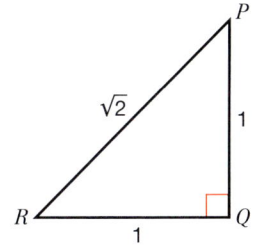

HINT

The graph of $\sin \theta$, where θ is in radians, has period 2π.

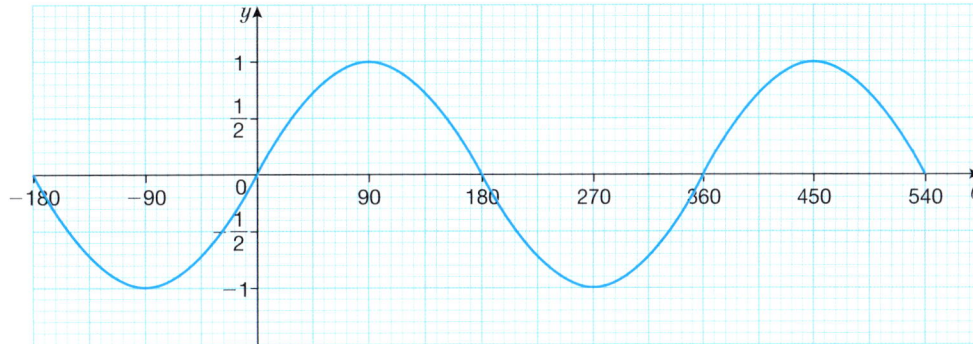

You need to be able to recognise the sine graph.

Functions that repeat themselves after a certain interval are called periodic functions, and the interval is called the **period** of the function. You can see that $\sin \theta$ is periodic with a period of 360°.

HINT

Because it is periodic.

There are many symmetry properties of $\sin \theta$ but you can see from the graph that

$\sin (\theta + 360°) = \sin \theta$ and $\sin (\theta - 360°) = \sin \theta$

$\sin (90° - \theta) = \sin (90° + \theta)$

You need to be able to recognise the cosine graph.

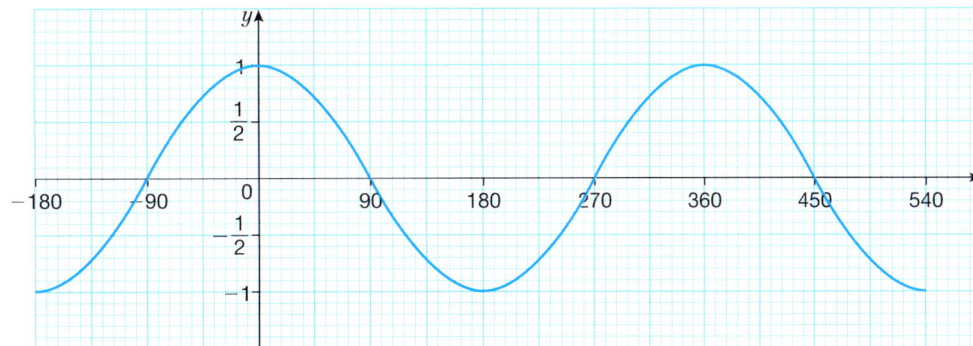

Like $\sin \theta$, $\cos \theta$ is periodic with a period of 360°. In fact, the graph of $\cos \theta$ is the same as that of $\sin \theta$ when it has been translated by 90°.

HINT

Because it is periodic.

Two further symmetry properties of $\cos \theta$ are

$\cos (\theta + 360°) = \cos \theta$ and $\cos (\theta - 360°) = \cos \theta$

HINT

Symmetry about $\theta = 0°$.

$\cos (-\theta) = \cos (\theta)$

You need to be able to recognise the tangent graph

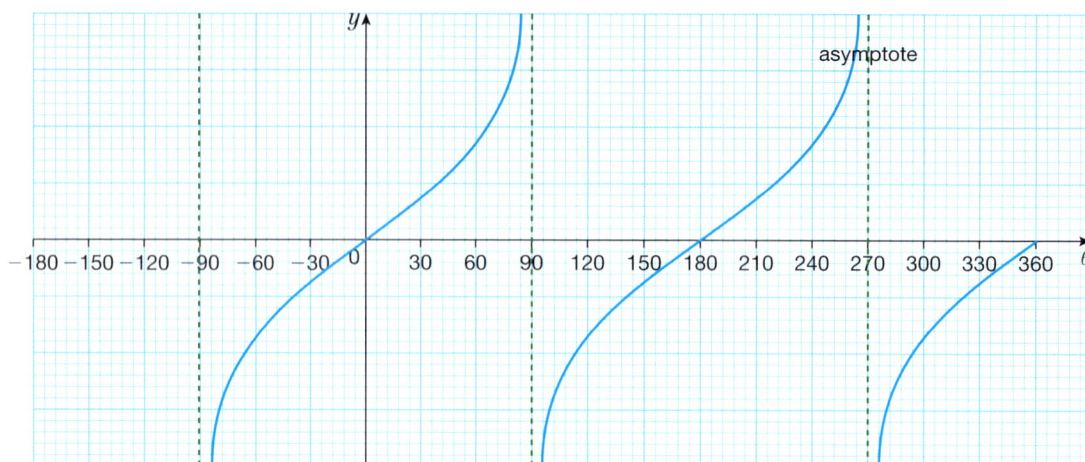

The tan function behaves very differently from the sine and cosine functions but it is still periodic, it repeats itself in cycles of 180° so its period is 180°.

The period symmetry properties of $\tan \theta$ are

$\tan(\theta + 180°) = \tan \theta$

$\tan(\theta - 180°) = \tan \theta$

EXAMPLE 9

Find the exact value of

a $\cos 405°$ **b** $\tan 120°$ **c** $\sin 300°$

a $\cos 405° = \cos(360° + 45°)$ You can see from the cosine graph that $\cos x$ has a period of 360°

$ = \cos 45°$

$ = \dfrac{1}{\sqrt{2}}$ Use triangle PRQ above

b $\tan 120° = \tan(180° - 60°)$ You can see from the tangent graph that $\tan x$ has a period of 180°

$ = \tan(-60°)$

$ = -\tan 60°$

$ = -\sqrt{3}$ Use triangle ABD above

c $\sin 300° = \sin(360° - 60°)$ You can see from the sine graph that $\sin x$ has a period of 360°

$ = \sin(-60°)$

$ = -\sin 60°$

$ = -\dfrac{\sqrt{3}}{2}$ Use triangle ABD above

EXERCISE 3

SKILLS

ANALYSIS

1 ▶ Express these trigonometric ratios using either 30°, 45° or 60°. (Do not use a calculator.)

a $\sin 135°$	**b** $\cos 120°$	**c** $\sin(-60°)$	**d** $\sin 330°$	**e** $\tan 210°$
f $\tan 135°$	**g** $\sin 405°$	**h** $\cos(-150°)$	**i** $\cos 330°$	**j** $\tan 300°$
k $\sin 420°$	**l** $\sin(-240°)$	**m** $\tan(-120°)$	**n** $\cos 225°$	**o** $\tan 330°$

2 ▶ The curve shows the graph $y = \cos x$ in the interval $-\dfrac{\pi}{2} \leqslant x \leqslant \dfrac{9\pi}{2}$ ($-90° \leqslant x \leqslant 810°$).

Write down in radians any points where the curve intersects the x-axis.

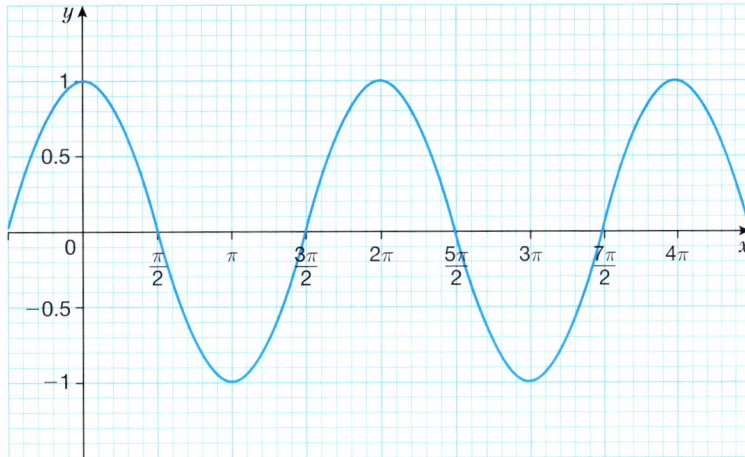

USE SINE AND COSINE RULES

In your IGCSE Mathematics course you should have met the **sine rule**, the **cosine rule** and the formula for the **area of a triangle**.

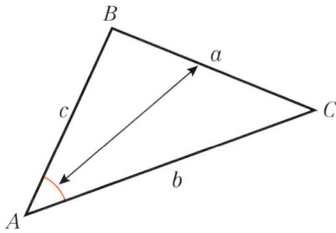

The formulae for these are

HINT

Note that side a is opposite angle A.

Sine Rule: $\dfrac{a}{\sin A} = \dfrac{b}{\sin B} = \dfrac{c}{\sin C}$ or $\dfrac{\sin A}{a} = \dfrac{\sin B}{b} = \dfrac{\sin C}{c}$

Cosine Rule: $a^2 = b^2 + c^2 - 2bc \cos A$

Area of a triangle: $\dfrac{1}{2} ab \sin C$

EXAMPLE 10 In the triangle ABC, $AB = 8\,\text{cm}$, the angle BAC is $30°$, and the angle BCA is $40°$. Find BC.

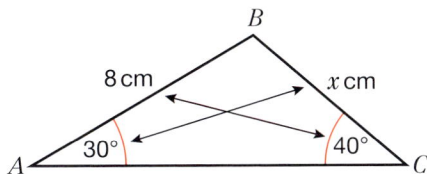

Using the sine rule $\dfrac{a}{\sin A} = \dfrac{c}{\sin C}$

gives $\dfrac{x}{\sin 30°} = \dfrac{8}{\sin 40°}$ Substitute $c = 8\,\text{cm}$, $C = 40°$, $A = 30°$, $a = x$

so $x = \dfrac{8 \sin 30°}{\sin 40°}$

$= 6.22$

Always draw a diagram and carefully then add the data

EXAMPLE 11 In the triangle ABC, $AB = 4\,\text{cm}$, $AC = 12\,\text{cm}$, and the angle ABC is $64°$. Find the angle ACB.

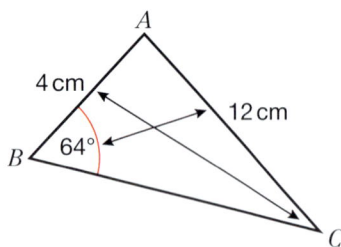

Using the sine rule $\dfrac{\sin C}{c} = \dfrac{\sin B}{b}$

gives $\dfrac{\sin C}{4} = \dfrac{\sin 64°}{12}$ Substitute $b = 12\,\text{cm}$, $c = 4\,\text{cm}$, $B = 64°$

so $\sin C = \dfrac{4\sin 64°}{12}$

$= \dfrac{\sin 64°}{3}$

and $C = \sin^{-1}\left(\dfrac{\sin 64°}{3}\right)$

$= 17.4°$

EXAMPLE 12 In the triangle ABC, $AB = 4\,\text{cm}$, $AC = 3\,\text{cm}$, and the angle ABC is $44°$. Work out two possible values for the angle ACB.

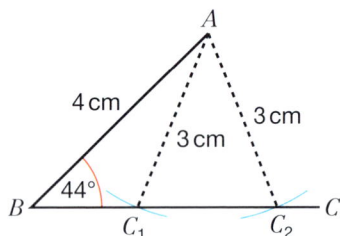

Here $b = 3\,\text{cm}$, $c = 4\,\text{cm}$, $B = 44°$.

Here $C > B$, as $c > b$, and so there will be two possible results. The diagram shows why.

With $B = 44°$ and $c = 4\,\text{cm}$ drawn, imagine putting a pair of compasses at A, then drawing an arc with centre A and radius $3\,\text{cm}$. This will intersect BC at C_1 and C_2 showing that there are two triangles ABC_1 and ABC_2 where $b = 3\,\text{cm}$, $c = 4\,\text{cm}$ and $B = 44°$.   This would not happen if $AC > 4\,\text{cm}$

Using the sine rule $\dfrac{3}{\sin 44°} = \dfrac{4}{\sin C}$

gives $\sin C = \dfrac{4\sin 44°}{3}$

One solution is $C = \sin^{-1}\left(\dfrac{4\sin 44°}{3}\right)$

$= 67.9°$

This corresponds to the triangle ABC_2.

The other solution is $C = 180° - 67.9°$ As $\sin(180° - x) = \sin x$

$= 112.1°$

This corresponds to the triangle ABC_1.

EXAMPLE 13 In the triangle PQR, $PQ = 5.9\,$cm, $QR = 8.2\,$cm and $PR = 10.6\,$cm. Find the size of the angle PQR.

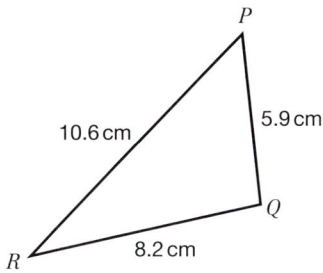

Using the cosine rule $\quad \cos Q = \dfrac{p^2 + r^2 - q^2}{2pr}$

gives $\qquad\qquad\qquad \cos Q = \dfrac{8.2^2 + 5.9^2 - 10.6^2}{2 \times 8.2 \times 5.9}$

Substitute $p = 8.2\,$cm, $r = 5.9\,$cm
and $q = 10.6\,$cm

$\qquad\qquad\qquad\qquad\quad = -0.1065...$

so $\qquad\qquad\qquad\quad Q = \cos^{-1}(-0.1065...)$

$\qquad\qquad\qquad\qquad\quad = 96.1°$

EXAMPLE 14 In the triangle ABC, $AB = 5\,$cm, $BC = 6\,$cm, and the angle ABC is $x°$. The area of the triangle ABC is $12\,$cm². Given that AC is the longest side, find the value of x.

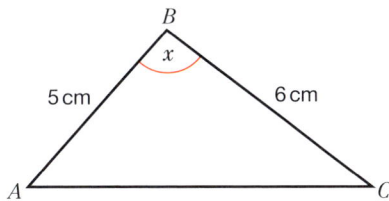

Using $\quad$ Area $= \dfrac{1}{2}ac\sin B$

gives $\quad 12 = \dfrac{1}{2} \times 6 \times 5 \times \sin x \qquad$ Substitute $a = 6\,$cm, $c = 5\,$cm, $B = x°$ and the area $= 12\,$cm²

so $\quad \sin x = 0.8$

There are two possible solutions for x.

One is $x = \sin^{-1}(0.8) = 53.1°$. However this cannot be the solution because B must be the largest angle, and if both A and C are smaller than $53.1°$, the sum of the angles of the triangle cannot be $180°$.

The other solution for x is $180° - 53.1° = 126.9°$. This is the correct solution.

It can be written as $127°$ to 3 significant figures.

1 ▶ In each triangle below find the values of x, y and z.

a

b

c

d

e

f

g

h

i

2 ▶ Find the area of each triangle.

a

b

c

3 ▶ In triangle ABC, $AB = 11$ cm, $BC = 9$ cm and $CA = 10$ cm. Find the area of the triangle.

4 ▶ A bird leaves a point A and flies 3.2 km, on a bearing of 128°, to a point B. It then flies 4.7 km, on a bearing of 066°, to point C. Show that angle ACB is 24°.

5 ▶ $ABCD$ is a quadrilateral. $AB = 7$ cm, $AD = 6$ cm and $BC = 9$ cm. Angle $ABC = 75°$ and angle $ADC = 90°$. Calculate the perimeter of $ABCD$.

6 ▶ Prove the sine rule for a general triangle ABC.

7 ▶ Prove the cosine rule for a general triangle ABC.

8 ▶ The longest side of a triangle has length $(2x - 1)$ cm. The other sides have lengths $(x - 1)$ cm and $(x + 1)$ cm. Given that the largest angle is 120°, find

    a the value of x.   **b** the area of the triangle.

USE SINE AND COSINE RULES TO SOLVE PROBLEMS IN 3D

You need to be able to solve problems in 3D.

EXAMPLE 15   The diagram below shows a **cuboid** with dimensions 8 cm, 6 cm and 5 cm.

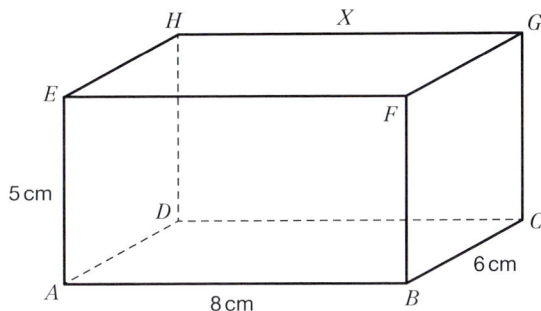

a   Find length AC.
b   Find length AG.
c   Find angle GAC.

---

a AC is the diagonal across the base $ABCD$ of the cuboid. Start by sketching this base and draw AC.

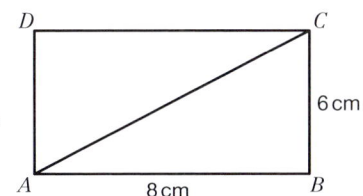

Identify a relevant right-angled triangle (triangle ABC in this case). Use Pythagoras' theorem to find AC.

$$AC^2 = AB^2 + BC^2$$
$$AC^2 = 6^2 + 8^2$$
$$AC^2 = 100$$
So $AC = 10$ cm

HINT

AC was calculated in part a.

b   Identify a relevant right-angled triangle. Use triangle AGC (you use this triangle because C is vertically below G).

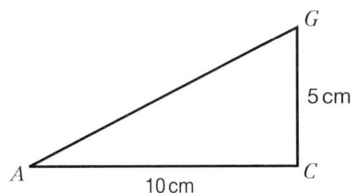

Use Pythagoras' theorem to find AG.

$$AG^2 = AC^2 + CG^2$$
$$AG^2 = 10^2 + 5^2$$
$$AG^2 = 125$$
So $AG = 11.2$ cm (3 s.f.)

c   Find angle GAC. This is the triangle drawn in part **b**. Use trigonometry to find angle GAC.

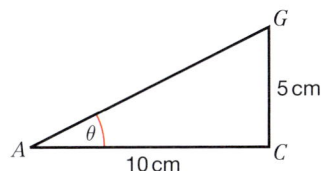

$\tan\theta = \dfrac{5}{10}$. therefore, $\theta = 26.6$ degrees.

1 ▶ The diagram below shows a square-based pyramid. The length AB is 8 cm. Point E is vertically above point X (not marked), the centre point of square $ABCD$. The height of the pyramid, EX, is 7 cm.

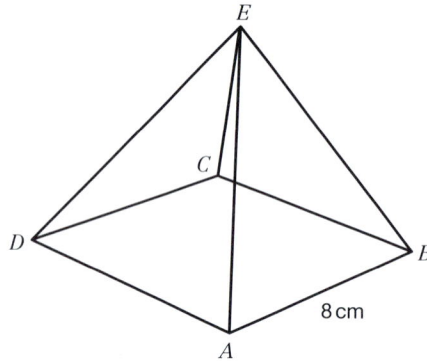

    a Calculate length AC.   **b** Calculate length AE.

    c Calculate angle EAC.   **d** Calculate the area of face AEB.

2 ▶ A **cube** has sides of 6 cm. Find

    a the length AB

    b the angle between AB and the horizontal **plane**.

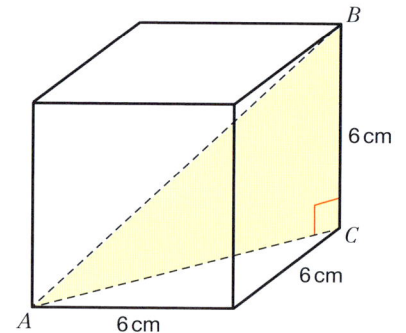

3 ▶ The diagram represents a cuboid $ABCDEFGH$. $CD = 10$ cm, $BC = 8$ cm and $BF = 4$ cm.

    a Calculate the length of AG. Give your answer to 3 significant figures.

    b Calculate the size of the angle between AG and the face $ABCD$. Give your answer to 3 significant figures.

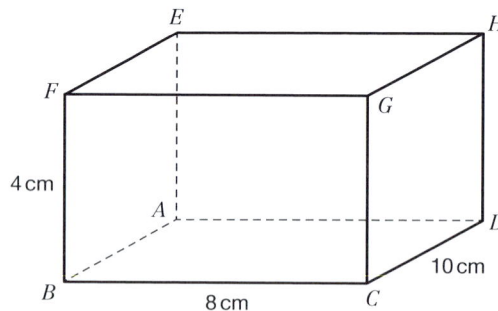

4 ▶ The diagram represents a ski slope. $AEFD$ is a rectangle. $ABCD$ is a square. EF and FC are perpendicular to plane $ABCD$. $AB = AD = 60$ m. Angle $ABE = 90°$. Angle $BAE = 30°$. Calculate the size of the angle that the line DE makes with the plane $ABCD$.

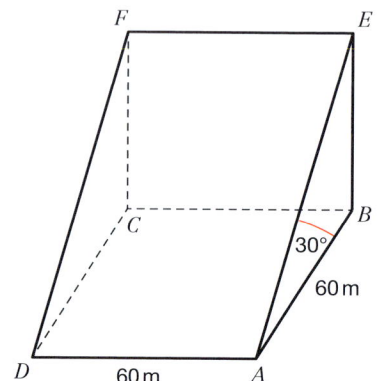

5 ▶ *ABCDEFGH* is a cuboid. *M* is the midpoint of *HG*. *N* is the midpoint of *DC*.

    a Calculate *BN*.

    b Work out the size of the **obtuse** angle between the planes *MNB* and *CDHG*.

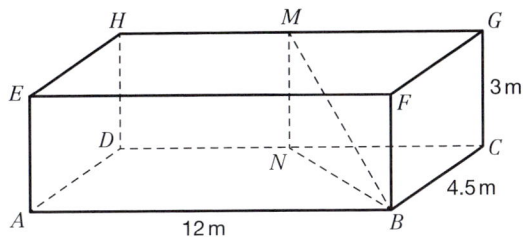

6 ▶ A mobile cell tower 150 m tall has two support cables running 300 metres due east and *x* metres due south, anchored at *A* and *B*. The angle of inclination to the horizontal of the latter cable is 50°

    a Find the length, *x*, of the cable attached to *B*.

    b Find the distance between *A* and *B*.

USE TRIGONOMETRY IDENTITIES TO SOLVE PROBLEMS

You should already know the **identity**

$$\tan\theta \equiv \frac{\sin\theta}{\cos\theta}$$

You also need to know the following. The first of these is not given in the exam.

$$\sin^2\theta + \cos^2\theta \equiv 1$$

$$\sin(A + B) \equiv \sin A\cos B + \cos A\sin B$$

$$\cos(A + B) \equiv \cos A\cos B - \sin A\sin B$$

$$\tan(A + B) \equiv \frac{\tan A + \tan B}{1 - \tan A\tan B}$$

EXAMPLE 16

Simplify these expressions.

a $\sin^2 3\theta + \cos^2 3\theta$

b $5 - 5\sin^2\theta$

c $\dfrac{\sin 2\theta}{\sqrt{1 - \sin^2 2\theta}}$

---

a $\sin^2 3\theta + \cos^2 3\theta = 1$ This is the same as $\sin^2\theta + \cos\theta = 1$ with θ replaced by 3θ

b $5 - 5\sin^2\theta = 5(1 - \sin^2\theta)$

           $= 5\cos^2\theta$ Use $\sin^2\theta + \cos^2\theta = 1$ which gives $1 - \sin^2\theta = \cos^2\theta$

c $\dfrac{\sin 2\theta}{\sqrt{1 - \sin^2 2\theta}} = \dfrac{\sin 2\theta}{\sqrt{\cos^2 2\theta}}$ Use $1 - \sin^2 2\theta = \cos^2 2\theta$

           $= \dfrac{\sin 2\theta}{|\cos 2\theta|}$.   Since $\sqrt{\cos^2 2\theta} = |\cos 2\theta|$

           $= \tan 2\theta$ or $-\tan 2\theta$ as $|\cos 2\theta| = \pm\cos 2\theta$

EXAMPLE 17

Show that $\dfrac{\cos^4\theta - \sin^4\theta}{\cos^2\theta} \equiv 1 - \tan^2\theta$

When you have to prove an identity like this, you often need to use basic identities you know like $\sin^2\theta + \cos^2\theta \equiv 1$

Usually the best strategy is to start with the more complicated side (here the left-hand side, LHS) and try to produce the expression on the other side.

$\text{LHS} = \dfrac{\cos^4\theta - \sin^4\theta}{\cos^2\theta}$

$\qquad = \dfrac{(\cos^2\theta - \sin^2\theta)(\cos^2\theta + \sin^2\theta)}{\cos^2\theta}$ Factorise the numerator as the difference of two squares

$\qquad = \dfrac{\cos^2\theta - \sin^2\theta}{\cos^2\theta}$ Use that $\cos^2\theta + \sin^2\theta \equiv 1$

$\qquad = \dfrac{\cos^2\theta}{\cos^2\theta} - \dfrac{\sin^2\theta}{\cos^2\theta}$

$\qquad = 1 - \tan^2\theta$

$\qquad = \text{RHS}$

EXAMPLE 18

Use the formula for $\sin(A+B)$ and $\cos(A+B)$ to prove that

a $\tan(A+B) \equiv \dfrac{\tan A + \tan B}{1 - \tan A \tan B}$ b $\tan(A-B) \equiv \dfrac{\tan A - \tan B}{1 - \tan A \tan B}$

a $\tan(A+B) \equiv \dfrac{\sin(A+B)}{\cos(A+B)} \equiv \dfrac{\sin A \cos B + \cos A \sin B}{\cos A \cos B - \sin A \sin B}$

Dividing the top and bottom by $\cos A \cos B$ gives

$\tan(A+B) \equiv \dfrac{\dfrac{\sin A \cos B}{\cos A \cos B} + \dfrac{\cos A \sin B}{\cos A \cos B}}{\dfrac{\cos A \cos B}{\cos A \cos B} - \dfrac{\sin A \sin B}{\cos A \cos B}}$ Cancel terms as shown and use the result $\tan\theta \equiv \dfrac{\sin\theta}{\cos\theta}$

$\qquad\qquad\quad \equiv \dfrac{\tan A + \tan B}{1 - \tan A \tan B}$

b Replace B by $-B$ in the result above.

$\tan(A-B) \equiv \dfrac{\tan A + \tan(-B)}{1 - \tan A \tan(-B)}$ Use the result $\tan(-\theta) \equiv -\tan\theta$

$\qquad\qquad\quad \equiv \dfrac{\tan A - \tan B}{1 + \tan A \tan B}$

EXAMPLE 19

Show, using the formula for $\sin(A-B)$, that $\sin 15° = \dfrac{\sqrt{6} - \sqrt{2}}{4}$

You know the exact form of sin and cos for many angles, for example 30°, 45°, 60°, 90°, 180°. You can use two of these to write 15°.

$\sin 15° = \sin(45° - 30°) = \sin 45° \cos 30° - \cos 45° \sin 30°$

$\qquad\qquad = \dfrac{\sqrt{2}}{2} \times \dfrac{\sqrt{3}}{2} - \dfrac{\sqrt{2}}{2} \times \dfrac{1}{2}$

$\qquad\qquad = \dfrac{1}{4}(\sqrt{2} \times \sqrt{3} - \sqrt{2})$

$\qquad\qquad = \dfrac{1}{4}(\sqrt{6} - \sqrt{2})$

EXAMPLE 20

Given that $2\sin(x + y) \equiv 3\cos(x - y)$, express $\tan x$ in terms of $\tan y$.

$2\sin x \cos y + 2\cos x \sin y \equiv 3\cos x \cos y + 3\sin x \sin y$ — Expand $\sin(x + y)$ and $\cos(x - y)$

$\dfrac{2\sin x \cos y}{\cos x \cos y} + \dfrac{2\cos x \sin y}{\cos x \cos y} \equiv \dfrac{3\cos x \cos y}{\cos x \cos y} + \dfrac{3\sin x \sin y}{\cos x \cos y}$ — Divide by $\cos x \cos y$, assuming it is non-zero

$2\tan x + 2\tan y \equiv 3 + 3\tan x \tan y$ — Use $\dfrac{\cos x}{\cos x} = \dfrac{\cos y}{\cos y} = 1$, $\dfrac{\sin x}{\cos x} \equiv \tan x$ and $\dfrac{\sin y}{\cos y} \equiv \tan y$

so $\quad \tan x(2 - 3\tan y) \equiv 3 - 2\tan y$

and $\quad \tan x \equiv \dfrac{3 - 2\tan y}{2 - 3\tan y}$

EXERCISE 6

SKILLS

CRITICAL
THINKING
DECISION
MAKING
ANALYSIS

1 ▶ Simplify each of these expressions.

a $1 - \sin^2\theta$
b $1 - \cos^2\frac{1}{2}\theta$
c $6\sin^2 4\theta + 6\cos^2 4\theta$

d $\cos^2 A - 1$
e $\dfrac{\sin 4\theta}{\tan 4\theta}$
f $\dfrac{\sqrt{1 - \cos^2\theta}}{\cos\theta}$

g $\dfrac{\sqrt{1 - \cos^2 3A}}{\sqrt{1 - \sin^2 3A}}$
h $(1 + \cos x)^2 + (1 - \cos x)^2 + 2\sin^2 x$

i $\sin^4 x + \sin^2 x \cos^2 x$
j $\sin^4 x + 2\sin^2 x \cos^2 x + \cos^4 x$

2 ▶ Prove that

a $(\cos x + \sin x)^2 \equiv 1 + 2\sin x \cos x$
b $\dfrac{1}{\cos\theta} - \cos\theta \equiv \tan\theta\sin\theta$

c $\dfrac{\cos^2\theta}{1 - \sin\theta} \equiv 1 + \sin\theta$
d $\dfrac{1 + \sin x}{\cos x} \equiv \dfrac{\cos x}{1 - \sin x}$

e $\tan x + \dfrac{1}{\tan x} \equiv \dfrac{1}{\cos x \sin x}$
f $\cos^2 A - \sin^2 A \equiv 2\cos^2 A - 1 \equiv 1 - 2\sin^2 A$

g $2 - (\sin x - \cos x)^2 \equiv (\sin x + \cos x)^2$
h $\sin^2 x \cos^2 y - \cos^2 x \sin^2 y \equiv \sin^2 x - \sin^2 y$

3 ▶ Express these as a single sine, cosine or tangent.

a $\sin 15° \cos 20° + \cos 15° \sin 20°$
b $\cos 130° \cos 80° - \sin 130° \sin 80°$

c $\dfrac{\tan 76° - \tan 45°}{1 + \tan 76° \tan 45°}$
d $\cos 2x \cos x - \sin 2x \sin x$

e $\cos 4\theta \cos 3\theta - \sin 4\theta \sin 3\theta$
f $\dfrac{\tan 2x + \tan 3x}{1 - \tan 2x \tan 3x}$

g $\sin(A + B)\cos B - \cos(A + B)\sin B$

h $\cos\left(\dfrac{3x + 2y}{2}\right)\cos\left(\dfrac{3x - 2y}{2}\right) - \sin\left(\dfrac{3x + 2y}{2}\right)\sin\left(\dfrac{3x - 2y}{2}\right)$

4 ▶ Calculate, without using your calculator, the exact value of

a $\sin 30° \cos 60° + \cos 30° \sin 60°$
b $\cos 110° \cos 20° + \sin 110° \sin 20°$

c $\sin 60° \cos 15° - \cos 60° \sin 15°$
d $\dfrac{\tan 45° + \tan 15°}{1 - \tan 45° \tan 15°}$

e $\dfrac{1 - \tan 15°}{1 + \tan 15°}$
f $\dfrac{\tan\dfrac{7\pi}{12} - \tan\dfrac{\pi}{3}}{1 + \tan\dfrac{7\pi}{12}\tan\dfrac{\pi}{3}}$

5 ▶ Prove these identities.

  a $\sin(A + 60°) + \sin(A - 60°) \equiv \sin A$

  b $\dfrac{\sin(x + y)}{\cos x \cos y} \equiv \tan x + \tan y$

  c $\cos\left(\theta + \dfrac{\pi}{3}\right) + \sqrt{3}\sin\theta \equiv \sin\left(\theta + \dfrac{\pi}{6}\right)$

SOLVE TRIGONOMETRIC EQUATIONS

You can use your calculator to find a solution to an equation such as $\sin x = 0.4$. Here, the solution is $x = 23.6°$

However, by analysing the sine, cosine and tangent graphs, you can see other possible solutions.

Here, the solutions are

$x = 180° - 23.6° = 156.4°$

$x = 23.6° + 360° = 383.6°$

and so on.

The below table summarises this situation for sine, cosine and tangent.

EQUATION	1st SOLUTION (CALC)	2nd SOLUTION	3rd SOLUTION	4th SOLUTION
$\sin x = k$	a	$180° - a$	All cases are $\pm 360°$	All cases are 2nd solution $\pm 360°$
$\cos x = k$	a	$360° - a$		
$\tan x = k$	a	$180° + a$		

EXAMPLE 21 ▶

Solve, in the interval $0° \leqslant x < 360°$, giving your answers to the nearest degree.

a $\sin x = 0.5$ **b** $4\sin x = -3$ **c** $2\tan(x + 1) = 0$

---

a $\sin x = 0.5$

  $x = 30°$ Using a formula table or a calculator

  or

  $x = 180° - 30°$

  $\quad = 150°$

b $4\sin x = -3$

  $\sin x = -\dfrac{3}{4}$ Rearrange into the form $\sin x = k$.

  $x = -48.6°$

This is outside the range so you need to find a second and third solution.

  $x = 180° - (-48.6°)$ Use the formula table to calculate the correct range of answers

  $\quad = 228.6°$

  or

  $x = -48.6° + 360° = 311.4°$ (to 3 s.f.)

Therefore, $x = 229°$ or $311°$

c $2\tan x + 1 = 0$

$\tan x = -\dfrac{1}{2}$ Rearrange into the form $\tan x = k$

$x = -26.6°$ Use the formula table to calculate the correct range of answers

or

$x = -26.6° + 180°$

  $= 153.4°$

$x = -26.6° + 360°$

  $= 333.4°$

so $x = 155°$ or $x = 333°$ (to 3 s.f.)

EXAMPLE 22   Solve, in the interval $0° \leqslant x < 360°$, giving your answers to the nearest degree.

a $\cos(x - 25°) = 0.4$

b $\tan 2x = 3$

---

a $\cos(x - 25°) = 0.4$

Let $y = x - 25°$

Then $\cos y = 0.4$ Substitute $y = x - 25°$ into the equation

$y = 66.4°$ Solve for $\cos y = 0.4$

or

$y = 360° - 66.4°$

  $= 293.6°$

Therefore,

$x - 25° = 66.4°$ or $293.6°$

$x = 91.4°$ or $319°$ Then use $x = y + 25°$ to find the x values to the nearest degree

b $\tan 2x = 3$

$y = 2x$ Substitute $y = 2x$ into the equation

$\tan y = 3$

$y = 71.6°$ or $251.6°$ or $431.6°$ or $611.6°$ Solve for $\tan y = 3$

Therefore

$x = 35.8°$ or $126°$ or $216°$ or $306°$ Then use $x = \dfrac{y}{2}$ to find the x values to the nearest degree

You may also need to solve equations in radians.

EXAMPLE 23

Solve $2\cos 2x + 1 = 0$ for $-\pi \leqslant x \leqslant \pi$. Give your answers in multiples of π.

Solve $2\cos 2x + 1 = 0$ for $-\pi \leqslant x \leqslant \pi$. Give your answers in multiples of π.

$2\cos 2x + 1 = 0$ First rearrange into the form $\cos 2x = k$

Let $y = 2x$

$\cos y = -\dfrac{1}{2}$

$y = \dfrac{2\pi}{3}$ Using a calculator gives $\dfrac{2\pi}{3}$

$x = \dfrac{\pi}{3}$ Since $y = 2x$ divide by 2 to find x. This is the first solution

or

$y = 2\pi - \dfrac{2\pi}{3}$ Use the formula table for the second solution

$\quad = \dfrac{4\pi}{3}$

$x = \dfrac{2\pi}{3}$ Since $y = 2x$ divide by 2 to find x. This is the second solution

$y = \dfrac{2\pi}{3} - 2\pi$ Use the formula table for the third solution

$\quad = -\dfrac{4\pi}{3}$

$x = -\dfrac{2\pi}{3}$ Since $y = 2x$ divide by 2 to find x. This is the third solution

or

$y = \left(2\pi - \dfrac{2\pi}{3}\right) - 2\pi$ Use the formula table for the fourth solution

$\quad = -\dfrac{2\pi}{3}$

$x = -\dfrac{\pi}{3}$ Since $y = 2x$ divide by 2 to find x. This is the third solution

So the solutions in the range $-\pi \leqslant x \leqslant \pi$ are

$x = \dfrac{\pi}{3}, \dfrac{2\pi}{3}, -\dfrac{2\pi}{3}, -\dfrac{\pi}{3}$

EXAMPLE 24

Solve, in the interval given, giving your answer to 3 significant figures.

a $\sin\left(x - \dfrac{\pi}{2}\right) = \dfrac{3}{4}$ $0 \leqslant x \leqslant 2\pi$

b $\sin^2\left(x + \dfrac{\pi}{6}\right) = \dfrac{1}{2}$ $-\pi \leqslant x \leqslant \pi$

a $\sin\left(x - \dfrac{\pi}{2}\right) = \dfrac{3}{4}$

Let $y = x - \dfrac{\pi}{2}$

Then $\sin y = \dfrac{3}{4}$ $\left(\text{Solve for } \sin y = \dfrac{3}{4}\right)$

$y = 0.848$ rad

or   (Use the table to find all the values in the acceptable range)

$y = 2.29$ rad

Therefore,

$x - \dfrac{\pi}{2} = 0.848$ or 2.29

$x = 2.42$ or 3.86

b $\sin^2\left(x + \dfrac{\pi}{6}\right) = \dfrac{1}{2}$

Let $y = x + \dfrac{\pi}{6}$

Then $\sin^2 y = \dfrac{1}{2}$

$\sin y = \pm\dfrac{\sqrt{2}}{2}$ $\left(\text{Solve for } \sin y = \dfrac{\sqrt{2}}{2}\right)$

$y = \dfrac{1}{4}\pi$ or $\dfrac{3}{4}\pi$ or $-\dfrac{3}{4}\pi$ or $-\dfrac{1}{4}\pi$ (Use the table to find all the values in the acceptable range)

Therefore,

$x = \dfrac{1}{12}\pi, \dfrac{7}{12}\pi, -\dfrac{11}{12}\pi, -\dfrac{5}{12}\pi$

EXERCISE 7

SKILLS

CRITICAL
THINKING
PROBLEM
SOLVING
ANALYSIS

1 ▶ Solve these equations for θ, in the interval $0° < \theta \leqslant 360°$.

    a $\sin\theta = -\dfrac{1}{2}$ **b** $\tan\theta = \sqrt{3}$ **c** $\cos\theta = -1$ **d** $\sin\theta = \sin 15$

    e $\cos\theta = -\cos 40$ **f** $2\tan\theta = 2$ **g** $\cos\theta = 0$ **h** $\sin\theta = -0.766$

    i $7\sin\theta = 5$ **j** $2\cos\theta = -\sqrt{2}$

2 ▶ Solve these equations for x or θ. Give your answers to 2 decimal places or in terms of π where appropriate, in the intervals indicated.

    a $\sin x = -\dfrac{\sqrt{3}}{2}, -180° \leqslant x \leqslant 180°$ **b** $2\sin x = -0.3, -180° \leqslant x \leqslant 180°$

    c $\cos x = -0.809, -180° \leqslant x \leqslant 180°$ **d** $\cos x = 0.84, -360° \leqslant x \leqslant 0°$

    e $\tan x = \dfrac{\sqrt{3}}{3}, 0° \leqslant x \leqslant 720°$ **f** $\tan x = 2.90, 80° \leqslant x \leqslant 440°$

    g $\sin\theta = 0, -2\pi \leqslant \theta \leqslant 2\pi$ **h** $\sin\theta = \dfrac{1}{\sqrt{2}}, -2\pi \leqslant \theta \leqslant \pi$

    i $\cos\theta = -\dfrac{1}{2}, -2\pi \leqslant \theta \leqslant \pi$ **j** $2(1 + \tan\theta) = 1 - 5\tan\theta, -\pi \leqslant \theta \leqslant 2\pi$

3 ▶ Find the values of θ, in the interval $0° \leqslant \theta \leqslant 360°$, for which

    a $\sin 4\theta = 0$ **b** $\cos 3\theta = -1$ **c** $\tan 2\theta = 2$

    d $\tan\dfrac{1}{2}\theta = -\dfrac{1}{\sqrt{3}}$ **e** $\sin(-\theta) = \dfrac{1}{\sqrt{2}}$ **f** $2\sin(\theta - 20°) = 1$

    g $\tan(\theta + 75°) = \sqrt{3}$

4 ▶ Solve, in the intervals indicated, these equations for θ, where θ is measured in radians. Give your answer in terms of π or to 2 decimal places.

    a $\sin\theta = 0, -2\pi \leqslant \theta \leqslant 2\pi$ **b** $\sin\theta = \dfrac{\sin\theta}{\cos\theta}, 0 \leqslant \theta \leqslant 2\pi$

5 ▶ Solve these equations in the interval given, giving your answers to 3 significant figures where appropriate.

    a $\cos(3x + 60°) = \dfrac{1}{2}, -90° \leqslant x \leqslant 90°$ **b** $\cos\left(x + \dfrac{\pi}{4}\right) = \dfrac{3}{4}, 0 \leqslant x \leqslant 2\pi$

    c $\tan(4x - 30°) = 2, 90° \leqslant x \leqslant 270°$ **d** $\sin(2x - \pi) = -\dfrac{1}{2}, -\pi \leqslant x \leqslant \pi$

    e $\cos^2\left(x - \dfrac{\pi}{16}\right) = \dfrac{1}{4}, -\pi \leqslant x \leqslant \pi$

USE TRIGONOMETRIC FORMULAE TO SOLVE EQUATIONS

EXAMPLE 24

Solve these equations for $0° \leqslant x \leqslant 360°$.

a $2\sin x = \tan x$ **b** $\sin^2(x - 30°) = \dfrac{1}{2}$

a $2\sin x = \tan x$

$$= \frac{\sin x}{\cos x}$$ Use that $\tan x = \dfrac{\sin x}{\cos x}$

HINT

When factorising $\sin x(2\cos x - 1)$ $= 0$, do not cancel. This would cause the solutions $x = 0°$, $180°$ to be lost.

so $2\cos x \sin x = \sin x$

and $\sin x(2\cos x - 1) = 0$ Rearrange

       $\sin x = 0$, which gives $x = 0°$ or $180°$ or $360°$

or $2\cos x - 1 = 0$

       $\cos x = \dfrac{1}{2}$, which gives $x = 60°$ or $300°$

The solutions are $x = 0°$ or $60°$ or $180°$ or $300°$ in the range $0° \leqslant x \leqslant 360°$

HINT

If one of the solutions was $x = 90°$, it would have been rejected. The reason is that the equation was multiplied by a factor $\cos x$ because there was a $\cos x$ in the denominator on the rhs of $2\sin x = \dfrac{\sin x}{\cos x}$. However, $\cos 90° = 0$, so this would have been incorrect. Take care when multiplying by trigonometric functions.

b $\sin^2(x - 30°) = \dfrac{1}{2}$

$\sin(x - 30°) = \pm\dfrac{1}{\sqrt{2}}$ Take the square root of both sides

Let $y = x - 30°$

So the solutions of $\sin y = \dfrac{1}{\sqrt{2}}$ in the interval $0° \leqslant x \leqslant 360°$ are

$y = 45°$ or $135°$ Recall that $\sin 45° = \dfrac{1}{\sqrt{2}}$

$x - 30° = 45°$ or $135°$ As $y = x - 30°$

$x = 75°$ or $165°$

The solutions of $\sin y = -\dfrac{1}{\sqrt{2}}$ in the interval $0° \leqslant x \leqslant 360°$ are

$y = -45°$ or $180° - (-45°)$ or $-45° + 360°$

$x - 30° = -45°$ or $225°$ or $315°$ As $y = x - 30°$

$x = -15°$ or $255°$ or $345°$

The solution $x = -15°$ is not in the range $0° \leqslant x \leqslant 360°$ so it is rejected.

The acceptable solutions are $x = 75°$ or $165°$ or $255°$ or $345°$

You may need to solve trigonometric equations in radians.

EXAMPLE 25

Find the values of x, in the interval $-\pi < x \leqslant \pi$, that satisfy the equation

$2\cos^2 x + 9\sin x = 3\sin^2 x$

Give your answers in radians correct to 3 significant figures.

$2\cos^2 x + 9\sin x = 3\sin^2 x$ Use $\cos^2 x + \sin^2 x = 1$ to replace $\cos^2 x = 1 - \sin^2 x$

$2(1 - \sin^2 x) + 9\sin x = 3\sin^2 x$

Let $\sin x = s$

$2 - 2s^2 + 9s = 3s^2$ Substitute $s = \sin x$

$5s^2 - 9s - 2 = 0$ Rearrange

$(5s + 1)(s - 2) = 0$ Factorise

$s = 2$ or $s = -\dfrac{1}{5}$

$\sin x = 2$ has no solutions

$\sin x = -\dfrac{1}{5}$

gives $x = -0.201$ (3 s.f.)

Use a calculator in 'rad' mode to get this solution. You can find another solution noting that $\sin(\pi - x) \equiv \sin x$ when x is in radians. This gives: $x = \pi - (-0.201) = 3.34$ (3 s.f.).

You can find further solutions considering $-0.201 \pm 2\pi$ and $3.34 \pm 2\pi$. You could also consider solutions like $-0.201 \pm 4\pi$, but it is clear that these would all be outside the interval $-\pi < x \leqslant \pi$.

EXERCISE 8

SKILLS

CRITICAL THINKING
PROBLEM SOLVING
ANALYSIS

1 ▶ Solve these equations for θ, in the interval $0° < \theta \leqslant 360°$.

   a $\cos\theta = \sqrt{3}\sin\theta$

   b $\sin\theta = -\cos\theta$

2 ▶ Solve $2\cos\theta - 3\sin\theta = 0$, $0 < \theta \leqslant 2\pi$ where θ is measured in radians.

3 ▶ Solve these equations for θ in the interval $0° < \theta \leqslant 360°$.

   a $4\cos^2\theta = 1$

   b $2\cos^2\theta = 5\cos\theta - 2$

   c $\sin\theta + 2\cos^2\theta + 1 = 0$

   d $4\cos^2\theta - 5\sin\theta = 5$

4 ▶ Solve these equations for x, in the interval $0 \leqslant x \leqslant 2\pi$. Give your answers to 3 significant figures or in the form $\dfrac{a}{b}\pi$, where a and b are integers.

   a $2\sin^2(x + \frac{\pi}{3}) = 1$

   b $6\sin^2 x + \cos x = 4$

   c $\cos^2 x - 6\sin x = 5$

EXAM PRACTICE: CHAPTER 11

1 The diagram below shows a sector of a circle of radius 6 cm with centre A. Given that the size of angle BAC is 0.95 radians, find

a the area of the sector ABC [2]

b the length of the arc BC. [2]

The point D lies on the line AC and is such that $AD = BD$. The length AD is 5.16 cm.

c Find the perimeter of R. [3]

d Find the area of R. [2]

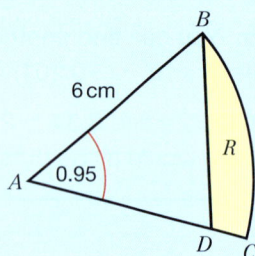

2

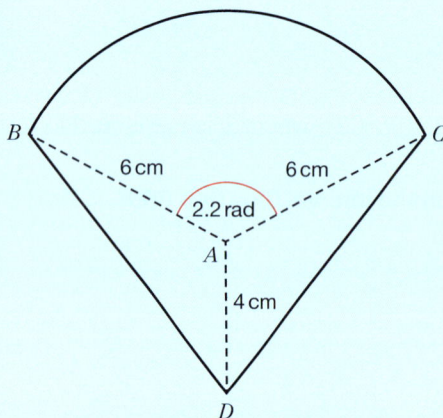

The shape BCD is shown above.

The straight lines DB and DC are equal in length. The curve BC is an arc of a circle with centre A and radius 6 cm. The size of $\angle BAC$ is 2.2 radians and $AD = 4$ cm.

a Show that the area of the sector BAC is 39.6 cm². [2]

b Calculate the size of $\angle DAC$, in radians. [3]

c Calculate the total area of the shape. [4]

3 In the triangle ABC, $AB = 11$ cm, $BC = 7$ cm and $CA = 8$ cm.

a Find the size of angle C, giving your answer in degrees to 3 significant figures. [2]

b Find the area of triangle ABC, giving your answer in cm² to 3 significant figures. [3]

4 Show that the area of a triangle is $\frac{1}{2}ab\sin C$ [3]

5 a Given that $\sin\theta = 5\cos\theta$, find $\tan\theta$.   [3]

   b Hence, or otherwise, find the values of θ in the interval $0° \leqslant \theta < 360°$ for which $\sin\theta = 5\cos\theta$.   [2]

6 Solve $2\cos 2x + 1 = 5\sin x$, for the interval $0 \leqslant x < 2\pi$.   [4]

7 Simplify

   a $\sin^2 3\theta - \sin^2 3\theta\cos^2 3\theta$ [4]

   b $\cos^4\theta + 2\sin^2\theta\cos^2\theta + \sin^4\theta$ [4]

8 a Given that $2(\sin x + 2\cos x) = \sin x + 5\cos x$, find the exact value of $\tan x$.   [4]

   b Given that $\sin x\cos y + 3\cos x\sin y = 2\sin x\sin y - 4\cos x\cos y$, express $\tan y$ in terms of $\tan x$.   [4]

9 Find, giving your answers in terms of π, all values of θ in the interval $0 < \theta < 2\pi$ for which

   a $\tan\left(\theta + \frac{\pi}{3}\right) = 1$ [3]

   b $\sin 2\theta = -\frac{\sqrt{3}}{2}$ [4]

10 Find the values of x in the interval $0° \leqslant x \leqslant 360°$ for $2\sin x = \cos(x - 60°)$.   [4]

11 Prove that $(\cos\theta - \tan\theta)^2 + (\sin\theta + 1)^2 \equiv 2 + \tan^2\theta$ [4]

12 a Sketch, for $0 \leqslant x \leqslant 2\pi$, the graph of $y = \sin\left(x + \frac{\pi}{6}\right)$.   [3]

   b Write down the exact coordinates of the points where the graph meets the axes.   [1]

13 Solve $3\sin^2\theta - 2\cos^2\theta = 1$ for the interval $0° \leqslant \theta < 360°$.   [4]

14 Prove that $\dfrac{\cos A}{\sin B} - \dfrac{\sin A}{\cos B} \equiv \dfrac{\cos(A + B)}{\sin B\cos B}$ [5]

15 The region R is bounded by the curve $y = \sin 2x$, the x-axis and the vertical lines $x = 0$ and $x = \frac{\pi}{2}$. Find the volume of the solid formed when the region is rotated 2π radians about the x-axis.   [6]

CHAPTER SUMMARY: CHAPTER 11

- 1 radian $= \dfrac{180}{\pi}$ degrees
- The length of an arc of a circle is $l = r\theta$
- The area of a sector is $A = \dfrac{1}{2}r^2\theta$

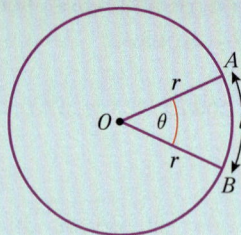

- The sine rule is

$$\frac{a}{\sin A} = \frac{b}{\sin B} = \frac{c}{\sin C}$$

or

$$\frac{\sin A}{a} = \frac{\sin B}{b} = \frac{\sin C}{c}$$

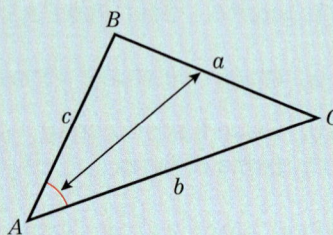

- The cosine rule is

$$a^2 = b^2 + c^2 - 2bc\cos A$$

or

$$b^2 = a^2 + c^2 - 2ac\cos B$$

or

$$c^2 = a^2 + b^2 - 2ab\cos C$$

- You can find an unknown angle using rearranged form of the cosine rule

$$\cos A = \frac{b^2 + c^2 - a^2}{2bc} \quad \text{or} \quad \cos B = \frac{a^2 + c^2 - b^2}{2ac} \quad \text{or} \quad \cos C = \frac{a^2 + b^2 - c^2}{2ab}$$

- You can find the area of a triangle using the formula

Area $= \dfrac{1}{2}ab\sin C$

if you know the length of two sides (a and b) and the value of the angle C between them

- You need to know these identities

  - $\tan\theta \equiv \dfrac{\sin\theta}{\cos\theta}$

  - $\sin^2\theta + \cos^2\theta \equiv 1$

  - $\sin(A + B) \equiv \sin A\cos B + \cos A\sin B$

  - $\cos(A + B) \equiv \cos A\cos B - \sin A\sin B$

  - $\tan(A + B) \equiv \dfrac{\tan A + \tan B}{1 - \tan A\tan B}$

- The table below will help you solve trigonometrical equations

EQUATION	1st SOLUTION (CALC)	2nd SOLUTION	3rd SOLUTION	4th SOLUTION
$\sin x = k$	α	$180° - \alpha$	All cases are $\pm 360°$	All cases are 2nd solution $\pm 360°$
$\cos x = k$	α	$360° - \alpha$		
$\tan x = k$	α	$180° + \alpha$		

GLOSSARY

acceleration the rate at which the velocity of an object increases

adjacent next to one another

approximation 'approximate' means 'almost exact'

area of a triangle $\frac{1}{2}ab\sin C$

arithmetic sequence where the terms have a **common difference**

asymptote a line that a curve approaches, but never reaches

attribute if people *attribute* something to a person, they believe that person did it, said it, etc

base of a logarithm $y = \lg x$ means the same as $10^y = x$. Here the *base* of the logarithm is 10. Another common base is the constant e. In this case can write $\log_e x$ as $\ln x$

bearing an angle measured clockwise from north. Always expressed with three digits, e.g. 045°

beehive a container where people keep bees

binomial series means the same as 'Binomial Expansion'

calculus the part of mathematics that deals with changing quantities, such as the speed of a falling object or the slope of a curve

Cartesian describes the standard x-y graph and its axes

chain rule $\frac{dy}{dx} = \frac{dy}{du} \times \frac{du}{dx}$

chime (of a clock) to sound a small bell

coefficient in the expression $3x^2 + 4x + 2$, 3 is the *coefficent* of x^2 and 4 is the *coefficient* of x

column vector e.g. $\begin{pmatrix} x \\ y \end{pmatrix}$

common difference the difference between any two consecutive terms in an arithmetic sequence (or series), shared by (*common* to) the whole sequence. In the arithmetic sequence 2, 4, 6, 8, 10 ... the *common difference* is 2

common ratio the same as a common difference (above), except that multiplication rather than addition is used. In the geometric sequence 2, 4, 8, 16, 32 ... the *common ratio* is 2

cosine rule $a^2 = b^2 + c^2 - 2bc\cos A$

constant a term that does not include a variable. In the expression $3x^2 + 4x + 2$, 2 is a *constant*

cube a six-sided solid whose sides are all squares

cuboid a six-sided solid whose sides are all rectangles, placed at right angles

dam a wall built across a river or stream to stop the water from flowing, especially in order to make a lake or produce electricity

deduce to reach a logical conclusion. If $x + 2 = 3$, you *deduce* that $x = 1$

derivative, derived function the result of differentiating

determine to find out. By analysing the equation of a curve, you can *determine* whether it is a circle or not

displacement change of position

divisible able to be divided without remainder. $x^2 + 3x + 2 = (x + 1)(x + 2)$, hence $x^2 + 3x + 2$ is *divisible* by $(x + 1)$ and $(x + 2)$, but no other expression

due north/south/east/west *directly* to the north/south/east/west

earnings the money that you receive for the work that you do

elongated longer than usual

equivalent having the same value or meaning as something else

expansion multiplying out terms in brackets. The opposite of **factorisation**

exponential function a function where the variable occurs as an exponent, e.g. $e^{2x + 1}$

factor theorem if f(x) is a polynomial and f$(p) = 0$ then $(x - p)$ is a factor of f(x)

factorial the result when you multiply an integer by all the integers below it, down to 1. It is written as an exclamation mark. $5! = 5 \times 4 \times 3 \times 2 \times 1$

factorise to rewrite an expression using brackets. You *factorise* $x^2 + 3x + 2$ to get $(x + 1)(x + 2)$

finite having an end

fluctuate if an amount *fluctuates*, it keeps changing both up and down

function $x + 2, 2x, x^2, \ln x, \sin x, e^x$ and so on are *functions* of x. An equation such as $y = 2x^2 + x$ can be written as f$(x) = 2x^2 + x$

geometric sequence (or **series**) each term is multiplied by a multiplier to produce the next term. 2, 4, 8, 16, 32 ... is a *geometric sequence* where the multiplier is 2

global warming the gradual heating up of the Earth

gradient slope

graph (verb) to draw a mathematical function as a graph

graphical calculator a calculator that can display graphs

hemisphere half of a sphere

hence means the same as 'therefore': $2x = 6$, *hence* $x = 3$

hexagon a shape with six sides

identity (e.g. trigonometrical identity) a statement which is always true, wherever the value of the variables involved. $\tan \theta \equiv \dfrac{\sin \theta}{\cos \theta}$ is an identity. Notice that you show this by using $\equiv$ instead of $=$

inequality the opposite of an equation. The equals sign $(=)$ is replaced by an *inequality* sign: $>$, $\geqslant$, $<$, $\leqslant$, $<>$ or $\neq$. For example '$x \geqslant 1$' means 'x is greater than or equal to 1'

infinite series doesn't end

integer a whole number

intercept where curves or lines cross the x-axis or y-axis

interpret to explain the meaning of something

interval the *interval* of $\int_a^b x \, \mathrm{d}x$ is $[a, b]$

invest to give money to a company such as a bank in order to obtain a profit

kinematics the study of moving objects

landslide a sudden fall of a lot of earth or rocks down a hill, cliff etc

legend a historical story that may not be true

LHS left-hand side

linear where the variables have the power 1. Hence $y = 2x + 3$ is *linear* but $y = x^2$ and $y = \dfrac{1}{x}$ (i.e. $y = x^{-1}$) are not. A *linear function* can be represented by a *straight line*

linear growth where the value over time can be expressed as a straight line

linear programming solving a problem by drawing graphs of inequalities

linear relationship where the power of the variables is 1. $y = 4x + 1$ (i.e. $y^1 = 4x^1 + 1$) shows a *linear relationship* between x and y, which can be plotted as a *line*. On the other hand, $y = x^2 + x + 1$, $y = \dfrac{1}{x}$, $y = \sin x$, $y = \lg(x)$ and $y = \mathrm{e}^x$ show *non-linear* relationships between x and y, which produce *curves*

local a *local* maximum is greater than *nearby* values on the curve, but not necessarily greater than values *further away*

long division in algebra, a method of dividing one polynomial by another

magnitude if a **vector** is drawn on a graph, its magnitude (or *size* or *modulus*) is the distance from the origin to its tip. The magnitude is not a vector itself, but a scalar.
By Pythagoras, the magnitude of $\begin{pmatrix} x \\ y \end{pmatrix}$ is $\sqrt{x^2 + y^2}$

manipulate (a mathematical expression) to work on it so as to change it into a simpler or more useful form

mathematical modelling using mathematics to understand and/or solve a real-world problem

midpoint a point that is half of the way through or along something

modulus of a vector the vector's **magnitude**

modulus the positive value of an expression, shown as $|x|$. $|1|$ and $|-1|$ are both equal to $+1$. Useful in statements such as $|x| < 1$, meaning that x is a fraction between -1 and $+1$. Note that the modulus of a *vector* has a different meaning

multiply out expand. If you *multiply out* $(x + 1)(x + 2)$, you get $x^2 + 3x + 2$

non-perfect square an expression that can't be factorised into the form $(ax \pm b)^2$

normal is perpendicular to a tangent

obtuse between $90°$ and $180°$ ($\dfrac{\pi}{2}$ and π)

outcome the final result of something – used especially when no one knows what it will be until it actually happens

overlap if two or more things *overlap*, part of one thing covers part of another

parallel two lines that are the same distance apart along their whole length

parallelogram a quadrilateral in which opposite sides are parallel and equal

Pascal's triangle a triangle of numbers where each number is the two numbers above it added together except for the edges, which are all 1.

per annum for each year

perfect square an expression that can be factorised into the form $(ax \pm b)^2$

perimeter the whole length of the border around an area or shape

period how often a curve repeats itself. $y = \sin\theta$ has a period of $360°$ (2π)

perpendicular gradient the gradient of a line at right angles (*perpendicular*) to another line

plane a flat surface, for example the side of a cuboid

plot a small piece of land for building or growing things on

polynomial usually has three or more terms, e.g. $x^2 + 5x + 2$

product rule if $y = uv$ then $\dfrac{dy}{dx} = u\dfrac{dv}{dx} + v\dfrac{du}{dx}$

quadratic an expression such as $x^2 + 2x + 3$, containing a variable to the power of 2 (but no higher)

quadrilateral a shape that has four sides

quotient rule $\dfrac{dy}{dx} = \dfrac{v\dfrac{du}{dx} - u\dfrac{dv}{dx}}{v^2}$

radians π radians $= 180$ degrees

rational any real number, including integers, that can be written as a fraction, even if it produces a repeating decimal. Many functions are irrational: most roots, logarithms and trigonometrical functions, and the constants π and e

rational exponent a rational power e.g. $(a + b)^3$, $(a + b)^{-3}$, $(a + b)^{\frac{2}{7}}$, $(a + b)^{-\frac{2}{7}}$. An expression with a rational *power* may not produce a rational *number*

real any number representing a quantity. 3, -3, $\sqrt{3}$, $\dfrac{1}{3}$, lg 3, sin 3, π and e are all real. $\sqrt{-3}$ and $\ln(-3)$ are both *unreal*. Not all real numbers are *rational*

rebound bounce

reciprocal $\dfrac{31}{4}$ is the *reciprocal* of $\dfrac{4}{31}$, and vice versa

reciprocal function $y = \dfrac{k}{x}$ where k is a constant. Called 'reciprocal' because the variable x has been moved to the denominator; the reciprocal of x is $\dfrac{1}{x}$

rectangular Cartesian coordinates (x, y)

recurrence relationship where the next term of a sequence is derived from the preceding term(s). The pattern repeats itself (*recurs*) throughout the sequence

remainder the expression left over after dividing

remainder theorem if a polynomial f(x) is divided by $(ax - b)$ then the remainder is f$\left(\dfrac{b}{a}\right)$

RHS right-hand side

rotate to turn around an axis or centre

rules of indices how to combine powers, e.g. $x^2 \times x^3 = x^5$

satisfy if a statement is true when another is true, the first *satisfies* the second. The statement $x = 2$ *satisfies* the equation $(x - 1)(x - 2) = 0$

savings account a bank account in which you keep money that you want to save, and which pays you interest on that money

scalar a single quantity (unlike a vector). A vector multiplied by a scalar gives another vector: $\begin{pmatrix} x \\ y \end{pmatrix} \times 3 = \begin{pmatrix} 3x \\ 3y \end{pmatrix}$

sector a part of a circle bounded by an arc and two radii

segment part of a line between two points

sequence a set of terms in which each term is defined by the previous one(s). A sequence may be arithmetic (3, 5, 7, 9, 11 ...), geometric (3, 6, 12, 24, 48 ...), Fibonacci (0, 1, 1, 2, 3...) and so on

series a **sequence** in which the terms are added together: $3 + 5 + 7 + 9 + 11$ ..

shift a change in position

Sigma notation/$\sum$ notation uses the Greek 'S' to indicate a Sum of elements, for example in a series

similar triangles have equal angles but not necessarily equal sides

simultaneous equations two or more equations, including two or more variables, that must be solved together. If the equations are linear, you will need as many equations as variables. $y = x + 1$ and $3y = 7x - 5$ are two simultaneous equations in two variables.

sine rule $\dfrac{a}{\sin A} = \dfrac{b}{\sin B} = \dfrac{c}{\sin C}$ or $\dfrac{\sin A}{a} = \dfrac{\sin B}{b} = \dfrac{\sin C}{c}$

size of a vector is the vector's **magnitude**

sketch (noun or verb) a sketch is a drawing that explains something without necessarily being accurate

spot to detect something that is hard to see

straight line graph where the variables have a **linear relationship**

stretch normally means 'enlarge in length, width, height or depth' but in mathematics it can also mean 'reduce in length, width, height or depth'

substitute to replace something (e.g. a variable) with something else (e.g. a value). Let $y = x + 1$. If you substitute $x = 2$, you find that $y = 2 + 1 = 3$

subtend the angle subtended by an arc is the angle at the centre of the circle formed by the two radii

tangent a line that touches a curve but does not cross it

tend to move in a particular direction

term a separate part of a mathematical expression. The function $ax^2 + bx + c$ has three terms. The sequence 1, 3, 5, 7 has four terms

the binomial coefficients the numbers preceding the variables in a binomial expansion. The expansion of $(a + b)^4$ is $(1)a^4$, $4a^3b$, $6a^2b^2$, $4ab^3$, $(1)b^4$. Here the binomial coefficients are 1, 4, 6, 4, 1

the binomial theorem shows how to expand expressions of the form $(a + b)^n$

the generalised binomial theorem the version (discovered by Newton) used nowadays.

to round (a number) **up** to increase a decimal fraction to the nearest whole number

transformation altering a curve or shape by using arithmetic to change its mathematical definition. Examples are **translation**, rotation, reflection and enlargement

translation (in mathematics) movement from one position to another

triangle pattern Pascal's triangle

variable a mathematical quantity that can represent different (varying) amounts, usually represented by a single letter such as x

vector a quantity that has both size and direction

vertex (plural **vertices**) where two lines meet at an angle, especially in a shape such as a triangle

visual realisation something, e.g. a mathematical expression, represented in a form like something that can be seen in the real world

vital very important

volume of revolution the volume of a solid formed by rotating a curve around a line (usually an axis)

x-intercept/y-intercept where the line or curve crosses the x-axis/y-axis

ANSWERS

CHAPTER 1 – SURDS AND LOGARITHMIC FUNCTIONS

STARTER ACTIVITIES

1 ▶ a y^{11} **b** $8q^7$ **c** $27k^6$
d x^8 **e** a^5 **f** $16x^3y^4$

2 ▶ a $m^{\frac{3}{2}}$ **b** $3p^{\frac{7}{2}}$ **c** $4c^{\frac{1}{3}}$
d 18 **e** $3p^{\frac{1}{2}}$ **f** $15y^{-1}$

3 ▶ a 4 **b** 5 **c** $\frac{1}{64}$
d $-\frac{1}{8}$ **e** 1 **f** $\frac{1}{3}$
g $\frac{64}{27}$

EXERCISE 1

1 ▶ a $3\sqrt{2}$ **b** $5\sqrt{2}$ **c** $5\sqrt{5}$
d $8\sqrt{2}$ **e** $2\sqrt{33}$ **f** $5\sqrt{345}$

2 ▶ a $\sqrt{15}$ **b** $\frac{3}{2}\sqrt{15}$ **c** $\sqrt{2}$
d $\frac{\sqrt{17}}{2}$ **e** $\frac{2\sqrt{6}}{3}$

3 ▶ a $4\sqrt{3}$ **b** $9\sqrt{3}$ **c** $\sqrt{7}+4\sqrt{43}$
d $24\sqrt{3}$ **e** $58\sqrt{2}$ **f** 30
g 168 **h** 192

4 ▶ a $24-12\sqrt{3}$ **b** $54-27\sqrt{29}$ **c** $13+10\sqrt{3}$
d $-8\sqrt{7}-2\sqrt{2}$ **e** 13 **f** $26-5\sqrt{42}$
g 3

5 ▶ 22.4%

6 ▶ $34+9\sqrt{2}$

EXERCISE 2

1 ▶ a $\frac{\sqrt{13}}{13}$ **b** $\frac{\sqrt{7}}{7}$ **c** $\frac{2\sqrt{3}}{3}$
d $\sqrt{2}$ **e** $4\sqrt{3}$ **f** $\sqrt{15}$
g $\frac{3\sqrt{6}}{2}$ **h** $2+\sqrt{3}$

2 ▶ a $2-\sqrt{2}$ **b** $7+4\sqrt{3}$ **c** $-5+2\sqrt{6}$
d $6\sqrt{6}-14$ **e** $4+\sqrt{10}$ **f** $\frac{5+\sqrt{21}}{2}$
g $\frac{19+\sqrt{55}}{34}$ **h** $\frac{10\sqrt{30}-8\sqrt{10}-15\sqrt{42}+12\sqrt{14}}{118}$
i $\sqrt{2}$ **j** $\frac{a\sqrt{b}+b\sqrt{a}}{a-b}$ **k** $\frac{a\sqrt{b}+b\sqrt{a}}{ab}$

EXERCISE 3

1 ▶
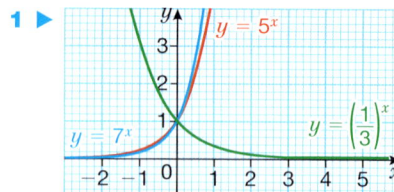

2 ▶
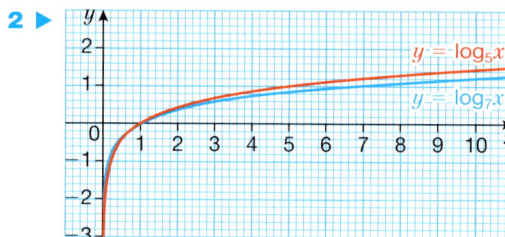

c Intersection occurs at $(1, 0)$.

3 ▶
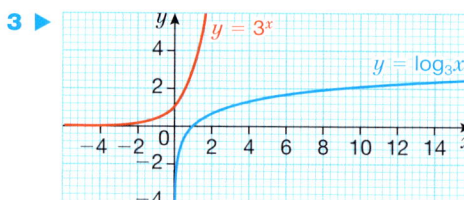

4 ▶
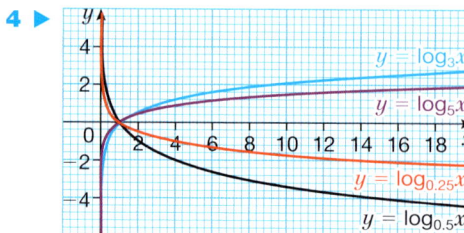

EXERCISE 4

1 ▶ a
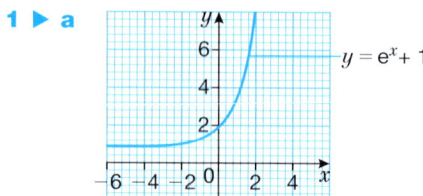

b
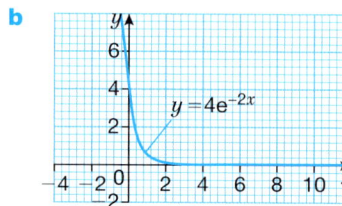

c

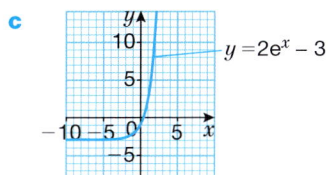

$y = 2e^x - 3$

d

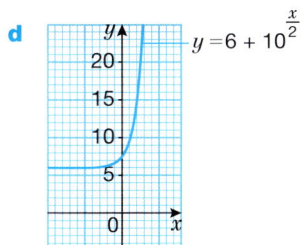

$y = 6 + 10^{\frac{x}{2}}$

e

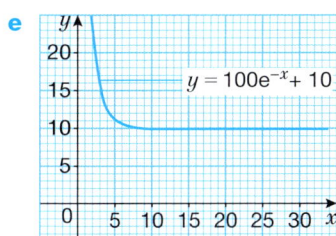

$y = 100e^{-x} + 10$

2 ▶ a Intersection at (0, 0)

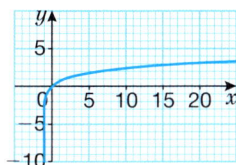

Vertical asymptote. $x = -1$

b Intersection at (1, 0), asymptote y-axis

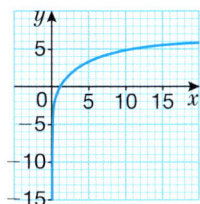

Vertical asymptote. $x = 0$

c Intersection at (0.5, 0), asymptote y-axis

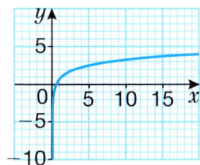

Vertical asymptote. $x = 0$

d Intersection at (3, 0)

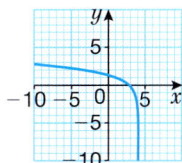

Vertical asymptote. $x = 4$

e Intersection at $x = -2 + \exp(-4)$, which is about −1.98

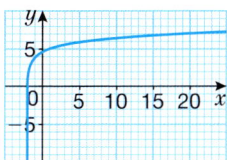

Vertical asymptote. $x = -2$

EXERCISE 5

1 ▶ a

$y = 3 + 2e^{-\frac{1}{2}x}$

b

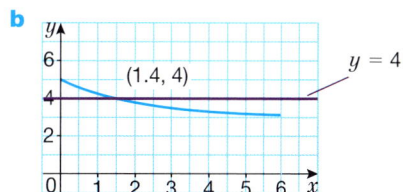

(1.4, 4) $y = 4$

The solution is approximately $x = 1.4$

c

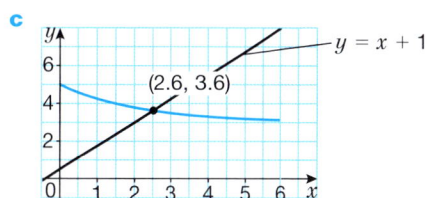

$y = x + 1$ (2.6, 3.6)

The solution is approximately $x = 2.6$

2 ▶ a

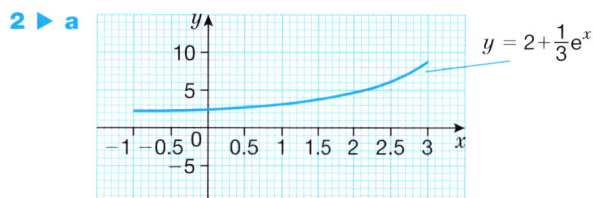

$y = 2 + \frac{1}{3}e^x$

b

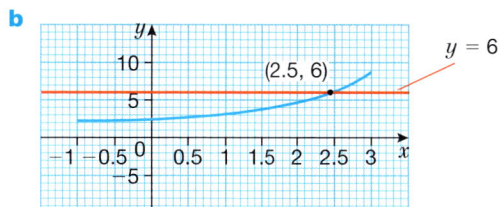

(2.5, 6) $y = 6$

The solution is approximately $x = 2.5$

c

(0.7, 2.6) $y = 4 - 2x$

The solution is approximately $x = 0.7$

3 ▶ a $x = 30, y = 2.60; x = 75, y = 1.98$

b

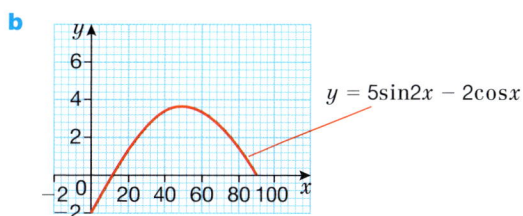

$y = 5\sin 2x - 2\cos x$

c $2 + 2\cos x = 5\sin 2x$
$\Rightarrow 2 = 5\sin 2x - 2\cos x$

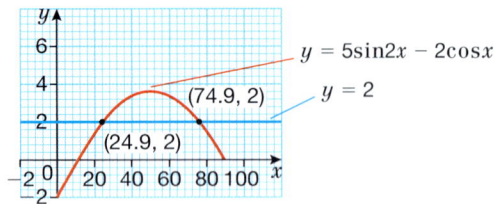

The two points of intersection are approximately at (24.9, 2) and (74.9, 2)

EXERCISE 6

1 ▶ a $\log_4 64 = 3$
b $\log_5\left(\dfrac{1}{25}\right) = -2$
c $\log_8(262\,144) = 6$
d $\log_3 9 = x$
e $\log_8 1 = x$
f $\log_2\left(\dfrac{1}{4}\right) = x$

2 ▶ a $3^4 = 81$
b $3^6 = 729$
c $5^4 = 625$
d $16^{\frac{1}{2}} = 4$
e $3^{-3} = \dfrac{1}{27}$
f $10^{-2} = 0.01$

3 ▶ a 2
b 3
c 4
d 4
e −3
f $\dfrac{1}{2}$
g $\dfrac{3}{2}$
h $\dfrac{1}{5}$

4 ▶ a 81
b 216
c 4
d 8
e 512

5 ▶ a 1.30
b 1.15
c −0.602
d −0.523
e 1.74

EXERCISE 7

1 ▶ a $\log_4 64$
b $\log_9 6$
c $\log_5 81$
d $\log_4 120$
e $-36\log_6 3$
f $\log_2 45$
g $\log_8 2$
h $\log_{12} 144$
i $\lg 10$

2 ▶ a $4\log_a x + 3\log_a y + \log_a z$ **b** $6\log_a x - 3\log_a y$
c $2\log_a x + 2\log_a z$
d $-\log_a x - \log_a y - \log_a z$
e $\dfrac{1}{2}\log_a x + \dfrac{1}{2}\log_a y$
f $2\log_a x + \log_a y + \dfrac{3}{2}\log_a z$
g $\dfrac{3}{2}\log_a x + \dfrac{7}{2}\log_a y - 3\log_a z$

EXERCISE 8

1 ▶ a 3.21
b 1.68
c 1.93
d 0.558
e −0.719

2 ▶ a 1.51
b 3.01
c 0.406
d 2.59
e 1.46
f 1
g 0.861

3 ▶ a $x = 512, x = \dfrac{1}{2}$
b $x = 216, x = 6$
c $x = \dfrac{1}{10}, x = \dfrac{1}{100\,000}$
d $x = 2^{\frac{4}{3}}$

EXERCISE 9

1 ▶ a $x = 1.79$
b $x = 1.86$
c $x = 1.91$
d $x = -0.712$
e $x = 1.45$
f $x = 0.421$

g $x = -3.71$
h $x = -58.4$
i $x = 4.99$
j $x = 0.542$

2 ▶ a $x = 0.792$
b $x = 1.23$ or -0.0733
c $x = 1.21$
d $x = 0.161$
e $x = 0, 1.26$
f $x = 2.00$

EXAM PRACTICE QUESTIONS

1 ▶ $7\sqrt{2}$

2 ▶ $3\sqrt{2} - 2$

3 ▶ a $16 - 4\sqrt{5}$
b $4 - \sqrt{5}$

4 ▶ $2\sqrt{3}$

5 ▶ $5 - \sqrt{5}$

6 ▶

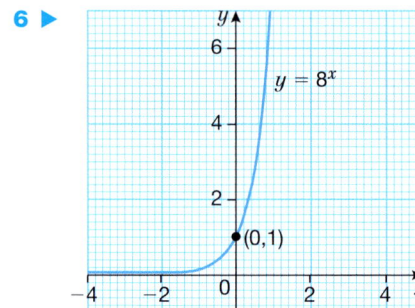

The graph crosses the y-axis at (0, 1)

7 ▶ $x = 0.739$

8 ▶ a $y = 6x^2$
$\log_6 y = \log_6 (6x^2)$
$\log_6 y = \log_6 6 + \log_6 (x^2)$
$\log_6 y = 1 + 2\log_6 x$
b $x = 9$ or $\dfrac{1}{3}$

9 ▶ $x = 6$ or 3

10 ▶ $y = 8$ or $\dfrac{1}{8}$

11 ▶ $y = \dfrac{1}{8}b^5$

12 ▶ $x = 1$ or 1.21

13 ▶ $x = 1.43$

14 ▶ $b = \left(\dfrac{1}{9}\right)(a - 5)$

15 ▶ $x = \dfrac{8}{9}$

16 ▶ $t = 0.683$

17 ▶ a $4 + p$
b $4p - 1$
c $x = 2\sqrt{2}$

18 ▶ $t = 1$

19 ▶ a

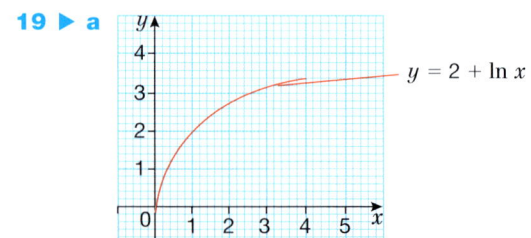

b Accept 1.6–1.7 range of answers

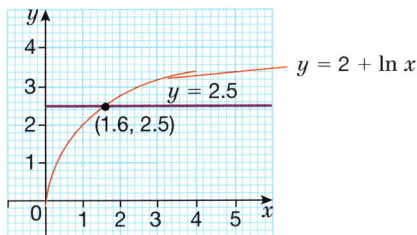

c Accept 0.1 to 0.2 and 3.1 to 3.2 as a range of answers

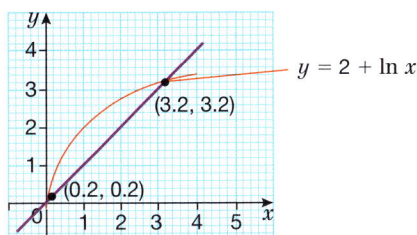

CHAPTER 2 – THE QUADRATIC FUNCTION

STARTER ACTIVITIES

1 ▶ a $3x(2x + 3)$ b $2b(b + 4)$

   c $9m(qm - 3)$ d $9xy(y + 4x)$

   e $8x(3 - 8x)$

2 ▶ a $(x + 3)(x + 6)$ b $(x - 3)(x - 4)$

   c $(x + 1)(x - 3)$ d $(x + 3)(x + 12)$

   e $(x + 3)(x + 9)$

3 ▶ a $(x + 3)(x - 3)$ b $(x + 5)(x - 5)$

   c $(3x + 4)(3x - 4)$ d $(5x + 4)(5x - 4)$

EXERCISE 1

1 ▶ a $(x - 3)(3x + 2)$ b $(2x + 1)(x + 5)$

   c $(2x + 1)(x - 4)$ d $(5x - 1)(x - 3)$

   e $(3x - 4)(2x + 3)$ f $(3x - 1)^2$

   g $(3x + 1)(3x - 7)$

2 ▶ a $x = -2$ or $-\dfrac{1}{2}$ b $x = -4$ or $x = -\dfrac{1}{4}$

   c $x = 4$ or $x = \dfrac{1}{3}$ d $x = 1$ or $\dfrac{2}{3}$

   e $x = -6$ or $\dfrac{1}{3}$ f $x = \dfrac{1}{5}$ or -3

   g $x = \dfrac{2}{3}$

EXERCISE 2

1 ▶ a $(x + 2)^2 - 4$ b $(x - 8)^2 - 64$

   c $3(x - 4)^2 - 48$ d $\left(x - \dfrac{1}{2}\right)^2 - \dfrac{49}{4}$

   e $\left(x + \dfrac{1}{2}\right)^2 - \dfrac{5}{4}$ f $3(x - 1)^2 - 2$

   g $2\left(x + \dfrac{3}{4}\right)^2 - \dfrac{17}{8}$ h $4\left(x + \dfrac{3}{4}\right)^2 - \dfrac{13}{4}$

2 ▶ a $x = -\dfrac{2}{3}, x = \dfrac{5}{2}$ b $x = \sqrt{3} - 1, -\sqrt{3} - 1$

   c $x = \dfrac{\sqrt{7} \pm 3}{2}$ d $x = -\dfrac{3}{4} \pm \dfrac{\sqrt{57}}{4}$

   e $x = 15, x = -\dfrac{1}{4}$ f $x = -1 \pm \dfrac{\sqrt{13}}{2}$

   g $x = -\dfrac{3}{2} \pm \dfrac{\sqrt{39}}{2}$ h $x = \dfrac{1}{8} \pm \dfrac{\sqrt{129}}{8}$

EXERCISE 3

1 ▶ a $x = 0, 6$ b $x = 0, x = -25$

   c $x = 3, -2$ d $p = 2 \pm \sqrt{2}$

   e $m = -1 \pm \sqrt{3}$ f $x = -5, -2$

   g $t = 6, -1$ h $x = 5, -7$

   i $n = 2$ j $x = -3 \pm \sqrt{3}$

2 ▶ a $x = \dfrac{1 + \sqrt{26}}{3}, x = \dfrac{1 - \sqrt{26}}{3}$

   b $x = \dfrac{3 + \sqrt{3}}{3}, x = \dfrac{3 - \sqrt{3}}{3}$

   c $x = \dfrac{3}{2}, x = -\dfrac{2}{3}$

   d $x = \dfrac{-3 + \sqrt{17}}{4}, x = \dfrac{-3 - \sqrt{17}}{4}$

   e $x = -\dfrac{1}{2}, x = -3$

   f $x = \dfrac{-7 + \sqrt{37}}{6}, x = \dfrac{-7 - \sqrt{37}}{6}$

   g $x = \dfrac{5}{2}, x = \dfrac{3}{2}$

   h $x = \dfrac{-5 + \sqrt{109}}{14}, x = \dfrac{-5 - \sqrt{109}}{14}$

   i $x = \dfrac{15 + \sqrt{545}}{20}, x = \dfrac{15 - \sqrt{545}}{20}$

   j $x = \dfrac{-3 + \sqrt{33}}{2}, x = \dfrac{-3 - \sqrt{33}}{2}$

   k $x = 3\sqrt{7} + 7, x = -3\sqrt{7} + 7$

   l $x = \dfrac{-15 + \sqrt{17}}{8}, x = \dfrac{-15 - \sqrt{17}}{8}$

3 ▶ $x = 2.26$

EXERCISE 4

1 ▶ a One repeated root   **b** Two distinct real roots

   c Two distinct real roots   **d** No roots

   e One repeated root   **f** Two distinct real roots

   g No roots   **h** Two distinct real roots

   i No roots   **j** One repeated root

   k No roots

2 ▶ $p > -\dfrac{1}{7}$ where $p \neq 0$

3 ▶ $m = \dfrac{1}{3}$

EXERCISE 5

1 ▶ a $x^2 + 8x - 1 = 0$

   b $x^2 - 6x + 8 = 0$

2 ▶ a $x^2 - 8 = 0$

   b $x^2 - 34x + 1 = 0$

3 ▶ a $x^2 + x - 1 = 0$

   b $x^2 - x - 1 = 0$

EXAM PRACTICE QUESTIONS

1 ▶ a i $3x^2 + 56x + 3 = 0$

    ii $9x^2 - 90x + 14 = 0$

   b $\dfrac{5}{3} \pm \dfrac{\sqrt{31}}{3}$

2 ▶ $5x^2 + 9x - 15 = 0$

3 ▶ a $\alpha + \beta = 7$ and $\alpha^2 + \beta^2 = 25$

    $(\alpha + \beta)^2 = 7^2$

    $\alpha^2 + 2\alpha\beta + \beta^2 = 49$

    $\alpha^2 + \beta^2 + 2\alpha\beta = 49$

    $25 + 2\alpha\beta = 49$

    $2\alpha\beta = 24$

    $\alpha\beta = 12$

   b $x^2 - 7x + 12 = 0$

   c $12x^2 - 25x + 12 = 0$

4 ▶ a $a = 1$, $b = (p - 3)$ and $c = (3 - 2p)$

    $b^2 - 4ac > 0$

    $(p - 3)^2 - 4 \times 1 \times (3 - 2p) > 0$

    $p^2 - 6p + 9 - 12 + 8p > 0$

    $p^2 + 2p - 3 > 0$

   b $p > 1$ or $p < -3$

5 ▶ a $x^2 + 6x + 11$

    $x^2 + 6x + 9 - 9 + 11$

    $(x + 3)^2 + 2$

   b -8

6 ▶ a $(x + 3)(5x + 1)$ **b** $(x - 1)(3x - 4)$

7 ▶ a $p = -1, -2$ **b** $x = \dfrac{2}{3}$ or -5

8 ▶ a $\dfrac{-3 \pm \sqrt{29}}{10}$ **b** $\dfrac{5 \pm \sqrt{7}}{2}$

9 ▶ a $a = -2, b = -1$ **b** 3

10 ▶ $x = 0, x = \dfrac{2}{3}$

CHAPTER 3 – INEQUALITIES AND IDENTITIES

STARTER ACTIVITIES

1 ▶ a $(9, 6)$ **b** $(4, 2)$ **c** $(6, 1)$ **d** $(-3, 2)$

2 ▶

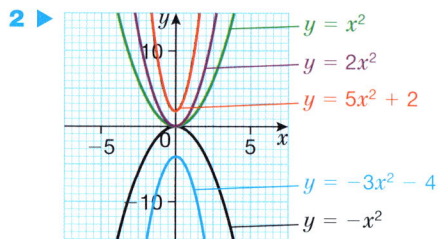

3 ▶ a 17.4 **b** 18.4 **c** 17.0 **d** 38.9

EXERCISE 1

1 ▶ a $(1, 2), (-2, -1)$ **b** $(2, 5), (1, 3)$

   c $(2, 1), (1, 2)$ **d** $(2, 5), (-2, -3)$

   e $(2, -1), (3, 1)$

   f $(5, 1), (-3, -3)$

   g $(-3, 4), \left(\dfrac{7}{2}, -\dfrac{5}{2}\right)$ **h** $(2, -1), \left(-\dfrac{7}{8}, \dfrac{19}{4}\right)$

   i $\left(-\dfrac{3}{2}, \dfrac{9}{4}\right), \left(4, -\dfrac{1}{2}\right)$ **j** $\left(\dfrac{21}{4}, \dfrac{8}{3}\right), (2, 7)$

   k $\left(0, \dfrac{7}{2}\right), (-3, -4)$ **l** $\left(\dfrac{13}{4}, \dfrac{5}{8}\right), \left(\dfrac{7}{2}, \dfrac{1}{2}\right)$

   m $(6, 3), (2, 7)$

2 ▶ a $(0, 0), (-3, 3), (4, 108)$ **b** $(0, 0), (2, 14), (-1, -4)$

   c $(0, 0), (0.5, -1.75), (3, -18)$

   d $(0, 0), (-2, 10), (1.5, 3)$

EXERCISE 2

1 ▶ **a** $x < 2$　　**b** $x > \dfrac{12}{7}$　　**c** $x \geq \dfrac{1}{2}$

d $x \geq \dfrac{1}{3}$　　**e** $x > -\dfrac{4}{41}$　　**f** $x < \dfrac{2}{13}$

g $x \leq -55$　　**h** $x \geq -\dfrac{17}{5}$

2 ▶ **a** $x \geq -\dfrac{7}{2}$　　**b** $x < -5$　　**c** $x > -22$

d $x \leq -\dfrac{11}{5}$　　**e** $x \geq \dfrac{3}{13}$　　**f** $x > -\dfrac{7}{3}$

g $x \geq \dfrac{43}{25}$　　**h** $x < \dfrac{1}{9}$

3 ▶ **a** $x > \dfrac{5}{2}$　　**b** $x > \dfrac{1}{5}$　　**c** $\dfrac{1}{7} \leq x \leq \dfrac{21}{11}$

d No solution　　**e** $x \geq \dfrac{31}{18}$　　**f** $-10 < x < -\dfrac{1}{13}$

EXERCISE 3

1 ▶ **a** $-3 < x < 2$　　**b** $-3 \leq x \leq 4$

c $-4 < x < -\dfrac{3}{2}$　　**d** $-\dfrac{8}{7} < x < \dfrac{2}{3}$

e $x \leq -\dfrac{1}{2}$ and $x \geq \dfrac{3}{4}$　　**f** $\dfrac{3}{4} \leq x \leq \dfrac{7}{5}$

2 ▶ **a** $-2 < x < 9$　　**b** $x = -3$

c $x \leq -12, x \geq -1$　　**d** $4 < x < 10$

e $x < -4, x > -3$　　**f** $-\dfrac{4}{7} \leq x \leq 5$

g $x < -7, x > -\dfrac{3}{2}$　　**h** $-\dfrac{9}{5} < x < 2$

i $x \leq -3, x \geq \dfrac{2}{3}$　　**j** $-5 \leq x \leq 5$

k $x \leq -4, x \geq 4$

EXERCISE 4

1 ▶ $x \leq -4$

2 ▶ $y < 3$

3 ▶ $y \geq 2, y < x$

4 ▶ $x \leq -3, y \geq -x$

5 ▶ $y \leq x, y > -6, x \leq 5$

6 ▶ $y < 3x + 6, y > 3x - 10$

7 ▶ $y \leq \dfrac{1}{2}x - 6, y \leq -2x - 6$

8 ▶

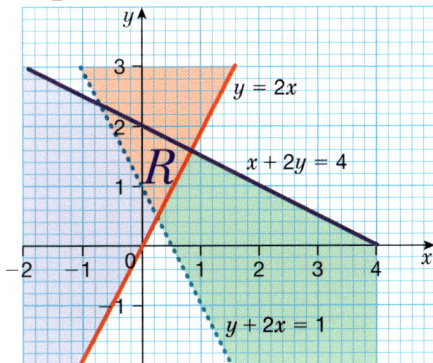

9 ▶

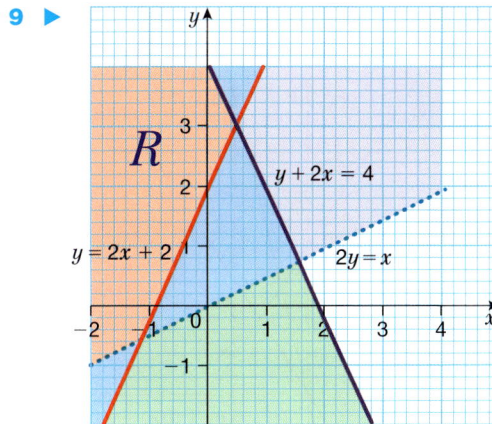

10 ▶

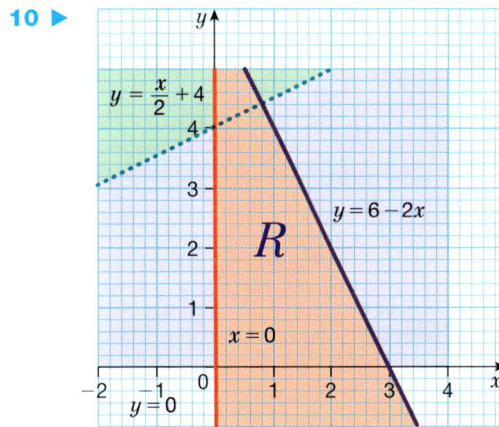

11 ▶

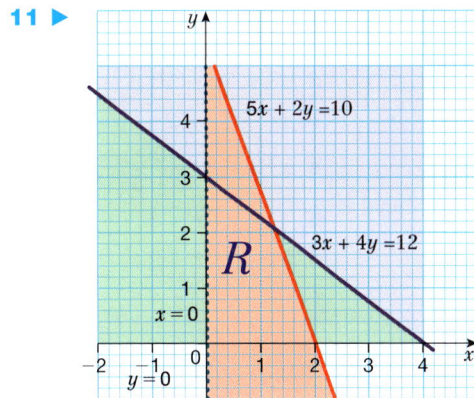

12 ▶ **a** $c + l \geq 10$

$l > c$

$120c + 200l \leq 1800$

b 3 chickens and 7 lambs for a profit of Y3600

13 ▶ She can earn a maximum of 184 JOD by working 12 hours as a wedding photographer and 8 hours as a studio photographer.

14 ▶ Let type A be x and type B be y

maximum profit is $15x + 12y$
maximise $P = 15x + 12y$
subject to

$x \geq 50$

$\dfrac{1}{5}(x + y) \leq x \Rightarrow y \leq 4x$

$x \leq \dfrac{2}{5}(x + y) \Rightarrow y \leq \dfrac{3}{2}x$

$3x + 2y \leqslant 200$

$y \geqslant 0$

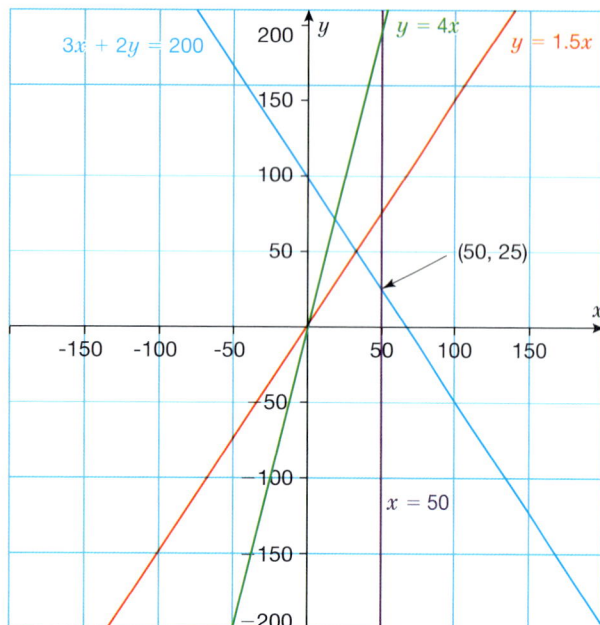

Therefore, for maximum profit $x = 50$ and $y = 25$

$p = 15(50) + 12(25)$

$p = £1050$

EXERCISE 5

1 ▶ **a** $x^2 - 2x - 15$ **b** $x^2 + 5x - 6$

    c $x^2 + 5x + 3$ **d** $x^2 + 7x + 10$

    e $x^2 - 3x + 7$ **f** $x^2 - 3x + 2$

    g $x^2 + 1$ **h** $x^2 + 2 - \dfrac{9}{x + 5}$

2 ▶ **a** $-2x^2 - x + 5$ **b** $4x^2 + 8x - 32$

    c $6x^2 + 3x + 2$ **d** $3x^2 + 2x - 2$

    e $-3x^2 - 3x + 90$ **f** $-5x^2 + 3x + 5$

    g $2x^2 + x - 1$

3 ▶ **a** $x^2 + 3x - 1$ **b** $2x^2 - 5x - 3$

    c $x^2 - 3x - 10$ **d** $x^2 - x - 6$

    e $2x^2 + x - 2$ **f** $x^2 + 3x + 2$

EXERCISE 6

1 ▶ **a** $f(-2) = 2(-2)^3 - 3(-2)^2 - 12(-2) + 4$

      $f(-2) = 0$

      Therefore $(x + 2)$ is a factor

    b $f(1) = 2(1)^4 - 3(1)^3 - (1)^2 + 2$

      $f(1) = 0$

      Therefore $(x - 1)$ is a factor

    c $f(-3) = 2(-3)^4 + 5(-3)^3 - 8(-3)^2 - 17(-3) - 6$

      $f(-3) = 0$

      Therefore $(x + 3)$ is a factor

    d $f(2) = (2)^3 - 5(2)^2 + 2(2) + 8$

      $f(2) = 0$

      Therefore $(x - 2)$ is a factor

    e $f(-4) = (-4)^7 + 10(-4)^6 + 27(-4)^5 - 57(-4)^3 - 30(-4)^2$
                   $+ 29(-4) + 20$

      $f(-4) = 0$

      Therefore $(x + 4)$ is a factor

2 ▶ $f(-1) = (-1)^4 - 3(-1)^2 + 2(-1) + 4$

    $f(-1) = 0$

    Therefore, $x^4 - 3x^2 + 2x + 4$ is exactly divisible by $(x + 1)$

    $f(2) = (2)^4 - 3(2)^2 + 2(2) + 4$

    $f(2) = 12$

    Therefore, $x^4 - 3x^2 + 2x + 4$ is not exactly divisible by $(x - 2)$

3 ▶ $(x - 1)(x^2 - x - 4)$

4 ▶ $(x - 1)(x + 2)(x - 3)$

5 ▶ $(x - 2)(x + 4)(2x - 1)$

6 ▶ $a = 4$

7 ▶ **a** $b = 2$ **b** $(x + 1)(x - 1)(3x + 2)$

8 ▶ $p = 6, q = -13$

9 ▶ **a** $a = 3, b = -1$ **b** $(x + 2)(x - 2)(3x - 1)$

EXERCISE 7

1 ▶ **a** 2   **b** 27   **c** 2   **d** -6

2 ▶ **a** -1 **b** 1   **c** 171

3 ▶ -80

4 ▶ $b = 7$

5 ▶ $16p - 176$

6 ▶ $b = 32$

7 ▶ $a = \dfrac{1}{3}, b = \dfrac{4}{3}$

8 ▶ **a** $a = 2, b = 4$ **b** $\dfrac{13}{27}$

9 ▶ $a = 5, b = -8$

10 ▶ $p = 8, q = 3$

EXAM PRACTICE QUESTIONS

1 ▶ $(-3, 5), \left(\dfrac{1}{3}, \dfrac{5}{3}\right)$

2 ▶ $(4, 10), \left(\dfrac{1}{3}, -1\right)$

3 ▶ $(1, 3), \left(-\dfrac{19}{5}, -\dfrac{9}{5}\right)$

4 ▶ **a** $x > 4$ **b** $x < -2, x > 6$

5 ▶ **a** $-1 < x < \dfrac{7}{2}$ **b** $x < \dfrac{14}{5}$

    c $-1 < x < \dfrac{14}{5}$

6 ▶ $x < -\dfrac{3}{2}, x > 4$

7 ▶ $\left(4, \dfrac{1}{2}\right), (-5, -1)$

8 ▶ **a** $p < -5$ or $p > \dfrac{1}{2}$ **b** $-5 < n < -2$

9 ▶ **a** $f(-2) = 2(-2)^3 - 7(-2)^2 - 10(-2) + 24$
        $= -16 - 28 + 20 + 24$
        $= 0$
    Therefore, $(x + 2)$ is a factor.

    b $(x + 2)(x - 4)(2x - 3)$

10 ▶ **a** $f(-5) = (-5)^3 + 8(-5)^2 + 17(-5) + 16$
        $= -125 + 200 - 85 + 16$
        $= 6$
    b $x^2 + 3x + 2 + \dfrac{6}{x + 5}$

11 ▶ **a** $f(4) = -3(4)^3 + 13(4)^2 - 6(4) + 8$
        $= -192 + 208 - 24 + 8$
        $= 0$
    Therefore, $(x + 4)$ is a factor.

    b $-(x - 4)(3x^2 - x + 2)$

12 ▶ $(x + 1)(x - 4)(2x - 1)$

13 ▶ **a** $p = -20$

    b $q = -6$

14 ▶ **a** $f(-3) = (-3)^3 - 2(-3) + 21$
        $= -27 + 6 + 21$
        $= 0$
    Therefore, $(x + 3)$ is a factor.

    b $(x + 3)(x^2 - 3x + 7)$

15 ▶ $p = -20$

16 ▶ **a** $a = -20$ **b** $(x - 4)(x^2 + 3x + 5)$

17 ▶ **a** $(x - 1)(x - 1)(2x + 3)$ **b** $x = 1$ and $x = -\dfrac{3}{2}$

18 ▶

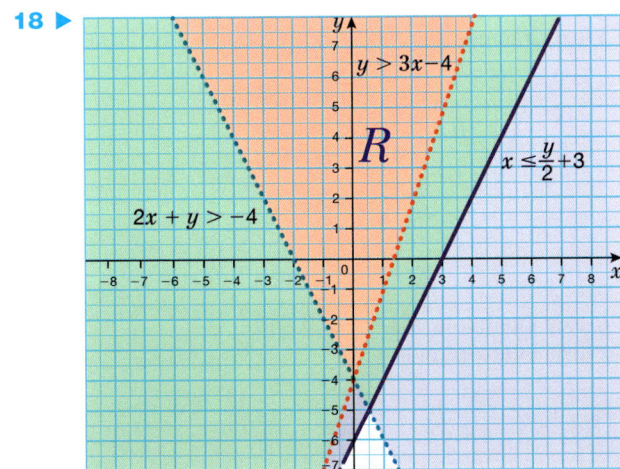

19 ▶ **a** Here is the summary.
    Let x be the number of desk top diaries bought.
    Let y be the number of pocket diaries bought.

Minimise $c = 6x + 3y$
Subject to $x \geqslant 200$
             $y \geqslant 80$
           $2x \leqslant y$
        $x + y \geqslant 400$

b

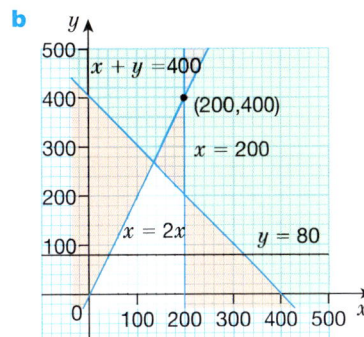

CHAPTER 4 – SKETCHING POLYNOMIALS

STARTER ACTIVITIES

1 ▶ **a–d**

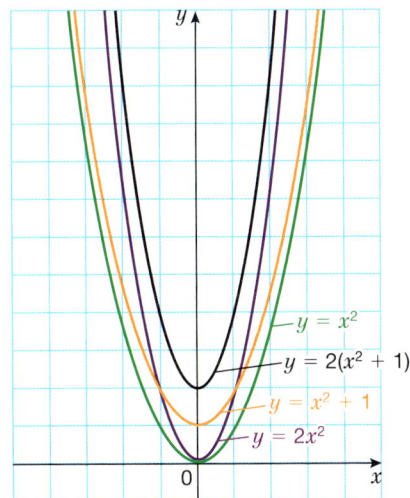

e–g

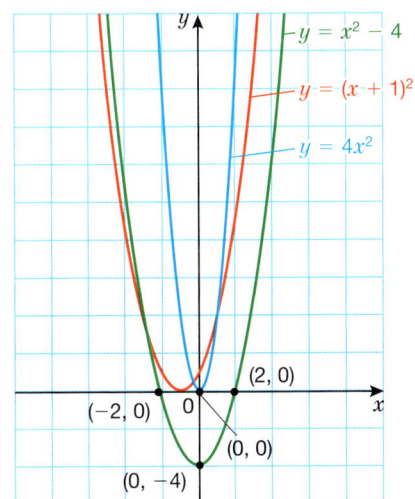

h–i

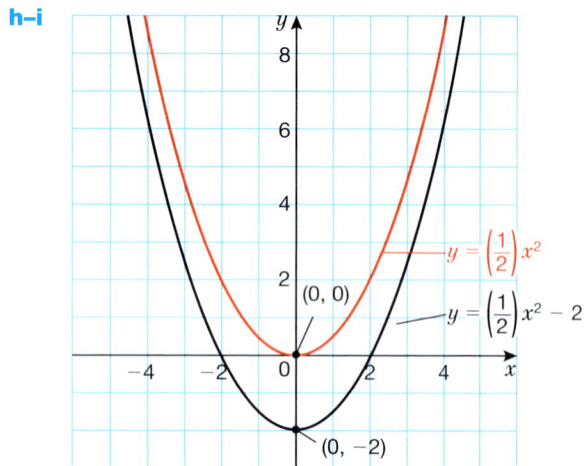

$y = \left(\frac{1}{2}\right)x^2$

$(0, 0)$

$y = \left(\frac{1}{2}\right)x^2 - 2$

$(0, -2)$

j–k

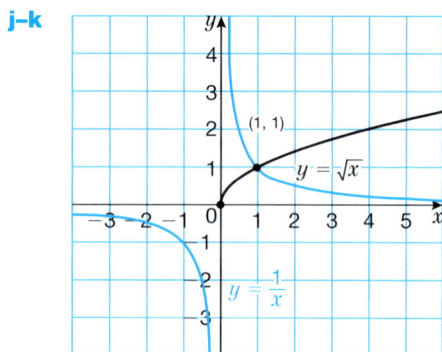

$(1, 1)$

$y = \sqrt{x}$

$y = \frac{1}{x}$

l–m

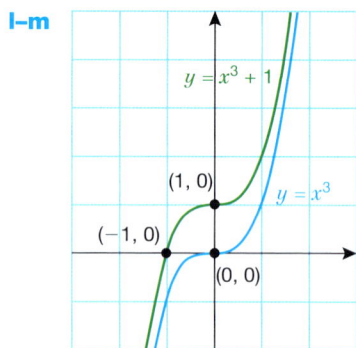

$y = x^3 + 1$

$(1, 0)$

$y = x^3$

$(-1, 0)$

$(0, 0)$

EXERCISE 1

1 ▶ a

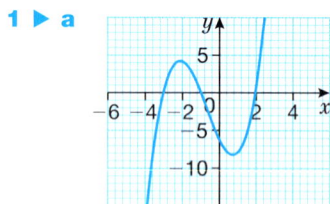

y-axis intercepts at $x = -3, -1$ and 2
x-axis intercept at $y = -6$

b

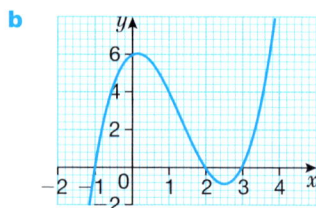

y-axis intercepts at $x = -1, 2$ and 3
x-axis intercept at $y = 6$

c

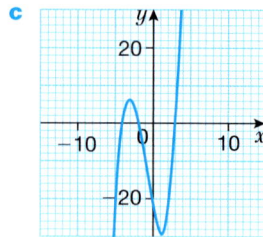

y-axis intercepts at $x = -4, -2$ and 3
x-axis intercept at $y = -24$

d

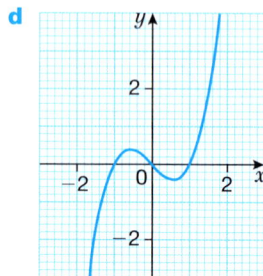

y-axis intercepts at $x = -1, 0$ and 1
x-axis intercept at $y = 0$

e

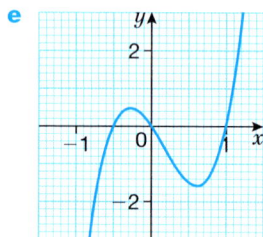

y-axis intercepts at $x = -\frac{1}{2}, 0$ and 1
x-axis intercept at $y = 0$

f

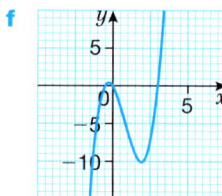

y-axis intercepts at $x = -\frac{1}{2}, 0$ and 3
x-axis intercept at $y = 0$

g

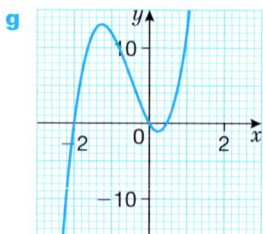

y-axis intercepts at $x = -2, 0$ and $\frac{1}{2}$
x-axis intercept at $y = 0$

h

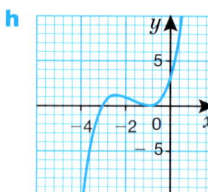

y-axis intercepts at $x = -1$ and -3
x-axis intercept at $y = 3$

i
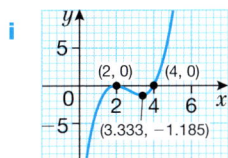
y-axis intercepts at $x = 2$ and 4
x-axis intercept at $y = -16$

j
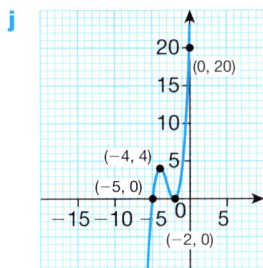
y-axis intercepts at $x = -2$ and -5
x-axis intercept at $y = 20$

k
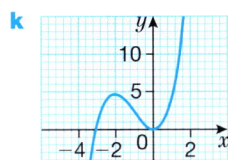
y-axis intercepts at $x = -3$ and 0
x-axis intercept at $y = 0$

l
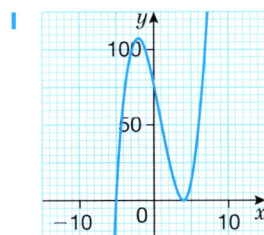
y-axis intercepts at $x = -5$ and 4
x-axis intercept at $y = 80$

2 ▶ a
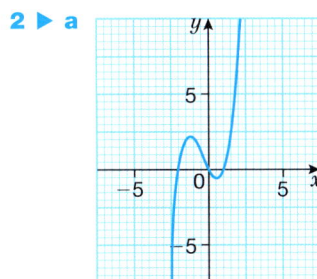
y-axis intercepts at $x = -2$, 0 and 1
x-axis intercept at $y = 0$

b
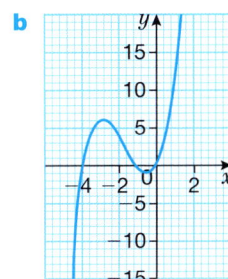
y-axis intercepts at $x = -4$, -1 and 0
x-axis intercept at $y = 0$

c
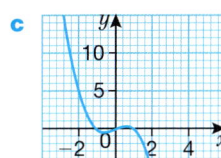
y-axis intercepts at $x = -1$, 0 and 1
x-axis intercept at $y = 0$

d
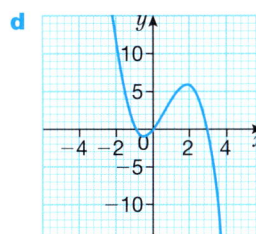
y-axis intercepts at $x = -1$, 0 and 3
x-axis intercept at $y = 0$

e
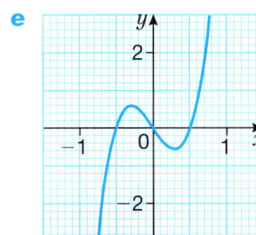
y-axis intercepts at $x = -\frac{1}{2}$, 0 and $\frac{1}{2}$
x-axis intercept at $y = 0$

f
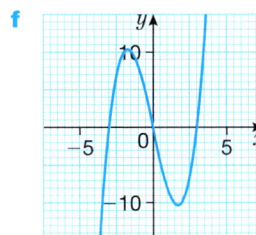
y-axis intercepts at $x = -3$, 0 and 3
x-axis intercept at $y = 0$

g
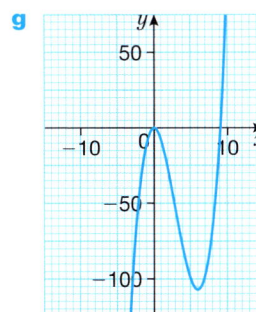
y-axis intercepts at $x = 0$ and 9
x-axis intercept at $y = 0$

EXERCISE 2

1 ▶ a

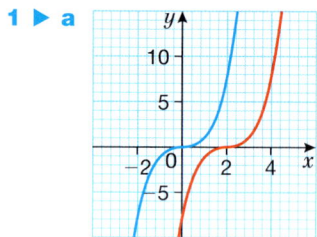

b

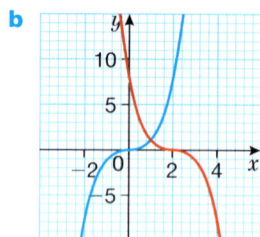

c

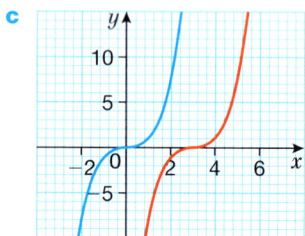

d

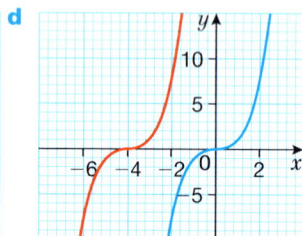

e

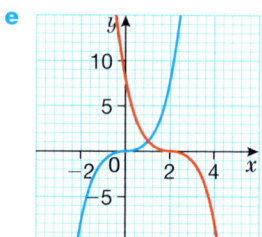

f

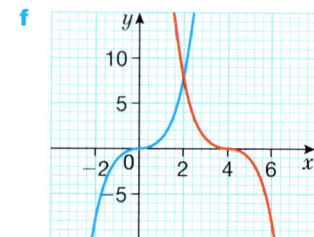

g

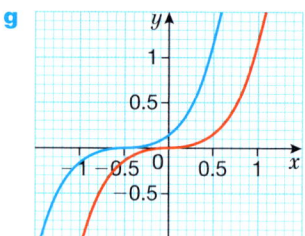

h

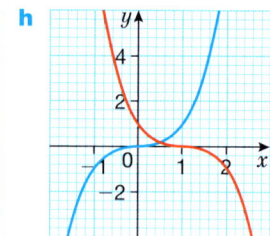

EXERCISE 3

1 ▶ a

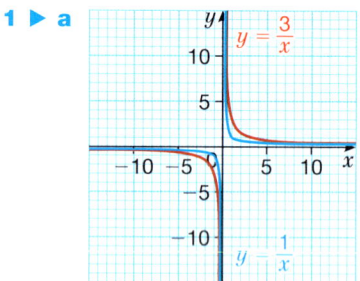

$y = \dfrac{3}{x}$

$y = \dfrac{1}{x}$

b

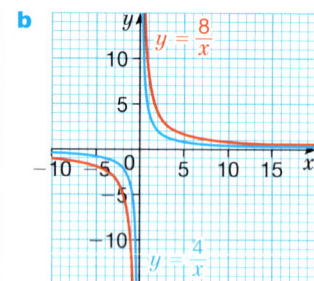

$y = \dfrac{8}{x}$

$y = \dfrac{4}{x}$

c

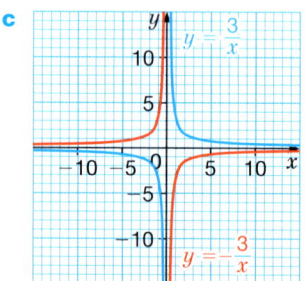

$y = \dfrac{3}{x}$

$y = -\dfrac{3}{x}$

d

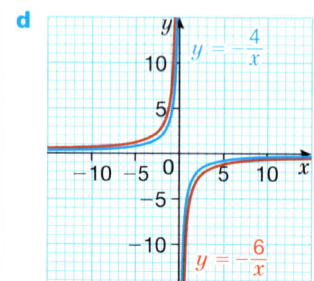

$y = -\dfrac{4}{x}$

$y = -\dfrac{6}{x}$

e

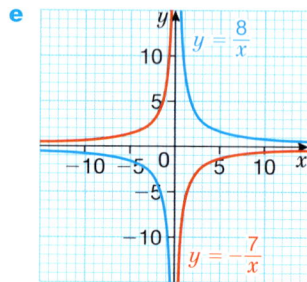

$y = \dfrac{8}{x}$

$y = -\dfrac{7}{x}$

f

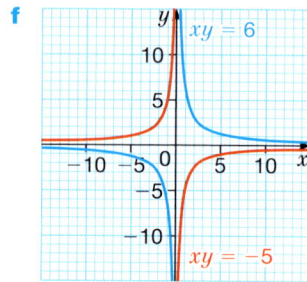

$xy = 6$

$xy = -5$

EXERCISE 4

1 ▶ a i

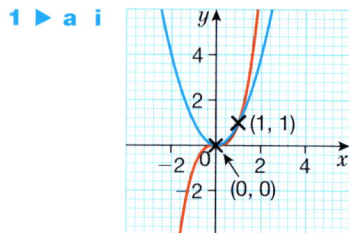

(1, 1)

(0, 0)

ii Two intersections   **iii** $x^2 = x^3$

b i

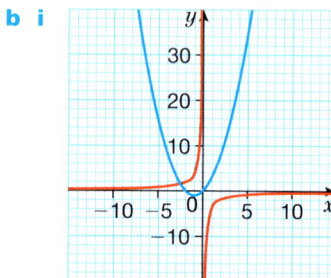

ii One intersection   **iii** $x(x + 2) = -\dfrac{3}{x}$

c i

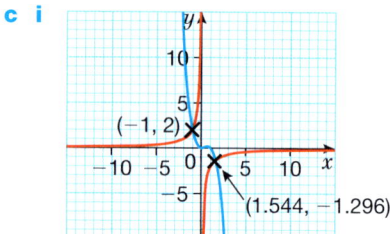

$(-1, 2)$

$(1.544, -1.296)$

ii Two intersections   **iii** $x^2(1 - x) = -\dfrac{2}{x}$

d i

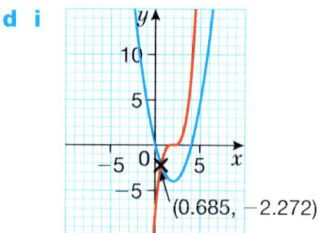

$(0.685, -2.272)$

ii One intersection   **iii** $x(x - 4) = (x - 2)^3$

e i

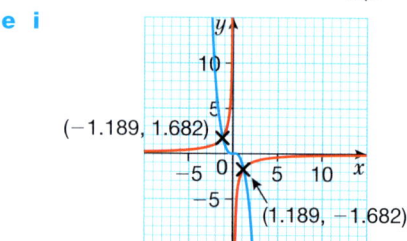

$(-1.189, 1.682)$

$(1.189, -1.682)$

ii Two intersections   **iii** $-x^3 = -\dfrac{2}{x}$

f i

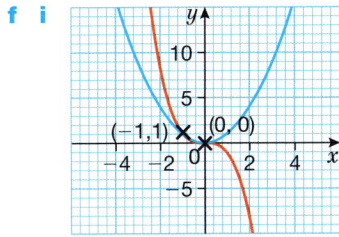

ii Two intersections   **iii** $x^2 = -x^3$

2 ▶ a

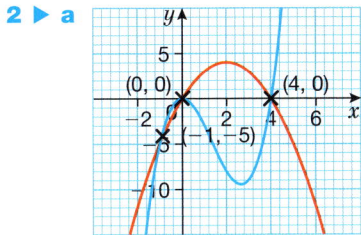

b (0, 0), (4, 0), (–1, –5)

3 ▶ a

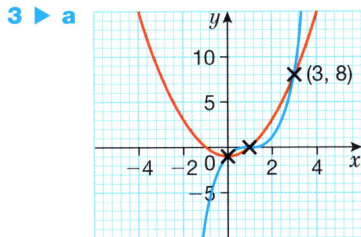

b (0, –1), (1, 0), (3, 8)

4 ▶

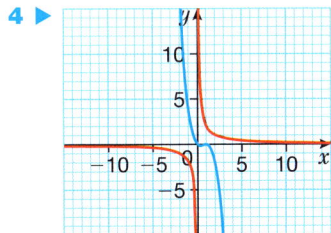

There is no intersection, therefore there is no solution to the equation.

5 ▶

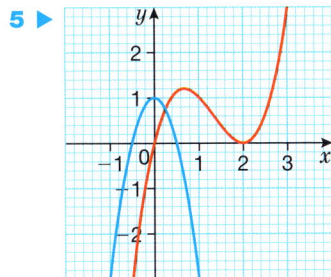

The curves intersect once, therefore there is one solution to the equation.

6 ▶

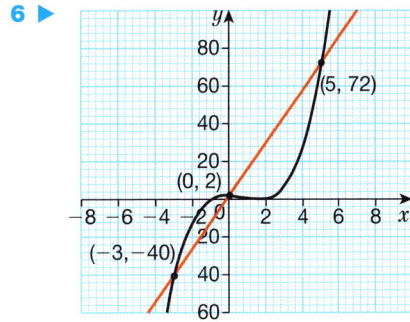

EXERCISE 5

1 ▶ a

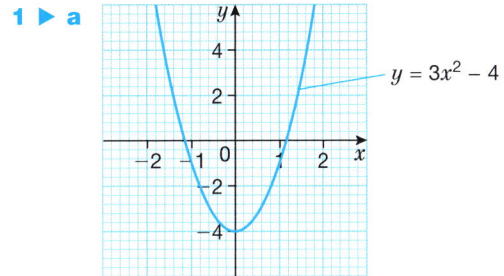

$y = 3x^2 - 4$

b

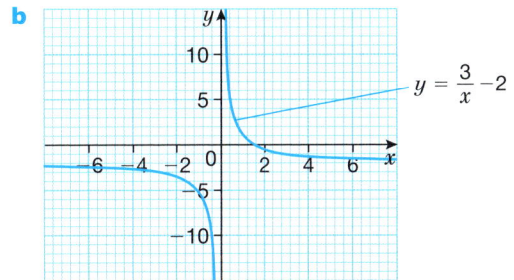

$y = \dfrac{3}{x} - 2$

c

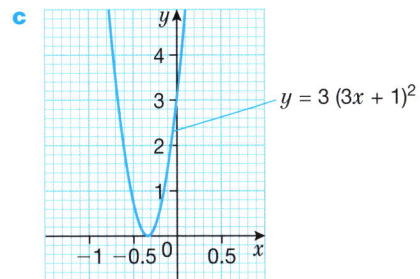

$y = 3(3x + 1)^2$

d

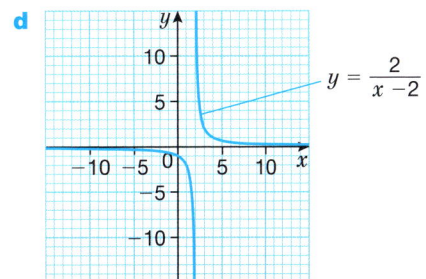

$y = \dfrac{2}{x - 2}$

e

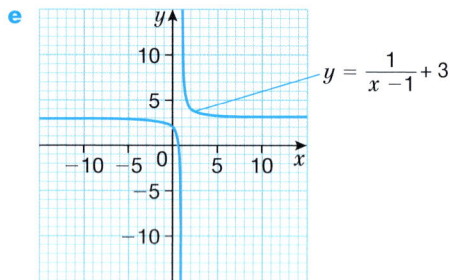

$y = \dfrac{1}{x-1} + 3$

f

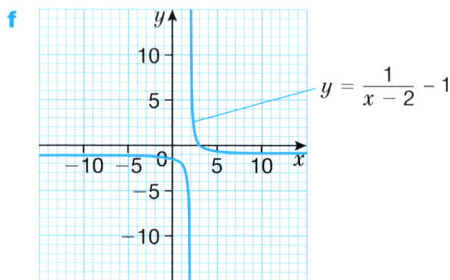

$y = \dfrac{1}{x-2} - 1$

g

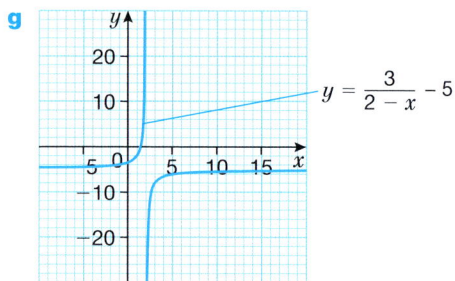

$y = \dfrac{3}{2-x} - 5$

h

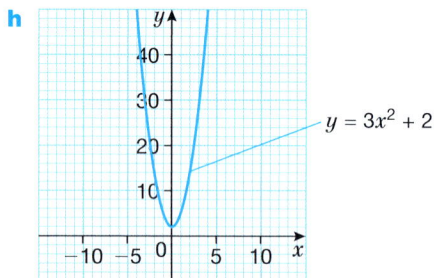

$y = 3x^2 + 2$

EXAM PRACTICE QUESTIONS

1 ▶ a

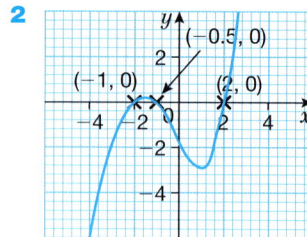

The curve $y = 2x + 5$ crosses the x-axis at $(-2.5, 0)$ and the y-axis at $(0, 5)$

b $(-3, -1)$, $(0.5, 6)$

2

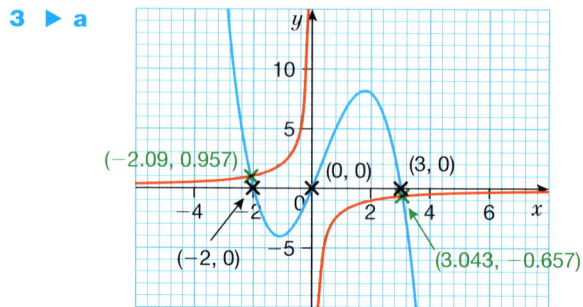

3 ▶ a

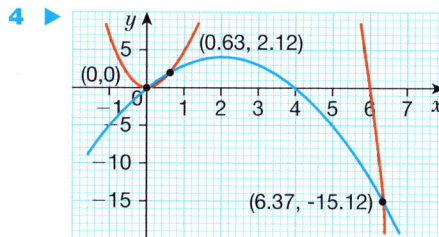

b There are two real solutions to the equation because the curves intersect twice: at $(-2.09, 0.957)$ and at $(3.043, -0.657)$

4 ▶

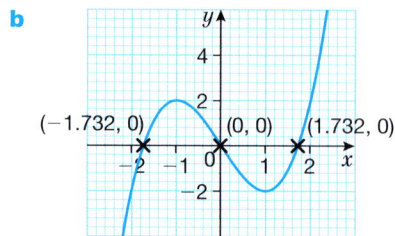

5 ▶ a $x(x^2 - 3)$

b

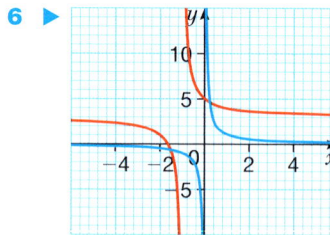

6 ▶

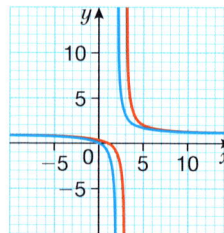

7 ▶ x asymptote is $x = 3$, y asymptote ($y = 0$) remains the same

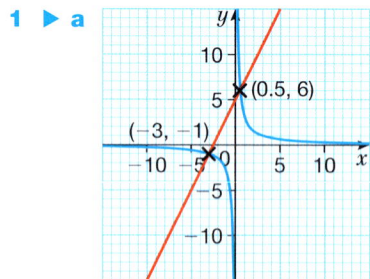

8 ▶ **a** $a = 1$ and $b = 5$

b
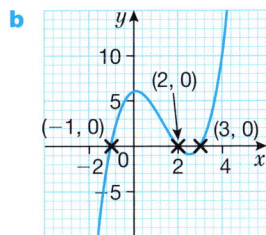

9 ▶
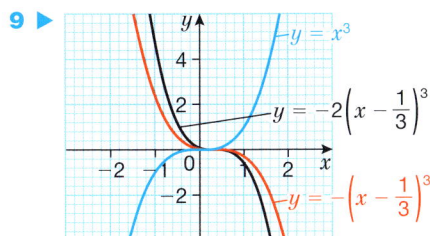

10 ▶
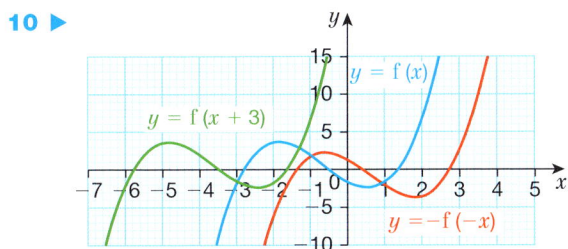

11 ▶ **a**
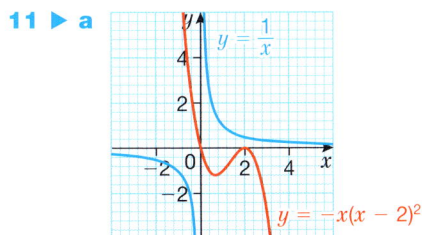

b There are no intersections.

CHAPTER 5 – SEQUENCES AND SERIES

EXERCISE 1

1 ▶ **a** No   **b** Yes   **c** Yes
     d No   **e** Yes   **f** Yes
     g No   **h** Yes   **i** Yes

2 ▶ **a** 21   **b** 11.5   **c** 105
     d $10x$ **e** $22 + 10a$

3 ▶ **a** \$5800   **b** $\$(4000 + 200(n - 1))$

4 ▶ **a** 33   **b** 17   **c** 21
     d 13   **e** 18   **f** n

EXERCISE 2

1 ▶ **a** 61, $3n + 1$ **b** 74, $3n + 14$
     c 26, $106 - 4n$ **d** -98, $22 - 6n$
     e $\dfrac{113}{15}$, $\dfrac{13}{15} + \dfrac{n}{3}$ **f** $39q$, $q(2n - 1)$
     g $-71k$, $k(9 - 4n)$

2 ▶ **a** 20   **b** 120   **c** 33   **d** 51   **e** 27   **f** 42

3 ▶ 4

4 ▶ **a** $a = 42$, $d = -15$ **b** 4th term

5 ▶ 22.12

6 ▶ $p = 5$;   25, 20, 15

7 ▶ $n = \dfrac{1}{2}$, $n = 8$

EXERCISE 3

1 ▶ **a** 650   **b** 960   **c** 1275
     d 2312.5   **e** $21(11x + 1)$

2 ▶ **a** 50   **b** 20   **c** 32   **d** 321

3 ▶ 900

4 ▶ \$652 200

5 ▶ 20 100

6 ▶ 1866.85 euros

7 ▶ 3876

8 ▶ 97 days

9 ▶ Sum required $1 + 2 + 3 + \ldots\ldots +2n$

This is an arithmetic series with $a = 1$, $d = 1$ and $n = 2n$

$$S_n = \frac{n}{2}[2a + (n - 1)d]$$
$$= \frac{2n}{2}[2 \times 1 + (2n - 1) \times 1]$$
$$= \frac{2n}{2}(2n + 1)$$
$$= n(2n + 1)$$

10 ▶ 1800°

11 ▶ **a** $\displaystyle\sum_{r=1}^{10}(2r + 1)$ **b** $\displaystyle\sum_{r=1}^{12}(8r + 1)$
     c $\displaystyle\sum_{r=1}^{10}4(10 - r)$ **d** $\displaystyle\sum_{r=1}^{18}4r$

12 ▶ We know that $a_n = a_1 + (n - 1)d$

Suppose the first term is a_1, second term is $a_1 + d$ and the third term $a_1 + 2d$ etc.

This leads to

$$S_n = a_1 + (a_1 + d) + (a_1 + 2d) + \ldots\ldots + [a_1 + (n - 1)d] \text{ (i)}$$

We could have also started with the nth term and successively subtracted the common difference, therefore

$S_n = a_n + (a_n - d) + (a_n - 2d) + \ldots\ldots + [a_n - (n-1)d]$ (ii)

If we add (i) and (ii)

$$S_n = a_1 + (a_1 + d) + (a_1 + 2d) + \ldots\ldots + [a_1 + (n-1)d]$$
$$\underline{S_n = a_n + (a_n - d) + (a_n - 2d) + \ldots\ldots + [a_n - (n-1)d]}$$
$$2S_n = (a_1 + a_n) + (a_1 + a_n) + (a_1 + a_n) + \ldots\ldots + (a_1 + a_n)$$

Therefore

$$2S_n = n(a_1 + a_n)$$

$$S_n = \frac{n(a_1 + a_n)}{2}$$

$$S_n = \frac{n}{2}(a_1 + a_n)$$

Substitute $a_n = a_1 + (n-1)d$ into the last formula

$$S_n = \frac{n}{2}[(a_1 + a_1 + (n-1)d]$$

As $L = a_1 + (n-1)d$

Therefore,

$$S_n = \frac{n}{2}(a + L)$$

13 ▶ a 465   **b** 630   **c** −432   **d** 511

14 ▶ 9

15 ▶ 33

EXERCISE 4

1 ▶ a Yes, $r = 5$ **b** No   **c** Yes, $r = 0.5$
   d No   **e** Yes, $r = -1$ **f** Yes, $r = 1$
   g Yes, $r = -\dfrac{1}{4}$ **h** No

2 ▶ a −3051, 9153, −27 459
   b 1280, 5120, 20 480
   c 6, 18, 54
   d 375, 1875, 9375
   e −0.015625, 0.00390625, −0.0009765625
   f x^3, x^4, x^5

3 ▶ a 8   **b** 64

EXERCISE 5

1 ▶ a 48, 192, $3(2^{n-1})$ **b** 10, 2.5, $\dfrac{160}{2^{n-1}}$
   c 162, 1458, $2(-3)^{n-1}$ **d** −16, −64, $-(2^{n-1})$

2 ▶ a $a = 3, r = 2$ **b** $a = 15, r = -2$
   c $a = -30, r = -0.5$ **d** $a = 0.5, r = 2$

3 ▶ a 3   **b** 1875

4 ▶ $\pm\dfrac{1}{4}$

5 ▶ −6 (when $p = 0$), 4 (when $p = 10$)

EXERCISE 6

1 ▶ a 1093   **b** 33.3 (3 s.f.)   **c** 28 697 812
   d 426.5625   **e** 97 655   **f** 4092
   g 544 (3 s.f.)   **h** 308 826

2 ▶ 18 446 744 073 709 551 615

3 ▶ 25 years

4 ▶ 10 644 rupees

5 ▶ The second option.

6 ▶ During the 37th day

7 ▶ 19

8 ▶ $n = 6, r = 4$

EXERCISE 7

1 ▶ a $\dfrac{10}{9}$ **b** Doesn't exist
   c Doesn't exist   **d** $\dfrac{1}{1 + 2y}$. If $|y| < \dfrac{1}{2}$

2 ▶ a $r = \dfrac{1}{2}$ **b** 8

3 ▶ a $\dfrac{9}{10}$ **b** 1000

4 ▶ 3

5 ▶ 20.25

6 ▶ 30 m

7 ▶ $625\pi\,\text{cm}^2$

8 ▶ £4 million

9 ▶ $r < 0$ because $S_\infty < S_3$. $a = 12, r = -\dfrac{1}{2}$

EXAM PRACTICE QUESTIONS

1 ▶ a $d = 27$ **b** $a = 13$ **c** 8425

2 ▶ a $q = 4.9$ **b** 58

3 ▶ 1017

4 ▶ a $a = 6$ and $d = 3$ **b** $n = 12$

5 ▶ a $a = 86$ and $d = -7$ **b** 50

6 ▶ a −1023
   b The positive terms of the series are the 1st, 3rd, 5th, etc. terms.

$$3(-2)^{1-1}, 3(-2)^{3-1}, 3(-2)^{5-1} \ldots\ldots 3(-2)^{17-1}$$

$$3(-2)^2, 3(-2)^4, 3(-2)^6 \ldots\ldots 3(-2)^{16}$$

3, 12, 48, 192, $\ldots\ldots$ 49152

Therefore, the common ratio is 4 and the first term is 3.

The sum of the first 8 terms is

$$\sum_{r=1}^{8} 12(4)^{n-1} = \frac{3(1-4^8)}{1-4} = 65\,535$$

7 ▶ 645

8 ▶ a 0.3   **b** $r = \dfrac{30}{a} = \dfrac{30}{0.3} = 100$ **c** 143

9 ▶ a $ar = 80$, $ar^4 = 5.12$ **b** 200

$$\frac{ar^4}{ar} = \frac{5.12}{80} = \frac{8}{125} = r^3$$

$$r = \frac{2}{5} = 0.4$$

c $333\frac{1}{3}$ **d** 8.95×10^{-4}

10 ▶ Proof

11 ▶ a Proof   **b** Proof

    c Common ratio $= \frac{3}{4}$ **d** 64

CHAPTER 6 – THE BINOMIAL SERIES

EXERCISE 1

1 ▶ a $27 + 27x + 9x^2 + x^3$ **b** $125 + 150x + 60x^2 + 8x^3$

    c $16 + 32x + 24x^2 + 8x^3 + x^z$

2 ▶ a 21875   **b** 9720

EXERCISE 2

1 ▶ a $27x^3 + 27x^2y + 9xy^2 + y^3$

    b $m^4 - 4m^3n + 6m^2n^2 - 4mn^3 + n^4$

    c $1 + 9x + 27x^2 + 27x^3$

    d $1 + y + \frac{3y^2}{8} + \frac{y^3}{16} + \frac{y^4}{256}$

    e $27y^3 + 108y^2x + 144yx^2 + 64x^3$

2 ▶ a $+43740$ **b** $+1400000$

    c $+5985$ **d** $+27405$

3 ▶ a $1 + 12x + 54x^2 + 108x^3$

    b $1 - \frac{7y}{4} + \frac{21y^2}{16} - \frac{35y^3}{64}$

    c $343 - 147b + 21b^2 - b^3$

    d $1024 + 15360x^2 + 103680x^4 + 414720x^6$

4 ▶ a $n = 5$ **b** $\frac{16x^4}{125}$

EXERCISE 3

1 ▶ a $1 + 9x + 36x^2 + 84x^3$

    b $1 - 15y + 90y^2 - 270y^3$

    c $1 + 28x + 336x^2 + 2240x^3$

    d $1 + \frac{9x}{2} + 9x^2 + \frac{21x^3}{2}$

    e $1 - 21x + 189x^2 - 945x^3$

    f $1 - 2x + \frac{5x^2}{3} - \frac{20x^3}{27}$

g $1 - \frac{3x}{2} + \frac{15x^2}{16} - \frac{5x^3}{16}$

2 ▶ a 8   **b** $+700$ **c** -7000

3 ▶ a $1 - 8x + 28x^2 - 56x^3$

    b 0.9227 (4 d.p.)

4 ▶ a $1 + 6x + 15x^2 + 20x^3$

    b 1.1262 (4 d.p.)

5 ▶ a -20 **b** 84   **c** 280

6 ▶ a $p = 6$ **b** $\frac{20}{3}$ **c** $-\frac{160}{27}$

EXERCISE 4

1 ▶ a $1 - 6x + 24x^2 - 80x^3$, $|x| < \frac{1}{2}$

    b $1 + 3x + 9x^2 + 27x^3$, $|x| < \frac{1}{3}$

    c $\frac{1}{2} - \frac{3}{8}x + \frac{27}{64}x^2 - \frac{135}{256}x^3$, $|x| < \frac{2}{3}$

2 ▶ a -1, $|x| < 1$ **b** $\frac{1}{2}$, $|x| < \frac{1}{2}$

    c 27, $|x| < \frac{1}{3}$ **d** $-\frac{5}{81}$, $|x| < 1$

3 ▶ a $1 - 3x + 9x^2 - 27x^3$

    b $1 - 4x + 12x^2 - 36x^3$

4 ▶ $b = \pm 8$, ∓ 160

5 ▶ a $1 + 2x - 4x^2 + \frac{40}{3}x^3$

    b Let $x = 0.004$:

    $(1 + 6x)^{\frac{1}{3}} \approx 1 + 2(0.004) - 4(0.004)^2 + \frac{40}{3}(0.004)^3$

    $= 1.007936853$

    $(1 + 0.024)^{\frac{1}{3}} = \sqrt[3]{1.024} = \sqrt[3]{\frac{512 \times 2}{1000}} = \frac{4}{5}\sqrt[3]{2}$

    $\sqrt[3]{2} = \frac{5}{4} \times 1.007936853 = 1.259921$ (7 s.f.)

6 ▶ -8

EXAM PRACTICE QUESTIONS

1 ▶ $1 + \frac{7x}{4} + \frac{21x^2}{16} + \frac{35x^3}{64}$

2 ▶ a $243 + 405ax + 270a^2x^2 + 90a^3x^3$

    b $a = 3$

3 ▶ $n = 9$

4 ▶

$$\sqrt{\left(\frac{1+x}{1-x}\right)} = \left(\frac{1+x}{1-x}\right)^{\frac{1}{2}}$$

$$= (1+x)^{\frac{1}{2}}(1-x)^{-\frac{1}{2}}$$

$$= \left[1+\left(\frac{1}{2}\right)(x)+\frac{\left(\frac{1}{2}\right)\left(-\frac{1}{2}\right)(x)^2}{2!}+...\right]\left[1+\left(-\frac{1}{2}\right)(-x)\right.$$

$$\left.+\frac{\left(-\frac{1}{2}\right)\left(-\frac{3}{2}\right)(-x)^2}{2!}+...\right]$$

$$= \left(1+\frac{1}{2}x-\frac{1}{8}x^2+...\right)\left(1+\frac{1}{2}x+\frac{3}{8}x^2+...\right)$$

$$= 1\left(1+\frac{1}{2}x+\frac{3}{8}x^2.....\right)+\frac{1}{2}x\left(1+\frac{1}{2}x+\frac{3}{8}x^2+...\right)$$

$$-\frac{1}{8}x^2\left(1+\frac{1}{2}x+\frac{3}{8}x^2+...\right)$$

$$= 1+\frac{1}{2}x+\frac{3}{8}x^2+\frac{1}{2}x+\frac{1}{4}x^2-\frac{1}{8}x^2+...$$

$$= 1+x+\frac{1}{2}x^2+..$$

Hence

$$\sqrt{\left(\frac{1+x}{1-x}\right)} \approx 1+x+\frac{1}{2}x^2$$

if terms larger than or equal to x^3 are ignored

5 ▶ **a** $= \frac{1}{2}-\frac{1}{16}x+\frac{3}{256}x^2-\frac{5}{2048}x^3+...$

    b $|x| < 4$

6 ▶ **a** $1+\frac{3}{2}x-\frac{9}{8}x^2+\frac{27}{16}x^3$

    b 10.14889188, accurate to 8 d.p.

    c Students should be writing something similar to 'accuracy is close to 100% or accurate to the 7th decimal place'.

7 ▶ 2

8 ▶ **a** $1-4x-8x^2-32x^3$

    b $|x| < \frac{1}{8}$

    c $= 4.79584$ (5 d.p.)

9 ▶ **a** $1-\frac{9}{2}x+\frac{27}{8}x^2+\frac{27}{16}x^3$

    b $x = 0.01, 955.3358$ (4 d.p.)

10 ▶ **a** $5+5x+\frac{15}{2}x^2+\frac{25}{2}x^3$

    b $|x| < \frac{1}{2}$

11 ▶ **a** $4-\frac{4}{3}x+\frac{2}{3}x^2$

    b $3\frac{131}{150}$

12 ▶ **a** $2-2x+3x^2-5x^3$

    b $|x| < \frac{1}{2}$

CHAPTER 7 – VECTORS

EXERCISE 1

1 ▶ **a**

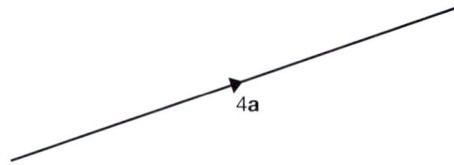
4**a**

    b

−2**a**

    c

$\frac{1}{4}$**a**

    d

$-\frac{1}{3}$**a**

2 ▶ **a**

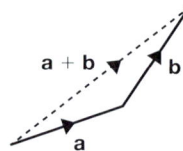
a + **b**   **b**   **a**

    b

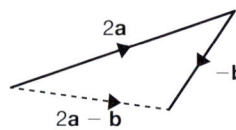
2**a**   −**b**   2**a** − **b**

    c

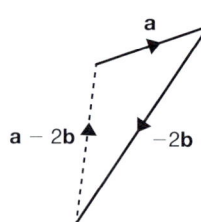
a   **a** − 2**b**   −2**b**

3 ▶ 36.49

4 ▶ 25.6

5 ▶ **a** **a** + **b**   **b** −**c** − **b** − **a**   **c** −**d** + **a** + **b**   **d** **d** − **a**

6 ▶ **a** $\frac{1}{2}$**a**   **b** $-\frac{1}{2}$**a** + **b**   **c** −**b** + $\frac{1}{2}$**a**

7 ▶ $\overrightarrow{PR} = \overrightarrow{PQ} + \overrightarrow{QR} = -\mathbf{a} + \mathbf{b}$

$\overrightarrow{RS} = \overrightarrow{RQ} + \overrightarrow{QS} = -\mathbf{b} + \mathbf{c}$

$\overrightarrow{PR} = \overrightarrow{RS}$ which means an equation can be created.

$-\mathbf{a} + \mathbf{b} = -\mathbf{b} + \mathbf{c}$

Rearranging the formula gives

$-\mathbf{a} + \mathbf{b} = -\mathbf{b} + \mathbf{c}$
$-\mathbf{a} + 2\mathbf{b} = \mathbf{c}$

EXERCISE 2

1 ▶ **a** 2**a** + **b**   **b** $\frac{1}{2}$(2**a** + **b**)   **c** $-\frac{1}{2}$(2**a** + **b**)

2 ▶ **a** **b**   **b** −**b**   **c** **b** + **a**

    d **b** + $\frac{1}{4}$**a**   **e** **b** − $\frac{3}{4}$**a**

3 ▶ **a** Yes   **b** No   **c** Yes   **d** No

4 ▶ **a** $\lambda = \frac{1}{2}, \mu = -4$ **b** $\lambda = -2, \mu = 3$

    c $\lambda = \frac{2}{5}, \mu = 4$ **d** $\lambda = -4, \mu = -3$

    e $\mu = -1, \lambda = 4,$ **f** $\lambda = \frac{1}{3}, \mu = \frac{16}{3}$

    g $\lambda = -1, \mu = 7$

5 ▶ **a** $\frac{1}{2}\mathbf{a}$ **b** $\mathbf{b} - \mathbf{a}$ **c** $\frac{1}{5}\mathbf{b}$

    d $-\frac{4}{5}\mathbf{b}$ **e** $-\mathbf{a} + \frac{1}{5}\mathbf{b}$

6 ▶ **a** $\mathbf{a} + \mathbf{b}$ **b** $\mathbf{b} - \mathbf{a}$ **c** $\mathbf{a} + 2\mathbf{b}$

7 ▶ **a** $6\mathbf{b} + 2\mathbf{a}$ **b** $6\mathbf{b} - 6\mathbf{a}$

EXERCISE 3

1 ▶ $\frac{5}{6}\mathbf{a} + \frac{1}{6}\mathbf{b}$

2 ▶ $-\frac{1}{2}\mathbf{a} - \frac{1}{2}\mathbf{b} + \mathbf{c}$

3 ▶ $\overrightarrow{OC} = -2\mathbf{a} + 2\mathbf{b}, \overrightarrow{OD} = -3\mathbf{a} + 2\mathbf{b}, \overrightarrow{OE} = -2\mathbf{a} + \mathbf{b}$

EXERCISE 4

1 ▶ **a** $\overrightarrow{AB} = \overrightarrow{AO} + \overrightarrow{OB} = -\mathbf{x} + \mathbf{y}$

$\overrightarrow{OM} = \overrightarrow{OA} + \frac{1}{2}\overrightarrow{AB} = \mathbf{x} + \frac{1}{2}(-\mathbf{x} + \mathbf{y}) = \mathbf{x} - \frac{1}{2}\mathbf{x} + \frac{1}{2}\mathbf{y}$

$= \frac{1}{2}\mathbf{x} + \frac{1}{2}\mathbf{y}$

$\overrightarrow{DC} = \overrightarrow{DO} + \overrightarrow{OC} = -2\mathbf{x} + 2\mathbf{y}$

    b $\overrightarrow{DC} = -2\mathbf{x} + 2\mathbf{y} = 2(-\mathbf{x} + \mathbf{y}) = 2\overrightarrow{AB}$

As $\overrightarrow{DC}$ is a multiple of $\overrightarrow{AB}$, they are parallel.

2 ▶ $\overrightarrow{ON} = \frac{1}{2}\overrightarrow{OB} = \frac{1}{2}\mathbf{b}$

$\overrightarrow{OM} = \frac{1}{2}\overrightarrow{OA} = \frac{1}{2}\mathbf{a}$

$\overrightarrow{AB} = \overrightarrow{AO} + \overrightarrow{OB} = -\mathbf{a} + \mathbf{b}$

$\overrightarrow{MN} = \overrightarrow{MO} + \overrightarrow{ON} = -\frac{1}{2}\mathbf{a} + \frac{1}{2}\mathbf{b}$

$= \frac{1}{2}(-\mathbf{a} + \mathbf{b}) = \frac{1}{2}\overrightarrow{AB}$

As $\overrightarrow{MN}$ is a multiple of $\overrightarrow{AB}$, they are parallel.

3 ▶ **a** $\overrightarrow{AB} = \overrightarrow{AO} + \overrightarrow{OB} = -\mathbf{x} + \mathbf{y}$

$OA : OC = 1 : 2$

$\overrightarrow{OC} = 2\overrightarrow{AO} = -2\mathbf{x}$

$OB : OD = 1 : 2$

$\overrightarrow{OD} = 2\overrightarrow{BO} = -2\mathbf{y}$

$\overrightarrow{DC} = \overrightarrow{DO} + \overrightarrow{OC} = 2\mathbf{y} - 2\mathbf{x}$

    b $\overrightarrow{DC} = 2\mathbf{y} - 2\mathbf{x} = 2(\mathbf{y} - \mathbf{x}) = 2(-\mathbf{x} + \mathbf{y}) = 2\overrightarrow{AB}$

4 ▶ Find the other vectors in terms of **a** and **b**.

$OM : MQ = 1 : 2$

$\overrightarrow{MQ} = \frac{2}{3}\overrightarrow{OQ} = \frac{2}{3}\mathbf{a}$

$\overrightarrow{PQ} = \overrightarrow{PO} + \overrightarrow{OQ} = -\mathbf{b} + \mathbf{a}$

$\overrightarrow{PN} = \frac{1}{3}\overrightarrow{PQ} = \frac{1}{3}(-\mathbf{b} + \mathbf{a})$

$\overrightarrow{NQ} = \frac{2}{3}\overrightarrow{PQ} = \frac{2}{3}(-\mathbf{b} + \mathbf{a})$

Finding $\overrightarrow{MN}$ in terms of **a** and **b**

$\overrightarrow{MN} = \overrightarrow{MQ} + \overrightarrow{QN} = \frac{2}{3}\mathbf{a} - \frac{2}{3}(-\mathbf{b} + \mathbf{a}) = \frac{2}{3}\mathbf{a} + \frac{2}{3}\mathbf{b} - \frac{2}{3}\mathbf{a} = \frac{2}{3}\mathbf{b}$

So $\overrightarrow{MN} = \frac{2}{3}\mathbf{b} = \frac{2}{3}\overrightarrow{OP}$, which means $\overrightarrow{MN}$ is a multiple of $\overrightarrow{OP}$ so they are parallel.

5 ▶ **a** $\overrightarrow{AB} = \overrightarrow{AO} + \overrightarrow{OB} = -\mathbf{a} + \mathbf{b}$

    b $AM : MB = 2 : 1$

$\overrightarrow{AM} = \frac{2}{3}\overrightarrow{AB} = \frac{2}{3}(-\mathbf{a} + \mathbf{b})$

We can now find $\overrightarrow{OM}$ in terms of **a** and **b**

$\overrightarrow{OM} = \overrightarrow{OA} + \overrightarrow{AM} = \mathbf{a} + \frac{2}{3}(-\mathbf{a} + \mathbf{b}) = \mathbf{a} - \frac{2}{3}\mathbf{a} + \frac{2}{3}\mathbf{b} = \frac{1}{3}\mathbf{a} + \frac{2}{3}\mathbf{b}$

$\overrightarrow{OM} = \frac{1}{3}\mathbf{a} + \frac{2}{3}\mathbf{b} = \frac{1}{3}(\mathbf{a} + 2\mathbf{b})$

    c First find the other vectors to help solve this problem.

$\overrightarrow{AC} = \overrightarrow{AO} + \overrightarrow{OC} = -\mathbf{a} + 4\mathbf{b}$

$AN : NC = 1 : 2$

$\overrightarrow{AN} = \frac{1}{3}\overrightarrow{AC} = \frac{1}{3}(-\mathbf{a} + 4\mathbf{b})$

Now we can find $\overrightarrow{ON}$ and $\overrightarrow{OM}$ in terms of **a** and **b** to show O, M and N are co-linear.

$\overrightarrow{ON} = \overrightarrow{OA} + \overrightarrow{AN} = \mathbf{a} + \frac{1}{3}(-\mathbf{a} + 4\mathbf{b}) = \mathbf{a} - \frac{1}{3}\mathbf{a} + \frac{4}{3}\mathbf{b}$

$= \frac{2}{3}\mathbf{a} + \frac{4}{3}\mathbf{b} = \frac{2}{3}(\mathbf{a} + 2\mathbf{b})$

$\overrightarrow{OM} = \frac{1}{3}\mathbf{a} + \frac{2}{3}\mathbf{b} = \frac{1}{3}(\mathbf{a} + 2\mathbf{b})$

$\overrightarrow{ON}$ and $\overrightarrow{OM}$ are multiples of the same vector, $(\mathbf{a} + 2\mathbf{b})$, and as they both originate from O it means O, M and N are co-linear.

6 ▶ **a** $OB : OD = 1 : 3$

$\overrightarrow{BD} = 2\overrightarrow{OB} = 2\mathbf{b}$

$\overrightarrow{OD} = \overrightarrow{OB} + \overrightarrow{BD} = \mathbf{b} + 2\mathbf{b} = 3\mathbf{b}$

$\overrightarrow{AD} = \overrightarrow{AO} + \overrightarrow{OD} = -\mathbf{a} + 3\mathbf{b}$

b $\overrightarrow{BC}$ and $\overrightarrow{OA}$ are parallel so $\overrightarrow{BC} = \mathbf{a}$

$\overrightarrow{BC} = \mathbf{a}$

$\overrightarrow{XC} = \frac{1}{3}\overrightarrow{BC} = \frac{1}{3}\mathbf{a}$

$\overrightarrow{AX} = \overrightarrow{AC} + \overrightarrow{CX} = \mathbf{b} - \frac{1}{3}\mathbf{a} = -\frac{1}{3}\mathbf{a} + \mathbf{b} = \frac{1}{3}(-\mathbf{a} + 3\mathbf{b})$

$\overrightarrow{AX}$ and $\overrightarrow{AD}$ are multiples of the same vector, $(-\mathbf{a} + 3\mathbf{b})$, and as they both originate from A it means A, X and D are co-linear.

7 ▶ a $\overrightarrow{PR} = \overrightarrow{PO} + \overrightarrow{OR} = -\mathbf{a} + \mathbf{b}$

$\overrightarrow{PM} : \overrightarrow{MR} = 2 : 1$

$\overrightarrow{PM} = \frac{2}{3}\overrightarrow{PR} = \frac{2}{3}(-\mathbf{a} + \mathbf{b})$

$\overrightarrow{OM} = \overrightarrow{OP} + \overrightarrow{PM} = \mathbf{a} + \frac{2}{3}(-\mathbf{a} + \mathbf{b}) = \mathbf{a} - \frac{2}{3}\mathbf{a} + \frac{2}{3}\mathbf{b}$

$\qquad\qquad = \frac{1}{3}\mathbf{a} + \frac{2}{3}\mathbf{b}$

b $\overrightarrow{PQ}$ and $\overrightarrow{OR}$ are parallel so $\overrightarrow{PQ} = \mathbf{b}$

$\overrightarrow{QN} = \overrightarrow{PQ} = \mathbf{b}$

$\overrightarrow{ON} = \overrightarrow{OP} + \overrightarrow{PQ} + \overrightarrow{QN} = \mathbf{a} + \mathbf{b} + \mathbf{b} = \mathbf{a} + 2\mathbf{b}$

$\overrightarrow{OM} = \frac{1}{3}\mathbf{a} + \frac{2}{3}\mathbf{b} + \frac{1}{3}(\mathbf{a} + 2\mathbf{b})$

$\overrightarrow{OM} = \frac{1}{3}\overrightarrow{ON}$

$\overrightarrow{OM}$ is a multiple of $\overrightarrow{ON}$ which means OMN is a straight line.

EXERCISE 5

1 ▶ a $6\mathbf{i} + 8\mathbf{j}$ **b** $6\mathbf{i} - 6\mathbf{j}$ **c** $\mathbf{i} + 6\mathbf{j}$

     d $-23\mathbf{i} - 12\mathbf{j}$

2 ▶ a $9\mathbf{i} + 14\mathbf{j}$ **b** $2\sqrt{34}$ **c** $\mathbf{i} + 8\mathbf{j}$

     d $\sqrt{65}$ **e** $-2\mathbf{i} + 8\mathbf{j}$

3 ▶ a $\overrightarrow{OA} = 4\mathbf{i} - 2\mathbf{j}, \overrightarrow{OB} = 6\mathbf{i} + 4\mathbf{j}, \overrightarrow{OC} = -2\mathbf{i} + 6\mathbf{j}$

     b $2\mathbf{i} + 6\mathbf{j}$ **c** $-6\mathbf{i} + 8\mathbf{j}$ **d** $2\sqrt{10}$

     e $2\sqrt{10}$ **f** 10

4 ▶ a $-\mathbf{i} + 5\mathbf{j}$ **b** $3\mathbf{i} - 4\mathbf{j}$ **c** $-2\mathbf{i} - \mathbf{j}$

5 ▶ $5\mathbf{i} + 6\mathbf{j}$

6 ▶ $\mathbf{a} = \frac{6\mathbf{i} + 3\mathbf{j}}{3\sqrt{5}}$, $\mathbf{b} = \frac{1}{10}(6\mathbf{i} - 8\mathbf{j})$, $\mathbf{c} = \frac{-5\mathbf{i} + 14\mathbf{j}}{\sqrt{221}}$

7 ▶ $m = 3, n = 1$

8 ▶ $p = -2, q = 5$

9 ▶ a $\begin{pmatrix} 8 \\ -15 \end{pmatrix}$ **b** 17 **c** $\begin{pmatrix} 12 \\ 0 \end{pmatrix}$ **d** 12

EXAM PRACTICE QUESTIONS

1 ▶ $\overrightarrow{OB} = \overrightarrow{OA} + \overrightarrow{AB} = 5\mathbf{i} - 6\mathbf{j} + \mathbf{i} + 11\mathbf{j} = 6\mathbf{i} + 5\mathbf{j}$

$|OA| = \sqrt{5^2 + (-6)^2} = \sqrt{25 + 36} = \sqrt{61}$

$|AB| = \sqrt{1^2 + 11^2} = \sqrt{1 + 121} = \sqrt{122}$

$|OB| = \sqrt{6^2 + 5^2} = \sqrt{36 + 25} = \sqrt{61}$

OB and OA have equal length, therefore the triangle OAB is an isosceles triangle.

2 ▶ First find vectors to help prove $\overrightarrow{BX}$ and $\overrightarrow{XE}$ are co-linear.

$\overrightarrow{AC} = \overrightarrow{AB} + \overrightarrow{BC} = -\mathbf{a} + \mathbf{b}$

$AX : XC = 3 : 2$

$\overrightarrow{AX} = \frac{3}{5}\overrightarrow{AC} = \frac{3}{5}(-\mathbf{a} + \mathbf{b})$

$DA : DE = 1 : 5$

$\overrightarrow{AE} = 4\overrightarrow{DA} = 4(\frac{1}{4}\mathbf{a} + \frac{3}{4}\mathbf{b}) = \mathbf{a} + 3\mathbf{b}$

Now we can find $\overrightarrow{BX}$ and $\overrightarrow{XE}$.

$\overrightarrow{BX} = \overrightarrow{BA} + \overrightarrow{AX} = \mathbf{a} + \frac{3}{5}(-\mathbf{a} + \mathbf{b}) = \mathbf{a} - \frac{3}{5}\mathbf{a} + \frac{3}{5}\mathbf{b} = \frac{2}{5}\mathbf{a} + \frac{3}{5}\mathbf{b}$

$\qquad = \frac{1}{5}(2\mathbf{a} + 3\mathbf{b})$

$\overrightarrow{XE} = \overrightarrow{XA} + \overrightarrow{AE} = -\frac{3}{5}(-\mathbf{a} + \mathbf{b}) + \mathbf{a} + 3\mathbf{b} = \frac{3}{5}\mathbf{a} - \frac{3}{5}\mathbf{b} + \mathbf{a} + 3\mathbf{b}$

$\qquad = \frac{8}{5}\mathbf{a} + \frac{12}{5}\mathbf{b} = \frac{4}{5}(2\mathbf{a} + 3\mathbf{b})$

$\overrightarrow{BX}$ and $\overrightarrow{XE}$ are multiples of the same vector, $(2\mathbf{a} + 3\mathbf{b})$, which means they are co-linear.

3 ▶ $\frac{4}{3}$

4 ▶ $-1\frac{1}{2}$

5 ▶ a $m = 3, n = -2$

     b $o = -4$

     c $\lambda = 5$

6 ▶ a Zaynab: $\begin{pmatrix} 10 \\ 14 \end{pmatrix}$ Asaad: $\begin{pmatrix} 8 \\ 10 \end{pmatrix}$ Alistair: $\begin{pmatrix} 6 \\ 4 \end{pmatrix}$

     b i Zaynab: 17.2 km   **ii** 2.9 km/h^{-1}

       i Asaad: 12.8 km   **ii** 2.1 km/h^{-1}

       i Alistair: 7.2 km   **ii** 1.2 km/h^{-1}

7 ▶ a As $OPQR$ is a parallelogram, $\overrightarrow{RQ} = \overrightarrow{OP}$ and $\overrightarrow{PQ} = \overrightarrow{OR}$

$\overrightarrow{OQ} = \overrightarrow{OP} + \overrightarrow{PQ} = 2\mathbf{a} + 2\mathbf{b}$

M is the midpoint of OQ so

$\overrightarrow{OM} = \frac{1}{2}\overrightarrow{OQ} = \frac{1}{2}(2\mathbf{a} + 2\mathbf{b}) = \mathbf{a} + \mathbf{b}$

     b $\overrightarrow{PR} = \overrightarrow{PO} + \overrightarrow{OR} = -2\mathbf{a} + 2\mathbf{b}$

$\overrightarrow{MR} = \overrightarrow{MO} + \overrightarrow{OR} = -(\mathbf{a} + \mathbf{b}) + 2\mathbf{b} = -\mathbf{a} - \mathbf{b} + 2\mathbf{b} = -\mathbf{a} + \mathbf{b}$

So $\overrightarrow{MR} = \frac{1}{2}\overrightarrow{PR}$ which means M is the midpoint of PR.

8 ▶ **a** $\overrightarrow{AB} = \overrightarrow{AO} + \overrightarrow{OB} = -4\mathbf{a} + 4\mathbf{b}$

b $\overrightarrow{EF}$ is parallel to $\overrightarrow{OA}$ which means $\overrightarrow{EF} = 4\mathbf{a}$

c $\overrightarrow{BC}$ is parallel to AO which means $\overrightarrow{BC} = -4\mathbf{a}$

$\overrightarrow{BX} = \frac{1}{2}\overrightarrow{BC} = -2\mathbf{a}$

$\overrightarrow{EO} = \overrightarrow{OB} = 4\mathbf{b}$

$\overrightarrow{EX} = \overrightarrow{EO} + \overrightarrow{OB} + \overrightarrow{BX} = 4\mathbf{b} + 4\mathbf{b} - 2\mathbf{a} = 8\mathbf{b} - 2\mathbf{a}$

d $AB : BY = 3 : 2$

$\overrightarrow{BY} = \frac{2}{3}\overrightarrow{AB} = \frac{2}{3}(-4\mathbf{a} + 4\mathbf{b}) = -\frac{8}{3}\mathbf{a} + \frac{8}{3}\mathbf{b}$

$\overrightarrow{EY} = \overrightarrow{EO} + \overrightarrow{OB} + \overrightarrow{BY} = 4\mathbf{b} + 4\mathbf{b} - \frac{8}{3}\mathbf{a} + \frac{8}{3}\mathbf{b} = \frac{32}{3}\mathbf{b} - \frac{8}{3}\mathbf{a}$

$= \frac{8}{3}(4\mathbf{b} - \mathbf{a})$

$\overrightarrow{EX} = 8\mathbf{b} - 2\mathbf{a} = 2(4\mathbf{b} - \mathbf{a})$

$\overrightarrow{EX} = \frac{3}{4}\overrightarrow{EY}$

$\overrightarrow{EX}$ is a multiple of $\overrightarrow{EY}$ which means E, X and Y lie on the same straight line.

9 ▶ If we label each of the vertices A, B and C. Then we have

$\overrightarrow{OA} = 2\mathbf{i} + 6\mathbf{j}$

$\overrightarrow{OB} = 6\mathbf{i} + 2\mathbf{j}$

$\overrightarrow{OC} = 11\mathbf{i} + 13\mathbf{j}$

We can then work out the vectors between A, B and C

$\overrightarrow{AB} = \overrightarrow{OB} - \overrightarrow{OA} = 6\mathbf{i} + 2\mathbf{j} - (2\mathbf{i} + 6\mathbf{j}) = 4\mathbf{i} - 4\mathbf{j}$

$\overrightarrow{AC} = \overrightarrow{OC} - \overrightarrow{OA} = 11\mathbf{i} + 13\mathbf{j} - (2\mathbf{i} + 6\mathbf{j}) = 9\mathbf{i} + 7\mathbf{j}$

$\overrightarrow{BC} = \overrightarrow{OC} - \overrightarrow{OB} = 11\mathbf{i} + 13\mathbf{j} - (6\mathbf{i} + 2\mathbf{j}) = 5\mathbf{i} + 9\mathbf{j}$

If we look at the lengths of $\overrightarrow{BC}$ and $\overrightarrow{AC}$

$|AC| = \sqrt{9^2 + 5^2} = \sqrt{81 + 25} = \sqrt{106}$

$|BC| = \sqrt{5^2 + 9^2} = \sqrt{25 + 81} = \sqrt{106}$

We can see they are equal which means the triangle is an isosceles triangle.

10 ▶ $\begin{pmatrix} -2 \\ 10 \end{pmatrix}$

11 ▶ M is the midpoint of $\overrightarrow{OA}$ which means $\overrightarrow{OA} = 2\overrightarrow{OM} = 2\mathbf{a}$

N is the midpoint of $\overrightarrow{OB}$ which means $\overrightarrow{OB} = 2\overrightarrow{ON} = 2\mathbf{b}$

$\overrightarrow{MN} = \overrightarrow{MO} + \overrightarrow{ON} = -\mathbf{a} + \mathbf{b}$

$\overrightarrow{AB} = \overrightarrow{AO} + \overrightarrow{OB} = -2\mathbf{a} + 2\mathbf{b} = 2(-\mathbf{a} + \mathbf{b})$

$\overrightarrow{AB} = 2\overrightarrow{MN}$

As $\overrightarrow{AB}$ is a multiple of $\overrightarrow{MN}$, this means they are parallel.

12 ▶ Since $\overrightarrow{AR} = k\overrightarrow{AB}$ they are parallel. Since they also both go through point A they must form a straight line.

CHAPTER 8 – RECTANGULAR CARTESIAN COORDINATES

STARTER ACTIVITIES

1 ▶ **a** $m = 2$, $c = 5$ **b** $m = 2$, $c = -3$

c $m = \frac{1}{3}$, $c = 0$ **d** $m = 0$, $c = 6$

e $m = \frac{2}{3}$, $c = 9$

EXERCISE 1

1 ▶ **a** 0.5 **b** 4 **c** $-\frac{5}{14}$ **d** $\frac{2}{3}$

2 ▶ $d = 5$

3 ▶ $a = 3$

4 ▶ $a = -4$

5 ▶ $a = 3.3$

6 ▶ $-10\frac{3}{22}$

7 ▶ **a** $AB : \frac{3}{2}$, $BC : -\frac{2}{3}$, $CD : \frac{3}{2}$, $DA : -\frac{2}{3}$

b The lines are parallel, therefore the quadrilateral is a parallelogram

EXERCISE 2

1 ▶ **a** $y = 3x$ **b** $y = 24 - 6x$ **c** $y = \frac{1}{2}x - 7$

2 ▶ $-7x + 19y - 219 = 0$

3 ▶ $y = \frac{1}{16}x + \frac{61}{8}$

4 ▶ $y = -\frac{3}{7}x + \frac{96}{7}$

5 ▶ $2x + 5y + 20 = 0$

6 ▶ $3y = 2x + 9$

7 ▶ $(3, 0)$

8 ▶ $y = -\frac{2}{3}x + 7$

EXERCISE 3

1 ▶ **a** Perpendicular   **b** Parallel   **c** Parallel

d Perpendicular   **e** Parallel   **f** Neither

2 ▶ $5y = -x + 37$

3 ▶ **a** $2y = x + 1$ **b** $4y = 22 - x$

c $2y = x + 1$ **d** $2y + 3x + 1 = 0$

4 ▶ $-3x + 4y + 25 = 0$

5 ▶ $5x + 4y - 42 = 0$

6 ▶ $3x + 2y - 27 = 0$

7 ▶ $4y = 3x - 33$

8 ▶

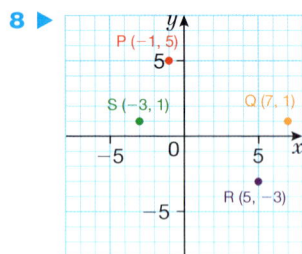

P (−1, 5), S (−3, 1), Q (7, 1), R (5, −3)

PQRS will be a rectangle if the line *PS* is perpendicular to *SR*, line *RQ* is perpendicular to *QP*, the line *SR* is parallel to *QP* and line *RQ* is parallel to *PS*.

Gradient of line $PS = \left(\dfrac{5-1}{-1-(-3)}\right) = \dfrac{4}{2} = 2$

Gradient of line $SR = \left(\dfrac{-3-1}{5-(-3)}\right) = \dfrac{-4}{8} = -\dfrac{1}{2}$

Gradient of line $RQ = \left(\dfrac{-3-1}{5-7}\right) = \dfrac{-4}{-2} = 2$

Gradient of line $QP = \left(\dfrac{1-5}{7-(-1)}\right) = \dfrac{-4}{8} = -\dfrac{1}{2}$

Therefore, the vertices of the quadrilateral PQRS form a rectangle.

EXERCISE 4

1 ▶ **a** 10 **b** 13 **c** 5
  d $4\sqrt{2}$ **e** $2\sqrt{34}$ **f** $a\sqrt{53}$
  g $b\sqrt{181}$ **h** $c\sqrt{10}$

EXERCISE 5

1 ▶ **a** (0, 6) **b** (0, 2) **c** $\left(2, \dfrac{23}{7}\right)$ **d** (5, 5)

2 ▶ $\left(-\dfrac{2}{7}, \dfrac{13}{7}\right)$

3 ▶ (−1, 3)

EXAM PRACTICE QUESTIONS

1 ▶ The line through *AB* is $y = \dfrac{4}{3}x + \dfrac{4}{3}$. The gradient of this line is $\dfrac{4}{3}$
Line *L* can be written as $y = -\dfrac{2}{3}x + \dfrac{4}{3}$. The gradient of *L* is $-\dfrac{2}{3}$
The lines are not parallel.

2 ▶ $-5x + 6y - 15 = 0$

3 ▶ **a** $\sqrt{41}$ **b** 8 **c** 20

4 ▶ $x + 2y - 21 = 0$

5 ▶ $x + 5y - 170 = 0$

6 ▶ $3x - y - 22 = 0$

7 ▶ **a** $\left(5, \dfrac{7}{2}\right)$ **b** $y = \dfrac{1}{2}x + 5$

8 ▶ The distances between adjacent vertices are equal, adjacent sides are perpendicular, and opposite sides are parallel.

9 ▶ 20 square units

10 ▶ 20.79 units

11 ▶ **a** $2y = x + 5$ **b** (7, 6)
  c $4\sqrt{5}$ **d** 30 square units

12 ▶ $\left(1, \dfrac{7}{2}\right)$

13 ▶ $\left(-\dfrac{3}{2}, \dfrac{3}{2}\right)$

14 ▶ **a** $x + 2y - 5 = 0$
  b $AB = \sqrt{(-2-5)^2 + (9-(-5))^2}$
  $= \sqrt{49+196}$
  $= \sqrt{245}$
  $= 7\sqrt{5}$

15 ▶ **a** $y = -x + 6$ **b** 18 square units

CHAPTER 9 – DIFFERENTIATION

STARTER ACTIVITIES

1 ▶ **a** a^{13} **b** a^{10} **c** a^{-14}
  d a^{-6} **e** a^{-2} **f** a^{-6}
  g a^8 **h** $a^{\frac{5}{2}}$ **i** $a^{-\frac{3}{2}}$
  j a^2 **k** a^{-3} **l** a^3
  m $\dfrac{a^2}{b^2}$ **n** $\dfrac{a^6}{b^{12}}$ **o** $a^{12}b^2$
  p $a^{-4}b^4$ **q** $\dfrac{a^8}{b^{12}}$ **r** $\dfrac{m^2}{n^6}$
  s $\dfrac{a^3}{b^5}$ **t** $\dfrac{m^2}{a}$ **u** $\dfrac{c^3}{a^4b}$
  v $\dfrac{x}{m^2}$ **w** $\dfrac{z^{12}}{x^8y^4}$ **x** $\dfrac{b^{\frac{16}{3}}}{a^2}$

EXERCISE 1

1 ▶ **a** $8x^7$ **b** $3x^2$ **c** $\dfrac{1}{2}x^{-\frac{1}{2}}$
  d $\dfrac{3}{2}x^{\frac{1}{2}}$ **e** $-3x^{-4}$ **f** $\dfrac{1}{2}x^{-\frac{1}{2}}$
  g $\dfrac{1}{3}x^{-\frac{2}{3}}$ **h** $-4x^{-5}$ **i** $-2x^{-3}$
  j $-\dfrac{1}{3}x^{-\frac{4}{3}}$ **k** 1 **l** $9x^8$
  m $-\dfrac{7}{2}x^{-\frac{9}{2}}$

2 ▶ **a** $6x$ **b** $28x^3$ **c** $-6x^{-3}$

    d $-3x^{-2}$ **e** $25x^4$ **f** $\frac{3}{2}x^{-\frac{1}{2}}$

    g $-\frac{3}{2}x^{-\frac{3}{2}}$ **h** $-\frac{5}{3}x^{-\frac{4}{3}}$

3 ▶ **a** $\dfrac{dy}{dx} = 5x^4 - 2x^{-3}$ **b** $\dfrac{dy}{dx} = -x^{-3} + 8x$

    c $\dfrac{dy}{dx} = \frac{1}{8}x^{-\frac{7}{8}} - 6x^{-3} + 3x^{-\frac{2}{3}}$

4 ▶ **a** $6x^5 + 2x + 2$ **b** $3x^2$

    c $18x^2 - 10x - 6x^{-3} + 6$

5 ▶ **a** $3 + \frac{2}{9}x^{-\frac{2}{3}}$ **b** $\frac{1}{2}x^{-\frac{5}{6}} + \frac{3}{2}x^{-\frac{1}{4}}$

    c $8x^{-2} - \frac{2}{3}x^{-\frac{5}{3}}$

6 ▶ **a** 6 **b** $\dfrac{23}{2}$ **c** $\dfrac{513}{16}$

7 ▶ **a** $\frac{4}{3}x^3 - 2x^2$ **b** $\frac{3}{2}x^{-\frac{1}{2}} - \frac{1}{2}x^{-2}$

    c $-3x^{-2}$ **d** $3 + 6x^{-2}$

    e $3x^2 - 2x + 2$ **f** $24x - 8 + 2x^{-2}$

EXERCISE 2

1 ▶ **a** $12(3x + 1)^3$ **b** $12(2x - 4)^5$ **c** $6x(1 + x^2)^2$

    d $-35(1 - 5x)^6$ **e** $-3(2 + 3x)^{-2}$ **f** $3(6x + 2)^{-\frac{1}{2}}$

    g $28x^3(x^4 + 3)^6$ **h** $-\frac{1}{2}(7 - x)^{-\frac{1}{2}}$ **i** $-112(2 - 7x)^3$

    j $54(7 - 3x)^{-4}$

2 ▶ **a** $24(2x + 1)$ **b** $20(1 + x)$

    c $-\dfrac{3}{(2 + x)^2}$ **d** $\dfrac{1}{2\sqrt{x + 1}}$

3 ▶ **a** $2\cos(2x + 1)$ **b** $-4x\sin(2x^2 + 3)$

    c $-\sin(x + 1)$ **d** $4\cos(2x + 1)$

4 ▶ -9

5 ▶ **a** $y = 128x - 240$ **b** $y = 2x + 6$

EXERCISE 3

1 ▶ **a** $3\cos 3x$ **b** $\sin x$

    c $-6\cos 2x$ **d** $2e^{2x}$

    e $3\cos x + 6\sin 3x$ **f** $4e^{2x} + 4$

2 ▶ **a** $6\cos 6x$ **b** $\frac{3}{2}\sin\frac{1}{2}x$

    c $4\cos 8x - 24\sin 8x$ **d** $12e^{4x}$

    e $-\frac{3}{2}e^{3x} + 15e^{5x} - 48$

3 ▶ -3

4 ▶ $\dfrac{3}{2}$

5 ▶ -10

EXERCISE 4

1 ▶ **a** $16x(1 + 4x)^3 + (1 + 4x)^4$

    b $24x^2(1 + 3x^2) + 2(1 + 3x^2)^2$

    c $\frac{1}{2}x(x - 2)^{-\frac{1}{2}} + (x - 2)^{\frac{1}{2}}$

    d $6x^4(5 + x)^2 + 8x^3(5 + x)^3$

    e $-20x^2(5x - 2)^{-2} + 8x(5x - 2)^{-1}$

    f $\frac{3}{2}x^3(3x + 1)^{-\frac{1}{2}} + 3x^2(3x + 1)^{\frac{1}{2}}$

2 ▶ **a** $(3x + 1)e^{3x}$ **b** $-2(x^2 - x - 4)e^{-2x}$

    c $2e^{-3x}(1 - 3x)$ **d** $4e^{x^3}(3x^3 + 1)$

    e $2(6x^2 + x + 3)e^{x^2}$ **f** $-(10x^2 + 4x - 5)e^{-x^2}$

3 ▶ **a** $\cos x - x\sin x$ **b** $\cos^3 x - \sin 2x\sin x$

    c $4(\sin 6x + 6x\cos 6x)$ **d** $e^x(\cos x - \sin x)$

    e $e^x(\cos x + \sin x)$

4 ▶ **a** 1700 **b** 14 **c** 224

5 ▶ $y = \dfrac{8}{\sqrt{3}}x - \dfrac{5}{\sqrt{3}}$

EXERCISE 5

1 ▶ **a** $-\dfrac{6}{(x - 1)^2}$ **b** $\dfrac{1}{(2x + 1)^2}$ **c** $-\dfrac{6x(x + 3)}{(2x - 3)^4}$

    d $\dfrac{24x}{(x + 2)^3}$ **e** $-\dfrac{3(x + 4)}{8x^3\sqrt{x + 3}}$ **f** $\dfrac{2x - 9}{(4x + 3)^{\frac{3}{2}}}$

2 ▶ **a** $\dfrac{1 - 3x}{e^{3x}}$ **b** $\dfrac{e^{x^2}(2x^2 + 2x - 1)}{(x + 1)^2}$

    c $2e^{x^2} - \dfrac{e^{x^2}}{x^2}$ **d** $\dfrac{3e^{3x}}{(1 - e^{3x})^2}$

3 ▶ **a** $-\left(\dfrac{x\sin x + \cos x}{x^2}\right)$ **b** $\dfrac{e^x\sin x - e^x\cos x}{\sin^2 x}$

    c $\dfrac{3x^2\sin x + \sin x + 6x\cos x}{\cos^2 x}$ **d** $\dfrac{2}{\sin x} - \dfrac{(2x - 1)\cos x}{\sin^2 x}$

4 ▶ **a** $y = \frac{1}{4}x + 1$ **b** $y = -\dfrac{x}{\pi} + 1$

EXERCISE 6

1 ▶ **a** Tangent: $y = -2x + 2$

    Normal: $y = \frac{1}{2}x - \dfrac{11}{2}$

    b Tangent: $y = 8x - \dfrac{5}{2}$

    Normal: $y = -\frac{1}{8}x + \dfrac{45}{8}$

    c Tangent: $y = \dfrac{13}{2}x - \dfrac{17}{2}$

    Normal: $y = -\dfrac{2}{13}x - \dfrac{24}{13}$

    d Tangent: $y = 2e^2x - e^2$

    Normal: $y = -\dfrac{1}{2e^2}x + \dfrac{2e^4 + 1}{2e^2}$

e Tangent: $y = -\dfrac{3}{e^3}(x-1) + \dfrac{1}{e^2}$

Normal: $y = \dfrac{e^3}{3}(x-1) + \dfrac{1}{e^2}$

EXERCISE 7

1 ▶ a $x = -6$ **b** $x = -\dfrac{3}{10}$

c $x = \dfrac{3}{8}$ **d** -3 or 3

2 ▶ a $x = -\dfrac{1}{6}$, minimum

b $x = \dfrac{7}{12}$, maximum

c $x = \dfrac{1}{4}$, minimum

d $x = 1$, minimum and $x = -\dfrac{1}{3}$, maximum

e $x = 1$, minimum and $x = -1$, maximum

f $x = 3$, minimum

EXERCISE 8

1 ▶ $20\,\text{m} \times 40\,\text{m} = 800\,\text{m}^2$

2 ▶ $2000\pi\,\text{cm}^3$

3 ▶ Maximum area is $\dfrac{800}{4+\pi}\,\text{cm}^2$

As $\dfrac{d^2A}{dr^2} = -4 - \pi < 0$ the area is a maximum, as required.

4 ▶ a $y = 1 - \dfrac{x}{2} - \dfrac{\pi x}{4}$

b $A = xy + \dfrac{1}{2}\pi\left(\dfrac{x}{2}\right)^2$

$A = x\left(1 - \dfrac{1}{2}x - \dfrac{\pi}{4}x\right) + \dfrac{\pi}{8}x^2$

$A = x - \dfrac{1}{2}x^2 - \dfrac{\pi}{4}x^2 + \dfrac{\pi}{8}x^2$

$A = \dfrac{x}{8}(8 - 4x - 2\pi x + \pi x)$

$A = \dfrac{x}{8}(8 - 4x - \pi x)$

5 ▶ $27\,216\,\text{mm}^2$

EXAM PRACTICE QUESTIONS

1 ▶ a $f'(x) = 3x^2 + 3$ **b** 2

2 ▶ $\dfrac{d}{dx}\left(5x - 7 + \dfrac{2\sqrt{x}+3}{x}\right) = 5 + \dfrac{x\left(x^{-\frac{1}{2}}\right) - \left(2\sqrt{x}+3\right)}{x^2}$

3 ▶ a $P = 16, Q = -24$ **b** $= \dfrac{16x-9}{2x^{\frac{3}{2}}}$ **c** $\dfrac{5}{2}$

4 ▶ a $6x^2 + 2kx$ **b** $k = \dfrac{31}{8}$ **c** $P = \dfrac{13}{2}$

5 ▶ a 7 **b** $y = 3x + 1$ **c** $\dfrac{1}{3}(2 + \sqrt{6})$

6 ▶ a $= 1 + \dfrac{24}{x^2}$ **b** $y = 7x - 29$

7 ▶ $15\cos 5x - 12\sin 3x$

8 ▶ $-\dfrac{1}{2}\sin\left(\dfrac{x}{2}\right)$

9 ▶ $2e^{2x} + 6x + 16\cos 4x$

10 ▶ -4

11 ▶ -8

12 ▶ $\dfrac{-3k}{(x-2k)^2}$

13 ▶ $2y + x = 35$

14 ▶ $36e^{2x^3}x^2$

15 ▶ $12\sin 2x\cos 2x$

16 ▶ $-\dfrac{e^x(e^x+2)}{(e^x-2)^3}$

17 ▶ $\dfrac{(4x\cos 4x - 3\sin 4x)}{x^4}$

18 ▶ $2x\cos 3x - 3x^2\sin 3x$

19 ▶ $12x^3 + 45x^2 + 10x - 5$

20 ▶ $y = -x$

21 ▶ a $(4, 6)$

b Maximum

22 ▶ a $y = x^2 - kx^{\frac{1}{2}}$ **b** $k > 32$

$\dfrac{dy}{dx} = 2x^{(2-1)} - \dfrac{1}{2}kx^{\left(\frac{1}{2}-1\right)}$

$\dfrac{dy}{dx} = 2x - \dfrac{1}{2}kx^{-\frac{1}{2}}$

23 ▶ a Let angle $MON = \theta$ radians

$Perimeter\ P = 2r + r\theta$

$Area\ A = \dfrac{1}{2}r^2\theta$

Area = 100, therefore,

$\dfrac{1}{2}r^2\theta = 100$

$r^2\theta = 200$

$r\theta = \dfrac{200}{r}$

Substituting $r\theta$ into the perimeter equation gives:

$P = 2r + \dfrac{200}{r}$

b $40\,\text{cm}$

CHAPTER 10 – INTEGRATION

STARTER ACTIVITIES

1 ▶ a i $2x - 3$ ii 1 iii -5 iv -3

b i $2x + 1$ ii 5 iii -1 iv 1

c i $6x^5 - 14x$ ii 164 iii 8 iv 0

d i $4x^3$ ii 32 iii -4 iv 0

e i $\dfrac{1}{4}$ ii $\dfrac{1}{4}$ iii $\dfrac{1}{4}$ iv $\dfrac{1}{4}$

f i $-2x - 2$ ii -6 iii 0 iv -2

EXERCISE 1

1 ▶ a $\dfrac{x^4}{4} + \dfrac{3x^2}{2} + c$ b $x^4 - x^2 + c$

c $4x - \dfrac{3}{x} + c$ d $-x^3 + \dfrac{10x^{\frac{3}{2}}}{3} + c$

e $10x^3 + \dfrac{1}{2}x^{-2} + c$ f $\dfrac{x^3}{3} - \dfrac{2x^{\frac{5}{2}}}{5} + 4x + 2\sqrt{x} + c$

g $\dfrac{4}{3}x^3 + x^{-3} + rx + c$ h $\dfrac{p}{5}x^5 + 2tx - 3x^{-1} + c$

i $-\dfrac{3}{4x} - \dfrac{x^2}{8} + c$

2 ▶ a $\dfrac{1}{2}x^4 + x^3 + c$ b $2x - \dfrac{3}{x} + c$

c $\dfrac{4}{3}x^3 + 6x^2 + 9x + c$ d $\dfrac{4}{3}x^{\frac{3}{2}} + 6x^{\frac{1}{2}} + c$

e $\dfrac{3}{x} - \dfrac{1}{8x^2} + c$ f $\dfrac{3x^{\frac{8}{3}}}{8} - \dfrac{4}{3x^{\frac{3}{4}}} + c$

3 ▶ a $2\sin x + c$ b $-\dfrac{2\cos 3x}{3} + c$

c $4e^x + c$ d $\dfrac{3e^{4x}}{4} + c$

e $= -3e^{-x} + c$ f $-\dfrac{5e^{-3x}}{3} + c$

g $-2\cos\dfrac{1}{2}x + c$ h $\dfrac{5}{3}\sin 3x + c$

i $-\dfrac{4}{3}\cos 3x + c$

4 ▶ a $2(\sin x + \cos x) + 3x^2 + c$

b $-3\cos x + 7e^x + \dfrac{2}{x} + c$

c $2\sin x - \cos x + e^x + c$

d $-\cos 2x + \dfrac{3e^{4x}}{4} + x^3 + c$

e $4\left(\sin x + e^x + \dfrac{x^3}{3}\right) + c$

EXERCISE 2

1 ▶ $v = 20t$

2 ▶ $v = 48 - 32t$

3 ▶ a $30 - 10t$ b $0\,\text{ms}^{-1}$

4 ▶ a $a = -32\,\text{ms}^{-2}$ b i $s = 384 + 160t - 16t^2$
  ii $t = 12$

5 ▶ a $a = 6 - 2t$ b $2\,\text{ms}^{-2}$ c $57.3\,\text{m}$ (3 s.f.)

EXERCISE 3

1 ▶ a $\dfrac{4}{3}$ square units

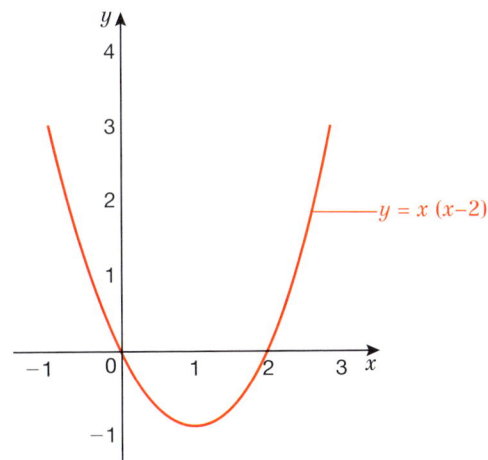

b $20\dfrac{5}{6}$ square units

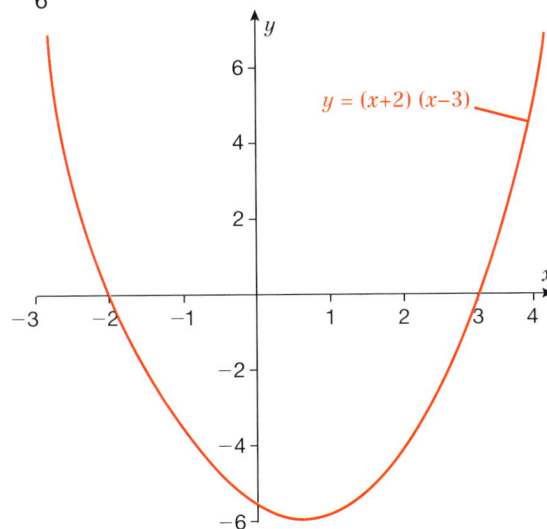

c $20\dfrac{5}{6}$ square units

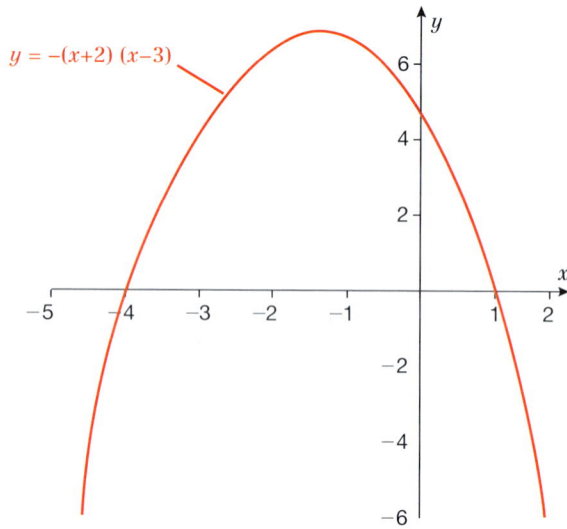

$y = -(x+2)(x-3)$

d $21\dfrac{1}{12}$ square units

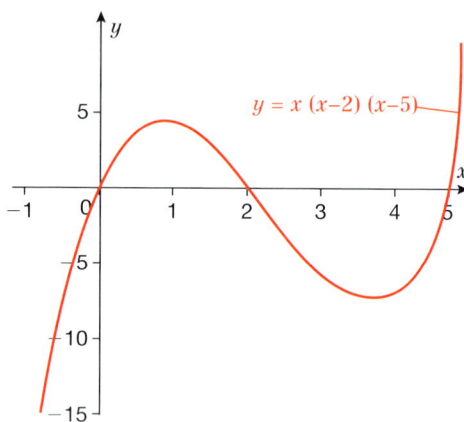

$y = x(x-2)(x-5)$

2 ▶ a 33 square units   **b** $5\dfrac{1}{6}$ square units

    c $\dfrac{9}{4}$ square units   **d** 8.48 square units

    e $8\dfrac{5}{12}$ square units

3 ▶ a $\dfrac{4}{3}$ square units   **b** $10\dfrac{2}{3}$ square units

    c $\dfrac{1}{6}$ square units   **d** $5\dfrac{1}{3}$ square units

    e $\dfrac{9}{2}$ square units

4 ▶ a 7   **b** 0.5

    c 2   **d** 32

5 ▶ $20\dfrac{5}{6}$ square units

6 ▶ 3 square units

7 ▶ a $(-3, 9), (3, 9)$ **b** 36 square units

8 ▶ a $(0, 1), (3, 4)$ **b** $\dfrac{9}{2}$ square units

9 ▶ $\dfrac{59}{6}$ square units

10 ▶ a $(2, 12)$

    b The area is found by taking $\displaystyle\int_{0}^{2} x(4+x)\,dx$ away from a rectangle of area $12 \times 2 = 24$

$$\text{Area} = 24 - \int_{0}^{2} x(4+x)\,dx$$

$$= 24 - \left[\frac{x^3}{3} + 2x^2\right]_{0}^{2}$$

$$= 24 - \left\{\left(\frac{8}{3}+8\right)-(0)\right\}$$

$$= 24 - \frac{32}{3}$$

$$= 13\frac{1}{3}$$

11 ▶ Plotting the curve of $y + 4x - x^2$ reveals that it crosses the x-axis at $x = 4$.

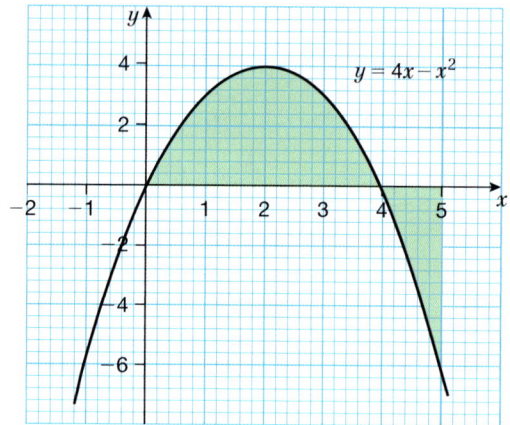

$y = 4x - x^2$

To find the area, we need to split the integral at $x = 4$

$$\text{Area above the } x\text{-axis} = \int_{0}^{4}(4x - x^2)\,dx = \left[2x^2 - \frac{x^3}{3}\right]_{0}^{4} = 10\frac{2}{3}$$

$$\text{Area below the } x\text{-axis} = \int_{5}^{4}(4x - x^2)\,dx = \left[2x^2 - \frac{x^3}{3}\right]_{5}^{4} = 2\frac{1}{3}$$

The total area is $10\dfrac{2}{3} + 2\dfrac{1}{3} = 13$

EXERCISE 4

1 ▶ $\dfrac{32}{5}\pi$ cubed units

2 ▶ $\dfrac{128}{7}\pi$ cubed units

3 ▶ $\dfrac{198}{7}\pi$ cubed units

4 ▶ a i $2\ln 2$ **ii** 2π

     b i $\dfrac{8}{3}$ **ii** $\dfrac{64}{15}\pi$

EXERCISE 5

1 ▶ $\dfrac{8}{9\pi}$

2 ▶ 6π

3 ▶ $15e^2$

4 ▶ $-\dfrac{9}{2}$

5 ▶ 2%

6 ▶ 3%

7 ▶ $\dfrac{dM}{dt} = -kM$

8 ▶ The gradient of the curve is given by $\dfrac{dy}{dx} \sim xy$

Therefore,

$$\dfrac{dy}{dx} = kxy$$

When $x = 4$ and $y = 2$, $\dfrac{dy}{dx} = \dfrac{1}{2}$

Therefore,

$$\dfrac{1}{2} = k \times 4 \times 2$$

$$k = \dfrac{1}{16}$$

$$\therefore \dfrac{dy}{dx} = \dfrac{xy}{16}$$

9 ▶ Rate of expansion of surface area is $\dfrac{dA}{dt}$

Using the chain rule:

$$\dfrac{dV}{dt} = \dfrac{dV}{dA} \times \dfrac{dA}{dt}$$

$$\dfrac{dA}{dt} = 2 \text{ and } \dfrac{dV}{dt} = 2\dfrac{dV}{dA}$$

Let the cube have edge of length x cm

Then $V = x^3$ and $A = 6x^2$

Eliminate x to give $A = 6V^{\frac{2}{3}}$

$$\therefore \dfrac{dA}{dV} = 4V^{-\frac{1}{3}}$$

From

$$\dfrac{dV}{dt} = 2\dfrac{dV}{dA}$$

$$\dfrac{dV}{dt} = \dfrac{2}{4V^{-\frac{1}{3}}}$$

$$= \dfrac{2V^{\frac{1}{3}}}{4}$$

$$= \dfrac{1}{2}V^{\frac{1}{3}}$$

10 ▶ $\dfrac{dh}{dt} = \dfrac{18}{\pi h^2}$

EXAM PRACTICE QUESTIONS

1 ▶ $y = \dfrac{1}{5}x^5 + 2x^3 + 9x - \dfrac{548}{5}$

2 ▶ $y = -\dfrac{1}{4}x^4 - 2x^{-1} + \dfrac{5}{4}x^{-2} + 8$

3 ▶ $\dfrac{5x^4}{4} + \dfrac{5}{x} + c$

4 ▶ $\dfrac{2\sqrt{x}(x + 27)}{3} + c$

5 ▶ $-4\sin x + 5e^x + \dfrac{x^4}{2} + c$

6 ▶ $12\dfrac{2}{3}$ square units

7 ▶ **a** (2, 8) and (9, 1)   **b** $57\dfrac{1}{6}$ square units

8 ▶ **a** $(-1, 0)$ and (4, 0)   **b** $\dfrac{125}{6}$ square units

9 ▶ 37.7 (3 s.f.)

10 ▶ $\dfrac{148}{3}$ square units

11 ▶ $\dfrac{11}{6}$ square units

12 ▶ $\dfrac{243}{2}$ square units

13 ▶ $\dfrac{128}{7}\pi$ cubed units

14 ▶ $\dfrac{16}{7}\pi$ cubed units

15 ▶ $\dfrac{146}{5}\pi$ cubed units

16 ▶ The distance of P from O when $t = 1$ is 12.25 m

17 ▶ **a** The acceleration of P when $t = 3$ is 19.5 ms^{-2}

     b 32 m

CHAPTER 11 – TRIGONOMETRY

STARTER ACTIVITIES

1 ▶ Sin
Opposite
Hypotenuse
Cosine
Adjacent
Hypotenuse
Tangent
Opposite
Adjacent

2 ▶ 1500 m

3 ▶ 41.2 m

EXERCISE 1

1 ▶ a 18°   **b** 9°   **c** 75°
d 90°   **e** 180°   **f** 540°
g 900°   **h** 140°   **i** 225°
j 270°

2 ▶ a 32.7°   **b** 57.3°   **c** 114.6°
d 78.5°   **e** 81.0°   **f** 179.9°
g 257.3°

3 ▶ a 0.247   **b** 6.334   **c** 0.847
d −0.998   **e** −0.058   **f** 0.0585

4 ▶ a $\dfrac{2\pi}{45}$ **b** $\dfrac{\pi}{18}$ **c** $\dfrac{\pi}{8}$
d $\dfrac{\pi}{6}$ **e** $\dfrac{5\pi}{8}$ **f** $\dfrac{2\pi}{3}$
g $\dfrac{3\pi}{4}$ **h** $\dfrac{4\pi}{3}$ **i** $\dfrac{3\pi}{2}$
j $\dfrac{7\pi}{4}$ **k** $\dfrac{11\pi}{6}$

5 ▶ a 0.873   **b** 1.31   **c** 1.75
d 2.09   **e** 4.10   **f** 5.67

EXERCISE 2

1 ▶ a i 3.6 cm   **ii** 25.9 cm   **iii** 15.4 cm
b i 20 cm   **ii** 3.34 cm   **iii** 1.91 cm
c i 1.19 rad   **ii** 0.978 rad   **iii** 2.45 rad
d i 13.8 cm²   **ii** 28.9 cm²   **iii** 169 cm²

2 ▶ a Area = 24.3 cm² and arc length = 5.4 cm
b Area = 6.73 cm² and arc length = 2.01 cm
c Area = 88.1 cm² and arc length = 26.3 cm

3 ▶ a 5.6 cm²   **b** 4.87 cm²

4 ▶ $\dfrac{16}{3}\pi$ cm²

5 ▶ a 4.13 radians   **b** 45.5 cm

6 ▶ Area = 39.6 cm² and perimeter = 25.2 cm

7 ▶ a Perimeter = 10 cm   **b** Area = 6 cm²

8 ▶ a Perimeter = 20.4 cm   **b** Area = 23.7 cm²

9 ▶ a $r = 20$ cm
b Area of minor sector $=\dfrac{1}{2}r^2\theta=\dfrac{1}{2}\times 20^2\times 0.25=50$ cm²
c 0.519 cm²

10 ▶ 42.3 cm²

11 ▶ a $(R-r)$ cm
b In $\triangle COE, \angle CEO=90°$
$\angle CEO=\theta$
(radius perpendicular to tangent)

(OT bisects $\angle AOB$)
Using $\sin \angle COE=\dfrac{CE}{OC}$
$\sin\theta=\dfrac{r}{R-r}$
$(R-r)\sin\theta=r$
$R\sin\theta-r\sin\theta=r$
$R\sin\theta=r+r\sin\theta$
$R\sin\theta=r(1+\sin\theta)$

c 5.68 cm

12 ▶ a Using the cosine rule
$\cos A=\dfrac{b^2+c^2-a^2}{2bc}$
$\cos A=\dfrac{10^2+12^2-14^2}{2\times 10\times 12}=0.2$
$A=\cos^{-1}(0.2)=1.37\text{ radians}$

b 34.1 m²

13 ▶ a

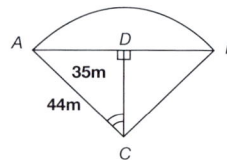

Using right-angled $\triangle ADC$
$\sin \angle ACD=\dfrac{35}{44}$
$\angle ACD=\sin^{-1}\left(\dfrac{35}{44}\right)$
and
$\angle ACB=2\sin^{-1}\left(\dfrac{35}{44}\right)$
$\angle ACB=1.84\text{ radians}$

b i 80.9 m   **ii** 26.7 m   **iii** 847 m²

EXERCISE 3

1 ▶ a $\dfrac{\sqrt{2}}{2}$ **b** $-\dfrac{1}{2}$ **c** $-\dfrac{\sqrt{3}}{2}$
d $-\dfrac{1}{2}$ **e** $\dfrac{\sqrt{3}}{3}$ **f** -1
g $\dfrac{\sqrt{2}}{2}$ **h** $-\dfrac{\sqrt{3}}{2}$ **i** $\dfrac{\sqrt{3}}{2}$
j $-\sqrt{3}$ **k** $\dfrac{\sqrt{3}}{2}$ **l** $\dfrac{\sqrt{3}}{2}$
m $\sqrt{3}$ **n** $-\dfrac{\sqrt{2}}{2}$ **o** $-\dfrac{\sqrt{3}}{3}$

2 ▶ $\dfrac{\pi}{2}, \dfrac{3\pi}{2}, \dfrac{5\pi}{2}, \dfrac{7\pi}{2}$

EXERCISE 4

1 ▶ a $x = 37.7°, y = 86.3°, z = 6.86$
b $x = 48°, y = 19.5, z = 14.6$

c $x = 30°, y = 11.5, z = 11.5$

d $x = 21.0°, y = 29.0°, z = 8.09$

e $x = 93.8°, y = 56.3°, z = 29.9$

f $x = 97.2°, y = 41.4°, z = 41.4°$

g $x = 45.3°, y = 94.7°, z = 14.7$
or $x = 134.7°, y = 5.27°, z = 1.36$

h $x = 7.07, y = 73.7°, z = 61.2°$
or $x = 7.07, y = 106°, z = 28.7°$

i $x = 49.8°, y = 93.2, z = 37.0°$

2 ▶ a $23.7\,cm^2$　　**b** $4.31\,cm^2$　　**c** $20.2\,cm^2$

3 ▶ $42.4\,cm^2$

4 ▶ $\angle CAB = 38°$ (Due to $180° - 128° = 52°$ ·

$\angle ABN = 52°$ (Using the North line from the bearing and due to alternate angles)

$\angle ABC = 52° + 66° = 118°$

$\angle ACB = 180° - \angle CAB - \angle ABC$

$\angle ACB = 180° - 38° - 118°$

$\angle ACB = 24°$

5 ▶ $29.8\,cm$

6 ▶

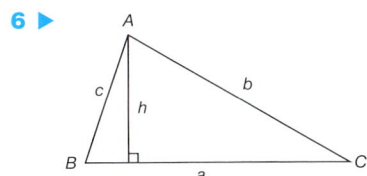

From the definition of the sine function

$$\sin B = \frac{h}{c} \text{ and } \sin C = \frac{h}{b}$$

or

$$h = c\sin B \text{ and } h = b\sin C$$

Since they are both equal to h:

$$\frac{c}{\sin C} = \frac{b}{\sin B}$$

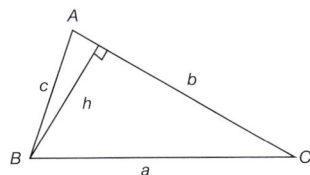

Repeat the above, this time the altitude is drawn from B

$$\frac{c}{\sin C} = \frac{a}{\sin A}$$

$$= \frac{a}{\sin A} = \frac{b}{\sin B} = \frac{c}{\sin C}$$

7 ▶

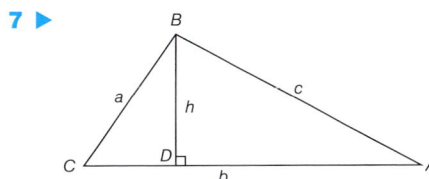

In the right-angled triangle BCD, from the definition of cosine:

$$\cos C = \frac{CD}{a} \text{ or } CD = a\cos C$$

Subtracting the above from side b

$$DA = b - a\cos C$$

In the triangle BCD, from the definition of sine

$$\sin C = \frac{BD}{a} \text{ or } BD = a\sin C$$

In the triangle ADB

$$c^2 = BD^2 + DA^2$$

Substituting for BD and DA

$$c^2 = (a\sin C)^2 + (b - a\cos C)^2$$

$$c^2 = a^2\sin^2 C + a^2\cos^2 C + b^2 - 2ab\cos C$$

$$c^2 = a^2(\sin^2 C + \cos^2 C) + b^2 - 2ab\cos C$$

$$c^2 = a^2 + b^2 - 2ab\cos C \quad (\sin^2\theta + \cos^2\theta = 1)$$

8 ▶ a $x = 4$　　**b** $6.50\,cm^2$

EXERCISE 5

1 ▶ a $11.3\,cm$　**b** $9\,cm$　**c** $51.1°$　**d** $32.2\,cm$

2 ▶ a $10.4\,cm$　　　　　**b** $35.3°$

3 ▶ a $13.4\,cm$　　　　　**b** $17.3°$

4 ▶ 22.2

5 ▶ a $7.5\,cm$　　　　　**b** $143°$

6 ▶ a $26.6°$　　　　　**b** $288.7\,m$

EXERCISE 6

1 ▶ a $\cos^2\theta$　**b** $\sin^2\left(\frac{\theta}{2}\right)$　**c** 6

d $-\sin^2 A$　**e** $\cos 4\theta$　**f** $\tan\theta$

g $\tan 3A$　**h** 4　**i** $\sin^2 x$

j 1

2 ▶ a $(\cos x + \sin x)^2$

$$= \cos^2 x + \sin^2 x + 2\sin x\cos x$$

$$= 1 + 2\sin x\cos x$$

b $\dfrac{1}{\cos\theta}-\cos\theta$

$=\dfrac{1}{\cos\theta}-\dfrac{\cos\theta}{1}$

$=\dfrac{1-\cos^2\theta}{\cos\theta}$

$=\dfrac{\sin^2\theta}{\cos\theta}$

$=\dfrac{\sin\theta}{\cos\theta}\times\dfrac{\sin\theta}{1}$

$=\tan\theta\sin\theta$

c $\dfrac{\cos^2\theta}{1-\sin\theta}$

$=\dfrac{1-\sin^2\theta}{1-\sin\theta}=\dfrac{(1-\sin\theta)(1+\sin\theta)}{1-\sin\theta}$

$=1+\sin\theta$

d $\dfrac{1+\sin x}{\cos x}\times\dfrac{(\sin x-1)}{(\sin x-1)}$

$=\dfrac{\sin x-1+\sin^2 x-\sin x}{\cos x(\sin x-1)}$

$=\dfrac{\sin^2 x-1}{\cos x(\sin x-1)}$

$=\dfrac{-\cos^2 x}{\cos x(\sin x-1)}$

$=-\dfrac{\cos^2 x}{\cos x(\sin x-1)}$

$=-\dfrac{\cos x}{(\sin x-1)}$

$=\dfrac{\cos x}{1-\sin x}$

e $\tan x+\dfrac{1}{\tan x}$

$=\dfrac{\sin x}{\cos x}+\dfrac{\cos x}{\sin x}$

$=\dfrac{\sin^2 x+\cos^2 x}{\cos x\sin x}$

$=\dfrac{1}{\cos x\sin x}$

f $\cos^2 A-\sin^2 A$

$=\cos^2 A+(\cos^2 A-1)$

$=2\cos^2 A-1$

and

$\cos^2 A-\sin^2 A$

$=1-\sin^2 A-\sin^2 A$

$=1-2\sin^2 A$

g $2-(\sin x-\cos x)^2$

$=2-(\sin^2 x-2\sin x\cos x+\cos^2 x)$

$=2-(1-2\sin x\cos x)$

$=1+2\sin x\cos x$

$=\sin^2 x+\cos^2 x+2\sin x\cos x$

$=(\sin x+\cos x)^2$

h $\sin^2 x\cos^2 y-\cos^2 x\sin^2 y$

$=\sin^2 x(1-\sin^2 y)-(1-\sin^2 x)\sin^2 y$

$=\sin^2 x-\sin^2 x\sin^2 y-\sin^2 y+\sin^2 x\sin^2 y$

$=\sin^2 x-\sin^2 y$

3 ▶ a $\sin 35°$ **b** $\cos 210°$ **c** $\tan 31°$

    d $\cos 3x$ **e** $\cos 7\theta$ **f** $\tan 5x$

    g $\sin A$ **h** $\cos 3x$

4 ▶ a 1 **b** 0 **c** $\dfrac{\sqrt{2}}{2}$

    d $\sqrt{3}$ **e** $\dfrac{\sqrt{3}}{3}$ **f** 1

5 ▶ a $\sin(A+60°)+\sin(A-60°)$

$=\sin A\cos 60°+\cos A\sin 60°+\sin A\cos 60°-\cos A\sin 60°$

$=2\sin A\cos 60°$

$=\sin A$

b $\dfrac{\sin(x+y)}{\cos x\cos y}$

$=\dfrac{\sin x\cos y+\cos x\sin y}{\cos x\cos y}$

$=\dfrac{\sin x\cos y}{\cos x\cos y}+\dfrac{\cos x\sin y}{\cos x\cos y}$

$=\dfrac{\sin x}{\cos x}+\dfrac{\sin y}{\cos y}$

$=\tan x+\tan y$

c $\cos(\theta+\dfrac{\pi}{3})+\sqrt{3}\sin\theta$

$=\cos\theta\cos\dfrac{\pi}{3}-\sin\theta\sin\dfrac{\pi}{3}+\sqrt{3}\sin\theta$

$=\dfrac{1}{2}\cos\theta-\dfrac{\sqrt{3}}{2}\sin\theta+\sqrt{3}\sin\theta$

$=\dfrac{\sqrt{3}}{2}\sin\theta+\dfrac{1}{2}\cos\theta$

$=\sin\theta\cos\dfrac{\pi}{6}+\cos\theta\sin\dfrac{\pi}{6}$

$=\sin(\theta+\dfrac{\pi}{6})\qquad[\sin(A+B)]$

EXERCISE 7

1 ▶ a $210°, 330°$ **b** $60°, 240°$

    c $180°$ **d** $15°, 165°$

    e $140°, 220°$ **f** $45°, 225°$

    g $90°, 270°$ **h** $230°, 310°$

i 45.6°, 134.4°   **j** 135°, 225°

2 ▶ a −120°, −60°   **b** −171.37°, −8.63°

c −144°, 144°   **d** −327.1°, −32.9°

e 30°, 150°, 330°, 510°, 690°   **f** 251°, 431°

g −2π, −π, 0, π, 2π   **h** $-\dfrac{7\pi}{4}, -\dfrac{5\pi}{4}, \dfrac{\pi}{4}, \dfrac{3\pi}{4}$

i $-\dfrac{4\pi}{3}, -\dfrac{2\pi}{3}, \dfrac{2\pi}{3}$ **j** −0.14, 3.00, 6.14 rad

3 ▶ a 0°, 45°, 90°, 135°, 180°, 225°, 270°, 315°, 360°

b 60°, 180°, 300°   **c** 22.5°, 112.5°, 202.5°, 292.5°

d 240°   **e** 225°, 315°

f 50°, 170°   **g** 165°, 345°

4 ▶ a −2π, −π, 0, π, 2π   **b** 0, π, 2π

5 ▶ a $x = -40°, 0°, 80°$

b 4.78^c, 6.22^c

c 113°, 158°, 203°, 248°

d $-\dfrac{11}{12}\pi, -\dfrac{7}{12}\pi, \dfrac{\pi}{12}, \dfrac{5}{12}\pi$

e $-\dfrac{29}{48}\pi, -\dfrac{13}{48}\pi, \dfrac{19}{48}\pi, -\dfrac{35}{48}\pi$

EXERCISE 8

1 ▶ a 30°, 210°   **b** 135°, 315°

2 ▶ 0.59, 3.73

3 ▶ a 60°, 120°, 240°, 300°

b 60°, 300°

c 270°

d 194°, 270°, 346°

4 ▶ a $\dfrac{5\pi}{12}, \dfrac{11\pi}{12}, \dfrac{17\pi}{12}, \dfrac{23\pi}{12}$ **b** 0.841, $\dfrac{2\pi}{3}, \dfrac{4\pi}{3}$, 5.44

c 4.01, 5.41

EXAM PRACTICE QUESTIONS

1 ▶ a 17.1 cm^2 **b** 5.7 cm

c 11.7 cm   **d** 4.5 cm^2

2 ▶ a Area of sector $BAC = \dfrac{1}{2}r^2\theta$

$= \dfrac{1}{2} \times 6^2 \times 2.2$

$= 39.6 \text{ cm}^2$

b 2.04 rad

c 61 cm^2

3 ▶ a 94°   **b** 27.9 cm^2

4 ▶

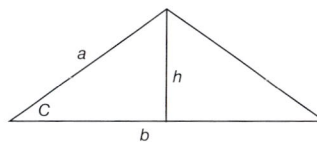

Suppose we have a triangle as shown above. The height can be found by:

$\sin C = \dfrac{h}{a}$ by using $\sin C = \dfrac{opposite}{hypotenuse}$

$\therefore h = a\sin C$

The area of a triangle (k) is $k = \dfrac{1}{2}bh$ (where b is the base

and h is the height)

Substituting $h = a\sin C$ into $k = \dfrac{1}{2}bh$ we get

$k = \dfrac{1}{2}b(a\sin C) = \dfrac{1}{2}ab\sin C$

5 ▶ a $\tan\theta = 5$ **b** 78.7°, 258.7°

6 ▶ 0.459, 2.683

7 ▶ a $\sin^4 3\theta$ **b** 1

8 ▶ a 1   **b** $\tan y = \dfrac{4 + \tan x}{2\tan x - 3}$

9 ▶ a $x = \dfrac{23\pi}{12}, x = \dfrac{11\pi}{12}$

b $x = \dfrac{2\pi}{3}, x = \dfrac{5\pi}{6}, x = \dfrac{11\pi}{6}, x = \dfrac{5\pi}{3}$

10 ▶ 23.8°, 203.8°

11 ▶ $(\cos\theta - \tan\theta)^2 + (\sin\theta + 1)^2$

$= \cos^2\theta - 2\cos\theta\tan\theta + \tan^2\theta + \sin^2\theta + 2\sin\theta + 1$

$= \cos^2\theta + \sin^2\theta + 1 - 2\cos\theta\tan\theta + 2\sin\theta + \tan^2\theta$

$= 2 - \dfrac{2\cos\theta}{1}\dfrac{\sin\theta}{\cos\theta} + \dfrac{2\sin\theta}{1} + \tan^2\theta$

$= 2 + \tan^2\theta$

12 ▶

13 ▶ 50.8°, 129.2°, 230.8°, 309.2°

14 ▶ $\dfrac{\cos A}{\sin B} - \dfrac{\sin A}{\cos B}$

$= \dfrac{\cos A\cos B - \sin A\sin B}{\sin B\cos B}$

$= \dfrac{\cos(A + B)}{\sin B\cos B}$

15 ▶ $\dfrac{\pi^2}{4}$

INDEX